Essential Strategies
of Argument

Essential Strategies of Argument

STUART HIRSCHBERG

*Rutgers: The State University
of New Jersey, Newark*

Allyn & Bacon
Boston ✦ *London* ✦ *Toronto* ✦ *Sydney* ✦ *Tokyo* ✦ *Singapore*

Vice President: Eben W. Ludlow
Editorial Assistant: Morgan Lance
Marketing Manager: Lisa Kimball
Production Administrator: Rowena Dores
Editorial-Production Service: Ruttle, Shaw, and Wetherill, Inc.
Text Designer: Denise Hoffman
Cover Administrator: Linda Knowles
Composition Buyer: Linda Cox
Manufacturing Buyer: Megan Cochran

Also published as Part One of *Strategies of Argument*, Second Edition, by Stuart
Hirschberg, copyright © 1996 by Allyn & Bacon.

Acknowledgments appear on pages 467–469, which constitute a continuation
of the copyright page.

Library of Congress Cataloging-in-Publication Data

Hirschberg, Stuart.
    Essential strategies of argument / Stuart Hirschberg.
        p.   cm.
    Includes bibliographical references and index.
    ISBN 0-205-17424-8
    1. English language—Rhetoric.   2. Persuasion (Rhetoric)
3. College readers.   I. Title.
PE1431.H57   1996
808'.042—dc20   95-43583
                                                              CIP

Printed in the United States of America

10   9   8   7   6   5   4   3   2   1   99   98   97   96

Roy Orbison
1936–1988
Z

Contents

3   *Arguing across the Disciplines*   131

7   *Writing an Argument from Sources*   364

Preface

——————◆——————

The *Essentials of Argument* is a rhetoric on argument. This book has two aims: (1) to offer instruction on understanding, analyzing, and evaluating different types of arguments and (2) to provide guidance on writing effective arguments.

Chapters 1, 2, 3, 4, and 5 introduce students to the skills of critical reading, note taking, summarizing, and the basic strategies of argument, in order to show them how to identify central ideas and techniques as a first step in understanding and analyzing arguments. The discussion, based on the Stephen Toulmin model of claim, warrant, backing, support, and qualifier, examines different kinds of arguments, explores basic argumentative strategies, and places particular emphasis on the importance of underlying assumptions, definition, and types of evidence in different disciplines. The uses (and abuses) of logic and language in argument are discussed in depth. Selections illustrating points in the discussion are on topics ranging from the serious—questions on AIDS, assisted suicide, and sexual harassment—to lighter analyses of training a pet, political correctness, and the unspoken rules governing friendship.

Chapter 6 provides guidance in writing effective arguments using a process model and discusses the important points of invention strategies, arriving at a thesis, adapting arguments for different audiences, using an outline, and revising a rough draft. The important role of critical thinking in bridging the gap between analyzing someone else's argument and generating one's own ideas is examined in detail. Students are introduced to the criteria important in evaluating the arguments of others and are provided with a sample student evaluation of an argument. The two short arguments for analysis with which the chapter ends include a tongue-in-cheek look at societal stereotyping of overweight people and a defense of the virtues of football for female fans.

Chapter 7 introduces students to the methods of inquiry used to generate an argument from sources. The process of writing an argument from sources is covered step by step, including the crucial aspects of finding a question to answer, using the print and computerized resources of the library, evaluating source materials, formulating the working thesis, note taking procedures, quoting, writing and revising a rough draft, and using both the MLA and APA styles of documentation.

In the text important principles of argument are illustrated by clear and timely examples. These readings include short editorials, advertisements, personal accounts, articles with graphs and tables, and selections written for academic audiences. Selections on AIDS, alcoholism, data bases, assisted suicide, ecology, immigration, gender roles, poverty, sexual harassment, friendship, pets, political correctness, alternate lifestyles, the jury system, democracy, football, black English, higher education, and primate behavior clarify important features of general reasoning and give students insight into specific characteristics of arguments across the disciplines.

Chapter 2, "Strategies of Argument," includes an in-depth treatment of different kinds of claims, specific advice on how different kinds of arguments might be developed, and full discussion of warrants in the Toulmin model of argument.

A full treatment of "Arguing Across the Disciplines" (Chapter 3) examines how claims are made and supported in different fields of study with sample arguments to analyze. Chapter 4 offers a discussion of traditional inductive and deductive reasoning (with illustrations of the most frequently encountered logical fallacies that appear in Appendix A). Chapter 5, "The Role of Language in Argument," features sections on advertising and other visual means of persuasion along with a discussion of humor, irony, parody, and satire, illustrated by four essays.

More than a hundred exercises and writing opportunities are integrated throughout the text at important stages to bring theory into practice. Many of these activities have been adapted to accommodate the Rogerian method.

Illustrative essays in different academic disciplines and a broad spectrum of exercises and activities give students ample opportunity to practice the skills they will need in writing their argument paper.

An up-to-date section on computerized data bases and on-line catalogs reflects changes in university libraries throughout the country. Chapter 7, "Writing an Argument from Sources," features student papers illustrating both the MLA and the APA styles of documentation, and reflects the latest *MLA Handbook* (1995, fourth edition).

The spectrum of subjects and points of view represented in the twenty-five readings and their varying lengths and levels of difficulty will accommodate a variety of teaching approaches. The annotated table of contents identifies the subject, purpose, and central idea of each selection. End-of-selection questions explore the substance of each reading and its argumentative strategies. These questions are intended to engage students' interest in the key issues in the text and to direct their attention to the ways in which authors adapt their arguments for specific audiences. Some of the end-of-selection questions might best be handled by analytical essays that evaluate the author's purpose in writing the selection, underlying assumption, tone or "voice" chosen, and success in adapting the presentation for a particular audience or occasion.

When the author's purpose in a selection is to argue for the acceptance of a proposition or to persuade the audience to take or approve an action, the student's analysis can assess the author's use of evidence (both for and against the position being presented) and his or her reasoning (whether it is clear, logical, compelling, and so forth). When the author's purpose is to demonstrate how to solve a problem or relate how a problem was solved, the student's analysis can address questions of (1) whether there is a clear definition of the problem, (2) whether there is sufficient background presented to demonstrate why there is a problem and what previous attempts have been made to solve it, and (3) why the solution of this problem would be important.

These selections also reveal that the assumptions underlying a particular reading are very closely tied to the author's purpose. For this reason, some questions ask students to draw up a list of these assumptions before deciding what the author's purpose might be. Once the assumptions are identified, students can compare the author's assumptions with their own beliefs, determine whether the assumptions are commonly held, and thus be in a better position to evaluate the validity of the author's statements. Discussion questions direct attention toward the tone or voice the author chooses to project to the audience. Other questions also ask students to evaluate this aspect of argument by focusing on the writer's choice of words, sentence structure, use of punctuation, choice of person, and success in matching the tone of the article with the subject, the audience, and the occasion.

The wide range of selections in this text will give students ample opportunity to see how writers attempt to persuade different audiences: the general public, scholars, or professionals in a particular academic field of study.

Instructor's Manual

An accompanying instructor's manual provides (1) strategies for teaching argumentative writing, (2) suggested answers to the end-of-selection questions, and (3) supplemental bibliographies of books and periodicals for students who wish to follow up any of the opposing viewpoints or in-depth thematic units for their argument papers from sources.

Acknowledgments

No expression of thanks can adequately convey my gratitude to all those teachers of composition who offered thoughtful comments and gave this book the benefit of their scholarship and teaching experience.

I would especially like to thank the instructors who reviewed the various stages of the manuscript, including Jennifer A. Black, McLennan Community College; Kathryn Fitzgerald, University of Utah; Christy Friend, University of Texas–Austin; and Stephen Wilhoit, The University of Dayton.

For their diligence and skill, I owe much to the able staff at Allyn and Bacon, to Morgan Lance, editorial assistant and to Rowena Dores for her work as production administrator. I would especially like to thank Stan Kushner for his invaluable advice. Most of all, Gloria Klaiman, of Ruttle, Shaw & Wetherill, Inc., for her outstanding efforts as production manager.

To Eben W. Ludlow I owe all the things that one owes to an extraordinarily gifted editor. Ultimately, to Terry I owe more than words can express.

1

Understanding Arguments

◆

Whether our argument concerns public affairs or some other sub-ject we must know some, if not all, of the facts about the subject on which we are to speak and argue. Otherwise, we can have no mate-rials out of which to construct arguments.

—Aristotle, *Rhetoric*

The Nature of Argument

Some of the most interesting and effective writing you will encounter takes the form of arguments that seek to persuade a specific audience of the validity of a proposition or claim through logical reasoning supported by facts, examples, data, or other kinds of evidence. Formal arguments differ from assertions based on likes and dislikes or personal opinion. Unlike questions of personal taste, arguments rest on evidence—whether in the form of facts, examples, the testimony of experts, or statistics—that can be brought forward to prove or disprove objectively the thesis in question.

Although the two are frequently confused, argumentation differs from persuasion. Argument is a form of discourse in which statements are offered in support of a claim or proposition. Argument is based on a rational appeal to the understanding and builds its case on a network of logical connections.

The term *argument* also refers to the practice of giving reasons to convince or persuade an audience to accept a claim or proposition. Argument is a form of advocacy and a process of reasoning designed to support a claim. Making an assertion, offering a hypothesis, presenting a claim, and putting forward a moral objection are all ways of arguing. Thus, the process of argument is valuable because it provides an arena for testing the validity, truth, or probability of specific ideas, propositions, and claims.

Whereas argument presents reasons and evidence to gain an audience's intellectual agreement with the validity of a proposition, persuasion also includes appeals to the emotional needs and values of an audience to move them to approve an action or to take an action that the writer recommends. In argument, the audience's agreement with the truth of the claim has more to do with the soundness of the evidence than with the audience's response to the speaker's character and personality. Because of this, arguments are usually addressed to a general, unspecified audience, whereas persuasion is usually keyed to the beliefs, prejudices, interests, values, and needs of a specific audience. For example, political speeches employing persuasive appeals are usually keyed to the specific needs of an immediate audience. Persuasion is influenced by the audience's sense of the speaker's character, presence, and reputation. The difference between argument and persuasion can be clearly seen by comparing the following two short paragraphs.

Kirkpatrick Sale in his book *Human Scale* (1980) cites the results of various studies as evidence to support his claim that smaller communities are more neighborly and healthier places in which to live:

> There is another way of coming at the question of the human limits of a community. Hans Blumenfeld, the urban planner, suggests starting with the idea of the size at which "every person knows every other person by face, by voice, and by name" and adds, "I would say that it begins to fade out in villages with much more than 500 or 600 population." Constantine Doxiadis, after reducing thousands of data from various centuries, came to the conclusion that what he called the "small neighborhood" would hold approximately 250 people, a large neighborhood some 1,500, with an average around 800–900. Gordon Rattray Taylor, the British science writer, has estimated that there is a "natural social unit" for humans, defined by "the largest group in which every individual can form some personal estimate of the significance of a majority of the other individuals in the group, in relation to himself," and he holds that the maximum size of such a group, depending on geography and ease of contact, is about 1,200 people.

Henry Fairlie, on the other hand, in *The Spoiled Child of the Western World* (1976) claims that life in a small community is subject to intrusion and loss of privacy and characterizes the typical village shop as follows:

> But the village shop, as one knew it personally, and as one can read about it in fiction, was usually an unattractive place, and frequently a malignant one. The gossip which was exchanged was, as often as not, inaccurate and cruel. Although there were exceptions, one's main memory of the village shopkeeper, man and wife, is of faces which were hard and sharp and mean, leaning forward to whisper in ears

that were cocked and turned to hear all that they could of the misfortunes or the disgrace of a neighbour. Whisper! Whisper! Whisper! This has always been the chief commodity of the village shop. And not only whispers, because the village shopkeeper, informed or misinformed, could always apply sanctions against those to whom disgrace or misfortune was imputed.

Notice how Sale relies on evidence and the testimony of experts to support his claim that small communities promote peace, social harmony, trust, and well-being. The character of Sale as a person is less important than the facts he presents to support his thesis or claim.

By contrast, Fairlie's description of the stifling character of small-town life is communicated by picturesque language that is designed to appeal to the imagination and arouse the emotions of his audience against this life. The audience's sense of Fairlie as a person is important, since his own observations are presented as a source of evidence drawn from his past experiences. There is no objective evidence as such in this passage. Fairlie's ability to appeal to the emotions of his audience through skillful use of provocative language is the only evidence he presents. Yet, it would be difficult to say which of these two passages is more persuasive. The point here is that the difference between argument and persuasion is one of degree. Arguments tend to emphasize appeals to logic, whereas persuasion tries to sway an audience through a calculated manipulation of the audience's needs and values. Real-world arguments, however, should be a blend of the two.

Rhetoric and Persuasion

Rhetoric came into existence as a specific field of study in the early part of the fifth century B.C. in Sicily to enable ordinary citizens to make an effective case concerning why they should be entitled to recover property that had been seized by a dictatorial tyrant. The claimants had to present their case without supporting documentation and construct an argument solely on the basis of inference and probability. This emphasis on discovering, arranging, and presenting arguments to enhance the probability of a claim defines the distinctive nature of argumentative discourse from this beginning to the present day.

The term *rhetoric* has acquired negative connotations of language calculated to deceive; "mere rhetoric" is associated with stylistic flourishes devoid of content, or empty talk without action. It was not always thus. For Aristotle, rhetoric meant discovering all the available means of persuasion in any given situation where the truth could not be known for certain (Aristotle, *Rhetoric*, Book I, Chapter 1, lines 26–27). Aristotle, of course, excluded coercive or violent means and concerned himself solely with systematic and skillful efforts that one person could use to get another to think in a certain way.

Rhetoric in its original context referred to the process of seeking out the best arguments, arranging them in the most effective way, and presenting them in the manner best calculated to win agreement from a particular audience.

Rhetoric is concerned with those questions in the realm of the contingent where the truth is not able to be known (Aristotle, *Rhetoric*, Book I, Chapter 2, line 15). It is up to arguers on all sides of the issues to find the most effective means for persuading audiences to believe or at least consider the probable truth of their claims.

Normally, the kinds of questions dealt with are those that are open to different interpretations; rhetoric, therefore, is concerned with the methods or strategies arguers may use in seeking acceptance of their position from an audience. Aristotle said there are three means by which people could persuade each other to adopt a certain point of view or approve a course of action. Broadly stated, these three elements—which are all present in some degree in every successful instance of persuasion—he identified as (1) the appeal to the audience's reason (*logos*), (2) the appeal to the audience's emotions (*pathos*), and (3) the degree of confidence that the speaker's character or personality could inspire in the audience (*ethos*) (Aristotle, *Rhetoric*, Book I, Chapter 2, lines 1–4).

The goal of all three of these appeals is the same, although each takes a different approach to achieve the same end of persuading or increasing the credibility or probable truth of the claim. The appeal to the audience's reason (*logos*) is often associated with formal logic and the citation of relevant facts and objective evidence (statistics, case histories, surveys, facts, examples, precedents). Well-constructed arguments that genuinely appeal to reason are indeed persuasive. And even though Aristotle made the point that appeals to an audience's deepest desires, needs, and values need not be deceptive, arguers soon became aware that appeals to the emotions, such as fear, greed, love of comfort, desire for status, or paranoia toward outsiders (*pathos*) could substitute for appeals to reason, especially in those cases where the persuader had little evidence or lacked the skill necessary to construct a logical argument. The third means Aristotle identified (*ethos*) depended on the degree to which the arguer could win the confidence of the audience. The credibility and persuasiveness of the arguer's claims would be in direct proportion to the audience's view of the speaker or writer as a person of good sense, good moral character, and good intentions (Aristotle, *Rhetoric*, Book I, Chapter 2, line 13).

It is in the context of these three methods that we will discuss arguments—what makes some persuasive, others ineffective, some legitimate, and others deceptive—and look at the separate elements that collectively constitute effective argumentation. Even though at points we may, for the sake of clarity, discuss elements of argumentation separately from elements of persuasion, the two are inextricably intertwined in any successful instance of persuasion.

The purpose, then, of argument is to persuade an audience to accept the validity or probability of an idea, proposition, or claim. Essentially, a claim is an assertion that would be met with skepticism if it were not supported with sound evidence and logical reasoning. Argument plays a key role for writers who use the forums provided by newspapers and popular magazines as well as the more specialized literary and scientific journals to persuade colleagues and the general public alike of the truth of their ideas, discoveries, viewpoints, and conclusions.

Critical Reading for Ideas and Organization

One of the most important skills to have in your repertoire is the ability to survey unfamiliar articles, essays, or excerpts and come away with an accurate understanding of what the author wanted to communicate and how the material is organized. On the first and in subsequent readings of any of the selections in this text, especially the longer ones, pay particular attention to the title, look for introductory and concluding paragraphs (with special emphasis on the author's statement or restatement of central ideas), identify the headings and subheadings (and determine the relationship between these and the title), and identify any unusual terms necessary to fully understand the author's concepts.

As you work your way through an essay, you might look for cues to enable you to recognize the main parts of the argument or help you perceive the overall organization of the article. Once you find the main thesis, underline it. Then work your way through fairly rapidly, identifying the main ideas and the sequence in which they are presented. As you identify an important idea, ask yourself how this idea relates to the thesis statement you underlined or to the idea expressed in the title.

Finding a Thesis

Finding a thesis involves discovering the idea that serves as the focus of the essay. The thesis is often stated in the form of a single sentence that asserts the author's response to an issue that others might respond to in different ways. For example, the opening paragraphs of "A Day in the Life of 'Salaryman'" present John Burgess's assessment of an important aspect of Japanese society:

The "salaryman," as the male white-collar worker is called in Japan, is what most of the 280,000 young men who graduate from universities each year quickly become.

The good salaryman devotes himself body and soul to the company. If the company thrives, so will he. He loves his wife and children, but in a pinch he can be counted on to put the office first.

The thesis (in bold type) represents the writer's view of a subject or topic from a certain perspective. Here, Burgess states a view of "salaryman" that will serve as a focus for his essay on Japanese culture. Writers often place the thesis in the first paragraph or group of paragraphs so that the readers will be able to perceive the relationship between the supporting evidence and this main idea.

As you read, you might wish to underline the topic sentence or main idea of each paragraph or section (since key ideas are often developed over the course of several paragraphs). Jot it down in your own words in the margins, identify supporting statements and evidence (such as examples, statistics, and the testimony of authorities), and try to discover how the author organizes the material to support the development of important ideas. To identify supporting material, look for any ideas more specific than the main idea that is used to support it. Also look for instances where the author uses examples, descriptions, statistics, quotations from authorities, comparisons, or graphs to make the main idea clearer or prove it to be true.

Pay particular attention to important transitional words, phrases, or paragraphs to better see the relationships among major sections of the selection. Noticing how certain words or phrases act as transitions to link paragraphs or sections together will dramatically improve your reading comprehension. Also look for section summaries, where the author draws together several preceding ideas.

Writers use certain words to signal the starting point of an argument. If you detect any of the following terms, look for the main idea they introduce:

since, because, for, as, follows from, as shown by, inasmuch as, otherwise, as indicated by, the reason is that, for the reason that, may be inferred from, may be derived from, may be deduced from, in view of the fact that

An especially important category of words is that which includes signals that the author will be stating a conclusion. Words to look for are these:

therefore, hence, thus, so, accordingly, in consequence, it follows that, we may infer, I conclude that, in conclusion, in summary, which shows that, which means that, and which entails, consequently, proves that, as a result, which implies that, which allows us to infer, points to the conclusion that

You may find it helpful to create a running dialogue with the author in the margins, posing and then trying to answer the basic questions *who, what, where, when,* and *why,* and to note observations on how the main idea of the article is related to the title. These notes can later be used to evaluate how effectively any specific section contributes to the overall line of thought.

Responding to What You Read

When reading an essay that seems to embody a certain value system, try to examine any assumptions or beliefs the writer expects the audience to share. How is this assumption related to the author's purpose? If you do not agree with these assumptions, has the writer provided sound reasons and evidence to persuade you to change your mind?

You might describe the author's tone or voice and try to assess how much it contributed to the essay. How effectively does the writer use authorities, statistics, or examples to support the claim? Does the author identify the assumptions or values on which his or her views are based? Are they ones with which you would agree or disagree? To what extent does the author use the emotional connotations of language to try to persuade his or her reader? Do you see anything unworkable or disadvantageous about the solutions offered as an answer to the problem the essay addresses? All these and many other ways of analyzing someone else's essay can be used to create your own. Here are some specific guidelines to help you.

When evaluating an essay, consider what the author's purpose is in writing it. Was it to inform, explain, solve a problem, make a recommendation, amuse, enlighten, or achieve some combination of these goals? How is the tone or voice the author projects toward the reader related to his or her purpose in writing the essay?

You may find it helpful to write short summaries after each major section to determine whether you understand what the writer is trying to communicate. These summaries can then serve as a basis for an analysis of how successfully the author employs reasons, examples, statistics, and expert testimony to support and develop his or her main points.

For example, if the essay you are analyzing cites authorities to support a claim, assess whether the authorities bring the most timely opinions to bear on the subject or display any obvious biases, and determine whether they are experts in that particular field. Watch for experts described as "often quoted" or "highly placed reliable sources"

without accompanying names, credentials, or appropriate documentation. If the experts cited offer what purports to be a reliable interpretation of facts, consider whether the writer also quotes equally
trustworthy experts who hold opposing views.

If statistics are cited to support a point, judge whether they derive
from verifiable and trustworthy sources. Also, evaluate whether the
author has interpreted them in ways that are beneficial to his or her
case, whereas someone who held an opposing view could interpret
them quite differently. If real-life examples are presented to support
the author's opinions, determine whether they are representative or
whether they are too atypical to be used as evidence. If the author relies
on hypothetical examples or analogies to dramatize ideas that otherwise would be hard to grasp, judge whether these examples are too far-
fetched to back up the claims being made. If the essay depends on the
stipulated definition of a term that might be defined in different ways,
check whether the author provides clear reasons to indicate why one
definition rather than another is preferable.

As you list observations about the various elements of the article
you are analyzing, take a closer look at the underlying assumptions
and see whether you can locate and distinguish between those assumptions that are explicitly stated and those that are implicit. Once
the author's assumptions are identified, you can compare them with
your own beliefs about the subject, determine whether these assumptions are commonly held, and make a judgment as to their validity.
Would you readily agree with these assumptions? If not, has the author
provided sound reasons and supporting evidence to persuade you to
change your mind?

Marking as You Read

The most effective way to think about what you read is to make notes
as you read. Making notes as you read forces you to go slowly and
think carefully about each sentence. This process is sometimes called
annotating the text, and all you need is a pen or a pencil. There are as
many styles of annotating as there are readers, and you will discover
your own favorite technique once you have done it a few times. Some
readers prefer to underline major points or statements and jot down
their reactions to them in the margin. Others prefer to summarize each
paragraph or section to help them follow the author's line of thinking.
Other readers circle key words or phrases necessary to understand the
main ideas. Feel free to use your notes as a kind of conversation with
the text. Ask questions. Express doubts. Mark unfamiliar words or
phrases to look up later. If the paragraphs are not already numbered,

you might wish to number them as you go to help you keep track of your responses. Try to distinguish the main ideas from supporting points and examples. Most importantly, go slowly and think about what you are reading. Try to discover whether the author makes a credible case for the conclusions he or she reaches. One last point: take a close look at the idea expressed in the title before and after you read the essay to see how it relates to the main idea.

Distinguishing between Fact and Opinion

As you read, distinguish between statements of fact and statements of opinion. Statements of fact relate information that is widely accepted and objectively verifiable; facts are used as evidence to support the claim made by the thesis. By contrast, an opinion is a personal interpretation of data or a belief or feeling that however strongly presented should not be mistaken by the reader for objective evidence. For example, consider the following claim by Edward T. Hall in "Hidden Culture":

> Each culture and each country has its own language of space, which is just as unique as the spoken language, frequently more so. In England, for example, there are no offices for the members of Parliament. In the United States, our congressmen and senators proliferate their offices and their office buildings and simply would not tolerate a no-office situation.

The only statement that could be verified or refuted on the basis of objective data is "In England . . . there are no offices for the members of Parliament." All the the other statements, *however persuasive they may seem*, are Hall's interpretations of a situation (multiple offices and office buildings for U.S. government officials) that might be interpreted quite differently by another observer. These statements should not be mistaken for statements of fact.

A reader who could not distinguish between facts and interpretations would be at a severe disadvantage in understanding Hall's essay. Part of the difficulty in separating fact from opinion stems from the difficulty of remaining objective about statements that match our own personal beliefs.

Take a few minutes to read and annotate the following essay. Feel free to "talk back" to the author. You can underline or circle key passages or key terms. You can make observations, raise questions, and express your reactions to what you read.

A SAMPLE ESSAY FOR
STUDENT ANNOTATION

Edward T. Hall

Hidden Culture

◆———————

1   A few years ago, I became involved in a sequence of events in Japan that completely mystified me, and only later did I learn how an overt act seen from the vantage point of one's own culture can have an entirely different meaning when looked at in the context of the foreign culture. I had been staying at a hotel in downtown Tokyo that had European as well as Japanese-type rooms. The clientele included a few Europeans but was predominantly Japanese. I had been a guest for about ten days and was returning to my room in the middle of an afternoon. Asking for my key at the desk, I took the elevator to my floor. Entering the room, I immediately sensed that something was wrong. Out of place. Different. I was in the wrong room! Someone else's things were distributed around the head of the bed and the table. Somebody else's toilet articles (those of a Japanese male) were in the bathroom. My first thoughts were, "What if I am discovered here? How do I explain my presence to a Japanese who may not even speak English?"

2   I was close to panic as I realized how incredibly territorial we in the West are. I checked my key again. Yes, it really was mine. Clearly they had moved somebody else into my room. But where was my room now? And where were my belongings? Baffled and mystified, I took the elevator to the lobby. Why hadn't they told me at the desk, instead of letting me risk embarrassment and loss of face by being caught in somebody else's room? Why had they moved me in the first place? It was a nice room and, being sensitive to spaces and how they work, I was loath to give it up. After all, I had told them I would be in the hotel for almost a month. Why this business of moving me around like someone who has been squeezed in without a reservation? Nothing made sense.

3   At the desk I was told by the clerk, as he sucked in his breath in deference (and embarrassment?) that indeed they had moved me. My particular room had been reserved in advance by somebody else. I was given the key to my new room and discovered that all my personal ef-

fects were distributed around the new room almost as though I had done it myself. This produced a fleeting and strange feeling that maybe I wasn't myself. How could somebody else do all those hundred and one little things just the way I did?

Three days later, I was moved again, but this time I was prepared. 4 There was no shock, just the simple realization that I had been moved and that it would now be doubly difficult for friends who had my old room number to reach me. *Tant pis,* I was in Japan. One thing did puzzle me. Earlier, when I had stayed at Frank Lloyd Wright's Imperial Hotel for several weeks, nothing like this had ever happened. What was different? What had changed? Eventually I got used to being moved and would even ask on my return each day whether I was still in the same room.

Later, at Hakone, a seaside resort where I was visiting with friends, 5 the first thing that happened was that we were asked to disrobe. We were given *okatas,* and our clothes were taken from us by the maid. (For those who have not visited Japan, the okata is a cotton print kimono.) We later learned, when we ventured out in the streets, that it was possible to recognize other guests from our hotel because we had all been equipped with identical okatas. (Each hotel had its own characteristic, clearly recognizable pattern.) Also, I noted that it was polite to wave or nod to these strangers from the same hotel.

Following Hakone, we visited Kyoto, site of many famous temples 6 and palaces, and the ancient capital of Japan.

There we were fortunate enough to stay in a wonderful little 7 country inn on the side of a hill overlooking the town. Kyoto is much more traditional and less industrialized than Tokyo. After we had been there about a week and had thoroughly settled into our new Japanese surroundings, we returned one night to be met at the door by an apologetic manager who was stammering something. I knew immediately that we had been moved, so I said, "You had to move us. Please don't let this bother you, because we understand. Just show us to our new rooms and it will be all right." Our interpreter explained as we started to go through the door that we weren't in that hotel any longer but had been moved to *another* hotel. What a blow! Again, without warning. We wondered what the new hotel would be like, and with our descent into the town our hearts sank further. Finally, when we could descend no more, the taxi took off into a part of the city we hadn't seen before. No Europeans here! The streets got narrower and narrower until we turned into a side street that could barely accommodate the tiny Japanese taxi into which we were squeezed. Clearly this was a hotel of another class. I found that, by then, I was getting a little paranoid, which is easy enough to do in a foreign land, and said to myself, "They must think we are very low-status people indeed to treat us this way."

8   As it turned out, the neighborhood, in fact the whole district, showed us an entirely different side of life from what we had seen before, much more interesting and authentic. True, we did have some communication problems, because no one was used to dealing with foreigners, but few of them were serious.

9   Yet, the whole matter of being moved like a piece of derelict luggage puzzled me. In the United States, the person who gets moved is often the lowest-ranking individual. This principle applies to all organizations, including the Army. Whether you can be moved or not is a function of your status, your performance, and your value to the organization. To move someone without telling him is almost worse than an insult, because it means he is below the point at which feelings matter. In these circumstances, moves can be unsettling and damaging to the ego. In addition, moves themselves are often accompanied by great anxiety, whether an entire organization or a small part of an organization moves. What makes people anxious is that the move usually presages organizational changes that have been co-ordinated with the move. Naturally, everyone wants to see how he comes out vis-à-vis everyone else. I have seen important men refuse to move into an office that was six inches smaller than someone else's of the same rank. While I have heard some American executives say they wouldn't employ such a person, the fact is that in actual practice, unless there is some compensating feature, the significance of space as a communication is so powerful that no employee in his right mind would allow his boss to give him a spatial demotion—unless of course he had already reached his crest and was on the way down.

10   These spatial messages are not simply conventions in the United States—unless you consider the size of your salary check a mere convention, or where your name appears on the masthead of a journal. Ranking is seldom a matter that people take lightly, particularly in a highly mobile society like that in the United States. Each culture and each country has its own language of space, which is just as unique as the spoken language, frequently more so. In England, for example, there are no offices for the members of Parliament. In the United States, our congressmen and senators proliferate their offices and their office buildings and simply would not tolerate a no-office situation. Constituents, associates, colleagues, and lobbyists would not respond properly. In England, status is internalized; it has its manifestations and markers—the upper-class received English accent, for example. We in the United States, a relatively new country, externalize status. The American in England has some trouble placing people in the social system, while the English can place each other quite accurately by reading ranking cues, but in general tend to look down on the importance that Americans attach to space. It is very easy and

very natural to look at things from one's own point of view and to read an event as though it were the same all over the world.

I knew that my emotions on being moved out of my room in Tokyo were of the gut type and quite strong. There was nothing intellectual about my initial response. Although I am a professional observer of cultural patterns, I had no notion of the meaning attached to being moved from hotel to hotel in Kyoto. I was well aware of the strong significance of moving in my own culture, going back to the time when the new baby displaces older children, right up to the world of business, where a complex dance is performed every time the organization moves to new quarters.

What was happening to me in Japan as I rode up and down elevators with various keys gripped in my hand was that I was reacting with the cultural part of my brain—the old, mammalian brain. Although my new brain, my symbolic brain—the neocortex—was saying something else, my mammalian brain kept repeating, "You are being treated shabbily." My neocortex was trying to fathom what was happening. Needless to say, neither part of the brain had been programmed to provide me with the answer in Japanese culture. I did have to put up a strong fight with myself to keep from interpreting what was going on as though the Japanese were the same as I. This is the conventional and most common response and one that is often found even among anthropologists. Any time you hear someone say, "Why *they* are no different than the folks back home—they are just like I am," even though you may understand the reasons behind these remarks you also know that the speaker is living in a single-context world (his own) and is incapable of describing either his world or the foreign one.

The "they are just like the folks back home" syndrome is one of the most persistent and widely held misconceptions of the Western world, if not the whole world. There is very little any outsider can do about this, because it expresses views that are very close to the core of the personality. Simply talking about "cultural differences" and how we must respect them is a hollow cliché. And in fact, intellectualizing isn't much more helpful either, at least at first. The logic of the man who won't move into an office that is six inches smaller than his rival's is *cultural* logic; it works at a lower, more basic level in the brain, a part of the brain that synthesizes but does not verbalize. The response is a total response that is difficult to explain to someone who doesn't already understand, because it is so dependent on context for correct interpretation. To do so, one must explain the entire system; otherwise, the man's behavior makes little sense. He may even appear to be acting childishly—which he most definitely is not.

It was my preoccupation with my own cultural mold that explained why I was puzzled for years about the significance of being

11

12

13

14

moved around in Japanese hotels. The answer finally came after further experiences in Japan and many discussions with Japanese friends. In Japan, one has to "belong" or he has no identity. When a man joins a company, he does just that—joins himself to the corporate body—and there is even a ceremony marking the occasion. Normally, he is hired for life, and the company plays a much more paternalistic role than in the United States. There are company songs, and the whole company meets frequently (usually at least once a week) for purposes of maintaining corporate identity and morale.

15   As a tourist (either European or Japanese) when you go on a tour, you *join* that tour and follow your guide everywhere as a group. She leads you with a little flag that she holds up for all to see. Such behavior strikes Americans as sheeplike; not so the Japanese. The reader may say that this pattern holds in Europe, because there people join Cook's tours and the American Express tours, which is true. Yet there is a big difference. I remember a very attractive young American woman who was traveling with the same group I was with in Japan. At first she was charmed and captivated, until she had spent several days visiting shrines and monuments. At this point, she observed that she could not take the regimentation of Japanese life. Clearly, she was picking up clues, such as the fact that our Japanese group, when it moved, marched in a phalanx rather than moving as a motley mob with stragglers. There was much more discipline in these sightseeing groups than the average Westerner is either used to or willing to accept.

16   It was my lack of understanding of the full impact of what it means to belong to a high-context culture that caused me to misread hotel behavior at Hakone. I should have known that I was in the grip of a pattern difference and that the significance of all guests being garbed in the same okata meant more than that an opportunistic management used the guests to advertise the hotel. The answer to my puzzle was revealed when a Japanese friend explained what it means to be a guest in a hotel. As soon as you register at the desk, you are no longer an outsider; instead, for the duration of your stay you are a member of a large, mobile family. *You belong.* The fact that I was moved was tangible evidence that I was being treated as a family member—a relationship in which one can afford to be "relaxed and informal and not stand on ceremony." This is very highly prized state in Japan, which offsets the official properness that is so common in public. Instead of putting me down, they were treating me as a member of the family. Needless to say, the large, luxury hotels that cater to Americans, like Wright's Imperial Hotel, have discovered that Americans do tenaciously stand on ceremony and want to be treated as they are at home in the States. Americans don't like to be moved around; it makes them anxious. Therefore, the Japanese in these establishments have learned not to treat them as family members.

Keeping a Reading Journal

The most effective way to keep track of your thoughts and impressions and to review what you have learned is to start a reading journal. The comments you record in your journal may express your reflections, observations, questions, and reactions to the essays you read. Normally, your journal would not contain lecture notes from class. A reading journal will allow you to keep a record of your progress during the term and can also reflect insights you gain during class discussions and questions you may want to ask, as well as unfamiliar words you intend to look up. Keeping a reading journal becomes a necessity if your composition course will require you to write a research paper that will be due at the end of the semester. Keep in mind that your journal is not something that will be corrected or graded, although some instructors may wish you to share your entries with the class.

TURNING ANNOTATIONS INTO JOURNAL ENTRIES

Although there is no set form for what a journal should look like, reading journals are most useful for converting your brief annotations into more complete entries that explore in depth your reactions to what you have read. Interestingly, the process of turning your annotations into journal entries will often produce surprising insights that will give you a new perspective. For example, a student who annotated Edward T. Hall's "Hidden Cultures" converted them into the following journal entries:

- Hall's personal experiences in Japan made him realize that interpreting an action depends on what culture you're from.
- Hall assumes hotels should treat long-term guests with more respect than overnight guests. "Like someone who had been squeezed in without a reservation" shows Hall's feelings.
- What does having your clothes replaced with an okata—cotton robe—have to do with being moved from room to room in a hotel? The plot thickens!
- The hotel in Hakone encourages guests—all wearing the same robes—to greet each other outside the hotel in a friendly, not formal, manner.
- Hall says that in America, size of office = personal value and salary. Hall compared how space works in the U.S. in order to understand Japanese attitudes towards space.
- Thesis—"culturally defined attitudes toward space are different for each culture." Proves this by showing how unimportant

space is to members of Parliament in England when compared with the great importance office size is to U.S. congresspersons and senators.

- Hall is an anthropologist. He realizes his reactions are instinctual. Hall wants to refute idea that people are the same all over the world. Says what culture you are from determines your attitudes and behavior.
- He learns from Japanese friends that workers are hired for life and view their companies as family. Would this be for me? In Japan, group identity is all-important.
- Hall describes two tour groups, one Japanese and one American, as an example of Japanese acceptance of regimentation, whereas Americans go off on their own.
- The answer to the mystery of why he was being moved: moving him meant he was accepted as a member of the hotel family. They were treating him informally, as if he were Japanese: a compliment not an insult. Informality is highly valued because the entire culture is based on the opposite—regimentation and conformity.

SUMMARIZING

Reading journals may also be used to record summaries of the essays you read. The value of summarizing is that it requires you to pay close attention to the reading in order to distinguish the main points from the supporting details. Summarizing tests your understanding of the material by requiring you to restate, concisely, the author's main ideas in your own words. First, create a list composed of sentences that express in your own words the essential idea of each paragraph, or each group of related paragraphs. Your previous underlining of topic sentences, main ideas, and key terms (as part of the process of critical reading) will help you follow the author's line of thought. Next, whittle down this list still further by eliminating repetitive ideas. Then formulate a thesis statement that expresses the main idea behind the article. Start your summary with this thesis statement, and combine your notes so that the summary flows together and reads easily.

Remember that summaries should be much shorter than the original text (whether the original is one page or twenty pages long) and should accurately reflect the central ideas of the article in as few words as possible. Try not to intrude your own opinions or critical evaluations into the summary. Besides requiring you to read the original piece more closely, summaries are necessary first steps in developing papers that synthesize materials from different sources. The test for a good summary, of course, is whether a person reading it without having read the original article would get an accurate, balanced, and complete account of the original material.

Writing an effective summary is easier if you first compose a rough summary, using no more than two complete sentences to summarize each of the paragraphs or group of paragraphs in the original article. A student's rough summary of Hall's essay might appear as follows. Numbers show which paragraphs are summarized from the article.

1–3 Hall describes how a seemingly inexplicable event that occurred while he was staying in a Tokyo hotel, frequented mostly by Japanese, led him to understand that the same action can have a completely different significance from another culture's perspective. Without telling him, the hotel management had moved his personal belongings to a new room and had given his room to another guest.

4 Three days later when Hall is again moved without warning, he is less startled but begins to wonder why this had never happened during his stay at Frank Lloyd Wright's Imperial Hotel in Tokyo.

5 At another hotel in Hakone, Hall is given an *okata*, a kind of cotton robe, to wear instead of his clothes and is encouraged to greet other guests wearing the same *okata* when he sees them outside the hotel.

6–7 At a third hotel, a country inn near Kyoto, Hall discovers that he has been moved again, this time to an entirely different hotel in what he initially perceives to be a less desirable section of town. Hall interprets this as an insult and becomes angry that the Japanese see him as someone who can be moved around without asking his permission.

8 The neighborhood he had initially seen as less desirable turns out to be much more interesting and authentic than the environs of hotels where tourists usually stay.

9 Hall relates his feelings of being treated shabbily ("like a piece of derelict luggage") to the principle that in the United States, the degree of one's power and status is shown by how much control one has over personal space, whether in the Army or in corporations, where being moved to a smaller office means one is considered less valuable to the company.

10–11 Hall speculates that the equation of control over space with power may pertain only to the United States, since in England, members of Parliament have no formal offices, while their counterparts in the United States—congressmen and senators—attach great importance to the size of their offices. Hall begins to realize that he has been unconsciously applying an American cultural perspective to actions that can be explained only in the context of Japanese culture.

12 Hall postulates the existence of an instinctive "cultural logic" that varies from culture to culture, and he concludes that it is necessary

to understand the cultural context in which an action takes place in order to interpret it as people would in that culture.

13–14 Once Hall suspends his own culturally based assumption that one's self-esteem depends on control over personal space, he learns from conversations with Japanese friends that in Japan one has an identity only as part of a group. Japanese workers are considered as family by the companies that hire them for life.

15 The emphasis Japanese society places on conforming to a group is evident in the behavior of Japanese tourists, who move as a coordinated group and closely follow their guide, while American tourists refuse to accept such discipline.

16 Hall realizes that wearing an *okata* and being moved to different rooms and to another, more authentic, hotel means that he is being treated in an informal manner reserved for family members. What Hall had misperceived as an insult—being moved without notice—was really intended as an honor signifying he had been accepted and was not being treated as a stranger.

Based on this list, a student's formulation of a thesis statement expressing the essential idea of Hall's essay appears this way:

> Every society has a hidden culture that governs behavior that might seem inexplicable to an outsider.

The final summary should contain both this thesis and your restatement of the author's main ideas without adding any comments that express personal feelings or responses to the ideas presented. Keep in mind that the purpose of a summary or concise restatement of the author's ideas in your own words is to test your understanding of the material. The summary would normally be introduced by mentioning the author as well as the title of the article:

> Edward T. Hall, writing in "Hidden Culture," believes every society has a hidden culture that governs behavior that might seem inexplicable to an outsider. In Japan, Hall's initial reactions of anger to being moved to another room in a hotel in Tokyo, having his clothes replaced by a cotton kimono or *okata* in Haykone, and being relocated to a different hotel in Kyoto led him to search for the reasons behind such seemingly bizarre events. Although control over space in America is related to status, Hall realizes that in other cultures, like England, where members of Parliament have no offices, this is not the case. Hall discovers that rather than being an insult, being treated informally meant he was considered to be a member of the hotel "family."

Although some features of the original essay might have been mentioned, such as the significance of office size in corporations in the

United States, the student's summary of Hall's essay is still an effective one. The summary accurately and fairly expresses the main ideas in the original.

USING YOUR READING JOURNAL TO GENERATE IDEAS FOR WRITING

You can use all the material in your reading journal (annotations converted to journal entries, reflections, observations, questions, rough and final summaries) to relate your own ideas to the ideas of the person who wrote the essay you are reading. Here are several different kinds of strategies you can use as you analyze an essay in order to generate material for your own:

1. What is missing in the essay? Information that is not mentioned is often just as significant as information the writer chose to include. First, you must have already summarized the main points in the article. Then, make up another list of points that are not discussed, that is, missing information that you would have expected an article of this kind to have covered or touched on. Write down the possible reasons why this missing material has been omitted, censored, or downplayed. What possible purpose could the author have had? Look for vested interests or biases that could explain why information of a certain kind is missing.

2. You might analyze an essay in terms of what you already know and what you didn't know about the issue. To do this, simply make a list of what concepts were already familiar to you and a second list of information or concepts that were new to you. Then write down three to five questions you would like answered about this new information and make a list of possible sources you might consult.

3. You might consider whether the author presents a solution to a problem. List the short-term and long-term effects or consequences of the action the writer recommends. You might wish to evaluate the solution to see whether positive short-term benefits are offset by possible negative long-term consequences not mentioned by the author. This might provide you with a starting point for your own essay.

4. After clearly stating what the author's position on an issue is, try to imagine other people in that society or culture who would view the same issue from a different perspective. How would the concerns of these people be different from those of the writer? Try to think of as many different people, representing as many different perspectives, as you can. Now, try to think of a solution that would satisfy both the author and at least one other person who holds a different viewpoint. Try to imagine that you are an arbitrator negotiating an agreement. How would your recommendation require both parties to compromise and reach an agreement?

TWO SHORT ARGUMENTS
FOR CRITICAL READING

Perhaps no issue in recent times illustrates the need to distinguish between the factual nature of a situation and the emotions it arouses as has the AIDS crisis. Almost every aspect connected with this disease elicits questions that can be answered in so many ways that proponents of different answers invariably find themselves constructing arguments to support their positions.

On June 2, 1987, the United States Senate unanimously approved a bill that would require AIDS testing for immigrants (the military was already screening applicants for the presence of the AIDS virus). Should testing of prospective marriage applicants for the AIDS virus be mandatory, like compulsory testing for syphilis? Should hospital patients be routinely tested to detect the presence of AIDS antibodies? Is it desirable or possible to guarantee the confidentiality of test results? What will be the direct and indirect costs of AIDS, and who should absorb the high cost of treatment, experimental therapies, and research? Should insurance companies be allowed to test for AIDS? How can the public be protected while preserving the civil rights of carriers of the virus so that they are not discriminated against by employers, landlords, insurance companies, and public schools? For example, should children with AIDS be allowed to attend public schools? When Clifford and Louise Ray tried to send their three AIDS-infected sons to public school (boys who, as hemophiliacs, had contracted the virus through blood transfusions before screening of the blood supply became mandatory in 1984), neighbors turned against them, their house was burned down, and they were forced to leave Arcadia, Florida. How have patterns of sexual behavior (homosexual and heterosexual) changed in response to the AIDS epidemic?

What arguments are advanced for and against the designation of hospitals in specific neighborhoods as centers solely for the treatment of AIDS victims? Perhaps the most controversial questions of all are those that pertain to society's attitude toward homosexuals, who are those most likely (although by no means exclusively) to contract and die from this inexorably fatal disease. For example, how would proposals recommending that homosexuals be barred from jobs as bartenders, waiters, food handlers, attendants at health care facilities, teachers, and employees at day-care centers come into conflict with current laws? Has the government's willingness to spend money on treatment centers, preventive education, and biomedical research been so slow to get off the ground because a majority of the victims are seen as disposable citizens (homosexuals, the poor, blacks, Hispanics, intravenous drug users)?

Every one of these questions (and untold others) is already, or will soon become, the center of an argument by individuals and groups who disagree about the basic facts and offer various hypotheses as to what caused the AIDS epidemic and what the consequences will be. The issue has provoked groups from every sector of American life to make value judgments and advocate various social, sexual, legal, medical, and educational policies.

A writer presenting an argument must keep an open mind, consider points of view other than his or her own, define or stipulate the meaning of key terms in the argument, and present a clear statement of the thesis. The writer must present the argument in logical order; cite the best and most relevant evidence, statistics, examples, and testimony available; state assumptions when necessary; draw conclusions that seem plausible and are consistent with the known facts; and effectively use rhetorical strategies to adapt the argument for a given audience.

Charles Krauthammer

AIDS: Getting More than Its Share?

◆

Charles Krauthammer served as Chief Resident in Psychiatry at Harvard Medical School. His views on public policy are expressed in his collection of essays Cutting Edges, 1985. *He has contributed articles to* The New Republic *and* Time *magazine, where this essay first appeared in 1990.*

1   Last month [May 1990] a thousand demonstrators camped outside the National Institutes of Health near Washington and with a talented display of street theater protested governmental and scientific neglect of AIDS. If not the angriest demonstration Washington has seen in a long time, it was certainly the most misdirected. The idea that American government or American society has been inattentive or unresponsive to AIDS is quite simply absurd. Consider:

2   *Treatment.* Congress is about to do something extremely rare: allocate money specifically for the treatment of one disease. The Senate voted $2.9 billion, the House $4 billion over five years for treating AIDS. And only AIDS. When Senator Malcolm Wallop introduced an amendment allowing rural districts with few AIDS patients to spend the money on other diseases, the amendment was voted down, 2 to 1.

3   *Research.* Except for cancer, AIDS now receives more Government research money than any other illness in America. AIDS gets $1.2 billion to $1.3 billion. Heart disease, for example, receives about half as much, $700 million. The AIDS research allocation is not just huge, it is hugely disproportionate. AIDS has killed 83,000 Americans in nine years. Heart disease kills that many every six weeks.

4   *Testing.* Under pressure from AIDS activists, the FDA has radically changed its regulations for testing new drugs. The Administration has proposed "parallel track" legislation that would make drugs available to certain patients before the usual testing process is complete. Nothing wrong with this. But this exception is for AIDS patients only—a fact that hardly supports the thesis that government is holding back an AIDS cure or discriminating against AIDS patients.

5   The suffering caused by AIDS is enormous. Sufferers deserve compassion, and their disease deserves scientific inquiry. But AIDS has got far more. AIDS has become the most privileged disease in America. Why? Mainly because its victims are young, in many cases creative and

famous. Their deaths are therefore particularly poignant and public. And because one of the two groups that AIDS disproportionately affects (gay men) is highly organized. This combination of conspicuousness and constituency has allowed AIDS activists to get more research funding, more treatment money and looser drug-testing restrictions than any comparable disease.

Nothing wrong with that. The system for allocating research and   6
treatment money in American medicine is archaic, chaotic and almost random anyway. Under the "Disease of the Month Club" syndrome, any disease that has in some way affected a Congressman or some relation gets special treatment. There is rough justice in this method of allocation because after a while Congressmen and their kin get to experience most of the medical tragedies that life has to offer. At the end of the day, therefore, funds tend to get allocated in a fairly proportionate way.

AIDS is now riding a crest of public support, won in the rough and   7
tumble of politics. All perfectly legitimate, and a tribute to the passion and commitment of AIDS activists. But that passion turns to mere stridency when they take to the streets to protest that a homophobic society has been ungenerous and stinting in its response to the tragedy of AIDS. In fact, American society is giving overwhelming and indeed disproportionate attention and resources to the fight.

At first the homosexual community was disoriented and defensive   8
in reaction to AIDS. In the quite understandable attempt to get public support, it fixed on a strategy of claiming that AIDS was everyone's problem. Since we were all potential sufferers—anyone can get AIDS, went the slogan—society as an act of self-protection should go all out for cure and care.

This campaign was initially successful. But then it ran into an ob-   9
stacle. It wasn't true. AIDS is not everyone's problem. It is extremely difficult to get AIDS. It requires the carrying out of specific and quite intentional acts. Nine out of ten people with AIDS have got it through homosexual sex and/or intravenous drug use. The NIH demonstrators, therefore, now appeal less to solidarity than to guilt: every person who dies is more blood on the hands of a society unwilling to give every dollar demanded for a cure.

But society has blood on its hands every time it refuses to give ev-   10
ery dollar demanded by the cancer lobby, the heart disease lobby, the diabetes lobby. So now a different tack: the claim that the AIDS epidemic is, of course, not an act of government but an act of God—and government has not done enough to help its helpless victims.

In fact, AIDS is far less an act of God than is, say, cancer or diabetes.   11
Apart from a small number of relentlessly exploited Ryan White–like exceptions, the overwhelming majority of sufferers get AIDS through some voluntary action: sex or drug abuse. You don't get AIDS the way you used to get TB, by having someone on the trolley cough in your

face. You don't get it the way you get, say, brain cancer, which is through some act of God that we don't understand at all.

12   AIDS is in the class of diseases whose origins we understand quite well. It is behaviorally induced and behaviorally preventable. In that sense it is in the same moral class as lung cancer, the majority of whose victims get it through voluntary behavior well known to be highly dangerous. For lung cancer the behavior is smoking; for AIDS, unsafe sex (not, it might be noted, homosexuality) and IV drug use.

13   As a society we do not refuse either to treat or research lung cancer simply because its sufferers brought it on themselves. But we would find it somewhat perverse and distasteful if lung cancer sufferers began demonstrating wildly, blaming society and government for their problems, and demanding that they be first in line for a cure.

14   Many people contracted AIDS before its causes became known, about six years ago. For them it is truly an act of God. For the rest (as the word has gone out, an ever increasing percentage), it is an act of man. They, of course, deserve our care and treatment. But it is hard to see from where they derive the claim to be first in line—ahead of those dying of leukemia and breast cancer and stroke—for the resources and compassion of a nation.

✦ Questions for Discussion and Writing

1. State Krauthammer's position in your own words.

2. To what extent might Krauthammer's description of "talented display of street theater" be seen as negative, although it is phrased positively?

3. Where else in his article do the emotional connotations of his descriptions seem to be designed to sway his audience?

4. How does Krauthammer characterize AIDS victims? How is his characterization intended to persuade his audience to agree with his thesis?

5. What are Krauthammer's major objections to the way the government spends money on AIDS? What means does he use to substantiate his overall objection?

6. Evaluate the persuasiveness of each of his counterarguments. Which do you disagree or agree with, and why?

7. In a paragraph of 150 words or less, write an objective summary of Krauthammer's essay. If you disagree with his thesis, try to identify the points at which you encountered difficulty in keeping your own views out of the summary.

Naomi Freundlich

No, Spending More on AIDS Isn't Unfair*

◆

Naomi Freundlich is the science and technology editor for Business Week *magazine, where this article first appeared in September 1990.*

Just a year or so ago, it would have been political suicide for a scientist, politician, or journalist to speak out against increased spending for AIDS research. After a regrettably slow start, the federal government took up the campaign in 1983 and has steadily increased research funding in an effort to curb the deadly epidemic. By the end of fiscal 1989, AIDS had garnered nearly $2.5 billion in government funds. And this year, the National Institutes of Health will kick in $740 million more. Last month, Congress allocated an additional $875 million for states to use for AIDS treatment. 1

Now, as activists stage protests demanding even more money for AIDS, a backlash is forming. For a few critics, the attack is a value judgment on the lifestyles of AIDS sufferers. Other critics just question whether AIDS research should be such a high priority. Politicians from rural states, for instance, complain that the funds Congress is allocating for AIDS can't be used to fight other diseases. And there is growing resentment among some cancer and other non-AIDS researchers. 2

They charge that a project without a mention of AIDS in the title runs an unfair risk of getting turned down. An Office of Technology Assessment report released last April [1990] shows how pervasive that feeling is. Of some 148 scientists who answered a poll on AIDS research, nearly half complained that too much funding has been diverted to AIDS. This year, some 1 million people will die of heart disease, and an additional 500,000 or so of cancer. So why, the argument goes, spend so much on a disease that has killed just 83,000 Americans in nine years? 3

It doesn't take much digging to come up with the answer. Heart disease and cancer occur at a fairly stable rate. AIDS, by contrast, is an infectious disease and can spread rapidly through a population. In fact, 4

*Reprinted from September 17, 1990 issue of *Business Week* by special permission, copyright by the McGraw-Hill Companies.

the number of cases is expected to triple in the U.S. by 1993. And in the next decade alone, doctors will be treating a million or more people who are already infected with HIV, the virus that leads to AIDS.

5   Beyond that, the most recent figures from the Centers for Disease Control in Atlanta show that the malady is no longer confined to gays and drug users. Countrywide, the ratio of men to women who carry the HIV virus has dropped from 11 to 1 early in the epidemic to close to 3 to 1 today. In some rural areas, says Dr. June E. Osborn, dean of the University of Michigan's School of Public Health and chairwoman of the National Commission on AIDS, the ratio is closer to 1 to 1. Because the number of people infected with HIV in these rural areas is growing faster than in urban centers, that raises the specter of a heterosexual epidemic such as is now sweeping parts of Africa. And unlike cancer and heart disease, which usually strike older people, AIDS is a disease of the young. Some 82% of its victims are below the age of 44—in the most productive years of their lives.

6   If all this isn't reason enough to fund AIDS work, there is one more factor. According to Osborn, AIDS research is yielding a wealth of knowledge about viruses, cancer, the brain, and, most important, the immune system. "We have already learned many broadly important facts about how the body works, and there have been more spin-offs for cancer and other diseases than for AIDS directly," she says. For example, she adds, before AIDS, there was only speculation that the immune system helps fight off cancer. Now, boosting the body's defenses has become a key part of cancer research. The [Office of Technology Assessment] OTA report came to the same conclusion, citing benefits in public health, epidemiology, and basic science from AIDS research.

7   If there is a problem of scarce resources, moreover, it's not that money used for AIDS is being taken away from cancer and heart disease. It's true that the AIDS share of the NIH budget is rising rapidly. Funding for AIDS is growing 23% this fiscal year, while support for non-AIDS research is rising by only 4.4%. But William F. Raub, acting director of the NIH, says there is no guarantee that AIDS money would have gone to other diseases. More likely, it would have been used elsewhere in the federal budget, he says.

8   The problem he and others see is too little funding for biomedical research in general. The U.S. spent $600 billion last year on health care—but just 2% of it went to research on disease. Only one-quarter of the research grants submitted to NIH are now approved, compared with 60% in 1975. That's because the funding pie is growing slower than both the cost of research and the number of scientists clamoring for a slice. As a result, young investigators are less able to get research funds, and even established researchers are leaving basic science to work in industry or to practice medicine.

9   For many researchers and other critics, AIDS funding is a convenient target. But ultimately, the real issue is how much should be spent on biomedical research. Giving AIDS short shrift while that question is hashed out would be a tragic mistake.

✦ *Questions for Discussion and Writing*

1. How does Freundlich characterize those who are critical of AIDS funding?

2. Evaluate the persuasiveness of Freundlich's main counterargument to the claim that AIDS receives disproportionate funding.

3. What role do hypothetical examples play in Freundlich's argument?

4. How do Krauthammer and Freundlich each use the characterization of people with AIDS as "young" to support their respective arguments against and for additional AIDS funding?

5. How does Freundlich's approach to persuading an audience that increased funding for AIDS is warranted depend on showing how this research can benefit precisely those diseases that Krauthammer felt were being underfunded? Evaluate this strategy.

6. Write a short summary of 150 words or less in which you run through the principal assertion and supporting reasons of Freundlich's essay. What special problems did you encounter, and what extra steps did you have to take to summarize this essay if you strongly disagreed or agreed with her position?

7. Whose arguments, those of Krauthammer or Freundlich, did you find more persuasive? Write a short essay that offers reasons for your evaluation. You may wish to present your evaluation to a classmate or small group as a basis for exchanging opinions. Can you find a compromise position that would be acceptable to all parties involved?

2

Strategies of Argument

◆

Introduction

What we usually call an *argument* is not the same thing as a formal written argument. Arguments in everyday life are usually spontaneous, often illogical, and usually not well thought through. Yet the goal of everyday debates is often the same as the most elegant, well-reasoned argument: persuasion of an audience to come around to your point of view. A well-reasoned argument not only makes a claim but presents reasons and evidence necessary to convince an audience that the claim is true. Arguments arise in any situation where a wide range of responses is possible. The most obvious example might be a court of law. The prosecution and the defense each tell one side of the story or one version of events. The judge or jury, acting as an audience, then decides which version of the events seems more plausible. As with a formal argument, the legal system requires evidence to meet certain standards and draws a distinction between admissible and inadmissible evidence. Expert witnesses also play the same role in the court as they do in a written argument. The adversary nature of the legal system assumes, as does a formal argument, that any reason that survives all objections raised against it is a valid one. Many other professions besides the law, such as journalism, science, and business, also depend on the formulation of convincing arguments to win an audience's assent. What all arguments have in common is the need to persuade an audience by means of exact and careful reasoning that a specific claim or assertion is true.

One of the most innovative researchers in the field of argumentation theory is British logician and philosopher Stephen Toulmin. Toulmin devised a precise means of identifying the important features of arguments as they are engaged in by people in real life. His analysis of the ways in which people actually reason led him to formulate what has become the leading approach to informal logic, that is, logic as it appears in natural language rather than in the form of syllogisms (fully discussed in Chapter 4). His approach began to be used at first in the field of speech communications and has been adopted by composition theorists as a useful method of analyzing existing arguments and/or planning one's own arguments. The model Toulmin proposed to reflect the way people actually reason has six elements, each of which plays a distinctive role. Toulmin first introduced this model in 1958 in his book *The Uses of Argument* and later proposed an expanded scheme (with Richard Reike and Allan Janik) in 1979 in *An Introduction to Reasoning.* The advantage of Toulmin's method is that it charts the different parts of an argument that an audience must reconstruct and helps us develop a complete picture of the unstated implicit components of the argument. This allows us to be in a better position to identify both the strengths and the weaknesses of any argument. In Toulmin's model, a fully developed individual argument has six elements instead of the three components of the traditional syllogism. The three basic parts are the *claim* (equivalent to the conclusion of a syllogism), the *warrant* (similar to the major premise), and the *grounds* (similar to the minor premise).

Using the three elements of grounds, warrant, and claim, let's see how they would work in a hypothetical argument.

> You have just purchased a ticket to the Super Bowl from a scalper outside the stadium, and as you present it you are told that you cannot go in. You argue that you should be allowed to gain admission.
>
> The grounds of this argument would be the factual basis that you possess a ticket inscribed with the correct date, time, and place. The warrant is the unstated but clearly understood general rule that "all bearers of a Super Bowl admission ticket are normally entitled to be admitted." On the basis of these grounds and this warrant, you claim that you are entitled to be admitted to the stadium.

Thus, the three basic elements to be considered in any argument include (1) the claim or proposition the audience is to consider, (2) the evidence, support, or grounds the writer will have to produce to back up the claim, and (3) the warrant, the underlying assumption, belief, or rule that spells out the relationship between the claim and the evidence offered to support it.

In addition to these three basic parts, Toulmin also identifies three elements that are not reflected in the traditional structure of deductive argument. They are the backing, the qualifier, and the rebuttal (see Figure 2-1). Each of these six elements serves a distinctive function in an argument. The term *grounds* refers to the facts that serve as the founda-

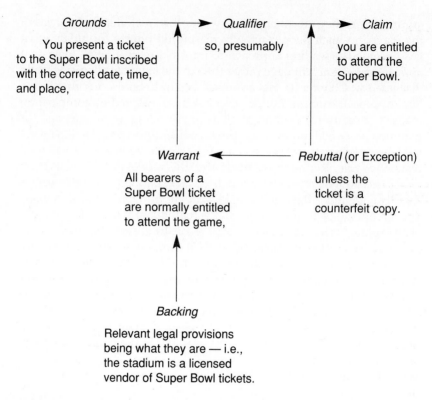

FIGURE 2-1 *Six Elements to Be Considered in an Argument, According to Toulmin.*

tion or support offered as evidence. Grounds may take the form of statistics, observations, testimony, or other factual data that literally "ground" the argument in something real. Grounds answer the question in the mind of an audience "What have you got to go on to support your claim?" The *claim*, in turn, is what the arguer wants the audience to believe or accept. The claim is the same as the conclusion or result of an argument. *Warrants* are the reasons for believing a claim or the principles or generalizations that serve as reasons for interpreting the data in support of the claim. Thus, the warrant is the principle or idea that provides the basis that literally "warrants" moving from the grounds to the claim. It answers the question in the minds of the audience "How do you get from the evidence to the claim?" The *backing* provides support for the warrant, showing why the warrant is safe to rely on in this particular argument, or it provides reasons why the warrant is true or in force. *Qualifiers* are words or phrases such as "probably," "sometimes," "in most cases," or "almost certainly" that express how reliable the speaker believes the claim to be. Qualifiers modulate the intensity of the claim. Toulmin's concept of *rebuttal*, like his analysis of other elements, is innovative and true to the ways in which people actually reason. The concept of rebuttal rests on the idea that the general rule or principle in the warrant may not always hold in every situation. The rebuttal identifies the circumstances or exceptions that might invalidate the claim in particular cases.

In the original example of being admitted to a Super Bowl game, the crucial role played by these additional three elements becomes clear. In diagram form, the argument might appear as shown in Figure 2-1.

Because warrants are often unstated, they often need to be spelled out explicitly. For example, a writer putting together a guidebook for travelers to Thailand would spell out rules and customs tourists would be wise to observe. She might warn tourists never to touch anyone—especially children—on the head, since Thais consider it to be the dwelling place of the soul. Other Thai customs based on assumptions every Thai knows but the tourist might not could, for example, necessitate explicitly warning the traveler never to cross the legs with one foot resting on the other knee. The feet are considered the lowliest part of the body, and pointing at anyone with your foot, even if inadvertently, is taken as an insult. Other customs could be assumed to be more self-evident—such as showing disrespect to images or statues of Buddha—and the warrants for them would not have to be spelled out explicitly for those of other religions.

Thus, any argument recommending certain kinds of behavior in Thailand would have to make explicit the underlying warrant rather than taking it for granted that readers would connect the evidence to the claim in the same way as would the writer. A traveler would need to understand the rationale or underlying principles of Thai culture in order to know how to act correctly. The assumptions or rules about what constitutes proper behavior assures (or warrants) the claim or advice about what is considered correct behavior in different circumstances.

In our example, the writer might quote authorities, cite anecdotes of travelers' experiences, and appeal to the need of travelers not to embarrass themselves when traveling in other cultures. In other arguments, support can also take the form of specific facts, data, statistics, personal testimony, results of experiments or surveys, and appeals to the emotions, needs, and values of the audience. The character of the author of the guidebook would also support the claim insofar as the reader perceived her as a seasoned traveler, familiar with the values and customs of different cultures. Both the citation of evidence and the appeal to needs and values of an audience are valid means by which writers support claims.

Kinds of Claims

The proposition that we wish our audience to agree with or act upon is called a claim. The claim is expressed as the thesis statement. Claims can be classified according to the kinds of questions that they answer.

> I. **Factual Claim:** Prices of generic drugs are often well below those of leading brands.
> Claims of fact seek to answer the question, what is the nature of [something]?
> II. **Causal Claim:** Sex differences cause differences in mathematical ability.
> Claims about cause or consequence try to answer the questions, what caused [something] to be the way it is? or what will happen as a result of [something]?
> III. **Value Claim:** Affirmative action is morally justifiable.
> Claims of value seek to answer the question, is [something] good or bad, right or wrong, moral or immoral, practical or impractical? These types of claims make value judgments.
> IV. **Policy Claim:** Automobiles should not be allowed in Yellowstone National Park.
> Claims about policy try to answer the question, what ought, should, or must we do about [something]? Claims of policy frequently appear as arguments that propose specific actions or policies as the best way to solve problems.

Claims may be phrased to suggest that there are certain kinds of conditions or limitations that prevent the claim from being advanced unconditionally. These qualifiers often take the form of adverbial phrases (*presumably, in all probability, apparently*) that indicate the provisional nature of the claim. In other cases, writers try to specify the sort of restrictions that limit the conditions under which the claim is true. For example, Dorothy Collier, in "Where Is My Child?" (*The London Sunday Times* [1977]), concludes her argument with a policy recommendation that includes a qualification. Collier, as a mother who has given up her son for adoption, believes that the natural parents should have the right to learn the identity and whereabouts of their children even though they have given them up for adoption. She argues the case on the grounds that adopted children have the right to learn who their natural parents are. She is careful to phrase her policy claim so that the reader understands she would apply the same restrictions as now govern the disclosure of information to adopted children:

> The law applies only to the child [the Children Act signed into law November 26, 1976, that permits adopted people to gain access to their

own birth records and thus to find out who they are]. He has all the rights and all the initiatives. If my son, the child that I bore, is dead, I am denied even the right to know where his body lies. I cannot believe that that right should be abrogated by the stroke of the pen at the time when the mind has ceased to function. I believe firmly that, with the same safeguards as now apply to the children, the right to know, the right to acquire basic information, should be granted to the natural parents of adopted persons.

How Collier qualifies her claim can be seen in the following sentence (the qualifying phrase is emphasized):

> POLICY CLAIM: I believe firmly that, **with the same safeguards as now apply to the children,** the right to know, the right to acquire basic information, should be granted to the natural parents of adopted persons.

Although we can more clearly see the distinctive qualities of each of these four types of claims (factual, causal, value, and policy) by discussing them separately, arguments frequently rely on more than just one type of claim. For example, Lori B. Andrews in an article titled "My Body, My Property" (*Hastings Center Report* [1986]) creates an argument that recommends changing the current system of voluntary donation of body parts (used in organ transplants) to permit the creation of a commercial market in organs and tissues (a claim about policy). In the course of her argument, Andrews defends the right of patients to sell their own body parts (a claim about value), defines the important difference between "regenerative" and "nonregenerative" organs and tissues (a claim about meaning), and discusses the benefits of such a market to donors, to recipients, and to society as a whole (a claim about consequences).

The Goals of Claims

Different kinds of arguments seek to accomplish different objectives or goals. Generally speaking, four kinds of goals can be identified.

People can disagree about the essential nature of the subject under discussion, what it is similar to or dissimilar to, how it should be defined. These are called *arguments of fact.* Even if people agree about the essential nature of X, they may disagree about what caused it or what effects it will cause in turn. These are *arguments of causation.* By the same token, even if all parties concerned agree what the nature of X is and what caused it and what the effects may be, they may disagree over whether it is good or bad or whether its effects are harmful or beneficial. These are *arguments about value.* The most complex form of argument, an argument about what should be done about X, is known as a *policy argument*. Policy arguments are complex because they may contain each of the preceding forms of argument.

For convenience, we will examine each of these four types of claims separately.

FACTUAL CLAIMS DEFINE AND DRAW DISTINCTIONS

Arguments that define and draw distinctions must identify the unique properties of the idea, term, or phenomenon being defined in a way that clearly distinguishes it from all other things with which it might be confused. Arguments that assert that a situation should be characterized in a certain way must identify the most important feature or crucial aspect of any situation, phenomenon, event, or idea.

Some arguments arise because of a lack of consensus about what commonly used terms actually mean. For example, in medicine, new technologies for prolonging life make it necessary to agree on what the terms *life* and *death* mean in this new context. Since machines can now prevent cessation of respiration, the traditional definition of death—as occurring when respiration ceases and the heart stops beating—must be stipulated as occurring with *brain death.* In these cases, decisions as to when to terminate life support or to remove organs for transplantation will obviously depend on which definition is applied. Thus, an argument seeking to establish what is most essential about the subject will often depend on the definition of a key term or concept.

For example, an argument against deinstitutionalization of the mentally ill might begin with a factual claim intended to establish the essential nature of one particular kind of mental illness: "schizophrenia is a mental disorder." In this case, the factual claim could easily be verified by citing the official definition published in the *Diagnostic Manual of the American Psychiatric Association.*

✦ *Questions for Discussion and Writing*

1. Explain how each of the following statements might serve as a premise or line of reasoning for an argument about the nature of something, that is, an argument that expresses a factual claim.

    a. Americans are pragmatists. Pragmatists believe that whatever works must be right. (William Schneider, *The Atlantic Monthly,* January, 1987.)

    b. Buddhism does not take its starting point on grand metaphysical questions like *who made the world?; what is the meaning of life?;* and *what happens to us after death?* It is not concerned with proving the existence of a God or gods. Rather its root focus is on the down-to-earth fact that all existence, including human existence, is imperfect in a very deep way. 'Suffering I teach—and the way out of suffering,' the Buddha declared. (John Snelling, *The Buddhist Handbook,* 1991.)

c. "Russian teenager Vitaly Klimakhin, who dropped out of high school to become a writer, finished his first book in 107 days. It consisted of the word 'Ford' written 400,000 times. 'My work is able to provoke a whole range of emotions in people,' he said. 'Some think it is just stupid. Others take it a bit more seriously.' (*News from the Fringe,* ed. by John Kohet and Roland Sweet, 1993.)

4. How does the following mini-argument define and draw distinctions about the basic current nature of journalism?

The Idiot Culture

For more than fifteen years we have been moving away from real journalism toward the creation of a sleazoid info-tainment culture in which the lines between Oprah and Phil and Geraldo and Diane and even Ted, between the *New York Post* and *Newsday,* are too often indistinguishable....

We are in the process of creating, in sum, what deserves to be called the idiot culture. Not an idiot *sub*culture, which every society has bubbling beneath the surface and which can provide harmless fun; but the culture itself.

I do not mean to attack popular culture. Good journalism *is* popular culture, but popular culture that stretches and informs its consumers rather than that which appeals to the ever descending lowest common denominator. If, by popular culture, we mean expressions of thought or feeling that require no work of those who consume them, then decent popular journalism is finished. What is happening today, unfortunately, is that the lowest form of popular culture—lack of information, misinformation, disinformation, and a contempt for the truth or the reality of most people's lives—has overrun real journalism.

—Carl Bernstein, *The New Republic,* June 8, 1992

EVALUATING THE RELIABILITY OF SOURCES OF INFORMATION

The persuasiveness of factual claims depends not only on specific reasons and evidence given to support the claim but on the reliability of the source of the information. The reliability of an authority depends on how reliable this expert has been in the past and on his or her ability to make accurate observations and draw sound conclusions. Both the way information is selected and the way judgments are made should be free from bias. For this reason, it is important to be able to distinguish statements that you merely believe to be true from those that you know to be true. You might try to do this with the following two descriptions of a Suzuki Samurai truck. The first paragraph appears as the advertising copy in the 1988 issue of *Motor Trend:*

It Has Fun Written All over It

—Take off your top with two piece removable hardtop.
—Haul your things around on a handy luggage rack.
—Fog lamps make great evening wear.
—Pull out of trouble with heavy duty compact winch.
—Protect your funmobile with durable brush guard.
—The Samurai logo. It has fun all over it.

The fun thing about a Suzuki Samurai™ is that you can give it a personality all your own. Genuine Suzuki accessories for America's favorite 4 × 4. We've got all kinds to choose from for the Suzuki look you want. Tops. Racks. Lamps. Western mirrors. Chrome bumpers. More. Make it sporty. Make it outdoorsy. Make it rugged. Make it yours. So go out and get a pure Suzuki. And make it your Suzuki.

The next series of paragraphs contain an evaluation of the Suzuki Samurai that appeared in the July 1988 issue of *Consumer Reports:*

Early this year a staff member was driving our new *Suzuki Samurai* slowly, in second gear, along a snow-covered dirt road leading to our auto test track when he felt the tires grab in a rut worn by earlier traffic. The driver turned the wheel to the right to steer clear. The front wheels pulled out of the rut and climbed approximately six inches up a ridge of plowed snow at the side of the road. Then, as the driver tried to straighten the wheels, the *Suzuki* flopped over on its side.

The driver climbed out uninjured, but with new respect for the laws of physics.

The Center for Auto Safety, a nonprofit consumer group, says it has received reports of 20 *Suzuki Samurai* rollover accidents resulting in 21 injuries and four deaths. It has also received reports of six rollovers in variants of the *Samurai,* such as the *Suzuki SJ410,* which is sold in Hawaii and the Virgin Islands; those resulted in seven injuries and one death. The National Highway Traffic Safety Administration has received 44 reports of *Samurai* rollovers, resulting in 16 deaths.

That's an ominous record of rollovers, considering that there are only 150,000 *Samurais* on U.S. roads so far, and that many of them have been in use for less than a year.

In our judgment, the *Suzuki Samurai* is so likely to roll over during a maneuver that could be demanded of any car at any time that it is unfit for its intended use. We therefore judge it Not Acceptable.

A rollover in a *Suzuki Samurai* would be even more dangerous than a rollover in a passenger car. Utility vehicles such as the *Suzuki* are not required to meet Federal safety standards for side-impact and rollover protection, which cover only passenger cars. Although widely advertised, sold, and used as a passenger car—indeed, as a car in which "to have a ball," as the advertising trade press puts it—the *Suzuki* we tested has no rollbar to reinforce its hardtop, as the *Jeep Wrangler* does.

Soon after our tests were complete, we called the results to the attention of the National Highway Traffic Safety Administration, in an effort to warn those who might have been considering a *Suzuki* before this issue of *Consumer Reports* came out. We have also petitioned NHTSA to establish minimum stability standards for all vehicles, so that cars and trucks as tippy as the *Suzuki Samurai* can no longer be sold here.

In comparing these two accounts of the *Suzuki Samurai* truck, we notice that the same vehicle is viewed very differently by the advertisers trying to sell their product and by the editors of *Consumer Reports,* a non-profit magazine that accepts no advertising and tests products and services and reports the findings. As you can see, if we are to accurately evaluate the source of information, we must be aware of the vested interests of the people reporting the information. We must also understand how these interests or purposes may have influenced the way the information has been presented. The key questions to ask in determining reliability of sources of information are these:

1. How knowledgeable or experienced is the source?
2. What sort of track record does the source of information have— that is, how reliable has this source been in the past?
3. Was the source able to make accurate observations in this particular case?
4. How could this information be objectively verified?
5. Do you have reason to believe that the information is incomplete or has been distorted by the self-interests of those relaying the information (due to the effects of income from advertising)?

Which of the following statements are simply expressions of personal preference or taste or claims that can be settled simply by looking up the facts in question? Which statements might serve as a basis for a genuine argument where evidence can be brought forward to support the disputed claim? After you have identified statements you believe can be the basis for an argument, follow it with the word "because" and provide a few reasons that would lead someone to believe that the claim was either probable or improbable.

1. Everyone who develops AIDS eventually dies.
2. Rich people don't get AIDS.
3. AIDS is God's punishment.

4. Only drug addicts get AIDS.
5. Old people don't get AIDS.
6. Women don't get AIDS.
7. Forty percent of hemophiliacs in North and South America are HIV positive.
8. AIDS was caused by radiation from French nuclear testing in the Sahara desert.
9. HIV positive women give birth to babies who test HIV positive.
10. The HIV virus is so tiny that over 500 million HIV viruses could fit on the top of the dot on this letter "i."
11. Humans caught the AIDS virus by eating raw monkey brains.
12. AIDS started in Africa brought in by white tourists.
13. AIDS is a CIA plot.

—Adapted from *COLORS: A Magazine About the Rest of the World*, No. 7, June, 1994, Rome, Italy

CAUSAL CLAIMS IDENTIFY POSSIBLE CAUSES FOR A GIVEN EFFECT OR POSSIBLE EFFECTS FOR A GIVEN CAUSE

Claims about causation assert that two events do not merely appear together but are in fact causally connected. That is, the writer argues that one event is caused by another or will cause another to occur. Whatever form they take, causal arguments must demonstrate the means (sometimes called the *agency*) by which an effect could have been produced.

Causal arguments are necessary when an audience might doubt that something could have caused the effect in question and needs to be shown *how* it was possible for X to have caused Y. For example, a writer who claimed that "cancer is caused by industrial chemicals" would be obligated to show the means by which specific industrial chemicals could produce certain kinds of cancer.

Causal arguments also offer plausible explanations as to the cause or causes of a series of events or a trend. A trend is the prevailing tendency or general direction of a phenomenon that takes an irregular course, like the upward or downward trend of the stock market, or the growing tendency to ban smoking in the workplace.

For example, Jonathan Broder, reporting for the *Chicago Tribune*, November 7, 1987, from New Delhi, describes an alarming increase of murder for profit among India's growing middle class ("An Unpaid Dowry Often Means Death"):

> Bride-burning, however, has grown common only during the last 20 years, coinciding with the upsurge—and rising greed—of India's middle classes, says Sarla Mudgal, president of the Salvation of Women organization, founded in 1947 after Indian independence.

"Bride-burning is mainly due to the increasing consumerism of the middle class," said Mudgal, adding that their appetite for consumer goods has joined the traditions of male chauvinism and dowry demands to produce what she calls a "vicious cycle of greed" that all too often ends in bride murder.

The reason why husbands choose to burn their brides, Jethmalani says, is because in most instances the death can be registered as a cooking accident or a suicide, making murder difficult to prove. Some men and their families go into bride-burning as a business, marrying and murdering over and over to collect as many dowries as possible, she says.

"Each morning, we open our newspapers to find one or two women burned while cooking food or in an apparent suicide. Surely, some are genuine suicides or accidents, but much of it is murder, attempted or successful."

A causal argument must present plausible grounds to support a claim as to why something happened or why something will happen. Writers may work backward from a given effect and attempt to demonstrate what cause or chain of causes could have produced the observed effect, or show how further effects could follow from a known cause. To see how this works, let's examine the following section drawn from William J. Darby's article "The Benefits of Drink" (*Human Nature* [November 1978]). The author, an emeritus professor of biochemistry at the Vanderbilt University School of Medicine, argues that persons who drink moderately tend to live longer than persons who abstain totally from drinking alcoholic beverages:

Klatsky and his colleagues evaluated the medical histories of 120,000 patients and found that moderate alcohol users were 30 percent less likely to have heart attacks than were non-drinking patients or matched controls or so-called risk controls—people who suffer from diabetes, hypertension, obesity, high serum cholesterol, or who smoke. (All of these factors are associated with increased risk of heart attacks.)

It was found that non-drinkers run a significantly greater risk of myocardial infarction than do users of alcohol. This finding was independent of age, sex, or prior related disease. In each of the groups of drinkers—those who drank up to two drinks daily, those who drank three or more drinks daily, and even those who drank six or more drinks per day—fewer heart attacks occurred than among the abstainers. The investigators concluded that "abstinence from alcohol may be a new risk factor." In a subsequent report from Massachusetts, where investigators studied 399 cases of infarction and evaluated 2,486 case histories, evidence persisted of a lower rate of heart attacks in subjects who consumed six or more drinks per day.

To substantiate his claim that contrary to popular belief moderate drinking is basically a healthy activity, Darby cites the results of several studies that seem to suggest that a causal argument could be made that alcohol consumption reduces the risk of heart attack in moderate drinkers. He cites a continuing study by Arthur Klatsky at the Kaiser-Permanente Medical Center in Oakland, California. (Klatsky first analyzed 464 heart attack patients and found that a large majority of them were persons who rarely or never consumed alcohol. He then broadened his study to 120,000 patients and found that moderate drinkers were 30 percent less likely to have heart attacks than teetotalers.) Darby also uses statistics drawn from a subsequent study to support his causal analysis. (For a fuller analysis of how writers use statistics to support a claim, see the discussion under "Support" later in this chapter.) A medical report in Massachusetts that included studies of 399 heart attack cases and 2,486 case histories found that the rate of heart attacks was significantly lower in persons who consumed six or more drinks in one day. It was especially important that Darby provide objective evidence, since his claim and its accompanying implication (that people who abstain from alcohol are actually at greater risk of having a heart attack than those who consume three to six drinks daily) are so controversial.

The rhetorical strategies that come into play in causal analysis require the writer to describe the subject in question, identify and discuss probable causes, provide reasons and evidence to support the causal claim, and consider and reject alternative explanations. Some writers reverse the sequence so that their own argument for a probable cause follows a thorough evaluation and rejection of competing explanations.

One way to substantiate a causal claim entails citing statistical evidence showing that a correlation exists between an increase or decrease of the stipulated cause and a simultaneous change in the effect. Demonstrating correlations remains one of the most difficult kinds of causal arguments. As Darrell Huff and Irving Geis, authors of *How to Lie with Statistics* (1954), have observed:

> Take the figures that show the suicide rate to be at its maximum rate in June. Do suicides produce June brides—or do June weddings precipitate suicides of the jilted? A somewhat more convincing (though equally unproved) explanation is that the fellow who licks his depression all through the winter with the thought that things will look rosier in the spring gives up when June comes and he still feels terrible.

Simply because two things change at the same time does not mean that there is causal correlation between them, that is, that the change in one has caused the change in the other.

Many studies in the social sciences investigate causal correlations. For example, the social psychologists John M. Darley and Bibb Latané in "Why People Don't Help in a Crisis" (*Psychology Today* [1968]) described experiments to identify what factors cause people, when part of a group, to be less likely to aid the same victims of street crime they would have helped on a one-to-one basis. Darley and Latané discovered a clear correlation between the numbers of people witnessing an emergency and the willingness of any one individual to come to the aid of the victim. Surprisingly, the more people in a group, the less likely any one person was to volunteer to help the victim. One such factor was peer pressure:

> A person trying to interpret a situation often looks at those around him to see how he should react. If everyone else is calm and indifferent, he will tend to remain so; if everyone else is reacting strongly, he is likely to become aroused. This tendency is not merely slavish conformity; ordinarily we derive much valuable information about new situations from how others around us behave. It's a rare traveler, who, in picking a roadside restaurant, chooses to stop at one where no other cars appear in the parking lot.

Darley and Latané's classic experiment disclosed a significant correlation between a measurable cause (number of bystanders) and an observable effect (willingness of any one individual to aid the victim). Causal analysis is an important tool used by researchers to discover the means by which social pressures control the behavior of people in groups. In this case, Darley and Latané's results challenged the traditional idea that apathy is the reason bystanders are unwilling to help victims of street crime.

Because of the complexity of causal relationships, writers must try to identify as precisely as possible the contributory factors in any causal sequence. The direct or immediate causes of the event are those most likely to have triggered the actual event, yet behind direct causes may lie indirect or remote causes that set the stage or create the framework in which the event could occur. Immediate or *precipitating* causes are those that can be identified as occurring just before the event, phenomenon, or trend. On the other hand, remote, indirect, or *background* causes occur in the past well before the actual event takes place.

For example, Aldous Huxley, political essayist and author of *Brave New World* (1932), distinguished between predisposing and triggering causes to explain why one segment of the German population was so easily swayed by Hitler's rhetoric:

> Hitler made his strongest appeal to those members of the lower middle class who had been ruined by the inflation of 1923, and then ruined all over again by the depression of 1929 and the following years. "The masses" of whom he speaks were these bewildered, frustrated and chronically anxious millions. To make them more masslike, more homogeneously subhuman, he assembled them, by the thousands and the tens of thousands, in vast halls and arenas, where individuals

could lose their personal identity, even their elementary humanity, and be merged with the crowd.

In this passage from "Propaganda Under a Dictatorship" in *Brave New World Revisited* (1958), Huxley uses causal analysis to emphasize that the people most likely to yield to propaganda were those whose security had been destroyed by previous financial disasters. That is, previous cycles of financial instability (the disastrous inflation of 1923 and the depression of 1929) played a crucial role in predisposing the lower middle classes, those whose security was most affected by the financial turmoil, to become receptive to Hitler's propaganda. Hitler, says Huxley, used techniques of propaganda—mass marches, repetition of slogans, scapegoating—to manipulate the segment of the population that was the least secure and most fearful.

Long-term future effects are much more difficult to make a case for than are short-term, immediate effects. Determining with any degree of certainty that X caused Y is more complicated in situations where one cause may have produced multiple effects or the same effect could have been produced by multiple causes.

For example, David Hilfiker in "A Doctor's View of Modern Medicine" (*The New York Times Magazine* [February 23, 1986]) analyzes several causes that have, in his words, resulted in "private medicine's abandonment of the poor." As part of his analysis identifying the cause that in his view plays the dominant role, Hilfiker must consider and evaluate all possible causes as well:

> There are of course many complex factors that have precipitated private medicine's abandonment of the poor. The urbanization and anonymity of the poor, the increasingly technological nature of medicine and the bureaucratic capriciousness of public medical assistance—all these serve to make private physicians feel less responsible for the medical needs of those who cannot afford the going rate.
>
> But the cause that is probably most obvious to the lay public is singularly invisible to the medical community: Medicine is less and less rooted in service and more and more based in money. With many wonderful exceptions all over the country, American physicians as a whole have been turned away from the ideals of service by an idolatry of money. Physicians are too seldom servants and too often entrepreneurs. A profitable practice has become primary. The change has been so dramatic and so far-reaching that most of us do not even recognize that a transformation has taken place, that there might be an alternative. We simply take it for granted that economic factors will be primary even for the physician.

In his article Hilfiker draws on his own experience as a practicing physician to illustrate how a variety of pressures transformed him from a caring physician into a businessman concerned only with the efficient management of his office and medical practice. The fact that the average medical student can accrue up to $100,000 of debt, the increasing cost of malpractice insurance, and the enormous amounts of money necessary to set up and maintain an office are identified by Hilfiker as contributory causes in transforming the practice of medicine into just another profit-oriented business. Hilfiker then cites a range of effects (including the use of ever more costly "procedures" and the assembly-line approach of seeing thirty or more patients a day) that dramatically illustrate the negative consequences for patients when doctors become little more than businesspeople.

Causal arguments can get off the track when writers confuse sequence with causation. Events that merely follow each other in sequence should not be confused with true cause and effect. Simply because A preceded B does not necessarily mean that A caused B. This confusion of antecedent or correlation with causation is called the *post hoc* fallacy, from the Latin *post hoc, ergo propter hoc* (literally, after this, therefore because of this).

Darrell Huff and Irving Geis, mentioned earlier, provide an amusing example of one form the *post hoc* fallacy can take:

> As an instance of the nonsense or spurious correlation that is a real statistical fact, someone has gleefully pointed to this: There is a close relationship between the salaries of Presbyterian ministers in Massachusetts and the price of rum in Havana.
>
> Which is the cause and which the effect? In other words, are the ministers benefiting from the rum trade or supporting it? All right. That's so farfetched that it is ridiculous at a glance. But watch out for other applications of post hoc logic that differ from this one only in being more subtle. In the case of the ministers and the rum it is easy to see that both figures are growing because of the influence of a third factor: the historic and world-wide rise in the price level of practically everything.

The confusion here is based on the erroneous assumption that simply because two events occur in the same time period there is also a cause and effect relationship. For example, a person who walked under a ladder and then, ten minutes later, tripped and fell, might attribute the fall to walking under the ladder. To avoid falling for the *post hoc* fallacy, writers need to examine every cause and effect relationship carefully.

Writers should also be wary of attempting to oversimplify events that have complex causes. A common error is to mistake a necessary condition for a sufficient one. A *necessary* condition is one that must be present if the effect is to occur. For example, if electricity is considered a cause for light in an electric bulb, then without electricity there can be no light. A *sufficient* condition is a condition in whose presence the effect will always occur. Using our example, a worn filament is a sufficient condition for the light to go out. But a worn filament is not a necessary condition; the light could also go out if the power lines were down because of a storm. To take another example, most people would agree that buying a lottery ticket is a necessary condition to winning a prize. That is, you cannot win without having bought a ticket. It is equally obvious that buying a lottery ticket, while necessary, does not of itself cause one to win the prize. By contrast, buying a lottery ticket with the correct numbers is a sufficient condition to cause one to win the prize—that is, it is a condition that will always ensure that the effect will occur.

Causes and effects can occur in connecting sequences of "chains of causation," where each effect itself becomes the cause of a further effect. Causal arguments must demonstrate how each cause produces an effect that then acts as a cause of a further effect. This type of causal argument often takes the form of a conditional prediction: if X happens then Y will occur.

For example, Carl Sagan's argument in "The Nuclear Winter" (*Parade Magazine* [1983]) is developed around the following conditional claim:

> Nuclear winter would be the result of even a small-scale nuclear war.

Sagan must show how an effect that has never been observed could be produced. Most people would not be convinced that the most devastating effect of even a small-scale nuclear war would be mass starvation. Yet, Sagan's research leads him to conclude that this would be the ultimate consequence of any nuclear exchange:

> In the baseline case, land temperatures, except for narrow strips of coastline, dropped to minus 25 Celsius (minus 13 degree Fahrenheit) and stayed below freezing for months—even for a summer war... Because the temperatures would drop so catastrophically, virtually all crops and farm animals, at least in the Northern Hemisphere, would be destroyed, as would most varieties of uncultivated or domesticated food supplies. Most of the human survivors would starve.

In Sagan's analysis, the fatal chain of consequences that even a small-scale nuclear war would produce begins with (1) dust lofted into the atmosphere, producing (2) a greater than expected drop in global temperatures, lasting (3) much longer than anticipated, and resulting in (4) the extinction of crops and animals and (5) mass starvation among human beings. In the article from which this passage is taken, Sagan draws on many kinds of evidence, including the computer's ability to simulate hypothetical scenarios, to support the "nuclear-winter" hypothesis. Because of the hypothetical nature of this thesis, Sagan is obligated to show how the ecosystem is much more vulnerable—and the consequences of even a small-scale nuclear war much more extreme—than scientists previously believed.

✦ Questions for Discussion and Writing

1. In a few paragraphs, identify the causes you believe were responsible for your decision to attend your present college or university. Try to distinguish between long-term (predisposing) and short-term (triggering) causes for your decision. Can you discover any connecting sequences of causation that would constitute a chain of cause and effect? Be sure to state *how* the cause or causes you identify could have produced the end result.

2. Describe an invention (car, airplanes, air-conditioning, etc.) that changed history or an invention that does not yet exist that would make the world a better place. State *how* the effects you describe were or could be produced by the invention.

3. Is there a sport that has failed to establish itself in the United States for which you have a plausible argument why it has not? For example, soccer or professional women's basketball.

4. How might Figure 2-2 serve as the basis for a causal argument? Sketch out a plausible sequence of cause and effect and identify the means by which the observed effect could have been produced.

FIGURE 2-2

Source: Copley News Service, Mike Ramirez: "Beat Your Parents With A Chair."

5. Analyze the following mini-argument on evolution. Sketch out or diagram, if you wish, the related sequences of cause and effect, chains of

causation, and contributing causes identified by Gould in supporting his claim. How persuasive do you find his argument?

Human Life Is an Accident

The human species has inhabited this planet for only 250,000 years or so—roughly .0015 percent of the history of life, the last inch of the cosmic mile. The world fared perfectly well without us for all but the last moment of earthly time—and this fact makes our appearance look more like an accidental afterthought than the culmination of a prefigured plan. Moreover, the pathways that have led to our evolution are quirky, improbable, unrepeatable and utterly unpredictable. Human evolution is not random; it makes sense and can be explained after the fact. But wind back life's tape to the dawn of time and let it play again—and you will never get humans a second time.

We are here because one odd group of fishes had a peculiar fin anatomy that could transform into legs for terrestrial creatures; because the earth never froze entirely during an ice age; because a small and tenuous species, arising in Africa a quarter of a million years ago, has managed, so far, to survive by hook and by crook. We may yearn for a "higher" answer—but none exists. This explanation, though superficially troubling, is not terrifying, is ultimately liberating and exhilarating. We cannot read the meaning of life passively in the facts of nature. We must construct these answers ourselves—from our own wisdom and ethical sense. There is no other way.

—Stephen Jay Gould in *The Meaning of Life*, 1991

6. From the following description of an observed effect, speculate on how the situation she describes might have come about. Identify relevant chains of causation as well as predisposing and triggering causes.

Racial Polarization

I'm beginning to see a disturbing pattern of identification among the [Berkeley] student population. Each group stays within its own boundaries, within its own territory. The black students sit together on the left side of Sproul Plaza, the Latinos occupy another corner, the Asian students assemble somewhere else and the whites mostly disappear to their sororities and fraternities.

What happened to socializing among the "diverse student population" of UC Berkeley? What happened to the goal of diversity: a mixed campus population conducive to promoting understanding of other customs and peoples?

Rather than gaining understanding and forming friendships, students seem less tolerant. Polarization along the lines of skin color is increasing at Berkeley.

—Lorenza Muñoz, *Los Angeles Times*, May 19, 1991

7. From your personal experience and observation, does competition strengthen or undermine friendship? Make a plausible causal case to support your opinion.

VALUE CLAIMS MAKE VALUE JUDGMENTS

As distinct from arguments that debate matters of fact, value arguments apply ethical, moral, aesthetic, or utilitarian criteria to produce judgments that measure a subject against an ideal standard. For example, consider the following cases:

> A sportswriter evaluates two teams and says that one has a better chance of winning the pennant because of better pitching.
>
> A writer for *Consumer Reports* evaluates different brands of microwave ovens and selects the best.
>
> A student writes an analysis arguing that the latest novel by a writer is her best work yet.
>
> A critic writes a review evaluating a new restaurant, movie, or software program.

In all these cases, the writers are not merely expressing personal taste but are making a reasoned judgment based on identifiable standards of value. Writers of value arguments must demonstrate that the standard being used as the yardstick is an appropriate one and must provide a convincing argument with reasons and evidence in order to influence the readers' judgment and perception of the subject. For example, a writer who contended that bilingual education was or was not worthwhile, or that euthanasia was or was not immoral, would be obligated to present clearly the ideal standard against which the subject was being evaluated. Arguments that evaluate whether something is good or bad must provide (1) sufficient and verifiable evidence of a phenomenon and (2) an appropriate standard by which to measure value.

Writers frequently use comparison and contrast as a rhetorical strategy in organizing value arguments. Whether the comparison is between two books, two candidates, two kinds of automobiles, or any two subjects in the same class or category, evaluations are structured so that one choice is clearly seen as superior to the other when the two are directly compared. To get a more accurate idea of how writers use this strategy, consider the following argument by Jennifer James, a social anthropologist. James presents her case in the article "The Prostitute as Victim" (1978):

> Violations of the prostitution statutes account for approximately 30% of most women's jail populations. Convicted prostitutes serve long jail sentences compared to other misdemeanants such as shoplifters or those involved in larceny or assault. The judicial attitude represented by these sentencing patterns has no justification when considered in reference to the traditional legal concerns of danger to person or property loss. Nor does the large number of women arrested for prostitution indicate the commitment of the criminal justice system to an effective realistic campaign to eliminate prostitution. Each act of pros-

titution, after all, requires at least two participants: a seller and a buyer. Despite this incontrovertible fact, the arrest rate for customers is only two for every eight prostitutes arrested (*Uniform Crime Reports*, 1976). It has been estimated that about 20% of the male population has some contact with prostitutes, and yet the prostitutes seem to bear virtually the entire weight of legal reprisals. Since the prostitution laws in almost every state are neutral on their face, holding the prostitute and the customer equally culpable, the figures prove that prostitutes are the victims of discriminatory law enforcement.

The traditional justification for discriminatory enforcement of prostitution laws was stated by K. David in 1937:

> The professional prostitute, being a social outcast, may be periodically punished without disturbing the usual course of society; no one misses her while she is serving out her term—no one, at least, about whom society has any concern. The man [customer], however, is something more than a partner in an immoral act; he discharges important social and business relations.... He cannot be imprisoned without deranging society.

In this society, there are some behaviors which are considered acceptable for men but not for women. Prostitutes are women who are simultaneously rewarded and punished for choosing to earn their living through patterns of behavior that are unacceptable for members of their sex. In other words, prostitutes are the victims of sex-role stereotyping.... Men who purchase the services of prostitutes are still considered normal (nondeviant), even though their action may be seen as unpalatable, or even immoral, according to the personal standards of the observer.... Men are expected to have a wide variety of sexual needs and to actively seek fulfillment of those needs. As part of that search, men are allowed to illegally purchase the sexual services of women with relative impunity, as arrest statistics demonstrate.... The provisions of sexual services to males by women is, in contrast, clearly labeled deviant. Males break few social rules in patronizing a prostitute; females break almost all the rules in becoming prostitutes. Streetwalkers, in particular, place themselves at the wrong end of the whore-madonna spectrum: they accept money for sex, they are promiscuous, they are not in love with their customers, they are not subtle, and they engage in "abnormal" or deviant sex acts—acts which "respectable" women are not expected to accept.

James identifies the essential issue as one of equal treatment under the law. Her strategy is to contrast how the law treats prostitutes in comparison with their clients. The fact that the arrest rate for customers is only "two for every eight prostitutes arrested" indicates that prostitutes are discriminated against by being treated much more harshly than their customers. James then speculates on why this discriminatory attitude exists and finds that it has its roots in the different value judgments society makes about the social worth of the prostitute in comparison with the presumed higher value of her customer as a contributing member of society.

Although the concept of equal protection under the law is a value standard with which few people would disagree, it is important to recognize that different people bring different value standards to bear within the same situation and therefore may produce very different value judgments. For example, a solution that might be perfectly acceptable on pragmatic or utilitarian grounds might be unacceptable or even repugnant when judged by moral or aesthetic standards. For this reason, it is important for readers to identify the particular value system the writer is using as a criterion.

Value systems shape perceptions by influencing what people see, how they make sense out of what they see, and, most important, how they interpret what they see. When people bring different value systems to the same situation, they perceive and understand the same events in radically different ways. Personal feelings, expectations, and interests strongly influence how people interpret events.

Michael Novak makes this point in his article "The Poor and Latin America" (*The Atlantic Monthly* [March 1982]):

> Latin Americans do not value the same moral qualities North Americans do. The two cultures see the world quite differently. . . . The "Catholic" aristocratic ethic of Latin America places more emphasis on luck, heroism, status, and *figura* than the relatively "Protestant" ethic of North America, which values diligence, regularity, and the responsible seizure of opportunity. Given two such different ways of looking at the world, intense love-hate relations are bound to develop.

As Novak's article illustrates, we should try to become aware of the extent to which value systems, our own and those of others, influence and shape our perceptions. This is crucial in arguments when we discover that our own perception differs drastically from that of others when we are seeing the same events. In these cases, we need to take a close look at the reasons and evidence that support the beliefs and decide whether the information on which the beliefs are based is reliable. This is one important function performed by value arguments: they challenge us to examine underlying assumptions that ordinarily remain unquestioned by forcing us to justify our view of the world.

✦ Questions for Discussion and Writing

1. How might the following quotations serve as the basis for value arguments? In each case, state your own value judgment, summarize opposing views (if applicable), and show how your conclusion meets the appropriate criteria.

   a. "A bad peace is even worse than war." (Tacitus)

   "The most disadvantageous peace is better than the most just war" (Erasmus).

   b. "We are not the policeman of mankind. We are not able to run the world, and we shouldn't pretend that we can." (Walter Lippmann, February 22, 1965)

   "We have learned that we cannot live alone, at peace; that our own well-being is dependent on the well-being of other nations, far away." (Franklin D. Roosevelt, fourth inaugural address, January 20, 1945)

   c. "Pornography is often grotesquely offensive; it is insulting, not only to women, but to men as well. But we cannot consider that a sufficient reason for banning it without destroying the principle that the speech we hate is as much entitled to protection as any other. The essence of negative liberty is freedom to offend and that applies to the tawdry as well as to the heroic." (Ronald Dworkin, *The New York Review of Books*, August 15, 1991)

   d. "It may be a strong statement to make, but in my opinion, a parent who says that he or she is not interested in sports and doesn't value athletics for their child is acting irresponsibly." (Eric Margenau, *Sports without Pressure*, 1990)

   e. "Group sex education amounts to a perversion of nature. It makes public and open that which is naturally private and intimate. Any teaching about sex in a public setting violates privacy and intimacy. Sex education in the classroom is an insidious and unnatural invitation to sexual activity; it is erotic seduction; and it is even a form of child molestation, violating the natural latency and post-latency periods of child development, periods which are crucial for normal development of the whole person." (Randy Engel, interviewed in *The New American*, January 27, 1992)

2. Extract the competing sets of values in Figure 2-3. Rank each of these value criteria in order of their importance to you. Summarize the opposing views and either refute or accommodate each of the objections that might be raised to your value claim.

3. How does the following mini-argument about giving alcoholics equal access to transplanted livers depend on moral values and value judgments? Would you apply different value criteria? If so, state what they are and give reasons why they would be more appropriate in this situation.

Experts are coming to recognize that there is no moral or medical reason to exclude alcoholics for liver transplantation just because they are

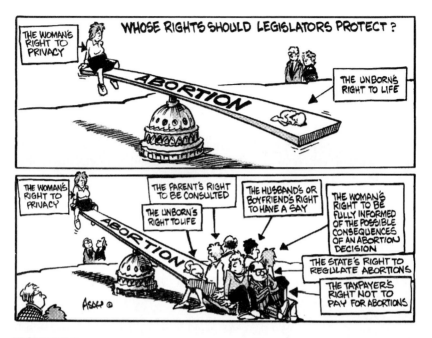

FIGURE 2-3

Source: Chuck Asay, by permission of the *Colorado Springs Gazette Telegraph.*

alcoholics. The limiting factors seem to be whether candidates are mentally or physically impaired from other well known complications of alcoholism that damage the brain, heart and blood system.

Several leaders have hammered away at the inconsistencies and the unique requirement from alcoholics that they abstain from alcohol. Those seeking transplants for other diseases are not held to the same standards. Smokers who need heart transplants are told to quit smoking, but they are not generally deprived of a suitable organ if they are unable to comply. . . .

Many would side with Dr. George D. Lundberg, the editor of the *Journal of the American Medical Association,* who said that if he had several possible recipients for a single organ, he would try to decide who was the most deserving recipient. He said he held to the view he expressed in an editorial in 1983: "If I had one liver to transplant and 50,000 possible recipients, I wouldn't let the fact that a great creative genius might drink deter me from giving him or her a needed new liver to allow another 30 years of creativity."

—Lawrence K. Altman, *The New York Times,* April 3, 1990

4. For each of the following situations, identify the criteria that you are applying, put them in the order of importance to you, and show how your choice meets your criteria.

a. Evaluate the comparative benefits of Eastern forms of exercise such as t'ai chi or yoga with Western exercises such as aerobics or jogging. According to criteria that you stipulate, which is better and why?

b. Would you rather be popular with an entire group without forming a really close friendship or have one very close friend but not be popular with the group?

c. Would you prefer to have a short, exciting life in which you had unusual powers (you may choose any you wish) or a long, uneventful life without those unusual powers?

POLICY CLAIMS MAKE RECOMMENDATIONS

In addition to arguments that characterize situations, make value judgments, or seek to establish causes or consequences, there are arguments that recommend policy changes. Many arguments in law and politics are of this kind, as are proposals in the fields of business, science, and technology.

A policy argument concerns itself first with establishing that a problem exists that is serious enough to need solving. The writer then analyzes the problem to discover the causes of the problem, puts forward a specific solution to the problem, and creates an argument that demonstrates that the proposed solution is workable (that is, can be implemented) and is superior to other proposed solutions.

An argument offering a proposed solution will often explore why there is a problem, investigate the circumstances that created it, describe who suffers because of the problem, and speculate about what will happen if the problem is not solved.

Frequently the proposed solution is put in the form of a recommendation using the terms *should, ought,* or *must.* For example, Siegfried and Therese Englemann in their book *Give Your Child a Superior Mind* (1981) argue that "parents *should* provide pre-school academic instruction for their children."

Likewise, an advocate for teaching creationism in the public schools might phrase the recommendation thus: "public schools *ought* to give equal weight to the teaching of creationism and the theory of evolution in the classrooms."

So, too, a staunch backer of drug testing might propose: "athletes competing in international sports events *must* be tested for steroids and other drugs."

Ideally, a policy argument should demonstrate that the way things are currently being done is producing negative consequences and that the recommended action or policy change would be capable of producing better results. For example, Dorothy W. Nelson, a judge in the United States Court of Appeals for the Ninth Circuit, in an article titled "Abolish the Blight of Plea Bargaining" (*The Christian Science Monitor* [February 12, 1979]) provides the following analysis to support her policy claim that "plea bargaining is a distorted and disgraceful blight on our criminal justice system which ought to be abolished":

> The prison conversations, a review of the empirical data available, and a conviction that there are alternative procedures available lead me to conclude that plea bargaining is a distorted and disgraceful blight on our criminal justice system which ought to be abolished. Admittedly, it would be folly to declare the abolition of plea bargaining merely to have the practice displaced to an earlier stage of the criminal justice system, or increased reliance on tacit rather than explicit plea bargaining. It is possible, however, to eliminate the bargaining or "bartering," as some would term it, through an expanded form of the felony preliminary hearing.

Nelson first defines the nature of the problem, demonstrates that it is serious enough to need solving, modifies her claim to take into account the counterclaim about the negative consequences of abolishing plea bargaining, and suggests a solution that from her perspective would provide a workable alternative to the current procedure.

Nelson's argument is typical in that it employs a problem–solution format. The author first defines the problem to be solved, carefully assesses alternative solutions (which she does in the full article), and then recommends and defends a particular course of action that will solve the problem more effectively than will other proposed ways.

Besides meeting the specific requirements of the problem-solving situation, solutions must be feasible, effective, and attractive to the audience to whom they are proposed. The audience must feel that the writer understands both the problem's causes and its consequences, is familiar with the history of past efforts to deal with it, and is united with them in their desire to remedy the problem.

For example, notice how Richard N. Goodwin devotes much of his article "Money Has Corrupted the Legislative Process" (*The Los Angeles Times* [December 12, 1985]) to demonstrating that a serious problem exists whose solution should be a matter of vital concern to his audience. He presents evidence to show that American government is being held hostage by special interest political action committee (PAC) groups. Implicit in Goodwin's article is the impression that he identifies with his reading public and is speaking out as any one of them might if he or she knew all the facts of the situation:

Power of wealth has [with honorable exceptions] achieved dominion over the legislative process and, hence, the conduct of democratic government. . . .

The principal instrument of this dominion is the political action committee, or PAC, which collects money from its members and gives it to the constitutional guardians of the public trust—members of Congress and aspirants to Congress.

Most of these committees belong to economic interests that have an important stake in the actions of government—insurance companies, real-estate developers, chemical and drug companies, for example. In less than a decade they have become the single most important force in the contest for federal office. . . . PAC money is neither a "gift" nor a "contribution."

It is an investment. The PACs expect recipients to give careful, and usually favorable, consideration to legislation that affects their economic well-being. Being experienced investors, they generally get what they expect. . . .

The meaning of the PACs is clear. Congress is not *influenced* by special interests. Congress does not *represent* special interests. Congress is *owned* by special interests. Morally the system is bribery. It is not criminal only because those who make the laws are themselves accomplices. Government is for sale. But the bids are sealed, and the prices are very high. There is an easy way out: Eliminate PACs. We should place a rigorous ceiling on all congressional campaigns, allocate public funds to finance campaigns and require television stations—the most costly component of modem political campaigns—to give a specified amount of air time to candidates.

As Goodwin's article illustrates, persuading readers to accept a recommendation means not only telling them what the best solution would be but also showing them through specific examples or hypothetical scenarios just how the solution would operate in practice. A writer who helps the reader visualize how the solution would work goes a long way toward refuting objections that the proposed solution might not be feasible, effective, or attractive; is too costly; or simply will not solve the problem. If possible, say who has the power to solve the problem.

It is important to keep in mind that because policy arguments are basically designed to motivate people to act, or to approve of an action that has been taken, the writer must make every attempt to make the audience aware of just how serious the problem really is. It must be serious enough to warrant doing something about it. For this reason, writers often begin by pointing out the negative consequences of failing to solve the problem and also provide an account of past attempts to solve the same problem.

Next, writers propose a solution and evaluate it against alternative solutions, giving sound reasons for rejecting the alternative solutions.

It is important that the writer be willing to admit honestly that difficulties could arise in carrying out his or her proposed solution and be willing to modify it in light of valid suggestions made by others.

Since policy arguments require not merely agreement, but action on the part of the audience, it is crucial for writers to try to anticipate how readers may react to the proposed solution. By putting yourself into the position of those you wish to persuade, you can generate a list of objections that might be made to your proposed solution. Would your critics reject your recommendation on any of the following grounds: your proposed action is too expensive, inefficient, unworkable, impractical, disrupting to the status quo, or unacceptable on the grounds that it is morally offensive or aesthetically unappealing?

If substantial costs are involved, the writer should specify who will bear those costs and explain how the benefits achieved will outweigh the costs involved.

Equally important as any substantive concerns, writers of policy arguments would be wise to adopt an appropriate tone for their argument. Usually the purposes of a policy argument are best served if the writer presents himself or herself as a reasonable person of good character who is well informed on the issue in question and who is sensitive to the needs and concerns of the audience.

✦ *Questions for Discussion and Writing*

1. Explain how each of the following examples might serve as a basis for a policy argument with which you might agree or disagree:

   a. Bilingual education tends to establish a limited English vocabulary and reduced language skills among Hispanics. A student taught in two languages, one intimate, easy and familiar, the other cold, formal and difficult, will naturally tend to use what is most pleasant and easy. As a result, Hispanics without real sensitivity to or capability in the English language will be competing with people who have immensely rich vocabularies in English. (Philip Vargas, *The Washington Post*, April 8, 1991.)

   b. It seems distressingly perverse that the very places where homeless people seek asylum, the shelters, are often, albeit by no means universally, the sites of greater risk than are the streets. Theft in shelters is rife: retention of personal belongings is accomplished by guile or domination, as even the best-staffed facilities can provide little real security. Shelter clients may fear their fellows—some recently released from jail, prison, or mental hospitals—who can be violent or exploitative; 34% of homeless people surveyed in Manhattan shelters and streets said they were afraid of being attacked in a shelter—a proportion similar to that of those who voiced fears of being attacked on the street. (Pamela J. Fischer, *Homelessness: A Prevention-Oriented Approach*, 1992.)

c.   *Fan Manipulation*

Professional sports management often means fan management, fan manipulation and exploitation of the fans' fantasies. Professional sports management has made viewing the game, in person or on television, less accessible, less affordable and less enjoyable....

Professional sports management has successfully adjusted to the demands of TV by orchestrating, what, when and how we view professional sports. The marriage of sports management to television, players to agents and the games to show business are the result of economic decisions that have sidelined the fan, discarded him like a ticket stub after a home-game loss.

The scenario runs like this: Make the "product" so desirable that ticket prices are unattainable for the average family. Introduce mismanagement scenarios such as strikes, lockouts and collective bargaining. Demand higher TV rights fees, send player salaries up and increase the cost to the fans, regardless of the quality of the game. And when TV revenue decreases, make sure pay-per-view is forced down fans' throats so the bottom line remains intact.

That is what professional sports management has done. And the American sports fan is tired, disgusted and wants a change.

—Nicholas F. Filla, *The Sporting News*, July 13, 1992

d. At some colleges and universities, traditional survey courses of world and English literature have been scrapped or diluted. At others they are in peril. At still others they will be. What replaces them is sometimes a mere option of electives, sometimes "multicultural" courses introducing material from Third World cultures and thinning out an already thin sampling of Western writings, and sometimes courses geared especially to issues of class, race, and gender. (Irving Howe, "Scrapping the Classics," *The New Republic*, Feb. 18, 1991.)

e.   *Protecting the Murderer*

There is a rule of evidence, used in all federal and state Courts in America, that defies logic, makes no sense whatsoever, and causes hundreds of serious miscarriages of justice each year. Its technical name is the Exclusionary Rule.

This pernicious rule prohibits the admission of evidence at trial if the evidence has been obtained by a policeman or other peace officer as a result of "unreasonable search and seizure" in violation of the Fourth Amendment to the U.S. Constitution....

The Exclusionary Rule has created an upside-down system of criminal justice which diverts the focus of the criminal prosecution from the guilt or innocence of the defendant to a trial of the police!...

The Exclusionary Rule holds, in effect, that it is better for a murderer to go free than for the State to take advantage of any illegal conduct on the part of its officers.

—L. Thaxton Hanson, from a brochure published by the Americanism Educational League, 1976

2. What problems confront students at your college or university? Which of them do you feel is most important and should be solved as soon as possible? Analyze the problem you consider most important in terms of the people who suffer because of it, the reasons why it exists, and the consequences of its failing to be solved. Speculate about why the problem has not been solved so far, and describe who (person, committee, student body, etc.) has the power to solve it. Offer a proposed solution specifying the benefits, the costs, and who will bear the costs. Why is your proposed solution better than alternative ones?

   Be prepared to defend your position in class. You may wish to present your essay in the context of a class discussion about the issue. What are the key interests that must be addressed in the process of mediating between conflicting parties? As a class, you might wish to evolve a collaborative statement that is acceptable to all parties involved.

3. You are empowered to decide that a building in your area should be demolished and replaced with a building whose appearance, uses, materials, and functions in the community are for you to determine. Make the case in terms of problem-solving criteria for the structure you would wish to create.

Support

EVIDENCE

Every assertion or claim put forward in an argument should be supported by appropriate, authoritative, and timely evidence. Evidence can appear in a variety of forms, including examples drawn from personal experience, hypothetical cases, analogies, the testimony of experts, and statistical data. Readers expect that evidence cited to substantiate or refute assertions will be sound, accurate, and relevant and that conclusions will be drawn logically from this evidence. Readers also expect that a writer arguing in support of a proposition will acknowledge and answer objections put forth by the opposing side in addition to providing compelling evidence to support his or her own position.

Examples Drawn from Personal Experience

Providing good examples is an essential part of effective argumentative writing. A single well-chosen example, or a range of illustrations, can provide clear cases that illustrate, document, and substantiate a writer's thesis. The report of a memorable incident, an account drawn from records, eyewitness reports, and a personal narrative account of a crucial incident are all important ways examples can serve to document the authenticity of the writer's thesis. For example, Loren C. Eiseley begins his review of Rachel Carson's *Silent Spring*, "Using a Plague to Fight a Plague" (1962), by drawing on personal experience to underscore the issue that is at the heart of Carson's book—the threat the widespread use of chemical pesticide poses to the environment:

> A few days ago I stood amidst the marshes of a well-known wildlife refuge. As I studied a group of herons through my glasses, there floated by the margin of my vision the soapy, unsightly froth of a detergent discharged into the slough's backwaters from some source upstream. Here nature, at first glance, seemed green and uncontaminated. As I left, however, I could not help wondering how long it would be before seeping industrial wastes destroyed the water—life on which those birds subsisted—how long it would be before poisonous and vacant mudflats had replaced the chirping frogs and waving cattails I loved to visit. I thought also of a sparkling stream in the Middle West in which, as a small boy, I used to catch sunfish, but which today is a muddy, lifeless treacle filled with oil from a nearby pumping station. No living thing now haunts its polluted waters.
>
> These two episodes out of my experiences are trifling, however, compared with that virulent facet of man's activities treated in Rachel Carson's latest book. It is a devastating, heavily documented, relentless attack upon human carelessness, greed, and irresponsibility—an irresponsibility that has let loose upon man and the countryside a flood of dangerous chemicals in a situation which, as Miss Carson states, is without parallel in medical history. "No one," she adds, "yet knows what the ultimate consequences may be."

These observations serve to illustrate the thesis of Carson's book and provide a context for Eiseley's discussion. It is significant that ecological effects documented by Carson are also confirmed by Eiseley's observations in two widely different areas of the country. His observations dramatize the consequences of chemical dumping and establish that the phenomenon identified by Carson has not occurred only in one section of the country; chemical pesticides pose a widespread threat to the environment.

One extremely effective way of substantiating a claim is by using a *case history*, that is, an in-depth account of the experience of one person that typifies the experience of many people in the same situation. The following account drawn from Michael Harrington's acclaimed sociological study *The Other America: Poverty in the United States* (1969) uses one woman's experiences to typify the plight of a whole class of older citizens:

> Sometimes in the course of an official Government report, a human being will suddenly emerge from the shadows of statistics and analyses. This happened in a summary statement of the Senate Subcommittee on the Problems of the Aged and Aging in 1960. Louise W— comes to life: Louise W—, age 73, lives by herself in a single furnished room on the third floor of a rooming house located in a substandard section of the city. In this one room, she cooks, eats and sleeps. She shares a bathroom with other lodgers. Widowed at 64, she has few friends remaining from her younger years. Those who do remain do not live near her, and it is difficult for her to see them. She feels that the other older men and women living in the same rooming house are not good enough for her company (conversations with these persons reveal that they have the same attitude, too: their fellow inhabitants are not good enough for them either).
>
> And so she stays confined to her one room and the bathroom shared by nine other people. When the weather is warm enough, she ventures down the long flight of stairs about once a week for a walk to the corner and back. Louise W— is symbolic of a growing and intense problem in American society. The nation venerates youth, yet the proportion of the population over sixty-five years of age is increasing. For many of these older people, their declining years are without dignity. They have no function; they are sick; they are without money. Millions of them wear out the last days of their existence in small apartments, in rooming houses, in nursing homes.
>
> This is no country for old men. The physical humiliation and the loneliness are real, but to them is added the indignity of living in a society that is obsessed by youth and tries to ignore age. These people are caught, as one witness before the Senate Committee testified, in a triple "chain of causality": they are plagued by ill health; they do not have enough money; and they are socially isolated. Some of them are new entrants to the world of the other America, drifting down from a working life of decent wages to an old age of dependency and social workers. A good many are old and poor because they were young and poor, middle-aged and poor. Taken together, they constitute a section of the culture of poverty with over 8,000,000 inhabitants.

The example of Louise W— serves as anecdotal proof that illustrates Harrington's claim that many of the elderly are among the most poverty-stricken people in the country. He shows, graphically and vividly, that many older people face a future very unlike the popular depiction of the "golden years."

+ *Questions for Discussion and Writing*

  1. Create a one or two paragraph mini-argument drawing on personal experience or the experiences of others (case history) that develops one or two of the following topics. (Support your claim with statements that refer to "a time when" or "a situation where," etc.) Specify the audience to whom you would be making this argument; think of an audience (person or group) whose opinion you would want to change.

     • The transition from living at home to living in the dorm
     • Friends who borrow money
     • Long-distance relationships and high telephone bills
     • Transportation issues (parking, bike lanes, etc.)
     • Coaches
     • First apartments, landlords, roommates
     • Having pets
     • Budgeting finances
     • The joys of cooking
     • Bosses, supervisors
     • Memorable dates, blind dates
     • Clubs, study groups, ethnic or activity-related gatherings such as Bible study groups, chorus
     • The mall's effect on socializing
     • Personal appearance, clothing, good or bad hair day
     • Substance abuse
     • Recreation, concerts (the Rainbow Gathering, etc.), games (virtual reality, etc.), museums
     • Dieting
     • Specialized pursuits, for example, cybersurfing, e-mail, Internet (Netscape, etc.)
     • Martial arts training
     • Computers
     • Culture clashes

Hypothetical Cases (Scenarios and "What If" Situations)

All examples need not be real. In some types of causal arguments where no real and observable effects can be cited as examples, the writer is obliged to show how an effect that has never been observed is possible or could be produced. In these circumstances, hypothetical examples are useful in clarifying possible future consequences. For example, in "The Case for Torture" (*Newsweek*, 1982) Michael Levin argues that in certain circumstances torture is "not merely permissible but morally mandatory." Levin uses a series of hypothetical examples to support this assertion. Levin's strategy is to begin with a very extreme hypothetical example of a terrorist who has "hidden an atomic bomb on Manhattan Island" in order to compel the reader to examine her own assumptions as to whether or not torture is, if ever, permissible:

> Suppose a terrorist had hidden an atomic bomb on Manhattan Island which will detonate at noon on July 4 unless . . . (here follow the usual demands for money and release of his friends from jail). Suppose, further, that he is caught at 10 A.M. of the fateful day, but—preferring death to failure—won't disclose where the bomb is. What do we do? If we follow due process—wait for his lawyer, arraign him—millions of people will die. If the only way to save those lives is to subject the terrorist to the most excruciating possible pain, what grounds can there be for not doing so? I suggest there are none. In any case, I ask you to face the question with an open mind. Torturing the terrorist is unconstitutional? Probably. But millions of lives surely outweigh constitutionality. Torture is barbaric? Mass murder is far more barbaric. Indeed, letting millions of innocents die in deference to one who flaunts his guilt is moral cowardice, an unwillingness to dirty one's hands. If you caught the terrorist, could you sleep nights knowing that millions died because you couldn't bring yourself to apply the electrodes?
>
> Once you concede that torture is justified in extreme cases, you have admitted that the decision to use torture is a matter of balancing innocent lives against the means needed to save them. You must now face more realistic cases involving more modest numbers. Someone plants a bomb on a jumbo jet. He alone can disarm it, and his demands cannot be met (or if they can, we refuse to set a precedent by yielding to his threats). Surely we can, we must, do anything to the extortionist to save the passengers. How can we tell 300, or 100, or 10 people who never asked to be put in danger, "I'm sorry, you'll have to die in agony, we just couldn't bring ourselves to . . ."
>
> Here are the results of an informal poll about a third, hypothetical, case. Suppose a terrorist group kidnapped a newborn baby from a hospital. I asked four mothers if they would approve of torturing kidnappers if that were necessary to get their own newborns back. All said yes, the most "liberal" adding that she would administer it herself.

Levin's strategy is extremely effective. If a reader accepts the use of torture in some cases, then he or she would have to consider more seriously whether torture is appropriate in nonhypothetical cases in real life. If torture is acceptable (1) to save the lives of millions of people from an atomic bomb hidden by terrorists, or (2) to save a few hundred people from a terrorist bomb on a jumbo jet, or (3) to save the life of one newborn child from kidnappers, then the reader must confront the question as to when torture is *not* appropriate. Levin imaginatively uses these scenarios to probe the issue and to compel his readers to seriously consider his claim that "the decision to use torture is a matter of balancing innocent lives against the means necessary to save them." Note how Levin uses results of an "informal poll" to suggest that even apart from extreme hypothetical cases, torture remains a viable option for those mothers whose children's lives are at stake. Levin's argumentative strategy is to work from extreme cases to more realistic ones, saying in effect, "If you agree with my first and second examples, then you must agree with my third." These invented episodes have the effect of provoking his audience to think beyond immediate responses and really consider whether or not torture is ever permissible.

Analogies

Analogies are useful for bringing out convincing similarities among ideas, situations, and people in order to persuade an audience that if two things are similar in several observed respects, they may well be similar in other ways as well. The distinguished philosopher David Hume observed that "in reality all arguments from experience are founded on the similarity which we discover among natural objects, and by which we are induced to expect effects similar to those which we have found to follow from such objects." Analogy is effective as a rhetorical strategy in that it persuades an audience if two subjects share a number of specific observable qualities, then they may probably share some unobserved qualities as well.

Analogies are an unparalleled means of clarifying complex ideas and abstract concepts. For example, the historian Arnold J. Toynbee employs an unusual analogy in "Challenge and Response" (from *A Study of History* [1946]) to illuminate his thesis that societies become civilizations when their normal routine is challenged by an outside force. The crucial difference Toynbee discovered between primitive and higher cultures is that primitive societies remain static, whereas higher cultures respond creatively to challenge:

> Primitive societies as we know them by direct observation, may be likened to people lying torpid upon a ledge on a mountainside with a precipice below and a precipice above; civilizations may be likened to companions of these sleepers who have just risen to their feet and have started to climb up the face of the cliff above . . . we can observe that, for every single one now strenuously climbing, twice that number . . . have fallen back onto the ledge defeated.

Toynbee's analogy of cliff climbers and ledge sitters is meant to reflect the contrast between dynamic civilizations on the one hand and stagnant cultures on the other. In his analogy, societies are represented by the dormant sleepers. The ledge below is the past they have risen above. The precipice above them is the next plateau they must reach to become flourishing civilizations. The analogy captures the readiness of some societies to risk a possible fall in order to leave the relative safety of the ledge and climb the precipice in search of the ledge above.

The preceding example illustrates one important aspect of creating effective analogies: every analogy is useful until the differences between the things being compared become greater than the similarities. Arguments based on analogy, however compelling, interesting, and imaginative the analogy might be, can only strive to demonstrate a high degree of probability, not absolute certainty. For this reason, the criteria for evaluating analogical arguments depend on comparing the number of respects in which the two subjects are said to be similar or analogous with the number of respects in which they are said to differ. A strong analogy is persuasive to the extent that the number of qualities shared by two subjects far outweigh the differences. Correspondingly, many points of difference between the two subjects greatly weaken the analogical argument by reducing the audience's perception that the two things are probably alike in many ways.

In the law, strong analogies serve as proof. When lawyers cite previously decided cases as legal precedents to argue that a case in question should be decided along the lines of the earlier cases, they are reasoning from strong analogies. For example, a lawyer might cite the *Miranda* case (Supreme Court decision, 1966) as a precedent in arguing that the defendant in the present case should not be tried because he was not advised of his rights (as the *Miranda* decision requires). The use of legal precedent in the courtroom is a form of reasoning from analogy. Lawyers may argue that the present case should be dismissed because a previous case was also dismissed on the same grounds. Such straightforward reasoning assumes that enough similarities between two cases exist to support the claim that what was true of one case is also true of the other.

By contrast, weak or figurative analogies can clarify or illustrate a claim but cannot serve as evidence to support it. For example, a striking figurative analogy by Isaac Asimov in "Science and Beauty" (1983) dramatically clarifies his claim of an intimate and precarious interrelationship between all living things and their environment:

> In fact, we can pursue the analogy. A man is composed of 50 trillion cells of a variety of types, all interrelated and interdependent. Loss of some of those cells, such as those making up an entire leg, will seriously handicap all the rest of the organism: serious damage to a relatively few cells in an organ, such as the heart or kidneys, may end by killing all 50 trillion.
>
> In the same way, on a planetary scale, the chopping down of an entire forest may not threaten Earth's life in general, but it will produce serious changes in the life forms of the region and even in the nature of the water runoff and, therefore, in the details of geological structure.

Asimov's analogy is designed to persuade his readers that many parallels exist between the life processes of a person and the life processes of the planet Earth. Asimov's analogy is quite effective as a way of clarifying the issues involved and alerting the audience to the vulnerability of the planet to environmental disturbance.

To discover if you can tell whether an analogy is strong enough to support a claim, consider the following argument from "The Scourge of This Society Is Drug Abuse: Testing is Clearly an Idea Whose Time Has Come" (*Miami Herald* March [1986]) by John Underwood:

> For if a drug test is an invasion of privacy, what is a blood test? A man's blood is certainly as private as his urine, and even if it might, in its course or of its type, communicate a deadly disease or produce a deformed child, the testing of it most assuredly requires an invasion. The common good, and every state in the union, nevertheless requires blood tests. Try to get a marriage license without one. Moreover, what is an eye test if not (by short extension of ACLU logic) an invasion of privacy? On the common sense basis that we already wreak havoc on our highways without allowing the physically disabled behind the wheels of our killer vehicles, the common good calls for eye tests. Try getting a driver's license without one.
>
> And what about the lie tests that are burgeoning in popularity as a means of screening security risks in both the government and private sectors? Is a lie test an invasion of privacy? Is a man's brain as sacred as his bladder, regardless of how much or little can be found in either? You betcha. What could be more intrusive than poking around in a man's thought processes? But we allow it. The common good demands it.

Underwood argues that drugs have caused such damage to society that civil liberties groups are wrong to stand in the way of drug testing. He argues by analogy that just as eye tests, blood tests, and lie detector tests are widely accepted even though they invade privacy, so widespread drug testing should be instituted although admittedly it is also an invasion of privacy.

On first reading, Underwood's use of an analogy seems rooted in real similarities in comparable situations. The analogy, however, breaks down in some respects: the results of blood tests and eye tests are used to diagnose illness or cite deficiencies that can then be remedied. In other words, the results of these tests are used for the benefit of the person being tested. By contrast, a urinanalysis drug test has only one purpose: to identify a drug abuser to his or her employer or the government. The results are not used to benefit the person being tested and may even be used to the detriment of that person. In short, information derived from the test is used against the person being tested.

Lie detector tests seem to offer a closer analogy. Here, however, Underwood does not take into account the fact that the results from lie detector tests are not admissible as evidence in court. Thus, a crucial number of differences weaken his argument and greatly undercut the validity of his conclusion.

✦ Questions for Discussion and Writing

1. Develop any of the following into a mini-argument in which you support a claim with either a hypothetical example or an analogy drawn from a precedent or a parallel instance. Evaluate your mini-argument for persuasiveness and credibility:

   a. Have you ever been romantically involved with someone from a different racial, religious, or political background? To what kinds of pressures from parents, relatives, friends, and society were you subjected? What was the outcome of the relationship? What beliefs, views, or opinions did you evolve as a result?

   b. In your opinion, what pressures create difficulties in second marriages for the new spouse, children, and step-children, in terms of fairness, financial equity, and other issues?

   c. What is your opinion about the issues raised in Figure 2-4?

FIGURE 2-4

Source: Mike Peters. Reprinted by permission: Tribune Media Services.

Testimony of Experts

The testimony of experts is an invaluable way of quickly demonstrating that the conclusions one has reached about a given issue are independently subscribed to by renowned authorities in the field. Writers rely on the opinion of authorities when their own ability to draw conclusions based on firsthand observations is limited. The authorities are presumed to have expertise based on many years of research and greater familiarity with the issues under investigation. The opinion of experts is no substitute for the process of reasoning by which you have arrived at your conclusion, but a well-known authority can add considerable weight to your opinion and a dimension of objective credibility to the argument.

When deciding whether to quote an authority, consider the following guidelines:

1. The expert must be an authority in the field.
2. His or her testimony must be free from bias and result from free and open inquiry that is subject to public verification.
3. The opinion must be timely and not open to question on the grounds that it might have been true in the past but is no longer relevant.

For example, Elizabeth W. and Robert A. Fernea in "A Look Behind the Veil" (*Human Nature* [1979]) cite the opinion of an expert on Islamic culture in their discussion of the changing attitudes toward wearing the veil in Mediterranean and Middle Eastern societies:

> The multiple meanings and uses of purdah and the veil do not explain how the pattern came to be so deeply embedded in Mediterranean society. Its origins lie somewhere in the basic Muslim attitudes about men's roles and women's roles. Women, according to Fatima Mernissi, a Moroccan sociologist, are seen by men in Islamic societies as in need of protection because they are unable to control their sexuality, are tempting to men, and hence are a danger to the social order. In other words, they need to be restrained and controlled so that society may function in an orderly way.

Three Forms Expert Opinion Can Take.   The opinion of experts offers an interpretation of a set of facts. The interpretation can take one of three forms: the expert (1) points out a causal connection, (2) offers a solution to a problem, or (3) makes a prediction about the future. Correspondingly, writers can use these "expert opinions" to support a causal claim (that is, to document the existence of causal correlation or connection), to support a proposed solution to a problem, or to authenticate the reliability of a prediction.

1. *Pointing out a causal connection.* For example, a writer wishing to support a claim that where you live influences your chances of getting cancer might quote Samuel S. Epstein, a professor of occupational and environmental medicine at the University of Illinois Medical Center, in "The Cancer-Producing Society" (*Science For the People* [July 1976]):

> A recent National Cancer Institute (NCI) atlas on cancer mortality rates, in different counties, has demonstrated marked geographical clustering of rates for various organs in the U.S. with populations in heavily industrialized areas. Such data suggest associations between cancer rates in the general community and the proximity of residence to certain industries.

The writer would probably mention Epstein's credentials and, to further enhance the credibility of the source, might cite the fact that Epstein's efforts were responsible for the enactment of legislation to control toxic substances.

2. *Offering a solution to a problem.* Besides citing experts to document the existence of causal connections, writers look to authorities for solutions to problems. For example, the philosopher Peter Singer's article "Rich and Poor" (1979) might be cited to support an argument that rich nations should help poor ones, since they can do so at a relatively low cost to themselves:

> Death and disease apart, absolute poverty remains a miserable condition of life, with inadequate food, shelter, clothing, sanitation, health services and education. According to World Bank estimates which define absolute poverty in terms of income levels insufficient to provide adequate nutrition, something like 800 million people—almost 40 percent of the people of developing countries—live in absolute poverty. Absolute poverty is probably the principal cause of human misery today.
>
> This is the background situation, the situation that prevails on our planet all the time. It does not make headlines. People died from malnutrition and related diseases yesterday, and more will die tomorrow. The occasional droughts, cyclones, earthquakes and floods that take the lives of tens of thousands in one place and at one time are more newsworthy. They add greatly to the total amount of human suffering; but it is wrong to assume that when there are no major calamities reported, all is well.
>
> The problem is not that the world cannot produce enough to feed and shelter its people. People in the poor countries consume, on average, 400 lbs. of grain a year, while North Americans average more than 2000 lbs. The difference is caused by the fact that in the rich countries we feed most of our grain to animals, converting it into meat, milk and eggs. Because this is an inefficient process, wasting up to 95 percent of the food value of the animal feed, people in rich countries are responsible for the consumption of far more food than those in poor countries

who eat few animal products. If we stopped feeding animals on grains, soybeans and fishmeal the amount of food saved would—if distributed to those who need it—be more than enough to end hunger throughout the world.

Note how the expert opinion here takes the form of a solution offered to the problem of world hunger.

3. *Making a prediction.* A third form in which the testimony of authorities can be used to support a claim is as a prediction. For example, a writer who argued against continued reliance on fossil fuels, because of the resulting increase in carbon dioxide concentration in the air, might quote the opinion of the meteorologist Harold W. Bernard, Jr., from *The Greenhouse Effect* (1980):

> CO_2 allows sunshine to heat the earth but then traps much of the heat near the earth's surface, rather than permitting it to radiate back to space. This *greenhouse* effect warms the earth. This is not a problem, of course, as long as the amount of CO_2 in the air remains fairly constant; the amounts of incoming sunshine and outgoing heat remain in balance, and our climate remains relatively comfortable.
>
> However, the amount of atmospheric CO_2 is increasing, and most scientists fear that this may lead to a significant warming of the earth's climate. Current estimates suggest that CO_2 induced warming may account for about a 1.8°F rise in global temperature by early next century. Within a hundred years, global warming could be on the order of 11°F, with temperature increases in polar regions as much as three times that.

The opinion of a meteorologist provides a highly credible source for the prediction of how increasing atmospheric carbon dioxide levels would lead to major alterations in weather patterns that would drastically affect climate (as the United States began to witness in the unusually hot and dry summer of 1988) and perhaps melt part of the polar ice caps, resulting in flooding of low-lying coastal areas on all continents. Keep in mind that the opinion of experts, however credible, is still only an interpretation of a set of facts. Other authorities might presumably reach diametrically opposite conclusions from the same evidence. This is why the writer should first create an independent, well-reasoned argument that can stand on its own and only then add the testimony of experts to strengthen the case.

Statistics

Statistical evidence is among the most compelling kinds of proof a writer can offer to support a thesis. To be effective, statistical data should be drawn from recent data and be as up-to-date as possible. It is important that statistics come from reliable and verifiable sources such as the United States Bureau of the Census, the Bureau of Labor, documented surveys conducted by well-established research centers or universities, or well-known polling organizations like those of Lou Harris, Burns and Roper, and George Gallup. Statistical data are useful in many kinds of argument because of the ease with which comparative differences can be evaluated in quantifiable form. For example, in an argument that the insanity defense is little more than a legal ploy mostly used to favor white, upper-middle-class defendants, Jonathan Rowe, in "Why Liberals Should Hate the Insanity Defense" (*The Washington Monthly* [May 1984]), cites available statistics to prove that the insanity defense is not employed in the majority of prosecutions:

> The insanity defense looms a good deal larger in our minds than it does in actual life. Somewhere between 1,000 and 2,000 criminals make use of it each year, or about 1 percent to 2 percent of felonies that go to trial (over 90 percent in many jurisdictions are plea-bargained before trial). The issue is important not because it arises frequently, but because it tends to arise in the most serious crimes: think of Son of Sam, for example, or the Hillside Strangler. Such people tend to be dangerous, and their trials attract so much publicity that they put our entire system of justice to a test.

It is important for Rowe to establish that the insanity defense is only rarely used because his argument recommends abolishing it in its present form. The way statistical evidence is used will depend on the nature of the claim. Evidence in the form of statistics may provide stronger support for a writer's claim than anecdotal cases or hypothetical examples.

Statistics are especially useful in arguments where writers use inductive reasoning (drawing an inference from specific cases) to support a generalization extrapolated from a representative sampling of all the evidence that might be examined. As with other uses of evidence in inductive reasoning, writers must be careful not to draw conclusions, even from reliable, objectively verifiable statistics, that go so far beyond what the available evidence warrants as to seem improbable. Perhaps the most famous illustration of unwarranted generalization from a relatively small sample was the erroneous prediction in the 1948 presidential election that the Republican governor of New York, Thomas E. Dewey, would definitely defeat the incumbent Democrat, Harry S. Truman. Unfortunately for the pollsters, the poll on which this prediction was made was drawn from an inadequate sample and did not represent the entire voting population. Since any prediction based on polls is essentially an inference drawn from a number of individual cases, this claim or conclusion will become more probable as the size of the sample becomes greater. The claim, therefore, can be expressed in quantitative or statistical terms. For example, William J. Darby (whose study we looked at earlier in this chapter as an example of a causal argument) in "The Benefits of Drink" (*Human Nature* [1978]) cites a study of 120,000 patients that discovered moderate drinkers were 30 percent less likely to have heart attacks than were teetotalers:

> A recent study by Arthur L. Klatsky and his colleagues at the Kaiser-Permanente Medical Center in Oakland, California, offers new evidence that moderate drinking may serve as a deterrent to heart attacks. They studied 464 patients who had been hospitalized with a first myocardial infarction (heart attack) and discovered that an unusually large proportion were teetotalers. Their curiosity aroused, Klatsky and his colleagues evaluated the medical histories of 120,000 patients and found that moderate alcohol users were 30 percent less likely to have heart attacks than were non-drinking patients or matched controls or so-called risk controls—people who suffer from diabetes, hypertension, obesity, high serum cholesterol, or who smoke. (All of these factors are associated with increased risk of heart attacks.)

Notice how the conclusion uses statistics to quantify the generalization about the mitigating effects of moderate drinking. In essence, the writer is saying, "On the basis of these 120,000 instances, I'm reasonably certain that similar results would be obtained in comparable studies on other groups of patients."

Three Types of Averages: The Arithmetic Mean, the Median, and the Mode. When a writer supports a claim by referring to the "average," he or she is purposely selecting a specific value to represent the qualities of a whole aggregate of things. But it is important for the reader to realize that there is more than one type of average and to know the writer has used the right kind to support his or her claim. There are three main types of averages, called (1) the *mean*, (2) the *median*, and (3) the *mode*. Each has its own characteristics, and the values they represent can, in different situations, be quite different from one another. The most commonly used kind of average is the *arithmetic mean*—or, as it is commonly called, the mean. To calculate it, you simply add up all the numerical values and divide by the total number. The resulting average is the arithmetic mean.

1. *The arithmetic mean.* One example of the mean might be in baseball, where a player's batting average shows statistically how often the batter has successfully hit the ball in comparison with the total number of times he has had at bat. While this kind of an average is useful for giving a sense of where the "center of gravity" of any set (total number of times at bat, in this case) is located, the useful information drawn from it can be distorted by very large or very small instances averaged in with all the others. For example, a brokerage firm, in order to recruit account executive trainees, advertises that the average starting salary

for new employees is $36,000 a year. Only later might a new account executive discover that the $36,000 was derived by averaging in the $108,000 starting salary of a senior account executive with ten years' experience (transferring in from another firm) along with the $18,000 starting salary of four new account executive trainees. Here, the average of $36,000 is reached by adding $108,000 + (4 × $18,000) (equaling $180,000) divided by the five new employees.

2. *The median.* Other ways of measuring the average would have provided prospective employees with a much more realistic figure of what starting salary they could expect. One of these more accurate kinds of averages is the median. The median is usually the central value in a set of values. The median also establishes a dividing line that separates higher from lower values in a set of numbers. In the preceding case, the median starting salary would be $18,000 (while the average or mean was $36,000). As the following list shows, the median establishes a dividing line with two salaries above and two salaries below:

$108,000
$18,000
$18,000 (the median)
$18,000
$18,000

3. *The mode.* Another way of arriving at an average that is useful for interpretive purposes is the mode. The mode is the value that occurs most frequently in any series of numbers. In the preceding case, more new employees (four out of five) start at $18,000 a year than any other amount; hence, $18,000 is the modal income. In this case, the median and the mode are both more reliable indicators for a prospective new employee than the more commonly relied upon average arithmetical mean. This case illustrates how important it is for readers to understand what kind of average writers are using to substantiate a claim. Keep in mind that the three uses of the word *average* in the preceding example all draw different conclusions from exactly the same information. The median is a much more representative measure than the mean or average because, in any example, extremely high or extremely low readings on the scale will distort the average but not the median.

Using Charts and Graphs.   Evidence drawn from statistical data can be expressed and presented in charts, graphs, or percentages. The reader should determine whether conclusions drawn from statistics are consistent with other evidence in the argument.

Statistical information can be represented in a variety of graphic forms. For example, Figure 2-5 shows how the statistical breakdown of responses to the question "Should people who are carriers of genetic diseases be allowed to have children?" might be represented in a *pie chart.*

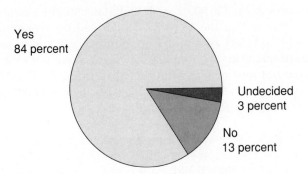

FIGURE 2-5   *Should People Who Are Carriers of Genetic Diseases Be Allowed to Have Children?*

Source: Adapted from Lou Harris, *Inside America,* Vintage Books, 1987, p. 139. *Business Week*/Harris Poll conducted by Lou Harris & Associates for *Business Week,* Nov. 1–4, 1985— national cross-section of 1,254 adults.

Statistical information can also appear in a *bar chart*. Figure 2-6 shows how the answer to the question "Would you engage in illegal insider trading if you got a tip?" might be shown.

The way statistical information is presented in graphic form can create, intentionally or unintentionally, a misleading impression. Examine the way the following two line graphs represent exactly the same information. The first graph (Figure 2-7) is designed to create the impression that not much is going on: over a twelve-month period the

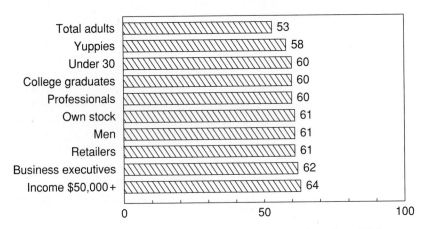

FIGURE 2-6   *Would You Engage in Illegal Insider Trading If You Got a Tip?*

Source: Adapted from Lou Harris, *Inside America,* Vintage Books, 1987, p. 110. *Business Week*/Harris Poll conducted by Lou Harris & Associates for *Business Week,* August 5–11, 1986—national cross-section of 1,248 adults.

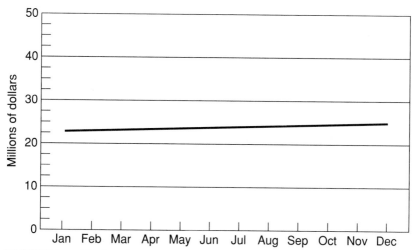

FIGURE 2-7 *Yearly Sales of the XYZ Widget Company.*

line marking changes in sales in millions of dollars barely manages to creep up from January to December.

Now look at the way the second graph (Figure 2-8) represents the same facts. By making the vertical axis cover a fraction of what it covered in the first graph, a misleading impression might be created by the way the graph line zooms into the stratosphere. For these reasons, it is important to look at the scale used on each axis of a graph.

The context in which statistics are presented is important. For example, the National Safety Council urges people to buckle up their seat

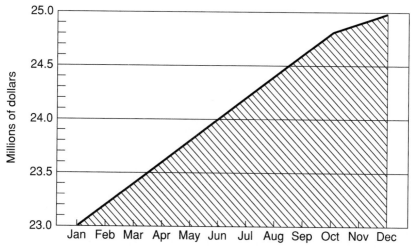

FIGURE 2-8 *Sales of the XYZ Widget Company.*

belts by announcing "80 percent of all fatal accidents occur five miles from home." Reading this, you're liable to have the mistaken impression that the area surrounding your house is more dangerous than other areas where you drive. Do you literally have to don a helmet and a flak jacket along with your seat belt whenever you enter this "danger zone"? What this public service announcement neglects to add is that 80 percent of *all* driving is done within five miles of where you live, which explains why 80 percent of all accidents, fatal and otherwise, occur in this area. The statistics themselves are true, but a proper context for evaluating what they mean has been omitted.

To evaluate the validity of a survey, readers should be aware of the size of the sample used to compile the data and the methods used to assure a fair cross section of the population under study. Opinion can be manipulated through seemingly impressive statistics where the sampling procedure used is subtly biased to support a preconceived opinion. For example, someone who reads that "nine out of ten dentists who recommend chewing gum, recommend XYZ gum" will probably overlook the key phrase "who recommend chewing gum." The statistics themselves might be true, but the sample has been skewed to survey only those dentists who recommend chewing gum—an atypical and miniscule subgroup of all dentists.

The most reliable technique for avoiding an error in sampling is to make sure the poll or study surveys a representative cross section of all those who might be polled. To ensure fairness, the sample must be random so that even if every individual cannot be polled, each member of the population has exactly the same chance of being included in the sample as any other.

This type of sampling procedure relies upon probability principles. It is implemented by dividing the population into separate categories, or *strata*. People interviewed are selected solely on a chance basis within each stratified category (for example, people who live in a certain part of town, or who earn a certain amount of money, or who have reached a certain level of education). The theory behind probability sampling is really quite straightforward. If one had a large barrel containing 10,000 marbles, half of which were red and half of which were blue, and wished to draw a probability sample of 200 marbles, one might draw the first marble while blindfolded to make sure that the marbles all stood an equal chance of being drawn. The barrel would be shaken after each trial to ensure that in subsequent drawings all the marbles still had an equal chance of being selected. The law of probability states that if this procedure were repeated an infinite number of times, the 200 marbles selected would be fairly close to a 50–50 division, with approximately 100 of them being red and 100 of them being blue. The next most likely combination would be either 99 red and 101 blue or 99 blue and 101 red. The next most likely combination after that would be 98 red and 102 blue or 98 blue and 102 red, and so on. The most unlikely combination would produce 200 marbles that were either all red or all blue.

For the same reason, if each member of a population being surveyed has an equal chance of being selected, probability theory states that the sample will wind up being sufficiently representative to provide an accurate index of the whole population. In practice, the expense of surveying a large number of people means that the size of the sample is frequently less than might be optimally desirable, since the larger the sample the smaller the sampling error that can be expected. *Sampling error* refers to the degree to which the results in the sample can be expected to differ from what the results would be if everyone in the population had been selected. It is expressed in terms of a range of percentage points above and below a reported percentage. For example, a survey based on 1,000 interviews might show that a candidate for governor might expect to be supported by 50 percent of the population. The margin of sampling error might be reported as plus or minus 4 percent. This means that if everyone in the population had been interviewed, rather than only 1,000, the actual results might see the candidate supported by as few as 46 percent of the people or as many as 54 percent. If the election were really close, a completely different outcome could be possible within the sampling error.

Therefore, any sampling procedure that automatically excludes any portion of the population is going to produce unrepresentative results of the kind that led pollsters to predict erroneously that Dewey would defeat Truman in the 1948 presidential election. The surveys that are used as evidence must be ones in which great efforts were made to ensure that all parts of the population are represented and not some arbitrarily selected group. It is also important to determine that those drawing up the survey have no vested interest in the outcome.

Thus, statistics play an important role in arguments where claims must be substantiated by reference to several cases where it would be impractical to test a whole population. At the same time, readers of arguments must be aware of the dangers of accepting statistics at face value without understanding both the procedures and the motives of those who gathered and interpreted the data.

✦ Questions for Discussion and Writing

1. Critically evaluate each of the following mini-arguments in terms of the credibility of the experts cited, the kind of testimony offered, and the quality and methodology of the statistical evidence presented.

a.   USA:
      Population: 255,000,000
      No. of lawyers: 750,000
      Lawyer/population ratio: 1:340
      No. of new lawyers/year: 36,000

      JAPAN:
      Population: 125,000,000 (roughly *half* that of the USA)
      Number of new lawyers/year: The Bar exam is the toughest
      professional examination in Japan; the failure rate is 98%; each
      year only about *500 new lawyers* are allowed to enter the legal
      system in the *entire* Japanese nation. (Source, *Japan Today,* PBS
      ch 13, 2/4/91)
          According to Professor Stephen Magee (economist, coauthor
      of *Black Hole Tariffs and Endogenous Policy Theory*), the nations with
      lawyer/population ratios most similar to USA: India and Bang-
      ladesh; the nations with lawyer/population ratios least similar to
      USA: Germany and Japan. Professor Magee believes these ratios
      are not coincidental and bode ill for the American economy.
          It's widely recognized that the multitude of rules, regula-
      tions, and lawsuits in the American legal system has a unseen,
      negative effect on our nation's economy. This negative effect
      inhibits the formation of new businesses and jobs, and drives ex-
      isting industries, companies, and jobs overseas or into bankrupt-
      cy. The net result is a diminished standard of living for all
      Americans.
          In an interview with the *Texas Lawyer,* Professor Magee esti-
      mated the annual drag on our Gross National Product (GNP)
      caused by our legal system to be *one million dollars per year per
      lawyer.* Compare this to the U.S. Department of Justice estimate
      that the average "societal cost" of each drug addict is $200,000
      per year. Loose implication: the average lawyer does *five times* as
      much harm to this nation's economy as the average drug addict.

      —Alfred Adask, "Just the Facts (and a few loose implications)," editor of *Anti-
      Shyster: A Critical Examination of the American Legal System,* Vol. 4, No. 2, 1994

b.   No serious student of crime claims that the solution to the crime
      puzzle is simple. There are many interrelated and complicated
      causes. However, one cause is clearcut: the economics of crime.
      Indeed, Gary Becker of the University of Chicago was awarded
      the Nobel Prize in 1992 for his work on that topic. Professor
      Becker's work shows that crimes are not irrational acts. Instead,
      they are voluntarily committed by people who compare the ex-
      pected benefits with the expected costs. Hence, one reason crime
      rates are surging is that, for many people, the benefits of criminal
      activity outweigh the costs.
          Crime pays, in part, because the cost of committing a crime
      is so low. That cost can be measured by determining the "expect-

ed punishment" associated with various criminal acts. Expected punishment is calculated by first multiplying four probabilities times each other: that of being arrested for a crime after it is committed, that of being prosecuted if arrested, that of being convicted if prosecuted and that of receiving punishment if convicted. The product of that arithmetic is the probability of being punished. To complete the calculation of expected punishment, we must next multiply the probability of being punished times the penalty for an offense.

—Steve Hanke, *The Washington Times*, January 1, 1993

c. James Ostrowski determined the per capita death rate for several drugs: tobacco, alcohol, heroin, cocaine, and marijuana. In his calculations, Ostrowski attempted to isolate only those deaths that were "intrinsically" connected to the drug being used. In other words, he attempted to determine whether an alcohol death was related to the use of alcohol per se rather than to some other influence. Thus, deaths resulting from diseases directly related to alcohol use are included while others such as DUI traffic deaths are not.

The data show that tobacco remains the number one killer, claiming 650 deaths per 100,000 users. Heroin use results in half the death rate of alcohol per capita. Not one death has been attributable to marijuana use. In fact, based on data concerning the number of repeat users of these drugs, Ostrowski notes that the illicit substances are less likely to lead to repeat use than either alcohol or tobacco.

Estimated per Capita Death Rates for Selected Drugs

Drug	Users	Deaths Per Year	Deaths/100,000
Tobacco	60 million	390,000	650
Alcohol	100 million	15,000	150
Heroin	500,000	400	80
Cocaine	5 million	200	4

Source: James Ostrowski, "Thinking About Drug Legalization," *Cato Policy Analysis No. 121* [Washington, D.C.: Cato Institute, 1989], 47, table 4.

Note: Deaths attributed to heroin and cocaine were adjusted downward to include only deaths attributed to drug use (e.g., not suicide). The unadjusted figure for heroin is 400 per 100,000 and for cocaine, 20 per 100,000.

—In Stan Staley, *Drug Policy and the Decline of American Cities*, 1992

d. How would voluntary prayer in public schools help society? The best answer to this question is to examine the direction of society from the time school prayer was deemed unconstitutional. Mr.

David Barton has done his best to study the correlation, if any, between the removal of school prayer and societal decline.

Mr. Barton, in his book *America: To Pray or Not to Pray*, has measured several social indices. For instance, the scholastic aptitude test [SAT] is an academic test measuring the developed verbal and math reasoning skills of students preparing to enter college. These results are used widely to gain admission to colleges and universities. The SAT has been administered to high school seniors since 1926. A scale was established in 1941 to allow comparison of scores from year to year.

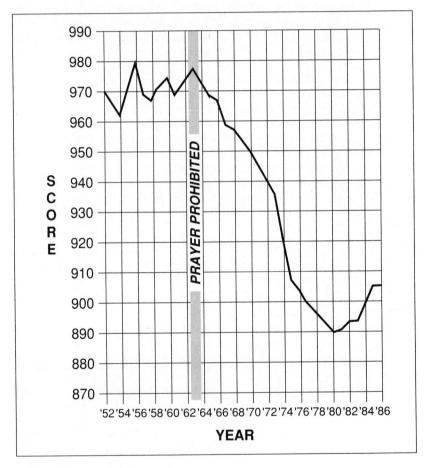

FIGURE 2-9   *Decline in SAT Scores.*

Source: *Congressional Record,* May 1, 1991.

—"Public Schools Should Allow Formal Prayer," Rep. William E. Dannemeyer, *Congressional Record,* May 1, 1991

Warrants

In everyday speech a "warranted" or "unwarranted" conclusion refers to the fact that some ways of connecting claims with supporting evidence are legitimate whereas others are not. For this reason, a third important element, in addition to the claim and the support, in understanding arguments, is the warrant.

The warrant is the reason or justification that links together the evidence offered and the conclusion drawn from that evidence. What Stephen Toulmin refers to as the warrant is simply what Aristotle referred to as the major premise in an argument: the overall justification for drawing a particular conclusion from the evidence offered to back up the claim. Sometimes the idea that justifies drawing the conclusion is assumed by the arguer and not explicitly stated. When this happens it is often more helpful to think of the warrant as the underlying assumption that serves as the unexpressed major premise in an argument.

For example, if the arguer claimed that the United States no longer has the highest standard of living and has been surpassed by other countries, including Sweden, Switzerland, and Denmark, the first thing we would want to know is the kind of evidence that would support this conclusion. If the arguer then brought forward comparative statistics measuring gross national product (GNP), infant mortality rate, and international rankings of students graduating from the educational systems of those countries, we might be more inclined to accept the claim (or conclusion). But, most importantly, we would have to accept the unexpressed warrant (or unstated major premise) that this kind of data or evidence (comparative statistics on economic output, quality of health care, and education) can logically justify drawing a particular conclusion. Within an argument, all claims are connected to evidence, examples, or other grounds by these stated or unstated assumptions.

For an argument to be persuasive, both the writer and the audience must have the same understanding of the logical justification or connection for drawing a particular conclusion from the data or evidence offered. If the audience did not believe that the GNP, infant mortality rate, international ranking of students, and so forth. were reliable criteria to measure a country's standard of living, they could not accept the conclusions drawn from this data.

All claims are based on warrants, or underlying assumptions. For an argument to be effective the writer and the audience should share the same underlying assumptions or beliefs regarding the issue. Moreover, the audience must agree with, or at least let pass unchallenged, the idea that a particular kind of evidence can be used in a specific way to support the claim. The warrant actually functions to guarantee the relationship between the claim and the support. Warrants guarantee (the ancient form of the word *guarantee* is *warrant*) that the evidence offered can really be used to support the claim in the way the writer says it does.

✦ Questions for Discussion and Writing

1. For each of the following mini-arguments, identify the reasons why a particular conclusion can be drawn from a particular set of grounds, data, or support. What logical justification does the arguer have in drawing conclusions from the data? How does the strength of the claim (or conclusion) vary according to the strength of the justification?

   a. Our own research has shown that male sexual orientation is substantially genetic. Over the last two years, we have studied the rates of homosexuality in identical and non-identical twin brothers of gay men, as well as adoptive brothers of gay men. Fifty-two percent of the identical twin brothers were gay, as against 22 percent of non-identical twins and 11 percent of the adoptive, genetically unrelated brothers. (Michael Bailey and Richard Pillard, *The New York Times*, Dec. 17, 1991.)

   b. If you define subliminal ads as those that appeal on an unconscious level as well as a conscious one, then subliminals surely exist. The best example is Newport's long-running and immensely successful "Alive with Pleasure!" campaign. The photos always show out-doorsy yuppies horsing around. But amid all this jollity, there is a strong undercurrent of sexual hostility, usually directed at women. Women are about to be clanged by a pair of cymbals, carried off on a pole, pulled along in a horse collar, or slam-dunked in the face by a basketball-wielding male. (John Leo, *U.S. News & World Report*, July 15, 1991.)

   c. The fathers of this nation never dreamed that separation of church and state meant that God should be separated from government. The government buildings in Washington bear ample testimony to the belief that faith in God is the basis for establishing laws and running the affairs of a nation. For example, the Ten Commandments hang over the head of the chief justice of the Supreme Court. In the rotunda, the words "in God we trust" are engraved, and on the Library of Congress we have "the heavens declare the glory of God and the firmament showeth his handiwork." The Washington monument and other governmental buildings contain phrases of Scripture. (Erwin J. Lutzer, *Exploding the Myths That Could Destroy America*, 1986.)

d. In India, 20,000 angry farmers protesting the state government gathered outside the legislature building and laughed for two hours. M. D. Nanjundaswamy, leader of the Karnataka Farmers Association, explained, "we want to laugh this government out." (*News From the Fringe,* ed. John J. Kohut and Roland Sweet, 1993.)

e. Though the educational establishment would rather die than admit it, multiculturalism is a desperate—and surely self-defeating—strategy for coping with the educational deficiencies, and associated social pathologies, of young blacks. Did these black students and their problems not exist, we would hear little of multiculturalism. There is no evidence that a substantial number of Hispanic parents would like their children to know more about Simon Bolivar and less about George Washington, or that Oriental parents feel that their children are being educationally deprived because their textbooks teach them more about ancient Greece than about ancient China. (Irving Kristol, *The Wall Street Journal,* July 31, 1991.)

UNDERLYING ASSUMPTIONS

Warrants provide a means of testing how the facts (in the form of statistics, real or hypothetical examples, expert opinion, and so on) are connected to a particular claim. If the support offered to prove the claim is relevant, then the warrant (in the form of a statute, precedent, rule, or principle) authorizes the writer to move from the evidence to the conclusion.

Warrants can take a variety of forms in different fields. In the law, warrants take the form of legal principles, statutes, licenses, or permits. The idea underlying a warrant survives today in the familiar term *arrest warrant.* In the natural and physical sciences, warrants take the form of scientific laws, formulas, and methods of calculation. In all these fields, warrants reflect acceptable methods of relating the evidence to the claim or chief assertion.

For example, in the law the warrant is an explicit statute laying out the specific circumstances under which someone can be found guilty of an offense. The warrant permits the judge or the court to conclude that a particular defendant is guilty of an offense if supporting evidence has been submitted and verified.

In other fields, like natural sciences and mathematics, warrants may take the form of relevant formulas that are used to confirm or reject a hypothesis or claim on the basis of evidence produced by experimentation and research. Within these fields warrants appear as commonly accepted principles or "laws." For example, Boyle's law in thermodynamics states that at relatively low pressures the pressure of an ideal gas kept at constant temperature varies inversely with the vol-

ume of the gas. Likewise, Einstein's discovery of the relationship between mass and energy is contained in the famous equation or law
$E = mc^2$.

In other fields, medicine, for example, warrants derive more from
principles generalized from the practitioner's past experience than
from formulas as such. A doctor making a diagnosis of a seven-year-
old patient's illness might discover an unusual rash of raised, circular,
small red spots and measure an elevated temperature (see Figure 2-10).
On the basis of principles generalized from past experience, the doctor
concludes that the patient has probably caught measles. To see how the
warrant serves as a kind of rule dictating how the evidence (rash, elevated temperature) should be related to the particular claim (the patient has caught measles), examine the following analysis of the
reasoning underlying the doctor's diagnosis:

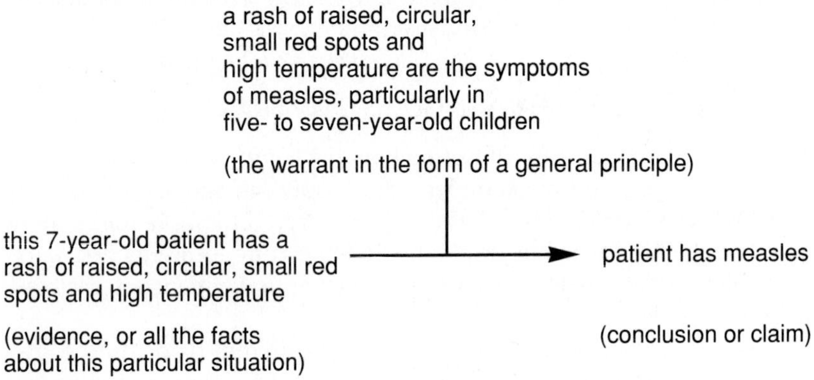

a rash of raised, circular,
small red spots and
high temperature are the symptoms
of measles, particularly in
five- to seven-year-old children

(the warrant in the form of a general principle)

this 7-year-old patient has a
rash of raised, circular, small red ⟶ patient has measles
spots and high temperature

(evidence, or all the facts   (conclusion or claim)
about this particular situation)

FIGURE 2-10   *Flowchart of Physician's Diagnostic Process.*

The warrant here is drawn from general principles of the kind that
might be familiar to the doctor from past experience and from information provided by a medical textbook.

Warrants can be either explicit or implicit; that is, they can take the
form of set rules or simply be assumptions and beliefs that both the
writer and the audience share. Whereas warrants take the form of
broad generalizations, rules of thumb, or general principles that could
apply to various circumstances, claims and support apply to specific
events and circumstances. In law or the sciences, warrants are generalizations based on extensive experience and data. Outside these formal
fields of study, in everyday conversation, warrants take the form of beliefs, assumptions, or rule-of-thumb generalizations.

As with all other generalizations, warrants must ultimately rest
on relevant facts and evidence. If the warrant or underlying assumption in an argument is challenged, the writer may have to produce

some of the primary information or backing on which the warrant itself is based.

This body of information supplies the *backing,* or justification for the warrant. The strength and credibility of the warrant therefore depends on the strength and credibility of the backing, or the information used to back it up. For example, an argument that examined the relationship between risk of injury and vehicle size might rest on the assumption (or warrant or major premise) that driver risk increased as a car's size and weight decreased irrespective of other factors such as air bags, safety belts, or kind of crash. If this assumption were challenged, the arguer would have to show how the warrant was justified by a credible and persuasive series of studies of driver fatalities in lighter as compared to heavier cars. These studies would serve as the backing for the warrant. This is important because people often bring different assumptions to the same situation without realizing it. For example, in her book *When Society Becomes an Addict* (1987), Anne Wilson Schaef, a psychotherapist, describes an episode of how two people "read" the same situation in different ways because of their different underlying assumptions:

> During one of my workshops an incident occurred that illustrates this lack of clarity very aptly. We had baked apples for dinner. I was too full to eat mine, so I took it back to the cottage I was sharing with another staff member and put it in the refrigerator, planning to eat it at my leisure. Since it was obviously mine, it did not occur to me that my cabin mate would eat it.
>
> Later, when I went to get my apple, it was gone. My cabin mate— a compulsive overeater—had, in fact, gobbled it down. I did not appreciate that, and I said so. Her response was, "I assumed you didn't want it since you hadn't eaten it." She had made two assumptions, neither of which she checked out with me: first, that I didn't want the apple, and second, that it was okay for her to eat it. Then she had used her assumptions to support her distorted thinking and feed her compulsive eating habit.

Identifying underlying beliefs is essential because many writers erroneously take it for granted that they and the audience share a common point of view. An audience that notices that they and the writer do not share the same assumptions might require the author to back up the warrant, since from the audience's point of view the warrant might be questionable.

Assumptions in an argument often remain implicit when the writer feels that the audience shares his or her underlying beliefs. If the audience already agrees with these beliefs, the writer can feel comfortable in bringing forth reasons to support the claim. The contrary is true in those arguments where the writer feels the audience may not share his or her basic values. In these cases, an assumption that might prove controversial may need to be stated explicitly and defended at the outset. The writer must win a hearing for the assumption on which the argument is based before going on to present evidence that specifically bears on the question or exact point that is the subject of the argument.

Not all warrants will be explicitly stated in the course of an argument. Sometimes the writer will not explicitly state the warrant because the writer feels that both she or he and the audience share a common perspective on the issue. In effect, the writer is depending on the audience to mentally supply the implicit warrant to connect the evidence with the claim. This is especially true when writers argue before partisan audiences who already share the same beliefs and can be depended upon to bring the same set of assumptions or warrants to the situation. For example, a lottery equipment manufacturer arguing for a national lottery before fellow manufacturers of lottery ticket printing equipment will not have to state or defend the assumption that a national lottery will mean more business for lottery equipment manufacturers. His or her audience can be depended upon to interpret any evidence the manufacturer presents in the light of this implicit warrant.

In other cases, the warrants will not be explicitly stated because the writer does not want the audience to be aware that they disagree on underlying assumptions. Such was the case in the baked apple incident where the cabin mate did not ask if she could eat the apple because she did not want to risk hearing that she could not.

✦ Questions for Discussion and Writing

1. For each of the following, state the implied premise/warrant/assumption and decide whether it is likely to be accepted by the audiences for whom it was written. Why or why not? How do these warrants justify accepting the arguer's descriptions and interpretations of problems? What commonly held beliefs do these warrants reflect? How might the same data be made more acceptable for the different specified audience by reliance on a different set of assumptions?

   a. The original audience for this argument was composed of ecologists. How could you reinterpret the same grounds (evidence, reasons) for an audience of real-estate developers or mining company executives?

   > If you have ever spent time with American Indians, you have noticed that their resistance to resource development is expressed as an effort to protect "Mother Earth." It is not only American Indians who use the phrase. So do Aborigines of the Australian desert, natives of the Pacific islands, Indians of the Ecuadorian jungles, Inuit from Arctic Canada; in fact, I have yet to find a native group that does not speak of the planet as "mother." And

they all mean it literally. Plants, animals, all life as we know it is nurtured at her breast. We have germinated within her, we are part of her, we burst into life from her, and we dissolve back into her to become new life.

Every culture that maintains this attitude about Mother Earth also has restrictions against any individual owning land, or mining it or selling it. Such ideas were unthinkable to native people until they met the invading Western cultures.

This fundamental difference in viewpoint between techno-logical cultures and land-based native peoples—whether the planet is alive or isn't—is the root of many conflicts between the two groups. Americans, for example, have a particularly hard time grasping the notion of a living earth. We scoff at the idea, in fact, and at anyone who speaks of it seriously. I have seen white people laugh aloud when young Indian activists stand at meet-ings to denounce some mining development as a "desecration of our mother, the earth." We find it particularly hard to take when such words are spoken by the more radical young Indian leaders of today.

—"Mother Earth" by Jerry Mander, from *The Absence of the Sacred,* 1991

b. The original audience for this argument was a group of female col-lege students. How could you reinterpret the same evidence and reasons for officials of campus fraternities?

College men are at their hormonal peak. They have just left their mothers and are questing for their male identity. In groups, they are dangerous. A woman going to a fraternity party is walking into Testosterone Flats, full of prickly cacti and blazing guns. If she goes, she should be armed with resolute alertness. She should arrive with girlfriends and leave with them. A girl who lets herself get dead drunk at a fraternity party is a fool. A girl who goes upstairs alone with a brother at a fraternity party is an idiot. Feminists call this "blaming the victim." I call it common sense.

—Camille Paglia, *Sex, Art and American Culture,* 1992

EVALUATING WARRANTS

Before you can evaluate the effectiveness of any particular warrant, you need to be able to identify all the warrants in any argument and to make explicit those that lie hidden beneath the surface. Writers must inquire (1) whether the warrant expresses a reliable generalization and (2) whether this generalization authorizes the connection between the facts and the conclusion in this particular case.

Evaluating how warrants work in a given argument means discov-ering whether the writer has used the correct kind of warrant to con-nect the evidence to the claim or has connected the evidence to the claim in the correct way. The first point has to do with the relevance of the evidence. The second concerns the quality of the writer's reasoning or use of logic.

A listing of the six main kinds of warrants writers use in creating arguments follows. The particular kind of warrant selected depends on the nature of the argument, the type of claim (of fact, causation, value, or policy), and the specific audience addressed or the context in which the argument is formulated.

Types of Warrants

Generalization Warrant.   A generalization warrant authorizes the movement from a number of specific examples offered as evidence to a generalization offered as a conclusion. The generalization warrant asserts that what is true of a sample is probably true of a group as a whole. The examples used must meet the test of being sufficiently representative, properly selected, and timely.

For example, Sigmund Freud in his classic essay "Typical Dreams (*Basic Writings of Sigmund Freud* [1938]) brings forward a whole range of examples from the dreams of children that illustrate one common theme—the death or disappearance of brothers or sisters. From these numerous case histories, Freud generalizes that children's dreams often reveal sibling rivalry, albeit in a disguised form. Freud's claim of the existence of sibling rivalry is an inference that should be verifiable as well in dreams of children whom Freud has not observed.

Looked at in terms of claim, support, and warrant, the argument appears this way:

CLAIM: The dreams of children featuring the death or disappearance of brothers or sisters reveal sibling rivalry in a disguised form.

SUPPORT: Numerous case histories in which Freud observed sibling rivalry in children who had these kinds of dreams.

GENERALIZATION WARRANT: Observations based on several case histories can be generalized to be true in as yet unobserved cases.

Everyday reasoning closely resembles arguments from generalizations, as do arguments whose claims are based on polls or surveys. For example, the Harris survey and the Gallup opinion poll generalize from results drawn from a sample cross section of 1,200 to 1,500 adults to infer what is true of the entire population. If the sample, by a margin of 80 percent to 20 percent, holds the view that "American business is not paying its fair share of taxes," Gallup or Harris will predict that this opinion would also be true in the same proportion if every adult in the United States were polled.

Cause and Effect Warrant.   Reasoning from cause assumes that one event can produce another. Causal generalization stipulates that if a particular cause is observed, a particular effect can be expected to follow. Conversely, the causal warrant may state that if a certain effect is observed, a particular cause may be assumed to have preceded it. Causal warrants may extend to chains of causation as well as multiple causes or multiple effects. For example, Wilson Bryan Key, a professor of communications, wanted to discover why many viewers of William Friedkin's movie *The Exorcist* became fearful, angry, and physically sick after seeing the film. As reported in his book *Media Sexploitation* (1976), Key discovered that Friedkin had accompanied the images on the screen with a sound track in which sounds of squealing pigs and the buzzing of infuriated bees were recorded at a level below the audience's conscious awareness. Key argues that this subliminal use of sound, though not consciously perceived, created an undertone of fear that amplified the frightening nature of the images on the screen. He interviewed theater staff who heard the sound track before they actually viewed the film and discovered that they often experienced the same reactions of hysteria and anxiety as did members of the audience who saw *and* heard the movie. In outline form, Key's causal argument might look like this (notice that the warrant acts as the cause, while the claim expresses the effect):

CLAIM: The anxiety of audiences watching *The Exorcist* was, in part, an unconscious reaction to the sounds of squealing pigs and infuriated bees interwoven into the sound track at a subliminal level.

SUPPORT: Theater staff who heard only the sound track of the movie experienced reactions of hysteria and anxiety. Friedkin admitted that he interwove sounds of pigs and bees in a way that coordinated with the visual images.

CAUSAL WARRANT: Even if the sounds were not consciously perceived, people instinctively fear the sounds of squealing pigs and infuriated bees.

Sign Warrant.   Arguments based on sign warrants point to a particular sign to support a claim that a certain event, condition, or situation exists. For example, a doctor may be reasoning from sign when he cites certain observable characteristics to justify the diagnosis that a patient is suffering from a particular disease. Anne Wilson Schaef uses the same reasoning process in *When Society Becomes an Addict* (1987):

An addiction is any process over which we are powerless. It takes control of us, causing us to do and think things that are inconsistent with our personal values and leading us to become progressively more compulsive and obsessive. A sure sign of an addiction is the sudden need to deceive ourselves and others—to lie, deny, and cover up. An addiction is anything we feel *tempted* to lie about.

Although one could certainly dispute her definition of addiction, Schaef clearly reasons from signs (need to lie, deny, and cover up) to support a claim about the presence of the phenomenon (addiction) to which the sign refers.

The philosopher C. S. Peirce defines *sign* this way: "a sign is something which stands to somebody for something else, in some respect or capacity." We reason from sign any time we drive down the highway, see a sign indicating a winding road, and slow down. The sign is used as a reliable indicator that a condition (a winding road) is or will be present. We do the same thing when we check our wallet before entering a restaurant in front of which we see a long green awning and a door attendant. The fancy facade is a usually reliable indicator that the restaurant is expensive.

In law, the concept of circumstantial evidence is based on the idea of reasoning from sign. A case may be constructed on a network of circumstantial facts based on the assumption or warrant that the defendant exhibits all the signs—that have been reliable indicators in past cases—of having committed the crime. In economics, economists look for signs of health or weakness in the nation's economy. These financial indicators (balance of trade, housing starts, unemployment figures, etc.) are believed to indicate the presence of a corresponding economic condition.

In "Notes on Class" (1980) Paul Fussell creates an amusing argument, based on a sign warrant, by pointing to features that he believes define different class levels in American society:

> Facade study is a badly neglected anthropological field. As we work down from the (largely white-painted) bank-like facades of the Upper and Upper Middle Classes, we encounter such Middle and Prole conventions as these, which I rank in order of social status:
>
> *Middle:*
> 1. A potted tree on either side of the front door, and the more pointy and symmetrical the better.
> 2. A large rectangular picture-window in a split-level "ranch" house, displaying a table-lamp between two side curtains. The cellophane on the lampshade must be visibly inviolate.
> 3. Two chairs, usually metal with pipe arms, disposed on the front porch as a "conversation group," in stubborn defiance of the traffic thundering past.

High-Prole
4. Religious shrines in the garden, which if small and understated, are slightly higher class than

Mid-Prole
5. Plaster gnomes and flamingos, and blue or lavender shiny spheres supported by fluted cast-concrete pedestals.

Low-Prole
6. Defunct truck tires painted white and enclosing flower beds. (Auto tires are a grade higher.)
7. Flower-bed designs worked in dead light bulbs or the butts of disused beer bottles.

> The Destitute have no facades to decorate, and of course the Bottom Out-of-Sights, being invisible, have none either, although both these classes can occasionally help others decorate theirs— painting tires white on an hourly basis, for example, or even watering and fertilizing the potted trees of the Middle Class.

Reduced to its essentials, Fussell's argument might look like this:

CLAIM: Although we like to pretend that American society is classless, "facade study" reveals a hierarchical class structure in American culture.

SUPPORT: Symmetrical plants, large rectangular picture windows, two chairs in middle-class homes; religious shrines in high-prole homes; plaster gnomes and flamingos in mid-prole homes; painted truck tires and disused beer bottles worked into designs in low-prole homes, and so on.

SIGN WARRANT: Statues, objects, and assorted bric-a-brac in front of people's houses are reliable signs of the social class to which they belong.

Much of advertising attempts to appropriate this form of reasoning to persuade potential customers to purchase a product. Advertisers are very clever in using warrants from sign in persuading audiences that purchasing, wearing, or using a particular product will enable the purchaser to partake of the reality (such as wealth, beauty, or health) of which the sign is an indicator. For example, an ad for expensive crystal glasses directed toward prospective brides might show a diamond ring and a wedding veil alongside the glasses. The ring and the veil are signs standing for marriage. The technique of advertising is based, in large part, on correlating attainable tangible objects with difficult-to-obtain feelings, moods, attitudes, and conditions. The advertiser can depend on the consumer's reasoning from sign that the purchase of the attainable will be accompanied by the difficult-to-obtain. For example, an ad for an expensive watch might show it on a night table alongside a gold money clip holding a stack of $100 bills. Reasoning from sign, the consumer might conclude that the purchase of this watch (as a sign of the possessions of a wealthy person) would somehow enable him or her to possess other items associated with wealth.

Analogy Warrant.   Reasoning from analogy assumes that there are sufficient similarities between two things to warrant the claim that what is true of one can reasonably be expected to be true of the other. Any time we look forward to reading a new novel by an author whose previous books we read and enjoyed, or to seeing a new movie by a favorite director, we are reasoning by analogy. We infer that the new book or movie will resemble the works we previously enjoyed.

It is important that shared characteristics be directly relevant to the claim and that no important differences exist that would undermine or weaken the analogy. For example, if a car manufacturer issues a recall of a certain model because a structural weakness in the frame has led rear bumpers to fall off, then it can reasonably be assumed that other cars of the same make and model are likely to develop the same problem. This would hold true despite differences in appearance or options. Since structural weakness in one model can reasonably be expected to be true of other cars in the line, the shared characteristics are directly relevant to the claim.

The more the analogy departs from the literally shared resemblances, the less useful it will be in supporting a claim. This is not to say that such analogies cannot be extraordinarily helpful in describing or explaining some point, but these analogies, sometimes called *figurative analogies,* cannot actually serve to warrant a claim. For example, Martin J. Rees and Joseph Silk writing in *Scientific American* ("The Origin of Galaxies" [August 1969]) formulated a figurative analogy to describe the phenomenon of an expanding universe:

> Perhaps the most startling discovery made in astronomy this century is that the universe is populated by billions of galaxies and that they are systematically receding from one another, like raisins in an expanding pudding.

The authors are not suggesting that the universe *is* an expanding pudding with raisins but are simply using a figurative analogy to describe and explain an otherwise hard-to-grasp concept. It is important for any reader of an argument using analogies to evaluate just how the analogy is being used. The question to ask is, does the analogy simply describe or explain something or does it actually support an inference and thereby warrant the claim?

Consider how David J. Armor, a professor, uses an analogy warrant in his argument against mandatory school busing in Statements Submitted to Committee on the Judiciary (U.S. Senate, Hearings on the Fourteenth Amendment and School Busing, 97th Congress, 1st Session, May 14, 1981):

> The school busing issue has been with us now for over ten years, and it shows no signs of abating. Massive mandatory busing has been ordered recently by courts in Los Angeles, Columbus (Ohio), and St. Louis; and major busing lawsuits are still pending in San Diego, Cincinnati, Kansas City (Missouri), and Indianapolis. Clearly, court-ordered busing is alive and well. This is a remarkable achievement for the most unpopular, least successful, and most harmful national policy since Prohibition.
>
> At the outset let me say I fully agree with the Supreme Court's policy that intentional segregation of the schools is prohibited by the United States constitution. Moreover, racial isolation and discrimination do exist in American society and in the schools, and these conditions should be combated wherever they are found.
>
> The real issue is the method chosen by the courts to remedy segregation. The courts adopted mandatory busing because they believed it to be the most effective way to end racial isolation. Therefore, it was also seen as the best way to end the harmful effects of segregation on race relations and on the educational opportunity of minority students. But, just as Prohibition was not a feasible remedy for alcohol abuse, so mandatory busing is not a feasible remedy for school segregation. Like Prohibition, the policy is not merely ineffective; it is counterproductive.

In schematic form the argument would appear this way:

CLAIM: Mandatory busing is an ineffective and undesirable remedy for racial segregation in the school systems.

SUPPORT: Like Prohibition, mandatory busing is not merely ineffective; it is counterproductive.

ANALOGY WARRANT: Prohibition as an intended solution that proved ineffective is comparable and analogous to the use of mandatory busing to solve the problem of racial segregation.

Armor's argument depends on the analogy warrant or assumption that court-ordered school busing is analogous to Prohibition. For him, the similarities between the two are more significant than the obvious differences. An opponent would assert that the fundamental dissimilarities between the two programs make any attempt to compare them unwarranted.

Authority Warrant.   Reasoning from authority presumes that the authority cited is in fact qualified to express an expert opinion on the subject of the claim. If the authority were to be challenged, the writer would have to supply backing for the warrant in the form of credentials and expertise that would qualify the authority in the particular circumstances.

In evaluating an argument based on authority, determine whether the writer clearly connects the claim and the authority's area of expertise. Also, try to determine whether the authority is acknowledged as such by other experts in the field and has made his or her investigations recently. Of course, the authority must be explicitly identified and not referred to as simply "a well-known expert." As an illustration, consider how Monroe Freedman in *Lawyers Ethics in an Adversary System* (1975) uses the testimony of widely respected figures to support his controversial claim that a lawyer's first obligation is to protect his or her client, not to search for the truth:

> Thus, the defense lawyer's professional obligation may well be to advise the client to withhold the truth. As Justice Jackson said: "any lawyer worth his salt will tell the suspect in no uncertain terms to make no statement to police under any circumstances." Similarly, the defense lawyer is obligated to prevent the introduction of evidence that may be wholly reliable, such as a murder weapon seized in violation of the Fourth Amendment, or a truthful but involuntary confession. Justice White has observed that although law enforcement officials must be dedicated to using only truthful evidence, "defense counsel has no comparable obligation to ascertain or present the truth. Our system assigns him a different mission. . . . We . . . insist that he defend his client whether he is innocent or guilty."
>
> Such conduct by defense counsel does not constitute obstruction of justice. On the contrary, it is "part of the duty imposed on the most honorable defense counsel," from whom "we countenance or require conduct which in many instances has little, if any, relation to the search for truth." The same observation has been made by Justice Harlan, who noted that "in fulfilling his professional responsibilities," the lawyer "of necessity may become an obstacle to truthfinding." Chief Justice Warren, too, has recognized that when the criminal defense attorney successfully obstructs efforts by the government to elicit truthful evidence in ways that violate constitutional rights, the attorney is "merely exercising . . . good professional judgment," and "carrying out what he is sworn to do under his oath—to protect to the extent of his ability the rights of his client." Chief Justice Warren concluded: "In fulfilling this responsibility the attorney plays a vital role in the administration of criminal justice under our Constitution."
>
> Obviously, such eminent jurists would not arrive lightly at the conclusion that an officer of the court has a professional obligation to place obstacles in the path of truth. Their reasons, again, go back to the

nature of our system of criminal justice and go to the fundamentals of our system of government. Before we will permit the state to deprive any person of life, liberty, or property, we require that certain processes be duly followed which ensure regard for the dignity of the individual, irrespective of the impact of those processes upon the determination of truth.

Freedman's point is that a lawyer may advise his or her client to withhold the truth in situations where disclosure of the truth will hurt the client. To support his claim that an attorney's main duty is to the client, not to the truth as such, Freedman cites the expert testimony of Supreme Court justices Jackson, White, Harlan, and Warren. Because each of these figures is a widely respected legal authority, their statements can be expected to persuade the reader to accept the claim. The three elements function as follows:

CLAIM: The defense lawyer's professional obligation may be to advise the client to withhold the truth.

SUPPORT: Supreme Court justices Jackson, White, Harlan, and Warren testify that this behavior is appropriate.

AUTHORITY WARRANT: The expert opinion of Supreme Court justices on matters of the law carries considerable weight because they are the nation's foremost legal authorities.

Also, notice how Freedman structures the argument to end with the remarks of the most important legal authority, the Chief Justice of the Supreme Court.

Value Warrant. Value warrants are moral or ethical principles or beliefs that the writer hopes will be shared by the audience. It is especially important that the value the warrant expresses be relevant to the claim and be a belief that the intended audience will perceive as important. Value warrants are frequently unexpressed in arguments, and readers must make every effort to make explicit the value, principle, or belief that the writer may have taken for granted. Value warrants function exactly as any other kind of warrant to guarantee a connection between the claim and the evidence. Value warrants frequently embody ethical principles that designate certain kinds of actions as right or wrong, acceptable or unacceptable; or stipulate what should be considered as good or bad; or express the standards by which some actions should be considered good or bad, preferable or objectionable. In some cases these value warrants will express societal consensus about the ethical propriety of certain kinds of actions. In other cases they may express a personal, rather than universal, moral value.

In the following paragraphs from "Abolish the Insanity Defense?—Not Yet" (*Rutgers Law Review* [1973]), John Monahan uses a value warrant to explain how the insanity defense is based on an underlying belief that people who are incapable of knowing the meaning or consequences of their actions should not be punished:

> The existing Anglo-American system of criminal justice is based on a model of man as a responsible agent with a free will. The insanity defense is closely tied to this model. Oversimplifying somewhat, "the defense of insanity rests upon the assumption that insanity negates free will, and the law does not punish people who lack the capacity for choice."
>
> If an individual has a complete inability to know the nature and quality of the act he has committed, that is, if he is insane by M'Naghten standards, then, it is argued, he is incapable of forming the cognitive or mental component (intent, recklessness, etc.) which is part of the definition of much serious crime. Since the insane person is held to be incapable of forming normal cognition, and since cognitive ability is part of the definition of crime, he has a complete defense to much criminal prosecution.

Split into the three elements, Monahan's case would appear thus:

CLAIM: Defendants who because of insanity are not consciously aware of the meaning of their acts should not be found guilty.

SUPPORT: A defendant is shown to be insane by M'Naghten standards.

VALUE WARRANT: The law does not punish people who lack the capacity for choice.

This argument is unusual in that it rests on a basic assumption on which the entire system of criminal law is built, but it reaches a conclusion with which increasing numbers of people disagree. When reading any argument based on a value warrant, try to identify any assumptions or unexamined beliefs that the writer expects the audience to share. Ask yourself how this assumption supports the author's purpose. Then compare this assumption (you may need to state it explicitly if the author does not) with your own beliefs on the issue, and decide whether the warrant, in fact, (1) is reliable and (2) actually applies to the particular case.

✦ *Questions for Study and Writing*

1. Develop a short argument on one or two of the following issues. For each mini-argument you construct, identify the kind of warrant or rationale your argument relies on to justify acceptance of the interpreta-

tion, conclusion, claim, or recommendation you make. If you feel the warrant or assumption might be challenged by an audience, supply the appropriate backing to let your audience see how you reached the decision to use the warrant you did. The warrants can include:

Generalization
Drawing a causal relationship
Sign warrant or reasoning from circumstantial evidence
Drawing analogies
Believing an authority
Applying an ethical or moral principle

a. Lawyers are expected to provide free (*pro bono*) legal services at some time in their careers. Physicians should or should not have the same obligation to provide free medical care at some time in their careers to those who cannot afford it.

b. What actions and reactions of your own or of someone you know can serve as reliable indicators of being in love?

c. Would an anchorwoman who wore a flowered sundress be more or less credible than the same person in a tailored suit? Why or why not?

d. Do you consider having children important in your future? From instances you have observed, are people with children happier than those without them?

e. Should juvenile offenders be treated differently from adult offenders? Why or why not? How might a researcher use statistics illustrating the relationship between lenient or harsh sentencing of juveniles and the percentage of those juveniles who subsequently commit worse crimes?

f. In any one day you encounter a variety of claims that reach you through the media, reading material, classrooms, and conversations. These claims take a variety of forms that may include commercials, religious services, lectures, movie or concert reviews, and so on. Evaluate the strength of any claim in relationship to who makes it.

g. What influence, if any, has any major religious text (Bible, Koran, Bhagavad Gita, etc.) had on shaping your ideals and attitudes toward life?

Audience

Most of the things people write are written with the expectation that someone will read what they have written. Since each audience has its own characteristic concerns and values, writers must be acutely sensitive to the audience's special needs. Without knowing what was important to an audience, it would be difficult for writers to assess what kinds of arguments, evidence, and supporting material a particular audience would be likely to find convincing.

Writers should try to identify who the audience is or is likely to be by creating an audience profile. For example, how might the audience, from its point of view, define the issue at the center of the argument? If the audience sees the issue differently, is there anything the writer can do to take this into account while characterizing the problem or issue? The key question is, how can the writer create a common meeting ground?

Matching the argument to the audience is largely a matter of figuring out what particular argumentative strategy would work best with a particular audience. In a typical persuasion situation, the writer is trying to influence readers who have not made up their minds on the topic and can be presumed to have open minds or at least to be neutral on the issue.

In this situation, the writer can announce the thesis of the argument at the outset and then present reasons and evidence in a straightforward way. The writer is obliged to present, directly and without apology, the most timely, up-to-date, and relevant information and the most cogent arguments he or she can muster.

In other situations, the writer attempts to persuade an audience that has already formed strong opinions and beliefs. Clearly, different tactics are required. For example, the writer might wish to present both sides of the argument before announcing the thesis. Or he or she might consider using deductive reasoning as a rhetorical strategy to win the audience's agreement to certain *premises* and then show how the conclusion must necessarily follow.

For many writers, a reasonable goal is not so much to change the readers' minds as to persuade them to give the writer's opposing point of view a fair hearing. The writer's goal is to get the audience to see the issue from a point of view or perspective different from their customary one.

There are several ways to enhance the probability that the writer's argument will address the readers' special concerns. But before this can happen, the writer must be able to define the issue in a way that will appeal to the audience's needs and values. At the very least, the writer must recognize and acknowledge the legitimacy of the audience's feelings on the issue. It is naive to assume that an audience will be persuaded by an argument, however well written or well supported, that fails to take into account psychological factors that can prevent each side from "hearing" the other.

THE ROGERIAN METHOD

One of the most useful attempts to study the factors that block communication was made by the prominent psychologist Carl R. Rogers. His article "Communication: Its Blocking and Its Facilitation," originally a paper delivered at Northwestern University's Centennial Conference on Communications, October 11, 1951, points out that people on both sides of an argument characteristically tend to dig in their heels and simply seek to justify their own opinion.

A variety of psychological reasons explains this intransigent mind set. First of all, people tend to identify with their positions on issues and are not able to separate themselves from their opinions. This automatic preference for one's own opinions makes it impossible to allow oneself to even consider another point of view. Because people identify with their opinions, they feel the need to defend their positions no matter how weak because in essence they are defending themselves against what they perceive to be a personal attack.

This basic frame of mind brings with it the tendency to rationalize. Rationalization is a self-deceptive form of reasoning in which evidence is distorted to fit a previously formed opinion. By contrast, authentic reasoning relies on logic and evidence to reveal a conclusion that may or may not agree with the preconceived opinion. Rogers has studied how the need to defend one's personal values and self-image shuts out potentially useful ideas. To get beyond these limitations Rogers recommends the following exercise:

> The next time you get into an argument with your wife, or your friend, or with a small group of friends, just stop the discussion for a moment and for an experiment, institute this rule. "Each person can speak up for himself only *after* he has first restated the ideas and feelings of the previous speaker accurately, and to that speaker's satisfaction." You see what this would mean. It would simply mean that before presenting your own point of view it would be necessary for you to really achieve the other speaker's frame of reference—to understand his thoughts and feelings so well that you could summarize them for him. . . . Once you have been able to see the other's point of view, your own comments will have to be drastically revised. You will also find the emotion going out of the discussion, the differences being reduced, and those differences which remain being of a rational and understandable sort.

This intriguing method of introducing some psychological perspective makes it more likely that the writer will be able to define the issue at the center of the argument in terms that reflect the values and beliefs of the audience. That is, by being able to summarize impartially an opponent's viewpoint on an issue, in language that the opponent would consider a fair restatement of the issue, the writer immeasurably increases the chances of reaching a middle ground. As Rogers observes:

> Real communication occurs and this evaluative tendency is avoided when we listen with understanding. What does that mean? It means *to*

see the expressed idea and attitude from the other person's point of view, to sense how it feels to him, to achieve his frame of reference in regard to the thing he is talking about.

Also, having a sense of the audience's values will allow the writer to allude to common experiences related to the issue. A knowledge of the readers' special concerns can suggest the kinds of hypothetical scenarios the writer might introduce to persuade the audience. In any case, it is important that writers make every attempt to adapt the argument to the needs and values of their particular audience. It is also crucial to set realistic persuasion goals in the context of the particular situation.

If the argument is well formulated, with effective examples, evidence, and cogent reasons, most audiences will want to try out the new viewpoint even if it means suspending their own views on the subject in the meantime. They will try on for size the writer's perspective simply to have the experience of seeing things from a different angle.

✦ Questions for Discussion and Writing

1. Rephrase the following mini-arguments in your own words, stating the issue impartially and using non-connotative language that the writer might consider a fair summary of his or her argument. Did you find it was easier to rephrase and summarize an argument with which you agreed than with one which you disagreed? What extra steps did you have to take to arrive at an impartial summary?

   a.   It is getting harder and harder to follow an American discussion. We used to chide worry warts with: "suppose one thing, suppose another, suppose a jackass was your brother?" Now, however, supposition is the handmaiden of political correctness. I often run into this because of my penchant for voicing unthinkable opinions. "I'm sick of women," and my opponent retorts, "suppose you substituted *blacks* for *women* in that sentence?" It goes on. "Bugger the spotted owls." Suppose you substituted *Jews* for *owls?* "Brand criminals on the forehead." Suppose you substituted *gays* for *criminals?* This is not sensitivity but rhetorical tumult.
   —Florence King, "The Misanthrope's Corner," from *National Review,* August 15, 1994

   b.   The worst day I ever had hunting was when I shot an elk in the neck, where I was aiming, but it made me feel strangely ashamed, after it was over. I broke the elk's neck, the way I always try to do—that instant drop—but he groaned when I walked up to him. He couldn't have been feeling anything, and I hope it was just air leaving his lungs—but it was still a groan.

For a fact—or rather, for me—hunting's better than killing. It takes a while, after it's over—sometimes a long while—before you can think of it as meat. You can't go straight from a living animal to 250 pounds of elk steaks. There's too much knife and ax work involved—and you're the one who has to do it—skinning the animal, and pulling the hide back to reveal your crime, the meat—and already, sometimes, the call of ravens drifting in, black-winged shapes flying through the treetops, past the sun....

Instead of trying to make that instantaneous conversion—which I cannot do—life to meat—what I do is pray, sort of. I give heartfelt, shaky thanks to the animal as I clean it—ravens calling to ravens—and I do this with deer and grouse too, and even, if I can remember—which I don't always—with fish. A man or a woman who apologizes for hunting is a fool. It's a man's, or a woman's, choice, and he or she must live with it.

I don't do it for profit or gain; and rarely do I tell anyone about it after I've done it.

—"Why I Hunt: A Predator's Meditation," by Rick Bass, *Esquire*, 1991

c. Rich people are pompous. Rich people are deluded. Rich people have to tell you every moment of their lives how rich they are. Rich people are stingy, coldhearted, mean, cowardly, immoral, furtive, dishonest, arrogant, petty, backbiting, ruthless, and pointless.

Well, maybe some of them are okay. The ones who came by their money inadvertently by doing something they really like, and some lost souls who inherited money and give it to weird performance artists can possibly be allowed to live. But mainly they're a scourge.

And here's the thing: It's not their fault. Rich people would be perfectly fine if we would all just stop sucking up to them.

We're all so busy trying to pry a little loose change out of them, trying to get them to buy this painting, that car, this precious little Ming vase. They start really thinking that maybe they are just too fabulous. And the more money they make, the more Porsches they buy, the more people seem to adore them! Rich people desperately want to believe their own press, they need so severely to think they are one of the chosen. This is what turns them into monsters.

—"Rich People: Blow Me" by Cynthia Heimel, *Get Your Tongue Out of My Mouth. I'm Kissing You Good-Bye!*, 1993

d. The senior citizen lobby seems to be approaching this frightful proportion. I mean what's with these old people? Where'd they come from? All of a sudden there are geezers and duffers and biddies and fusspots every place you look. Not a highway in the nation is safe from Florida-bound codgers swaying lane to lane at 52 mph in their Cruise Master motor homes with the novelty license plates bolted to the front: "Retired—No Job—No Phone—No Excuse for Living." Every Sun Belt plane flight has its aisles jammed to impassibility with blue-rinse wide loads and their carry-on cat boxes. Fogies crowd shopping centers in mall-walking packs and swamp the ten-items-or-less supermarket checkout lanes with case-lot purchases of Campbell's soup for one. Turn on the television, and the ads are all for bran, PeptoBis-mol, hemorrhoid medications and high-fiber this and that. *Sic transit* the Pepsi generation. Everyone in commercials is over seventy and has something wrong with his butt.

—"Graft for the Millions: Social Security," P. J. O'Rourke, *Parliament of Whores*, 1991, p. 212

2. Speculate for any of the preceding mini-arguments on who the audi-ence might be. Create a brief audience profile as to political leanings, economic class, level of education, gender or ethnicity (if relevant), and profession. What can you assume they know or care about? What might their attitude be toward the issue? What common assumptions or values might the audience share with the arguer? What kind of de-sired effect is the argument designed to produce on this specified audi-ence according to your profile of their characteristics and values?

BACKING

Sometimes merely considering the argument as it appears to an audi-ence will not be sufficient. It is at this point that the concept of *backing* becomes important. An audience may not be satisfied that the warrant used to connect the evidence or grounds to the claim is an appropriate one to apply to the present case. Backing supplies additional evidence necessary to support the warrant, and it provides the assurance that the assumptions used in formulating the argument really rest on solid and trustworthy grounds. Of course, not all arguments will require the writer to produce the broader foundation of backing. Only when read-ers can be presumed to view the claims of an argument with doubt or skepticism need backing be produced. For example, you and a friend might be arguing over whether a particular tennis player would win Wimbledon. You might claim that player X was a sure bet to win Wim-bledon this year and back up your claim with statistics about the rela-tive strengths of the serve and volley game of this year's crop of tournament players. You might even state your warrant in the form of an assumption that "only a tennis player who had a strong serve and volley game has a real chance to take the Wimbledon title."

At this point, your skeptical friend might question the validity of your assumption. You would then have to produce the backing on which your warrant rests to clarify your claim and answer your friend's doubts. In this case, backing might take the form of an analysis of the serve and volley game of past winners of Wimbledon. Thus, warrants or assumptions that are not accepted by your audience at face value must be supported to clarify and substantiate the underlying structure of your claim.

Backing is required so often that it should be considered a basic part of any argument, satisfying the doubts of an audience that wants to know that the writer can, if challenged, provide further support.

QUALIFIERS

Another way writers take audiences into account is by using what are called *qualifiers*. Realistically, no claim is ever presented in a vacuum. The qualifier represents the writer's assessment of the relative strength or weakness of the claim. Qualifiers express limitations that may have to be attached to a claim in order to pass the scrutiny of a particular audience. Frequently qualifiers take the form of phrases such as *in all probability, very likely, presumably,* or *very possibly.*

For example, let's say you're having a discussion with a friend about computer software and you want to recommend the use of a new spreadsheet program. Rather than making your recommendation in an unqualified way without conditions or restrictions, you phrase your recommendation so as to indicate the kind of strength you wish to be attributed to your claim. To do this you need to include a qualifying word or phrase such as "program X, *as far as I can tell,* will make the job much easier." In this way, arguers take their audiences into account by modifying a claim to include a restriction whose effect is to enhance the persuasiveness of the message.

REBUTTALS OR EXCEPTIONS

While the addition of *backing* and *qualifiers* to the basic structure of claim–support–warrant goes a long way to adapting an argument to cope with the contrary beliefs, expectations, or skepticism of an audience, writers are aware that one further element is required to create a persuasive case. This element, called the *rebuttal* or *exception,* arises from the writer's responsibility in confronting special circumstances or extraordinary instances that challenge the claim being made. Inserting the rebuttal or exception into the structure of the argument enhances the persuasiveness of the claim by honestly recognizing that there may be some particularly exceptional circumstances under which the claim could not be directly supported by the grounds. For example, a typical use of the rebuttal or exception is in the form of warnings printed by pharmaceutical companies regarding contraindications or situations where an otherwise safe-to-prescribe drug should not be used. This type of argument might appear as follows:

GROUNDS: This patient is on a weight control program.

BACKING: Clinical experience shows that—

WARRANT: As part of a weight control program, D-amphetamine may be prescribed.

QUALIFIER: It appears very likely that—

CLAIM: This patient needs D-amphetamine as part of a weight control program.

REBUTTAL OR EXCEPTION: Unless the patient has a history of heart disease, high blood pressure, thyroid disease, or glaucoma, or is allergic to any amphetamine or has a history of abusing amphetamine medications, or is pregnant (because of possible links to birth defects).

To illustrate how backing, qualifiers, and rebuttals work in a real situation, consider the following speech given by Bruce Springsteen at the induction of Roy Orbison into the Rock and Roll Hall of Fame, January 21, 1987 (*Roy Orbison In Dreams* [1987]):

In 1970, I rode for 15 hours in the back of a U-Haul truck to open for Roy Orbison at the Nashville Music Fair. It was a summer night and I was 20 years old and he came out in dark glasses, a dark suit and he played some dark music.

In 74, just prior to going in the studio to make *Born To Run*, I was looking at Duane Eddy for his guitar sound and I was listening to a collection of Phil Spector records and I was listening to Roy Orbison's *All-Time Greatest Hits*. I'd lay in bed at night with just the lights of my stereo on and I'd hear *Cryin', Love Hurts, Runnin' Scared, Only The Lonely* and *It's Over* fillin' my room. Some rock 'n' roll reinforces friendship and community, but for me, Roy's ballads were always best when you were alone and in the dark. Roy scrapped the idea that you need verse-chorus-verse-chorus-bridge-verse-chorus to have a hit.

His arrangements were complex and operatic, they had rhythm and movement and they addressed the underside of pop romance. They were scary. His voice was unearthly.

He had the ability, like all great rock 'n' rollers, to sound like he'd dropped in from another planet and yet get the stuff that was right to the heart of what you were livin' in today, and that was how he opened up your vision. He made a little town in New Jersey feel as big as the sound of his records.

I always remember layin' in bed and right at the end of *It's Over*, when he hits that note where it sounds like the world's going to end, I'd be laying there promising myself that I was never going to go outside again and never going to talk to another woman.

Right about that time my needle would slip back to the first cut and I'd hear … (the opening riff to) Pretty Woman/I don't believe you/You're not the truth/No one could look as good as you. And that was when I understood.

I carry his records with me when I go on tour today, and I'll always remember what he means to me and what he meant to me when I was young and afraid to love.

In 75, when I went into the studio to make *Born To Run*, I wanted to make a record with words like Bob Dylan that sounded like Phil Spector, but most of all I wanted to sing like Roy Orbison. Now everybody knows that nobody sings like Roy Orbison.

The two opening paragraphs let the audience see Orbison from Springsteen's perspective like two snapshots in time. The first reveals the difference in stature between Orbison and the young Springsteen who "rode for 15 hours in the back of a U-Haul truck" to open for Orbison. The second lets the audience know how important Orbison's music was to Springsteen just before he recorded his own very successful album *Born to Run*. The heart of the speech is really an argument. The claim appears in this sentence:

Some rock 'n' roll reinforces friendship and community, but for me, Roy's ballads were always best when you were alone and in the dark.

Notice how this assertion is qualified by the words "for me" and includes an exception that anticipates an implied objection: "some rock 'n' roll reinforces friendship and community."

The evidence to support the basic claim that "Roy's ballads were always best when you were alone and in the dark" can be found in the following paragraphs:

His arrangements were complex and operatic, they had rhythm and movement and they addressed the underside of pop romance. They were scary. His voice was unearthly.

He had the ability, like all great rock 'n' rollers, to sound like he'd dropped in from another planet and yet get the stuff that was right to the heart of what you were livin' in today, and that was how he opened up your vision. He made a little town in New Jersey feel as big as the sound of his records.

The warrant or assumption that links the assertion with the evidence that supports it might be stated as follows:

Great rock 'n' roll ballads let you know you are not alone, not the only person who has suffered, and help you get beyond the suffering.

At this point, the argument as such is complete, but notice how Springsteen intuitively adds what might be considered backing to clarify and support his implicit warrant for those members of the audience who might feel differently about what great rock 'n' roll ballads should be. The backing appears in the form of Springsteen's personal recollections that reveal how important Orbison's music was for him in echoing his own heartache and getting him beyond it to love again:

> I always remember layin' in bed and right at the end of *It's Over*, when he hits that note where it sounds like the world's going to end, I'd be laying there promising myself that I was never going to go outside again and never going to talk to another woman.
>
> Right about that time my needle would slip back to the first cut and I'd hear... (the opening riff to) Pretty Woman/I don't believe you/You're not the truth/No one could look as good as you. And that was when I understood.
>
> I carry his records with me when I go on tour today, and I'll always remember what he means to me and what he meant to me when I was young and afraid to love.

The argument now complete, Springsteen ends by evoking the opening paragraphs, almost as if the speech itself were a kind of song, ending with his now wiser perspective that "now everybody knows that nobody sings like Roy Orbison."

In diagram form (Figure 2-11) the relationship of the parts of Springsteen's speech might appear as follows:

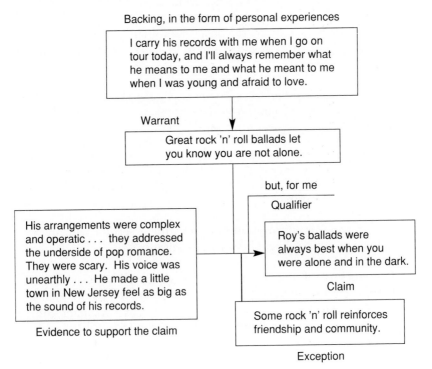

FIGURE 2-11   *The Relationship of the Parts of Springsteen's Speech.*

✦ *Questions for Discussion and Writing*

1. For any of the following issues, what kinds of information would you want to have before writing an argument?

2. For any of the following issues, what specific audience would you wish to persuade?

3. Select an issue for which you have specified an audience and write a short essay that expresses your views on the issue and takes opposing views into account. As your draft your argument, consider whether you need to qualify your claim, present significant exceptions, or provide backing for assumptions.

4. If you and some other members of your class have written arguments taking opposing views on the same issue, form groups that identify the key interests of each perspective. Drawing upon the Rogerian approach, try to summarize all positions involved as a first step toward mediating the conflicts. The class may wish to appoint a student to act as a mediator posing questions to each of the opposing parties. Try to come to a compromise that takes into consideration the interests of all parties involved, and as a class write a collaborative statement formalizing your resolution. Identify the principles the class has agreed on as a basis for the compromise.

   • Should schools be given the task of offering explicit sex education for children? In your opinion, at what age should this be started, if at all? When children are six, eight, ten, or some other age? Identify the assumptions underlying your opinion.
   • Should people who smoke cigarettes have to pay for their own health insurance? Why or why not?
   • Should religious institutions be required to pay taxes?
   • Should television networks be allowed to televise pornographic material after 11 P.M.?
   • Should speech codes be imposed on college campuses?
   • Should the content of records, compact discs, and cassette tapes be censored?
   • Should advertising on television directed at children be restricted?
   • Is the United States solving its immigration problem?
   • Should a tuition tax credit or voucher system be instituted to enable parents to send their children to schools of their choice?
   • How does the issue about when life begins underlie the abortion controversy?
   • Should welfare be made contingent on a willingness to work?
   • Does society have an obligation to rehabilitate criminals?

- Is there a date rape crisis on college campuses? What should be the legal distinction between rape and seduction?
- Should women be allowed to serve in combat in the Army and the Marines (the Navy and Air Force already assign combat missions to women)?
- Should executions be broadcast on television? Why or why not?
- Should colleges take race into account when awarding financial aid?
- Do student athletes receive a genuine academic education?
- What changes in the social behavior of young people are directly attributable to shopping malls?
- Should the names of all the persons testing positive for the HIV virus be reported to the Health Department?
- What local environmental problem is the subject of recent controversy? Why is the issue significant and what should be done about it?

FIVE SHORT ARGUMENTS FOR ANALYSIS: CLAIMS OF FACT, CAUSATION, VALUE, AND POLICY

George E. Vaillant

We Should Retain the Disease Concept of Alcoholism

———————◆———————

George E. Vaillant is Director of Adult Development at Harvard University (from which he received an M. D. in 1965). He is the author of The Wisdom of the Ego, *1993, and is the recipient of the Jellinck Prize for alcoholism research. This article appeared originally in the August 1990* Harvard Medical School Mental Health Letter.

When I read expert discussions of why alcoholism is not a disease, 1 I am reminded of the equally learned discussions by "the best and the brightest" of why the Viet Nam War was a good idea. These discussants had intelligence, advanced degrees, scholarship, prestige, literacy—every qualification but one. They lacked experience. None had spent much time in Viet Nam. Just so, the philosopher Herbert Fingarette, the psychoanalyst Thomas Szasz, the sociologist and theoretician Robin Room, and provocative, thoughtful psychologists like Stanton Peele and Nicholas Heather have every qualification but one for explaining why alcoholism is not a disease—they have never worked in an alcohol clinic. Why, I wonder, do experienced alcohol workers and recovering alcoholics, the thousands of competent common folk in the trenches, accept the view that alcoholism is a disease? Why is it mainly less competent people, the active alcoholics, who agree with Professor Fingarette that they are just "heavy drinkers"?

Let me summarize the evidence provided by the learned academics who have pointed out the folly of the medical model of alcoholism. First, alcohol abuse—unlike coughing from pneumonia, for example—is a habit under considerable volitional control. Second, there is compelling evidence that variations in alcohol consumption are distributed along a smooth continuum, although a medical model would suggest that in any individual, alcoholism is either present or absent. Third, when alcoholism is treated as a disease it can be used both by individuals and by society to explain away major underlying problems—poverty, mental deficiency, crime, and the like—which require our attention if efforts at prevention, treatment and understanding are to succeed. Fourth, to diagnose people as alcoholic is to label them in a way that can damage both self-esteem and public acceptance. Fifth, alcoholism should not be considered a disease if it is regarded as merely a symptom of underlying personality or depression.

Refutation of Objections

3   Let me try to refute these objections one by one. First, it may be true that there is no known underlying biological defect in alcoholism. Rather, alcohol abuse is a multidetermined continuum of drinking behaviors whose causes are differently weighted for different people and include culture, habits, and genes. But the same can be said of high blood pressure and coronary heart disease. The incidence of hypertension varies with measurement procedures and psychological circumstances. It lies on a physiological continuum which defies precise definition. It has no known specific cause. It is powerfully affected by social factors; for example, it has become epidemic among young urban black males. The point of using the term 'disease' for alcoholism is simply to underscore that once a person has lost the capacity to control consistently how much and how often he or she drinks, continued use of alcohol can be both a necessary and a sufficient cause of a syndrome that produces millions of invalids and causes millions of deaths.

4   The second objection to the medical model of alcoholism is that only opinion separates the alcoholic from the heavy drinker. Supposedly one either has a disease or does not have it; diagnosis should depend on signs and symptoms, not value judgments. But consider the example of coronary heart disease. We regard it as a medical illness, although its causes are diverse and often poorly understood and there is no fixed point at which we can decide that coronary arteries become abnormal. So it is with alcoholism. Normal drinking merges imperceptibly with pathological drinking. Culture and idiosyncratic viewpoints will always determine where the line is drawn.

5   The third objection is that alcoholism is affected by so many situational and psychological factors that the drinking must often be viewed as reactive. Some people drink uncontrollably only after a serious loss or in certain specific situations, and some alcoholics return to normal drinking by an act of will. But these observations are equally true of hypertension, which often has an extremely important psychological

component. Nevertheless, prospective studies show that alcohol dependence causes depression, anxiety, and poverty far more often than the other way around. In citing psychological problems as a cause of alcoholism, Fingarette reverses the position of cart and horse.

The fourth objection to calling alcoholism a disease is that it involves both labeling and a disparagement of free will. But in this case both labeling and the denial of free will are therapeutic. Some people believe that the label 'alcoholic' transforms a person into an outcast, akin to a leper. Well, should a doctor who knows that a person has leprosy keep the fact secret lest the patient be labeled a leper? Some people believe that if alcoholics are taught to regard alcoholism as a disease they will use this label as an excuse to drink or a reason why they should not be held responsible for their own recovery. It does not work out that way. Like people with high blood pressure, alcoholics who understand that they have a disease become more rather than less willing to take responsibility for self-care. That is why the self-help group, Alcoholics Anonymous, places such single-minded emphasis on the idea that alcoholism is a disease.

Diagnosis Helps

Once patients accept the diagnosis, they can be shown how to assume responsibility for their own care. Physicians stress the value of diagnosing hypertension early because it can provide a rational explanation for headaches and other symptoms that were hitherto regarded as neurotic or irrational. For years alcoholics themselves have labeled themselves 'wicked,' 'weak,' and 'reprehensible.' The offer of a medical explanation does not lead to irresponsibility, only to hope and improved morale.

The fifth argument against calling alcoholism a disease is the most compelling; it is said that uncontrolled maladaptive ingestion of alcohol is not a biological disorder but a disorder of behavior. Like compulsive fingernail biting, gambling, or child molesting, this form of deviant behavior can often be better classified by sociologists than by physiologists, and better treated by psychologists skilled in behavior therapy than by physicians with their medical armamentarium.

But unlike giving up gambling or fingernail biting, giving up alcohol abuse often requires skilled medical attention during acute withdrawal. Unlike gamblers and fingernail biters, most alcoholics develop secondary symptoms that do require medical care. Unlike child molesters, but like people with high blood pressure, alcoholics have a mortality rate two to four times as high as the average. In order to receive the medical treatment they require, alcoholics need a label that will allow them unprejudiced access to emergency rooms, detoxification clinics, and medical insurance.

10   The final argument for regarding alcoholism as a disease rather than a behavior disorder is that it often causes alcoholics to mistreat persons they love. Very few sustained human experiences involve as much abuse as the average close family member of an alcoholic must tolerate. Fingarette's "heavy drinking" model (which conveys a concept of misbehavior) only generates more denial in the already profoundly guilt-ridden alcoholic. Calling alcoholism a disease rather than a behavior disorder is a useful device both to persuade the alcoholic to acknowledge the problem and to provide a ticket for admission to the health care system. In short, in our attempts to understand and study alcoholism, we should employ the models of the social scientist and the learning theorist. But in order to treat alcoholics effectively we need to invoke the medical model.

11   Let me close with an anecdote. My research associate, reviewing the lives of 100 patients who had been hospitalized eight years previously for detoxification from alcohol, wrote to me that she mistrusted the diagnosis of alcoholism. To illustrate, she described one man who drank heavily for seven years after his initial detoxification. Although the alcohol clinic's staff agreed that his drinking was alcoholic, neither he nor his wife acknowledged that it was a problem. Finally he required a second detoxification, and the clinic staff claimed that they had been right.

12   "How can you call such behavior a disease," my associate wrote, "when you cannot decide if it represents a social problem [that is, requires a value judgment] or alcohol-dependent drinking?" Then she shifted her attention to the ninety-nine other tortured lives she had been reviewing. Oblivious of the contradiction, she concluded: "I don't think I ever fully realized before I did this follow-up what an absolutely devastating disease alcoholism is." I respectfully submit that if Professor Fingarette were to work in an alcohol clinic for two years, he would agree with the last half of my research associate's letter rather than the first half.

✦ Questions for Discussion and Writing

1. How do the structure of the argument and the way Vaillant raises points and deals with them enhance the credibility of his position?

2. What defining criteria does Vaillant propose by which to evaluate whether alcoholism is or is not a disease? Do they make sense to you?

3. According to Vaillant, what would be the disadvantages of failing to view alcoholism as a disease? What would be the advantages?

4. How does Vaillant draw correspondences to hypertension in order to develop his case?

5. Of the various kinds of evidence Vaillant presents to support his thesis or claim, which, in your opinion, seems the strongest and which the weakest? Which of his reasons seem the most compelling or the least compelling? Is there one phase of his argument that you feel he should have developed more fully in order to make his overall case more persuasive? If so, identify it and say what additional support you would have wished him to present.

6. What kinds of assumptions, whether implicit or explicit, does Vaillant rely on in his argument? Do some of them seem less valid than others?

7. On the basis of your personal experience or that of others you have observed, would you agree that alcoholism is less a matter of psychological and social factors than it is an inherited tendency?

8. Drawing on the format employed by Vaillant, write a short essay in which you make a case for the distinctive nature of some phenomenon that is classified as a form of "addictive behavior." For example, you might develop criteria, specify attributes, and offer examples that would lead your audience to have a clearer idea of food-related disorders such as anorexia, bulimia, chocoholism, or overeating; compulsive behaviors such as gambling, sexual activity, or shopping; exercising, such as jogging, weight lifting, or aerobics; or addictions to drugs, pornography, or sports (either as a participant or as a fan). Make sure you provide evidence to back up your claims, take opposing perspectives into account, and explain your assumptions that justify drawing the conclusions from the data you present. Where necessary, offer backing for these warrants or assumptions, and phrase your thesis using qualifiers and mentioning exceptions to make your argument more persuasive.

The Lays of Ancient ROM

◆

The following article was written by the editors of The Economist *and first appeared in the issue of August 27, 1994. This publication is known for its free-market orientation.*

1   In 1987 a budding classicist from the University of Lausanne finished four years of labour. She had spent them scouring ancient Greek tomes searching for the classical sources of 2,000 anonymous fragments of medieval text. Then, just when she was getting down to writing her doctoral dissertation, all that effort was eclipsed. In a few dozen hours working with a new database she found every one of her 600 hard-won sources again—and 300 more that had passed her by.

2   That database, the Thesaurus Linguae Grecae, was the first of the tools that is transforming the staid world of what used to be bookish learning. When computers were mere calculating machines, only the sciences had need of them. Now that they can be easily used to scan vast memories at inhuman speeds, the humanities have every reason to catch up. Whole libraries are vanishing into the digital domain, where their contents can be analyzed exhaustively. The changes in the practice of scholarship may be greater than any since Gutenberg.

3   The process seems now to have been inevitable, but even the inevitable has to start somewhere. In the 1970s a group of classicists at the University of California, Irvine, thought up a then extraordinary goal: having every extant word of ancient Greek literature in a single database; 3,000 authors, 66m words; all searchable, accessible and printable. With the help of nearby computer companies, this idea became the Thesaurus Linguae Grecae. There are now 1,400 places around the world where a classicist can use it to do a lifetime's worth of scanning for allusions or collecting references just for a single essay. On compact disc, the whole thesaurus costs about $300.

4   Scholars using the growing electronic-text archives at such places as Oxford University, the University of Virginia and Rutgers University, New Jersey, have more than the classics to play with. There are at least five different competing software bibles, some with parallel texts that provide Greek and Hebrew, and several with full concordances and indexing. Shakespeare's words have been done as well as God's; indeed, the entire canon of British poetry prior to this century is now digitised. So is Aquinas. Wittgenstein's unpublished fragments—20,000 pages of them—are expected soon; so are 221 volumes of Migne's Patrologia Latina, a collection of theological writings that date from between 200AD and the Council of Florence in 1439.

Some of this is the work of governments and charities: half the $7m   5
needed for the Thesaurus Linguae Grecae came from America's National Endowment for the Humanities, the other half from foundations
and private patrons. Some of it is done for profit, just like traditional
publishing. The English Poetry Full-Text Database (EPFTD), released in
June on four compact discs by Chadwyck Healey, a company in Cambridge, England, costs £30,000 ($46,500). It took four years to assemble
from roughly 4,500 volumes of verse; it is easy to use, and is poised to
become an indispensable research tool. Chadwyck Healey says it has
sold more than 100 copies. The company is now working on an index
to the entire runs of more than 2,000 scholarly journals.

Typing in every word of a nation's literary heritage is a time-   6
consuming and expensive task, even when the work is exported to take
advantage of cheap labour in Asia, as it almost always is. Another approach is to record the appearance of books and other writings, rather
than their contents, by scanning in images of them. The Archive of the
Indies in Seville has used IBM scanners and software to put near-perfect
facsimiles of the letters of Columbus, Cortes and their contemporaries
on to the screen. Years of scanning by a full-time staff of 30 people has
put more than 10m handwritten pages—one-seventh of the total—into
the archive's memory banks.

The computers store the pages as images, not text, so they cannot   7
be searched and compared in the way that the EPFTD can. They offer
scholars other compensations, though. Scanners like those originally
designed for medical imaging provide extremely detailed and subtle
digitisation. This can then be fed through image-enhancement software
so ancient smudges and ink-spills can be filtered out. And since the users cannot damage the copies as they might the originals, humble students can have access to documents previously available only to a
handful of elite scholars. The Seville project is proving so successful
that IBM and El Corte Ingles, a big Spanish retailer, have founded a company to market the techniques used. Half-a-dozen ventures are already
under way, including a proposal to digitise the gargantuan (and recent-
ly-opened) Comintern archives in Moscow.

Logos and Log-Ons

It is possible to combine the image of a page with searchable elec-   8
tronic text, simply by having both stored in the same system with
cross-references. A Chaucer archive that offers multiple manuscripts
and searchable texts is being released one Canterbury tale at a time
("The Wife of Bath" comes first). Of course, putting both together costs
even more than a straight text database, and those can be pretty expensive. The EPFTD works out at a quite reasonable $10-or-so per volume—
but that still makes it a pricey proposition when bought, as it must be,

all at once. The cost of such commercially compiled databases worries some scholars, not to mention librarians. It is not their only worry.

9   The difference between a printed page and the text it contains is not just one of aesthetics; there can be meaning in the way typefaces are chosen, in how pages are laid out, in the indentations before lines and the gaps in between them. There are data on the title page that apply to the whole text. A good database has to encode all this information somehow, and has to offer ways in which it can be used in searches.

10   That is why databases have "mark-up languages", which allow the text and the spaces within it to be tagged with particular meanings. Mark-up languages tell the computer, for example, that a title is a title and a footnote is a footnote; the computer can then display them as such, with typefaces to taste, and the interested user can search the text for titles and footnotes. The more complex the search, the more extensive the mark-up required. The mark-up for the EPFTD allows the computer to identify things like stanzas, verses, dates and names.

11   In a perfect world mark-ups would be neutral and descriptive, capable of applying equally well to almost any texts. In practice individual mark-up languages have sprung up like mushrooms. There is now a move to concentrate on using the Standard Generalised Mark-up Language (SGML) to define the codes that tag text. It was developed at IBM for lawyers, and adopted by the Pentagon for its mountains of manuals. At present SGML is probably the most widely used mark-up language; officially, it is an international standard. But it is not necessarily ideal for academics, who are aware that the way a text is marked up will have far-reaching implications for the kind of research that is possible. Marking up is an invisible act of interpretation; the scholars want the interpreting left to them.

12   That is why so much effort has gone into a specific way of using SGML for prose, verse, drama and other forms of text that are pored over by scholars. The Text Encoding Initiative is the sort of huge multinational research effort that nuclear physicists are used to but that scholars in the humanities can still be shocked by. After six years of work, supported financially by the American government, the European Union and others, the TEI published its guidelines in May—all 1,300 pages of them. More than 100 TEI scholars have had to decide everything from how poetry should be distinguished from prose to whether footnotes to footnotes are admissible in conforming texts. Their peers seem happy with the work.

13   Standardised formats will enable electronic texts to move on-line. That will make them available from any computer hooked up to a telephone line, not just from a dedicated terminal devoted to a single database and nothing else. That is good for the far-flung; the University of Dubrovnik, its library destroyed, has just been given a networked com-

puter terminal that puts it on-line to a host of foreign databases. It is also good for the independent researcher. Texts will be freed from academia's grip, just as books before them were freed from the church and the wealthy by printing.

More research; different research, too. Speculative hypotheses about influence or style will be rigorously testable by textual comparisons as cheap and plentiful as the numerical calculations in a computer model of the weather. Critics still raise the spectre of great literature passing under the die-stamp of conformity, but some degree of conformity may be a price of new forms of access. The first die-stamp for literature was a printing press. The passing of the illuminated manuscript made the world a slightly poorer place; the coming of print made it a far, far richer one. 14

✦ *Questions for Discussion and Writing*

1. What features of modern electronic data bases have superseded the efforts that humanities scholars had to make in the past?

2. If you have used data bases, draw on these experiences as a basis for an argument that makes a case for how data bases in your personal experience have changed the way you do research or locate information. You may have used InfoTrac, ProQuest, Newsbank Electronic Information System, CIS/Masterfile, Silver Platter, or any of the specialized Wilsondisc Data Bases (for example, what do you need to do to conduct efficient searches that go beyond what you would do in looking up information in an index of a book)?

3. What important difference in the way information can be accessed distinguishes text that has been digitized and text whose image has simply been scanned to put it into a data base? How does the way the information is entered affect its ability to be retrieved and manipulated?

4. What advantages do data bases have over books, and what advantages do books still possess over computer data bases?

5. Why are "mark-up" languages necessary to make text information more usable? How do these languages provide information that would be automatically available on any page of any text?

6. How do the editors use the analogy contained in their assessment that "texts will be freed from academia's grip, just as books before them were freed from the church and the wealthy by printing" to illustrate the consequences of using the available electronic data bases? Explore the social implications of this idea in a short essay. Do data bases really destroy elitism or simply transfer it to those with access to computers?

7. How does the following example suggest other consequences for traditional biological or other kinds of research that go beyond the effects described by the editors?

> When Dr. Thomas Hudson wants to share his latest research with other geneticists around the world, he doesn't publish it in the usual sense of the word.
>
> That takes too long. Besides, each time the researcher at the Whitehead Institute in Cambridge, Mass., makes a quarterly report, the data would more than fill the customary three pages allotted in printed journals.
>
> So like many other genetic researchers today Hudson uses the Internet to make his data electronically available to other scientists. As a result, Hudson says, other researchers can examine his findings sooner and in more complete detail than would be possible with traditional publishing.
>
> —Ted Bunker, "How Internet, Data Base Technologies Are Advancing Gene Research," *Investor's Business Daily,* September 14, 1994

8. If it is applicable, draw on your personal experiences to make a case for the consequences of any of the following:

   a. Under what circumstances do the rights of individuals conflict with new information technologies?

   b. What problems (ethical, financial) are involved in on-line searching?

   c. Specialized BBs.

   d. Software piracy.

   e. Hacking.

   f. ATM machines.

   g. Games subversive and otherwise. New game boxes, the Internet (and specific resources like MOSAIC, Gopher, Wais, Veronica, Archie, etc.), the Infobahn, news groups, virtual reality products, cyberspace, interactive cable, satellite T.V., wireless technologies, digital art, or synthesizers (MIDI, etc.), developments in video technologies (multimedia), amusements (karaoke), and so on. What new concepts, products, or ideas and technologies being developed are you aware of that would have profound social consequences? Explore any of these in a short essay.

   h. E-mail, flaming, etc.

   i. Faxing, cellular phones.

Daniel Callahan

Physician-Assisted Suicide
Should Not Be Legal

◆

*Daniel Callahan is a medical ethicist who is the co-founder and director of
The Hastings Center, an educational organization. The following article
originally appeared in the August 9, 1991 issue of* Commonweal.

The fear of dying is powerful. Even more powerful sometimes is   1
the fear of not dying, of being forced to endure destructive pain, or to
live out a life of unrelieved, pointless suffering. The movement to legal-
ize euthanasia and assisted suicide is a strong and, seemingly, historically inevitable response to that fear. It draws part of its strength from
the failure of modern medicine to reassure us that it can manage our
dying with dignity and comfort. It draws another part from the desire
to be masters of our fate. Why must we endure that which need not be
endured? If medicine cannot always bring us the kind of death we
might like through its technical skills, why can it not use them to give
us a quick and merciful release? Why can we not have "aid-in-
dying"?...

Individual Right

Exactly a century ago, in the 1891 *Union Pacific* v. *Bostford* case, the   2
Supreme Court held that "No right is more sacred, or is more carefully
guarded, by the common law, than the right of the individual to the
possession and control of his own person." That right has been reaf-
firmed time and again, and especially underscored in those rulings that
declare our right to terminate medical treatment and thus to die.

But if it should happen to be impossible for us to so easily bring   3
about our own death, would it not be reasonable to ask someone else,
specifically a doctor, to help us to die? Would it not, moreover, be an act
of mercy for a doctor to give us that kind of a release? Is not the relief of
suffering a high moral good?

To say "no" in response to questions of that kind seems both re-   4
pressive and cruel. They invoke our cherished political values of liberty
and self-determination. They draw upon our deep and long-standing
moral commitment to the relief of suffering. They bespeak our ancient
efforts to triumph over death, to find a way to bring it to heel.

5   Nonetheless, we should as a society say no, and decisively so, to euthanasia and assisted suicide.... If a death marked by pain or suffering is a nasty death, a natural biological evil of a supreme kind, euthanasia and assisted suicide are wrong and harmful responses to that evil. To directly kill another person in the name of mercy (as I will define "euthanasia" here), or to assist another to commit suicide (which seems to me logically little different from euthanasia) would add to a society already burdened with man-made evils still another....

Dire Social Consequences

6   Legalization would also provide an important social sanction for euthanasia, affecting many aspects of our society beyond the immediate relief of suffering individuals. The implications of that sanction are profound. It would change the traditional role of the physician. It would require the regulation and oversight of government. It would add to the acceptable range of permissible killing in our society still another occasion for one person to take the life of another.

7   We might decide that we are as a people prepared to live with those implications. But we should not deceive ourselves into thinking of euthanasia or assisted suicide as merely personal acts, just a slight extension of the already-established right to control our bodies and to have medical treatment terminated. It is a radical move into an entirely different realm of morality: that of the killing of one person by another....

Historical Perspectives

8   Traditionally, only three circumstances have been acceptable for the taking of life: killing in self-defense or to protect another life, killing in the course of a just war, and, in the case of capital punishment, killing by agents of the state. Killing in both war and capital punishment has been opposed by some, and most successfully in the case of capital punishment, now banned in many countries, particularly those of Western Europe.

9   Apart from those long-standing debates, what is most notable about the historically licit conditions of killing is (1) the requirement that killing is permissible only when relatively objective standards have been met (in war or self-defense, a genuine threat to life or vital goods, and the absence of an alternative means of meeting those threats); and (2) when the public good is thereby served. (Even in self-defense, the permission to kill has some element of fostering a sense of public security in the face of personal threats.) ...

10   The law does not now allow, in the United States or elsewhere, the right of one person to kill another even if the latter requests, or consents, that it be done. All civilized societies have also outlawed private

killings, either in the name of honor (dueling, for instance), or to right private wrongs (to revenge adulterous relationships, for instance).

Yet if we generally accept in our society a right to control our own life and body, why has the extension of that right to private killing been denied? The most obvious reason is a reluctance to give one person absolute and irrevocable power over the life of another, whether there is consent or not. That prohibition is a way of saying that the social stakes in the legitimization of killing are extraordinarily high. It is to recognize that a society should—for the mutual protection of all—be exceedingly parsimonious about conferring a right to kill on anyone, for whatever reason.... 11

Fatally Flawed

We come here to a striking pitfall of the common argument for euthanasia and assisted suicide. Once the key premises of that argument are accepted, there will remain no logical way in the future to: (1) deny euthanasia to anyone who requests it for whatever reason, terminal illness or not; or to (2) deny it to the suffering incompetent, even if they do not request it. We can erect legal safeguards and specify required procedures to keep that from happening. But over time they will provide poor protection if the logic of the moral premises upon which they are based are fatally flawed. 12

Where are the flaws here? Recall that there are two classical arguments in favor of euthanasia and assisted suicide: our right of self-determination, and our claim upon the mercy of others, especially doctors, to relieve our suffering if they can do so. These two arguments are typically spliced together and presented as a single contention. Yet if they are considered independently—and there is no inherent reason why they must be linked—they display serious problems. Consider, first, the argument for our right of self-determination. It is said that a competent, adult person should have a right to euthanasia for the relief of suffering. But why must the person be suffering? Does not that stipulation already compromise the right of self-determination? How can self-determination have any limits? Why are not the person's desires or motives, whatever they may be, sufficient? How can we justify this arbitrary limitation of self-determination? The standard arguments for euthanasia offer no answers to those questions. 13

Consider next the person who is suffering but not competent, who is perhaps demented or mentally retarded. The standard argument...would deny euthanasia to that person. But why? If a person is suffering but not competent, then it would seem grossly unfair to deny relief simply because that person lacks competence. Are the incompetent less entitled to relief from suffering than the competent? Will it only be affluent middle-class people, mentally fit and able, who can 14 qualify? Will those who are incompetent but suffering be denied that which those who are intellectually and emotionally better off can have? Would that be fair? Do they suffer less for being incompetent? The standard argument about our duty to relieve suffering offers no response to those questions either.

Jerry-Rigged Combination

15   Is it, however, fair to euthanasia advocates to do what I have done, to separate, and treat individually, the two customary arguments in favor of a legal right to euthanasia? The implicit reason for so joining them is no doubt the desire to avoid abuse. By requiring a showing of suffering and terminal illness, the aim is to exclude perfectly healthy people from demanding that, in the name of self-determination and for their own private reasons, another person can be called upon to kill them. By requiring a show of mental competence to effect self-determination, the aim is to exclude the nonvoluntary killing of the depressed, the retarded, and the demented.

16   My contention is that the joining of those two requirements is perfectly arbitrary, a jerry-rigged combination if ever there was one. Each has its own logic, and each could be used to justify euthanasia. But in the nature of the case that logic, it seems evident, offers little resistance to denying any competent person the right to be killed, sick or not; and little resistance to killing the incompetent, so long as there is good reason to believe they are suffering. There is no principled reason to reject that logic, and no reason to think it could long remain suppressed by the expedient of arbitrary legal stipulations. . . .

Justifying Moral Grounds

17   The doctor will not be able to use a medical standard. He or she will only be able to use a moral standard. Faced with a patient reporting great suffering, a doctor cannot, therefore, justify euthanasia on purely medical grounds (because suffering is unmeasurable and scientifically undiagnosable). To maintain professional and personal integrity, the doctor will have to justify it on his or her own moral grounds. The doctor must believe that a life of subjectively experienced intense suffering is not worth living. He must believe that himself if he is to be justified in taking the decisive and ultimate step of killing the patient: it must be his moral reason to act, not the patient's reason (even though they may coincide). But if he believes that a life of some forms of suffering is not worth living, then how can he deny the same relief to a person who cannot request it, or who requests it, but whose competence is in doubt? This is simply a different way of making the point that there is no self-evident reason why the supposed duty to relieve suffering

must be limited to competent patients claiming self-determination. Or why patients who claim death as their right under self-determination must be either suffering or dying.

There is, moreover, the possibility that what begins as a right of doc-   18
tors to kill under specified conditions will soon become a duty to kill. On what grounds could a doctor deny a request by a competent person for euthanasia? It will not do, I think, just to specify that no doctor should be required to do that which violates her conscience. As commonly articulated, the argument about why a doctor has a right to perform euthanasia—the dual duty to respect patient self-determination and to relieve suffering—is said to be central to the vocation of being a doctor. Why should duties as weighty as those be set aside on the grounds of "conscience" or "personal values"?

These puzzles make clear that the moral situation is radically   19
changed once our self-determination requires the participation and assistance of a doctor. It is then that doctor's moral life, that doctor's integrity, that is also and no less encompassed in the act of euthanasia. What, we might then ask, should be the appropriate moral standards for a person asked to kill another? What are the appropriate virtues and sensitivities of such a person? How should that person think of his or her own life and find, within that life, a place for the killing of another person? The language of a presumed right of someone to kill another to relieve suffering obscures questions of that kind. . . .

Our duty to relieve suffering cannot justify the introduction of new   20
evils into society. The risk of doing just that in the legalization of "aid-in-dying" is too great, particularly since the number of people whose pain and suffering could not be relieved would never be a large one (so even most euthanasia advocates recognize). It is too great because it would take a disproportionate social change to bring it about, one whose implications extend far beyond the sick and dying. It is too great because, as the history of the twentieth century should demonstrate, killing is a contagious disease, not easy to stop once unleashed in society. It is too great a risk because it would offer medicine too convenient a way out of its hardest cases, those where there is ample room for further, more benign reforms. We are far from exhausting the known remedies for the relief of pain (frequently, even routinely, underused), and a long way from providing decent psychological support for those who suffer from despair and a sense of futility in continuing life.

Pain and suffering in the critically ill and dying are great evils. The   21
attempt to relieve them by the introduction of euthanasia and assisted suicide is even greater. Those practices threaten the future security of the living. They no less threaten the dying themselves. Once a society allows one person to take the life of another based on their mutual private standards of a life worth living, there can be no safe or sure way to contain the deadly virus thus introduced. It will go where it will thereafter.

✦ *Questions for Discussion and Writing*

1. How is Callahan's restatement of the moral objections traditionally associated with suicide intended to enhance the persuasiveness of his argument?

2. Briefly summarize the moral criteria Callahan advances to refute the permissibility of assisted suicide. Which of his objections seems the most persuasive; which the least? In your view, has he made an effective case against assisted suicide? Why or why not?

3. How does the crux of Callahan's argument depend on the reasons brought forward to support his claim that assisted suicide cannot be seen as an extension of the right of self-determination? Why can't one person (the patient) turn that power over to another (the doctor)?

4. Why according to Callahan is it unfair and unwise to burden a physician with the moral decision when to take a patient's life?

5. How does Callahan use the examples of those who are incompetent or otherwise able to speak for themselves to support his claim?

6. Rhetorically, what effect is Callahan trying to achieve by characterizing the introduction of assisted suicide as a "deadly virus"? Does this help or hurt his case?

7. Are there any circumstances where you could foresee assigning the decision to take your life to someone else? If so, describe the circumstances and your reasons. Are there any circumstances where you could foresee agreeing to take the life of someone else who requested it of you? If so, describe those circumstances and your reasons.

Timothy E. Quill

My Patient's Suicide

———————◆———————

Timothy E. Quill is Professor of Medicine and Psychiatry at the University of Rochester School of Medicine. He is the director of the university's program for Biopsycho-Social Studies. He writes extensively on physician–patient relationships and end-of-life decisions. He is the author of Death and Dignity: Making Choices and Taking Charge *(1993). The following article appeared in the March 7, 1991 issue of* The New England Journal of Medicine.

Diane was feeling tired and had a rash. Her hematocrit was 22, and her white-cell count was 43 with some metamyelocytes and unusual white cells. I called Diane and told her it might be serious. When she pressed for the possibilities, I reluctantly opened the door to leukemia. Hearing the word seemed to make it exist. "Oh, shit!" she said. "Don't tell me that." I thought, I wish I didn't have to. 1

Diane was raised in an alcoholic family and had felt alone for much of her life. She had vaginal cancer as a young woman, and had struggled with depression and her own alcoholism for most of her adult life. I had come to know, respect, and admire her over the previous eight years as she confronted and gradually overcame these problems. During the previous three and half years, she had abstained from alcohol and had established much deeper connections with her husband, her college-age son, and several friends. Her business and artistic work was blossoming. She felt she was living fully for the first time. 2

Unfortunately, a bone-marrow biopsy confirmed the worst. Acute myelomonocytic leukemia. In the face of this tragedy, I looked for signs of hope. This is an area of medicine in which technological intervention has been successful, with long-term cures occurring 25 percent of the time. As I probed the costs of these cures, I learned about induction chemotherapy (three weeks in the hospital, probable infections, and hair loss; 75 percent of patients respond, 25 percent do not). Those who respond are then given consolidation chemotherapy (with similar side effects; another 25 percent die, thus a net of 50 percent survive). For those still alive to have a reasonable chance of long-term survival, they must undergo bone-marrow transplants (hospitalization for two months, a whole-body irradiation—with complete killing of the bone marrow—infectious complications; 50 percent of this group survive, or 25 percent of the original group). Though hematologists may argue over the exact percentage of people who will 3

123

benefit from therapy, they don't argue about the outcome of not having any treatment—certain death in days, weeks, or months.

4   Believing that delay was dangerous, the hospital's oncologist broke the news to Diane and made plans to begin induction chemotherapy that afternoon. When I saw her soon after, she was enraged at his presumption that she would want treatment and devastated by the finality of the diagnosis. All she wanted to do was go home and be with her family. She had no further questions about treatment and, in fact, had decided that she wanted none. Together we lamented her tragedy. I felt the need to make sure that she and her husband understood that there was some risk in delaying, that the problem would not go away, and that we needed to keep considering the options over the next several days.

5   Two days later Diane, her husband, and her son came to see me. They had talked at length about the problem and the options. She remained very clear about her wish not to undergo chemotherapy and to live whatever time she had left outside of the hospital. Her family wished she would choose treatment but accepted her decision. She articulated very clearly that it was she who would be experiencing all the side effects of treatment and that one-in-four odds were not good enough for her to undergo so toxic a course of therapy. I had her repeat her understanding of the treatment, the odds, and the consequences of forgoing treatment. I clarified a few misunderstandings, but she had a remarkable grasp of the options and implications.

6   I have long been an advocate of the idea that an informed patient should have the right to choose or refuse treatment, and to die with as much control and dignity as possible. Yet there was something that disturbed me about Diane's decision to give up a 25 percent chance of long-term survival in favor of almost certain death. Diane and I met several times that week to discuss her situation, and I gradually came to understand the decision from her perspective. We arranged for home hospice care, and left the door open for her to change her mind.

7   Just as I was adjusting to her decision, she opened up another area that further complicated my feelings. It was extraordinarily important to Diane to maintain her dignity during the time remaining to her. When this was no longer possible, she clearly wanted to die. She had known of people lingering in what was called "relative comfort," and she wanted no part of it. We spoke at length about her wish. Though I felt it was perfectly legitimate, I also knew that it was outside of the realm of currently accepted medical practice and that it was more than I could offer or promise. I told Diane that information that might be helpful was available from the Hemlock Society.

8   A week later she phoned me with a request for barbiturates for sleep. Since I knew that this was an essential ingredient in a Hemlock Society suicide, I asked her to come to the office to talk things over. She was more than willing to protect me by participating in a superficial conversation about her insomnia, but it was important to me to know how she

planned to use the drugs and to be sure that she was not in despair or overwhelmed in a way that might color her judgment. In our discussion, it was apparent that she was having trouble sleeping, but it was also evident that the security of having enough barbiturates available to commit suicide, if and when the time came, would give her the peace of mind she needed to live fully in the present. She was not despondent and, in fact, was making deep, personal connections with her family and close friends. I made sure that she knew how to use the barbiturates for sleep, and how to use them to commit suicide. We agreed to meet regularly, and she promised to meet with me before taking her life. I wrote the prescriptions with an uneasy feeling about the boundaries I was exploring—spiritual, legal, professional, and personal. Yet I also felt strongly that I was making it possible for her to get the most out of the time she had left.

The next several months were very intense and important for Diane. Her son did not return to college, and the two were able to say much that had not been said earlier. Her husband worked at home so that he and Diane could spend more time together. Unfortunately, bone weakness, fatigue, and fevers began to dominate Diane's life. Although the hospice workers, family members, and I tried our best to minimize her suffering and promote comfort, it was clear that the end was approaching. Diane's immediate future held what she feared the most: increasing discomfort, dependence, and hard choices between pain and sedation. She called her closest friends and asked them to visit her to say good-bye, telling them that she was leaving soon. As we had agreed, she let me know as well. When we met, it was clear that she knew what she was doing, that she was sad and frightened to be leaving but that she would be even more terrified to stay and suffer.

Two days later her husband called to say that Diane had died. She had said her final good-byes to her husband and son that morning, and had asked them to leave her alone for an hour. After an hour, which must have seemed like an eternity, they found her on the couch, very still and covered by her favorite shawl. They called me for advice about how to proceed. When I arrived at their house we talked about what a remarkable person she had been. They seemed to have no doubts about the course she had chosen, or about their cooperation, although the unfairness of her illness and the finality of her death were overwhelming to us all.

I called the medical examiner to inform him that a hospice patient had died. When asked about the cause of death, I said acute leukemia. He said that was fine and that we should call a funeral director. Although acute leukemia was the truth, it was not the whole story. But any mention of suicide would probably have brought an ambulance, efforts at resuscitation, and a police investigation. Diane would have become a "coroner's case," and the decision to perform an autopsy would have been made at the discretion of the medical examiner. The family or I could have been subjected to criminal prosecution; I could have been subjected to a professional review. Although I truly believe that the family and I gave her the best care possible, allowing her to define her limits and directions, I am not sure the law, society, or the medical profession would agree.

12   Diane taught me about the range of help I can provide people if I know them well and if I allow them to express what they really want. She taught me about taking charge and facing tragedy squarely when it strikes. She taught me about life, death, and honesty, and that I can take small risks for people I really know and care about.

✦ Questions for Discussion and Writing

1. What features of Diane's predicament and her reaction to it, and the dilemma her physician faced, reflect important issues brought up by Daniel Callahan?

2. Does Callahan's description of how the moral burden falls upon the physician apply in this case? How does Quill react to this burden? Does either Diane or Quill seem aware of or take into account Callahan's claim that no one has the right to assign putting an end to his or her life to another person? Discuss their reactions in relation to Callahan's assertions.

3. How might the editorial cartoon in Figure 2-12 serve as a basis for an argument against the current laws against suicide and assisted suicide? How does the point made in the cartoon relate to similar points raised in Quill's account?

FIGURE 2-12

Source: Don Wright/*The Palm Beach Post.* Reprinted with permission.

4. How might the passage of the "Death with Dignity Act" on November 8, 1994 in Oregon, allowing assisted suicide under limited circumstances, change national perceptions of this issue?

Jeremy Rifkin

Big, Bad Beef

————◆————

Jeremy Rifkin is head of the Foundation on Economic Trends, Washington, D. C. He has written extensively on the relationship between economic concerns and ecology in such works as Biosphere of Politics *(1991),* Voting Green *(1992), and* Beyond Beef: The Rise and Fall of the Cattle Culture *(1992). The following article is reprinted from the March 23, 1992 issue of* The New York Times.

1   In the U.S., beef is king. More than six billion hamburgers were sold last year at fast-food restaurants alone. The average American consumes the meat of seven 1,100-pound steers in a lifetime. Some 100,000 cows are slaughtered every 24 hours. In South America, the cattle population is approaching the human population. In Australia, cattle outnumber people.

2   Beef has been central to the American experience. Entrance into the beef culture was viewed by many immigrants as a rite of passage into the middle class. Commenting on the failure of European socialism to gain a foothold in America, Werner Sombart, the German economist, wrote, "On the shoals of roast beef and apple pie, all socialist utopias founder."

3   Now, the good life promised by the beef culture has metamorphosed into an environmental and social nightmare for the planet.

4   Cattle raising is a major factor in the destruction of remaining rain forests. Since 1960, more than a quarter of Central American forests have been razed to make cattle pastures. In South America, 38 percent of the Amazon forest cleared has been for ranching.

5   The impact of cattle extends well beyond rain forests. According to a 1991 report for the UN, as much as 85 percent of rangeland in the Western U.S. is being destroyed, largely by overgrazing. Nearly half the water used each year in the U.S. goes to grow feed for cattle and other livestock. A 1992 study by the California Department of Water Resources reported that more than 1,200 gallons of water are required to produce an eight-ounce boneless steak in California.

6   Cattle raising is even a significant factor in global warming. The burning of tropical forests to clear land for pasture releases millions of tons of carbon dioxide into the atmosphere each year. In addition, it is estimated that the earth's 1.28 billion cattle and other cud-chewing animals are responsible for 12 percent of the methane emitted into the atmosphere.

128

The beef addiction of the U.S. and other industrialized nations has 7
also contributed to the global food crisis. Cattle and other livestock
consume more than 70 percent of the grain produced in the U.S. and
about a third of the world's total grain harvest—while nearly a billion
people suffer from chronic under-nutrition. If the U.S. land now used
to grow livestock feed were converted to grow grain for human consumption, we could feed an additional 400 million people.

Despite the grim facts, the government continues to pursue poli- 8
cies that support cattle production and beef consumption. For example,
at the same time the Surgeon General is warning Americans to reduce
their consumption of saturated fat, the Agriculture Department's Beef
Promotion and Research Board is trying to persuade Americans to eat
more beef. This year, the board is expected to spend $45 million on
advertising.

Equally troubling is the government's grading system to measure 9
the value of beef. Established in 1927, the system grades beef on its fat
content: the higher the fat "marbling," the better the beef. By favoring
fat over lean beef, the Agriculture Department has helped promote
greater amounts of saturated fat in the American diet and, in so doing,
has contributed to rising health care costs.

Finally, the government has been virtually subsidizing Western cat- 10
tle ranchers, providing them with cheap access to millions of acres of
public land. Today, 30,000 ranchers in 11 Western states pay less than
$1.92 a month per cow for the right to graze cattle on nearly 300 million
acres of public land.

In 1986, the Reagan Administration estimated the market value for 11
pasturing cattle on the same grasslands to be between $6.40 and $9.50 a
month. This giveaway program has resulted in land erosion and the
destruction of native habitats and wildlife.

The government's antiquated cattle and beef policies must be over- 12
hauled. The Agriculture Department needs to shift its priorities from
promoting beef consumption to promoting a more balanced diet. Last
year, the agency tried to do this by recommending a new "eating right"
pyramid, which emphasized vegetables, fruit and grains. The effort
was abandoned under pressure from the meat industry. The department's grading system should also be restructured, with new classifica-
tions that elevate the status of leaner cuts of beef.

In addition, Congress must pass legislation to insure that ranchers 13
pay the market value for leased public lands. It should also reduce the
public acreage available to ranchers, to help restore the Western grasslands and preserve the native wildlife and habitat.

If we reduce our beef consumption by at least 50 percent, we can 14
help restore the global environment, free up arable land to grow food
for hungry people, protect our own health and reduce the suffering of
cattle and other animals.

✦ Questions for Discussion and Writing

1. What purpose is served by Rifkin's statement that "entrance into the beef culture was viewed by many immigrants as a rite of passage into the middle class"? By stating it in this way, does Rifkin hope to distance his audience from a value that once was appropriate but is now outdated?

2. What purpose is served by characterizing those who eat beef as part of a "beef culture"? How does he use this characterization to encourage his audience to distance themselves from those who continue to eat beef?

3. How compelling do you find the evidence that Rifkin advances to support his contention that beef eating has become "an environmental and social nightmare for the planet"? Is the evidence adequate to support such a far-reaching claim?

4. Although compact, Rifkin's policy recommendation rests upon the three other kinds of claims. Where does he define the nature of the situation, offer criteria for evaluating whether it is good or bad, present causes and consequences of the phenomena—all as a way of justifying why current attitudes and policies should be changed? How successfully does he construct his argument so that each claim builds on the strength of the preceding one?

5. Sketch out the causal chain of intermediate and long-term consequences in any one of Rifkin's lines of reasoning. Has he plausibly shown how an effect he claims (that might seem unlikely) is capable of being produced by the events that precede it? Has he made the case that the consequences of beef eating are grave enough to warrant the changes he proposes? Why or why not?

6. Which of the arguments Rifkin presents seem most compelling and least compelling?

7. If you don't agree with Rifkin, what counterarguments or compromise proposals can you offer that would offset his analysis and conclusions?

8. To what extent might you consider Rifkin's argument less compelling because it fails to summarize or take into account opposing views?

9. Would any of Rifkin's arguments be persuasive enough to cause you to become a vegetarian? Why or why not? What other arguments (economic, philosophical, religious, health-related, etc.) might you consider that would lead you to this course of action?

3

Arguing across the Disciplines

◆

Some of the most interesting and effective writing in various disciplines takes the form of arguments that seek to persuade a specific audience (colleagues, fellow researchers, or the general public) of the validity of a proposition or claim through logical reasoning supported by facts, examples, or other kinds of evidence. Writers and researchers in all academic disciplines are often compelled to convince others of the validity of their ideas and discoveries. Discussion and debate accompany the development of central ideas, concepts, and laws in all fields of study. Writers in the liberal arts, the political and social sciences, and the physical and natural sciences use strategies of argument to support new interpretations of known facts or establish plausible cases for new hypotheses.

Although arguments explore important issues and espouse specific theories, the forms in which they appear vary according to the style and format of the individual discipline. Evidence in different disciplines can appear in a variety of formats, including the interpretation of statistics, laws, and precedents, or the citation of authorities. The means used to construct arguments depends on the audience within the discipline being addressed, the nature of the thesis being proposed, and the accepted methodology for that particular discipline.

Like general arguments, the structure of arguments within the disciplines requires (1) a clear statement of a proposition or claim, (2) grounds that are relevant to the claim and sufficient to support it, and (3) a warrant based on solid backing that guarantees the appropriateness and applicability of the grounds in supporting the claim. So, too, appropriate qualifiers or possible exceptions to the claim must be stated as part of the argument.

The Nature of Inquiry across the Disciplines

Each of the three broad areas in the curriculum—liberal arts, political and social sciences, and sciences—seeks different kinds of knowledge and, therefore, has a different method of inquiry. That is to say, each area stipulates what kinds of problems or issues it considers worth addressing.

In the liberal arts, critics evaluate and interpret works of art; review music, dance, drama, and film; and write literary analyses. Philosophers probe the moral and ethical implications of people's actions and advocate specific ways of meeting the ethical challenges posed by new technologies. Historians interpret political, military, and constitutional events; analyze their causes; and theorize about how the past has influenced the present.

In the political and social sciences, lawyers and constitutional scholars argue for specific ways of applying legal and constitutional theory to everyday problems. Economists debate issues related to changes wrought by technology, distribution of income, unemployment, and commerce. Political scientists look into how effectively governments initiate and manage social change and ask basic questions about the limits of governmental intrusion into individual rights. Sociologists analyze statistics and trends to evaluate how successfully institutions accommodate social change.

In the sciences, biologists, as well as biochemists, zoologists, botanists, and other natural scientists, propose theories to explain the interdependence of living things and their natural environment. Psychologists champion hypotheses based on physiological, experimental, social, and clinical research to explain various aspects of human behavior. Physicists, as well as mathematicians, astronomers, engineers, and computer scientists, put forward and defend hypotheses about the basic laws underlying the manifestations of the physical world, from the microscopic to the cosmic.

The broad areas of the curriculum function as specific audiences. Each discipline has its own needs, aims, interests, and expectations and sets its own standards about what constitutes acceptable reasoning.

The kinds of knowledge sought and the procedures used by the political and social sciences are quite different from those of the liberal arts. These disciplines have, to a large extent, adapted the techniques and objectives of the physical and natural sciences to study how human beings interact within the context of social, political, business, legal, psychological, and cultural relationships.

The types of information sought and the methods employed within the domain of the sciences aim at providing an accurate, systematic, and comprehensive account of the world around us, as well as a framework within which new hypotheses can be put forward and evaluated.

We can appreciate the relevance of claims only in the context of the requirements of the larger fields within which the claims are advanced. That is, there are certain defining features and distinctive goals of each discipline that determine which items, data, or evidence will be seen as relevant to the claim. Training in different fields consists in learning what kinds of evidence are accepted as appropriate in supporting claims within that particular field. (The following discussions applying the Toulmin model to a range of disciplines have been adapted from Stephen Toulmin, Richard Rieke, and Allan Janik, *An Introduction to Reasoning* (1984). Future in-text citations refer to this source; page numbers are given in parentheses.)

Different fields have different concepts of what constitutes evidence to be introduced to support a claim. Grounds, evidence, and data that are appropriate in a legal argument will be of a different kind and will be judged differently from evidence in a scientific argument or in an argument in the arts. As in general arguments, warrants in the disciplines are statements, formulas, and rules that authorize the way evidence (all data: pertinent information, all that is known about a situation, the known variables, and so on) can be interpreted so as to justify the conclusion reached or the claim being made.

In fields such as natural and physical sciences, computer science, engineering, and mathematics, warrants most frequently take the form of exact formulas used to convert raw data (in the form of known variables) into a significant conclusion (50). In mathematics, for example, the circumference of a circle can be discovered by applying a relevant formula, $2\pi r$. For example, if the radius is measured at 3 feet, you apply the formula multiplying 2 times π times the radius to discover the value of the circumference. Of course, many more complex formulas govern other applied and theoretical sciences. These warrants are known, reliable, and exact, and they can be depended upon.

By contrast, the law, assuming there is no disagreement about what the facts of the situation are, applies warrants in the form of relevant statutes or precedents to discover whether one has or has not violated the law in a given situation (51).

As in general arguments, warrants are backed up in different ways. In science, the backing is the theoretical and experimental basis on which the warrant relies for its authority. In law, all the legal history of a particular statute would constitute the backing (whereas the warrant would be the statute that is appropriate to apply in that particular case).

In medicine, the backing for a diagnosis would be all the research that the physician might consult to make sure that the diagnosis was based on a generalization (the warrant) that provided the most accurate interpretation of the facts (symptoms, results of laboratory work, past medical history, etc.) of a particular case (53). Backing in all disciplines always refers to the underlying body of research in that specific field that justifies using a particular warrant (67).

Professional training is designed to familiarize students with concepts of evidence and with how the methodology of any particular field is related to its larger purposes or goals. Apprenticeship in various disciplines involves the process of discovering what warrants are appropriate to apply in different circumstances. In many fields, warrants do not take the form of exact formulas or statutes but rather are general principles, capable of being learned only through years of experience in that field. For example, in medicine, a skillful diagnostician draws on years of accumulated experience as well as information learned in medical school.

The way a veterinarian reaches a conclusion is characteristic of medical diagnoses. In *All Creatures Great and Small* (1972), James Herriot diagnoses the true causes of a cow's sudden illness:

> I have a vivid recollection of a summer evening when I had to carry out a rumenotomy on a cow. As a rule, I was inclined to play for time when I suspected a foreign body—there were so many other conditions with similar symptoms that I was never in a hurry to make a hole in the animal's side. But this time diagnosis was easy; the sudden fall in milk yield, loss of cudding; grunting, and the rigid sunken-eyed appearance of the cow. And to clinch it the farmer told me he had been repairing a hen house in the cow pasture—nailing up loose boards. I knew where one of the nails had gone.

The way Herriot reaches his conclusion is characteristic of a veterinary or medical diagnosis. Herriot is able to relate the meaning of the signs of illness the cow displays to general principles drawn from his experience and presumably from veterinary textbooks. In effect, he says, these kinds of symptoms can mean the cow has ingested a foreign body like a nail, and in this particular case there is a good chance that is what happened. Therefore, he concludes that a rumenotomy, or surgical incision into the cow's stomach to remove a foreign body, should be performed.

Broken down into the separate elements in the argument, Herriot's line of thought appears as follows:

GROUNDS: Sudden fall in milk yield, loss of cudding, grunting, rigid sunken-eyed appearance, nails used to repair loose boards in a hen house in the cow pasture.

WARRANT: A cow that swallows a foreign body like a nail can be expected to display characteristic symptoms of sudden fall in milk yield, and so forth.

record of people's everyday gestures, habits, manners, customs, styles of furniture, clothing, decoration, styles of traveling, eating, keeping house, modes of behaving toward children, superiors, inferiors, plus various looks, glances, poses, styles of walking, and other details symbolic of the entire pattern of behavior through which people express their position in the world.

CLAIM: You, as a nonfiction writer, should try to use all the techniques of novelists to obtain the effects of immediacy, concrete reality, emotional involvement, and a gripping or absorbing quality.

The audiences for whom the arts are created judge an artist's work from a different perspective (353). For the audience, the key question is how effectively the artist's work succeeds in deepening, enriching, or extending the sense of being human and conveying insight into human nature. As representative of and mediator for the audience's reactions, the critic or reviewer evaluates the work of art or artist's performance. For example, in "The Boo Taboo" (*New York Magazine* [1987]) the acerbic theater critic John Simon offers this evaluation of Richard Tucker's performance in the opera *Carmen:*

> The most illuminating occurrence for me was a recent Saturday matinee at the Met. It was Barrault's wretched staging of *Carmen,* with Richard Tucker as Don Jose. Now Tucker had once been in possession of a good, strong voice; but he had never been a genuine artist with a sense of shading, expressive range, a feeling for the emotional depth of the part or the language in which he was singing. By this time, with even his basic organ gone, Tucker is long overdue for retirement. In this Don Jose, Tucker's voice was as off as it had been for years, his phrasing as unlovely as it had always been. Visually, he was a geriatric travesty; histrionically, even by the shockingly low standards of operatic acting, a farce. Even his French was, let us say, hyper-Tourelian. After he got through mangling the Flower Song, and after the orchestra was through as well, I added to the general applause three loud *phooeys*—a *phooey* cuts through applause better than a boo or hiss.

When each of the elements in Simon's critique is identified, the outline of his argument appears this way:

GROUNDS: Tucker's basic singing voice, although once good and strong, was gone. His phrasing was unlovely; visually he was a geriatric travesty; his acting fell below even the "shockingly low standards of operatic acting." His French was not authentic. He mangled the "Flower Song" from *Carmen.*

BACKING: Viewers, listeners, and critics of operatic performances have generally agreed that:

WARRANT: Good operatic singing requires a strong voice, a sense of shading, expressive range, a feeling for the emotional depth of the part or the language in which the performer is singing, appropriate visual appearance, and competent acting ability.

CLAIM: Richard Tucker should not be performing, since he can no longer meet the standards required for professional operatic singing.

QUALIFIER OR EXCEPTION: Despite the fact that there was general applause for Tucker's performance.

The broadest perspectives are brought to bear by academic disciplines in the liberal arts that interpret the meaning of an individual work as it relates to other works of that type and to the historical context in which it was produced (354). For example, the art historian Alan Wallach views particular paintings by William L. Haney and Jan van Eyck as they relate to larger social and cultural contexts. Open-endedness of interpretive issues and problems are characteristic of the humanities and liberal arts. That is, although arguments take the form of interpretations (however well supported and effective the arguments may be), they do not foreclose the possibility of new, different, and equally convincing interpretations in the future. Reduced to its essentials, Wallach's argument in "William L. Haney and Jan van Eyck" (1984) appears like this:

GROUNDS: In Haney's *The Root of it All,* the gold ring of the American Stock Exchange is drastically foreshortened and made to resemble a casino gambling table. Haney further complicates things by placing near the front of the gold ring an anamorphic image of a black man's severed head.... Another composite technique Haney shares with van Eyck is a picture within a picture. Van Eyck's *Giovanni Arnolfini and His Bride* contains a convex mirror at the rear of the marriage chamber which reflects in extraordinary detail the couple and the otherwise invisible witnesses to the scene. In *A Present Tense of Extinct Too,* Haney's painting of a CBS sound stage, five television monitors play a similar role, commenting on the picture and augmenting its meaning with images of the Vietnam War, a nineteenth-century buffalo hunt, a mushroom cloud, and so on.

WARRANT: Artists, even those who live centuries apart, belonging to different worlds and different social conditions, often use the same techniques to express artistic judgments about the societies in which they live.

CLAIM: Both Haney and van Eyck solved problems of showing how spirituality was ruthlessly subordinated to materialism by (1) creating the illusion of unified compositions that break down upon closer inspection, (2) using architecture surrounding figures to bring together seemingly unrelated scenes, (3) using the technique of painting a picture within a picture, and (4) employing submerged symbolism to comment on the materialism of their respective societies.

Arguing in Ethics

Originally a branch of philosophy, the field of ethics as a discipline in its own right has grown increasingly important as society has become more specialized and technological. As people are more locked into specialized roles and see things only from narrow viewpoints, an ethical view is required as a counterbalance so that they can evaluate the consequences of their actions in relation to society as a whole.

Ethics as a field tries to mediate claims between traditional professional or societal demands and those larger overriding human concerns by providing a systematic procedure that makes it possible to discover which course of action, among many choices, is preferable. Because ethical dilemmas involve a choice of actions, the ability to create hypothetical or "what if" situations is invaluable, as it allows one to construct different scenarios in which the effects of different kinds of choices can be dramatized. A consideration of ethical choices should always involve understanding the consequences of choices for all those who will be affected.

Ethics is concerned with questions of what should be done because it seeks to investigate what kinds of actions are acceptable or unacceptable, right or wrong, good or bad when judged according to a specified moral or ethical criterion. Thus, typical arguments require the writer to apply a general ethical principle in the form of a warrant to discover whether an action that has already happened or is being considered is good or bad, desirable or regrettable, and is to be chosen or avoided (402–3).

We can see how this works by examining the argument made by Terence Cardinal Cooke in an address delivered to the First Annual American Health Congress (1972). Cooke argues that doctors, nurses, and other health care professionals need to think about their professional obligations in light of equally compelling ethical and moral considerations. The occasion prompting Cooke's speech was the imminent passage of a "death with dignity" bill in the state legislature that would require health care professionals to take an active role in disconnecting life-support systems of terminally ill patients (without any immediate family with whom to confer) whose life, in the opinion of three physicians, was meaningless.

This is a typical ethical argument in that Cooke is addressing a conflict between a role health care professionals would be obligated to play and equally compelling moral considerations. Cooke argues that medical professionals should not be put in a situation where they are able to "play God" and decide when a patient's life is or is not meaningful.

The ethical principle Cooke applies as a warrant is based on the assumption that life is a God-given gift and that no human being has the right to take the life of another regardless of the circumstances. Represented in outline form, Cooke's argument appears thus:

> GROUNDS: Allowing "death with dignity" would become an accepted part of health care professionals' duties because the bill under consideration by the state legislature stated that any disabled person with no immediate family, and for whom, in the opinion of three physicians, the prolongation of life would be meaningless, could be granted "death with dignity."

> WARRANT: Permitting a patient's life to be terminated on the grounds that it is meaningless is against the law of God and should be justly labeled as "murdering a human being."

> CLAIM: Health care professionals should not be party to a practice labeled "death with dignity" because it is against the law of God and constitutes murder.

Arguing in History

History explains how the present has been affected by the past and provides a clear account of the conditions in which societies have lived. Historical research brings to life important military, social, economic, and political events from the past. To create a persuasive reconstruction of past events, historians need to examine a wide range of records (private journals, letters, newspaper accounts, photographs if available, and other primary documents from the period under study), as well as secondary documents (such as interpretations of the same events by other historians). In seeking to delineate a plausible explanation for past events, historians may also draw on the information and research methods of political science (which studies how governments manage their affairs), sociology (which investigates the relationships between individuals and institutions in society), anthropology and archeology (which reconstruct past cultures and inquire into why they have different customs and patterns of development), and psychology (which studies human behavior). Historians may also use statistical and computer analyses to form a more accurate picture of past events.

The methods of inquiry used in history attempt to provide a clear picture of who, what, where, when, and how events took place. Some historians go beyond these basic issues and offer interpretations of why the events took place. Arguments in history often take the form of revising older interpretations or taking into account new information that forces a reevaluation of previously held beliefs. For example, in *The Peculiar Institution: Slavery in the Ante-Bellum South* (1956), Kenneth M. Stampp, a distinguished American historian, has investigated the relationship between the southern plantation system and slavery. In contrast to previous historians, such as Ulrich B. Phillips, who claimed in *American Negro Slavery* (1918) that slavery was part of the social structure of the plantation system, Stampp asserted that a shortage of labor and a desire to increase profits were the real reasons behind the phenomenon of slave labor.

In one section of his book—"To Make Them Stand in Fear"—Stampp uses a variety of source documents, including recorded testimony of slave owners in Mississippi, South Carolina, North Carolina, and Virginia, as well as quotations from the actual manuals written to advise plantation owners on the management of slaves, to support his analysis of the conditioning procedures used to instill fear and dependency in newly arrived blacks. In outline form Stampp's argument appears as follows:

> GROUNDS: The manual *Discourses on the Management of Slaves* provided specific instructions on all phases of the "programming process." Stampp identifies five separate steps: (1) establishing strict discipline modeled on army regulations, (2) implanting in the bondsman a consciousness of inferiority, (3) instilling a sense of awe at the master's enormous power, (4) persuading the bondsman to value the success of the master's enterprise, and (5) creating a habit of perfect dependence.

> WARRANT: The study of original source documents provides valuable new information with which to reevaluate and revise previously held interpretations of events in history. (The warrant expresses the methodology underlying the concept of historical revisionism practiced by Stampp.)

> CLAIM: Contrary to historical interpretations that view slavery as an integral component of the plantation system, original source documents reveal a calculated effort on the part of slave owners to transform newly arrived blacks into slaves who

would be psychologically conditioned to believe that what was good for the plantation owners was good for them as well.

Arguing in the Social Sciences

The social sciences are often referred to as the behavioral sciences because they focus on what can be observed objectively about human beings—their actions, or behavior. These disciplines seek to discover causal connections (sometimes expressed as statistical laws) that have both descriptive and predictive value and that can be confirmed or refuted by data from subsequent research.

The social sciences have adapted in some measure both the techniques and the objectives of the physical and natural sciences in order to study how human beings interact in the context of social, political, business, legal, psychological, and cultural relationships.

To ensure an objectivity comparable to that of the physical and natural sciences, social science researchers rely on statistical surveys, questionnaires, and other data-gathering techniques. Social scientists draw upon a whole range of theoretical models to explain human behavior and explore how individual behavior may be conditioned by expectations of the surrounding culture. The range of theories available often raises the question as to which theoretical model should be applied to explain the data in question. Social scientists strive to achieve results in quantifiable and repeatable form so that other researchers can repeat and thereby confirm the validity of the results of their experiments.

The ways in which social sciences have adapted methodology from the natural and physical sciences can be seen in the procedures social scientists use for gathering evidence through observation and controlled experiments. First and foremost, social sciences (including sociology, psychology, anthropology, archeology, education, economics, political sciences, business and management, and so forth) emphasize the importance of systematic and objective observation of events and people recorded in concrete language, without interposing any personal opinion as to motives. Events and human behavior must be recorded as objectively as possible so other social scientists can verify the observations and authenticate the findings. Of course, some social sciences such as archeology have to gather information after the event has taken place and must gather data in the form of artifacts and records.

To look at this methodology more closely, we might examine its use in sociology, a discipline that is concerned with the observation, description, and explanation of the behavior of people in groups. Sociologists investigate institutions within society, their origins, their capacity for accommodating social change, and the mechanisms within them that influence the behavior of individuals.

Questions to be answered or problems to be solved are expressed in the form of hypotheses whose validity can be measured by empirical means. For example, in a classic experiment John Darley and Bibb Latané used small groups of people to test their "diffusion of responsibility" theory to answer the question of why people don't help in a crisis. By varying the number of people who thought others also were aware of a crisis, Darley and Latané demonstrated in quantifiable form a plausible mechanism to explain the real causes of seeming apathy in bystanders.

Since it would be impractical for social scientists to test everyone in a particular population in order to gather evidence, researchers test a sample or small group of people from a specific population. Darley and Latané's research took the typical form of an experimental study in which they manipulated one variable (the number of people in the group in a room filling with smoke) and observed the effect on a second variable (the likelihood that any of the subjects would report the smoke to an external authority).

The professional journal in which the results of their study appeared is an appropriate forum within which arguments can be tested and evaluated. By studying the methodology of this experiment, other researchers could set up comparable experiments to test for themselves the validity of Darley and Latané's conclusions. The authors explain the design of the experiment, the hypothesis being tested, and the results in a brief abstract that precedes their article, "Group Inhibition of Bystander Intervention in Emergencies" (1968):

> Male undergraduates found themselves in a smoke-filling room, either alone, with 2 non-reacting others, or in groups of 3. Ss [subjects] were less likely to report the smoke when in the presence of passive others (10%) or in groups of 3 (38% of groups) than when alone (75%). These results seemed to have been mediated by the way Ss interpreted the ambiguous situation; seeing other people remaining passive led Ss to decide the smoke was not dangerous.

In outline form, Darley and Latané's argument appears as follows:

GROUNDS: Male undergraduates found themselves in a smoke-filling room, either alone, with two nonreacting others, or in groups of three. Ss (subjects) were less likely to report the smoke when in the presence of passive others (10 percent) or in groups of three (38 percent of groups) than when alone (75 percent).

BACKING: Prior research by social psychologists (Darley and Latané, Latané and D. C. Glass, S. Schacter, E. Goffman, R. Brown) makes it probable that the diffusion of responsibility model determines how people in groups react to a crisis.

WARRANT: The diffusion of responsibility hypothesis states that if an individual is alone when an emergency occurs, he or she feels solely responsible. When others are present, individuals feel that their own responsibility for taking action is lessened, making them less likely to help.

CLAIM: The behavior of the people in the situation is explained by the diffusion of responsibility model. As Darley and Latané conclude, "seeing other people remaining passive led Ss to decide the smoke was not dangerous."

QUALIFIERS OR EXCEPTIONS: (1) Unless Ss felt that the presence of others increased their collective ability to cope with fire, and therefore were less afraid *because* they were in a group, or (2) unless desire to hide fear and exhibit bravery compels people to appear less apprehensive when others are watching.

Arguing in the Law

Features of legal arguments are determined by the purpose of the law, that is, to provide protection for individuals in society and for society as a whole. Accordingly, legal decisions have to do with protecting life and liberty, property, and public order and with providing systematic guidelines in ensuring the performance of contractual relationships (281).

The law provides a procedure for reaching decisions that is binding on all parties. Beyond the immediate goal of reaching decisions, the law strives to make decisions that are consistent with previous statutes, codes, and precedents and with what society considers to be fair, equitable, and just (284). As with other arguments, the process of legal reasoning depends on the interplay between evidence or grounds and claims and warrants to produce the legal decision expressed as a claim. For example, the features of a regular legal argument can be seen in the following hypothetical case: A man whose name is Dan Webster petitions the court to have his name legally changed to 666. Dan Webster testifies that the number 666 has great personal meaning for him but that the State Motor Vehicle Bureau would not agree to accept the name 666 without a legal name change. In analytical form, the legal argument would look like this:

GROUNDS: A man whose name is Dan Webster petitions the court to have his name legally changed to 666. Dan Webster testifies that the number 666 has great personal meaning for him but that the State Motor Vehicle Bureau would not agree to accept the name 666 without a legal name change.

WARRANT: Laws governing name changes passed by the state where Dan Webster resides require names to be changed to ones composed of letters.

CLAIM: Dan Webster should not be allowed to change his name legally to 666.

QUALIFIER OR EXCEPTION: Unless Dan Webster wishes to change his name to a spelled-out version of Six Six Six.

In court, legal reasoning makes use of an adversarial procedure whereby two opposing parties present the strongest case they can assemble for their proposed claims. Each party tells its story, or version of the truth, and the court (judge or jury) decides which version is more credible (284). The court chooses between the two opposing versions rather than working out a negotiated settlement that would be acceptable to both parties. The adversary character of legal reasoning can be seen in other legal forums where arguments are heard, such as congressional hearings where individuals provide competing versions of the facts.

The examination of evidence is at the center of legal reasoning. Evidence is entered in the form of exhibits. Letters, documents, contracts, tape recordings, videotapes, and a wide range of physical evidence are then evaluated to see whose claim they best support (302).

Evidence or grounds can also take the form of testimony of witnesses, to be tested by cross-examination, or of the expert opinion of authorities, which is also subjected to cross-examination. Cross-examination is an important feature of legal reasoning, as are rules governing what evidence the jury will or will not be allowed to hear (302). For example, evidence cannot be admitted from certain kinds of protected relationships (doctor–patient, lawyer–client, priest–parishioner, husband–wife). In other cases, the court must rule whether particular circumstantial or hearsay evidence is admissible.

As with other types of arguments, a range of warrants specific to the law authorizes a connection between the claim and the evidence (304). Some warrants justify the use of expert testimony (for example, taking the form of an assumption that the testimony of a person with extensive experience and expertise in a particular field can be taken as authoritative). Other legal warrants justify the use of circumstantial, physical evidence to reach a conclusion. Still others take the form of particular cases to be used as precedents in reaching a decision on a current case (307).

In all disciplines a distinction is usually drawn between arguments that rely on laws, rules, procedures, accepted ways of thinking, and formulas and those arguments that challenge the very procedures or rules used in arriving at judgments. This latter kind of argument challenges the accepted methodology, the theoretical model upon which the discipline is based, whereas regular legal arguments simply apply the rules (308).

To see how rule-setting decisions become precedents that lawyers can use in ordinary legal arguments, we might examine the legal reasoning underlying the historic 1954 Supreme Court ruling on segregation in public schools (*Brown* v. *Board of Education of Topeka*). The decision was written by Earl Warren, then Chief Justice of the Supreme Court. In outline form, Warren's decision on behalf of the Court appears this way:

GROUNDS: Warren cites the results of psychological studies showing that segregated schools instill a sense of inferiority, retard mental development, and deprive the children of minority groups of equal educational opportunities.

WARRANT: A crucial clause in the Fourteenth Amendment, namely, "no state shall ... deny to any person within its jurisdiction the equal protection of the laws," empowers the court to evaluate how well states manage the important function of education for citizens.

CLAIM: Warren concluded that "in the field of public education the doctrine of 'separate but equal' has no place." The Court ruled that separate educational facilities are inherently unequal and found that segregation in the public schools deprives children of minorities of the educational opportunities they should rightfully enjoy under the Fourteenth Amendment.

An argument like this, which challenges the very interpretation of what the law is, is obviously of a different order than an argument that simply applies accepted rules or methodology. This Supreme Court decision served as a catalyst for the civil rights movement, bringing about a series of public demonstrations, marches, and sit-ins, that, in conjunction with changes in the law, permanently altered existing social attitudes toward the acceptability of racial discrimination.

Arguing in Business

Every phase of business production—finance, research and development, purchasing, marketing, and organizational development—entails a variety of decisions. Business in the present context refers to the part of the economy that provides goods and services for society.

Arguments in business differ from arguments advanced by scientists, historians, literary critics, ethicists, and so forth in several important respects. Because the goal of business is to make a profit, arguments tend to focus on questions of tactics or strategy in accomplishing this purpose.

In contrast to law, where arguments take place in an adversary framework, business and management decisions require all the parties involved to arrive at a consensus or practical compromise (370). Furthermore, most business decisions have to be made within a certain time. Not to decide within the time available is equivalent to not making the decision at all. Moreover, business decisions sometimes have to be made despite the fact that circumstances are not completely understood or information is incomplete. In this respect, business decisions are unlike those arguments advanced by historians and scientists where time constraints play almost no part and where the emphasis is on taking as much time as necessary to understand circumstances as fully as possible (371).

The forums within which business arguments take place include boardroom conferences, stockholder meetings, consultations between managers, and any other administrative setting where management must explain the basis of its decision to others both inside and outside the company—that is, to employees, stockholders, and government officials (370).

Claims in business take the form of policy recommendations. These proposals may concern actions that should be taken to introduce a new product or service, decisions as to whether to invest in a new plant, and proposals covering a wide range of issues (383). For example, should the company branch out, change its pricing strategies? How should it best respond to the marketing strategies of the competition? What use should be made of market research data in order to market a product more effectively? Most business arguments are utilitarian, short- or medium-term proposals and are concerned with questions of strategies and tactics rather than discussions of ultimate goals and purposes.

Grounds or support in business arguments consists of all the information on which claims can be based (383–84). This includes economic information and data gleaned from market research, as well as relevant government regulations. Information used to support claims frequently appears as a detailed breakdown of all types of expenses (administrative, market research, and costs of development). Business today also avails itself of a whole range of systematized information in the form of data bases.

The manipulation of information in business uses a problem-solving model that defines the nature of the problem, uses a variety of search techniques (brainstorming, breaking the problem into subproblems, and so forth), and generates a list of alternative solutions. The most feasible solution is presented as a proposal or claim. Solutions are evaluated in terms of what constitutes the best match of the company's resources and proven competence consistent with government regulations and expectations of society

Most business warrants relate directly to the underlying purpose of business itself; that is, whatever promises to produce a greater profit consistent with the proven methods should be selected from any field of alternatives (385–86). Likewise, whatever promises to lessen the cost of operation in producing a product or service, or promises to promote the more efficient functioning of the company, should be chosen from any field of alternatives.

We can see these basic elements operating in a typical situation where a municipality has entered into a long-term agreement to have trash collected by a private contractor. Town officials must now decide whether to sell their own equipment (trucks, shovels, plows) that the municipality no longer needs for the present and probably will not need for some years in the future.

Arguments in favor of selling the equipment emphasize the cost of maintaining and repairing it and the revenue its sale could generate. Arguments against selling the equipment refer to the experience of other municipalities that, having sold their trucks and so on, were at the mercy of the contractor when the agreement came up for renegotiation. Ultimately, the municipality officials decided not to sell in order to avoid a situation where they would be dependent on private contractors who would know they would be forced to pay because they could not provide the service themselves. In outline form, the argument appears as follows:

GROUNDS: The projected cost of maintaining the equipment, the revenue its sale would generate, and the projected costs of keeping a private contractor to collect the trash.

BACKING: Precedents are provided by other municipalities that initially entered into long-term service contracts because of low prices, sold their equipment, and subsequently were at the mercy of contractors who raised their prices dramatically when the service agreement came up for renewal.

WARRANT: In the short term the sale would produce apparent savings, but in the long term it might prove very costly. In weighing two alternatives, long-term disadvantages outweigh short-term advantages.

CLAIM: The municipality should keep its equipment (trucks, plows, etc.) rather than put it up for sale.

QUALIFIERS OR EXCEPTIONS: Unless unforeseen costs in maintenance and storage become excessive.

BUSINESS IN A CHANGING ENVIRONMENT

Recent times have seen a change in societal expectations about business that have created what might be called a new theoretical model for this discipline. Whereas traditional obligations for businesses ended with making profits, new expectations mean that business has to change accordingly if it is to fulfill its underlying mandate of responding to society's needs (380). The question whether or not business should assume social responsibilities beyond basic obligations to earn a profit is increasingly the subject of debate.

A traditionalist like Milton Friedman in "The Social Responsibility of Business Is to Increase Its Profits" (reprinted in Chapter 8) claims that economic values should be the only criteria to which businesses should be held accountable. From this viewpoint, money used to meet social responsibilities is money taken illegally from shareholders that must be recovered through higher product costs. If these firms were attempting to compete with other companies internationally, they would be at a severe disadvantage. Moreover, says Friedman, businessmen and women should not assume governmental functions and try to determine how resources should best be allocated.

The opposing position is well presented by Robert Almeder in "Morality in the Marketplace" (also in Chapter 8). Almeder asserts that as society's needs and expectations change, businesses must change accordingly. It is not inconceivable that a corporation's efforts to be socially responsible will gain more customers ultimately and make more money in the long run precisely because of the good will generated by the company's actions. More pragmatically, says Almeder, businesses that do not act in a socially responsible manner will compel the government to step in and regulate them on behalf of society. Thus, his position is that social irresponsibility on the part of businesses is not only self-destructive but will be unprofitable in the long run.

Business must also fulfill its obligation to consumers through truth in advertising, warranty service, and the production of products that do not pose a danger to the consumers. In relation to stockholders, there are standards of financial disclosure that must be met. At the same time, management's new relationship with labor has led to pension plans, concern for occupational health and safety issues, and profit-sharing plans. Many businesses now routinely fulfill obligations to minorities in terms of training and equal opportunity employment, and some businesses participate in solving community problems, establishing health care facilities, and participating in other local projects. How great the change in underlying warrants has been can be seen by comparing, in diagram form, the same set of circumstances when first the traditional warrant is applied and then one in which the newer assumption has been used:

GROUNDS: The Alaska reserves of untapped oil constitute the largest single remaining source of energy-producing fossil fuel left available to the United States.

WARRANT (TRADITIONAL): The dependence of society on fossil fuel for energy requires the exploitation of any domestic energy source that is discovered.

CLAIM: Oil companies must be granted the right to drill for oil in the Alaska oil reserve.

Observe how a change in the underlying assumption or warrant would produce a completely opposite conclusion. This warrant, if commonly accepted, would bring about a major paradigm shift in the world of business.

GROUNDS: The Alaska reserves of untapped oil constitute the largest single remaining source of energy-producing fossil fuel left available to the United States.

WARRANT (NEW): The long-term impact of the burning of fossil fuels on the environment (including the greenhouse effect) requires oil companies to act in such a way that harm is not caused to society as a whole.

CLAIM: Oil companies must not be granted the right to drill for oil in the Alaska oil reserve.

Arguing in the Sciences

The types of information sought and the methods employed within the domain of the sciences aim at providing an accurate, systematic, and comprehensive account of the world around us as well as a framework within which new hypotheses can be put forward and evaluated (315).

The forums in which argumentation takes place in the sciences include professional meetings, refereed journals, and conferences. These public forums guarantee that all ideas will be tested to determine their underlying validity.

Scientists, even those on the losing side of an argument, have a common interest in gaining a more accurate picture of the natural world, its origin, makeup, and functioning (317). Thus, the putting forth and disputing of claims is not an end in itself as it is in the law, but a means to clarify and improve a picture of the world.

The way science solves problems and generates new knowledge can be seen by examining procedures used by the biologists Arthur D.

Hasler and James A. Larsen in "The Homing Salmon" (1955). Their experiments solved the mystery of how salmon could find their way back to the exact streams where they were born, even from distances as great as 900 miles, by pinpointing the role played by the salmon's olfactory sense.

Well-documented observations based on the recovery of tagged salmon in the streams where they were originally born had established that the homing instinct was a scientific problem worth investigating. For scientists, observation plays a crucial role in identifying mysterious phenomena or anomalies (319). How salmon remember their birthplace and find their way back to the stream in which they were born, sometimes from great distances, is an enigma that has fascinated naturalists for many years.

Once observations show the existence of a problem needing explanation, scientists formulate a tentative explanation or hypothesis to account for this otherwise inexplicable event.

Scientists then design specific experiments to measure in objective and quantifiable form whether the hypothesis provides an adequate explanation of the phenomenon. A scientific hypothesis, if true, should have both descriptive and predictive value. That is, it must accurately predict that in particular circumstances (that other scientists can duplicate) certain kinds of measurable effects can be observed. These effects should confirm the truth of the hypothesis.

For this reason, the design of the experiment is the essential feature of scientific research. The experiment should make it possible to isolate, control, and measure the role played by one key variable. In Hasler and Larsen's experiment, half of a group of salmon were marked and deprived of their olfactory sense and the other half were used as a control group. When all the salmon were released downstream, it was determined that the control group correctly returned as usual to the original stream, whereas the "odor-blinded" fish migrated in random fashion "picking the wrong stream as often as the right one."

The way in which evidence or grounds, warrants, and claims play a part in scientific problem solving as a method of inquiring into the truth (as opposed to advocating a position, as in the law) can be seen in the following outline:

GROUNDS

We took water from two creeks in Wisconsin and investigated whether fish could learn to discriminate between them. Our subjects, first minnows, then salmon, were indeed able to detect a difference. If, however, we destroyed a fish's nose tissue, it was no longer able to distinguish between the two water samples. Chemical analysis indicated that the only major difference between the two waters lay in the organic material. By testing the fish with various fractions of the water, separated by distillation, we confirmed that the identifying material was some volatile organic substance. The idea that fish are guided by odors in their migrations was further supported by a field test. From each of the two different branches of the Issaquah River in the state of Washington, we took a number of sexually ripe silver salmon which had come home to spawn. We then plugged with cotton the noses of half the fish in each group and placed all the salmon in the river below the fork to make the upstream run again. Most of the fish with unplugged noses swam back to the stream they had selected the first time. But the "odor-blinded" fish migrated back in random fashion, picking the wrong stream as often as the right one.

BACKING: The experience of scientists in developing systematic procedures for testing hypotheses that claim to account for otherwise inexplicable phenomena.

WARRANT: The established procedures of scientific research state that the results of an experiment designed in such a way as to make it possible to isolate, control, and measure the role played by one key variable can be reliably depended upon to explain and predict a previously inexplicable phenomenon.

CLAIM (TAKES THE FORM OF A CLEAR-CUT WORKING HYPOTHESIS FOR INVESTIGATING THE MYSTERY OF THE HOMING SALMON):

We can suppose that every little stream has its own characteristic odor, which stays the same year after year; that young salmon become conditioned to this odor before they go to sea; that they remember the odor as they grow to maturity, and that they are able to find it and follow it to its source when they come back upstream to spawn.

QUALIFIER OR EXCEPTION: Unless the salmon's homing instincts are due to other causes such as salinity, water temperature, or the earth's magnetic field.

Sometimes the anomalies observed and theories formulated to explain them are in such conflict with existing paradigms or agreed-upon scientific laws that they demand the establishment of new theoretical models to guide further research (328–29). Charles Darwin's observations *On the Origin of Species By Means of Natural Selection* (1859) in the Galapagos Islands of adaptive mutations in finches, tortoises, and other species ultimately led him to formulate a theory of evolution that proposed that both humans and apes evolved from a common primate ancestor. By challenging existing theories and replacing them with a new theoretical model, Darwin advanced all of science.

Claims in the Humanities, Social Sciences, and Sciences

The statement of claims in arguments across the disciplines takes the same form as in general arguments. That is, claims appear as assertions of fact, causation, value, or policy. As we have seen, the humanities (including literary study, history, philosophy, and the arts) offer interpretations and evaluations, usually based on specific texts (documents and manuscripts). The social sciences make claims that seek correlations between the behavior of individuals and that of groups. Arguments in the sciences first make claims that define anomalies (unexplained phenomena) and then make causal claims that identify the means by which these anomalies occurred.

FACTUAL ARGUMENTS THAT DEFINE KEY TERMS OR CONCEPTS

All arguments generated in the context of the disciplines require the writer to clearly formulate a position, provide a context to explain why the issue is important, define ambiguous terms, and discover reasons and evidence that support the argument. An entire argument will often hinge on the definition of a key term or concept. Definition arguments identify the unique properties of the thing being defined in a way that clearly distinguishes it from all other things with which it might be confused.

Arguments can arise between disciplines over lack of consensus of what commonly used terms mean. Thus, in the liberal arts, different fields of study might bring very different perspectives and methods to bear on defining "Impressionism." A writer wishing to contend that there are certain qualities that characterize "Impressionism"—whether in the paintings of Monet and Pissarro, the sculpture of Rodin, the music of Debussy, the poetry of Carl Sandburg, or the short stories of Sherwood Anderson—would have to distinguish the different meanings of this term in the different contexts of art, music, and literature, and then show how "Impressionism" possessed certain generic qualities that transcended the individual disciplines.

Arguments of definition can arise in connection with general terms, along with questions raised by the specialized vocabulary of particular disciplines. For example, in the field of medicine, the American Psychiatric Association in 1981 decided to remove the term *homosexuality* from its diagnostic manual as a category of mental disorder on the grounds that "homosexuality does not meet the criteria for being a psychiatric disorder." This redefinition met with opposition from the American Medical Association's Council of Scientific Affairs.

Later in this chapter, Donald R. Griffin, a specialist in the field of comparative physiology, reviews evidence produced by researchers who believe that chimpanzees can be taught to communicate with humans, in "Wordy Apes." The crucial issue is one of definition. What criteria should be used to identify the existence of intelligent behavior in animals?

> A heated debate has raged about the extent to which such learned communication resembles human language. Sebeok and Umiker-Sebeok (1980) and Sebeok and Rosenthal (1981) have argued vehemently that the whole business is merely wishful and mistaken reading into the ape's behavior of much more than is really there. They stress that apes are very clever at learning to do what gets them food, praise, social companionship, or other things they want and enjoy. They believe that insufficiently critical scientists have overinterpreted the behavior of their charges and that the apes have really learned only something like: "If I do this she will give me candy," or "If I do that she will play with me," and so forth.

A precise definition of what constitutes "animal intelligence" depends on whether examples of lever pressing or signing activities of apes are interpreted as evidence of imitative or initiative behavior. On the basis of his summary of results obtained from different fields of study, Griffin favors continued research because he believes that real proof will eventually be found that apes are capable of communication with human beings.

ARGUMENTS THAT ESTABLISH CAUSES OR PREDICT CONSEQUENCES

Arguments across the disciplines over causation (such as "Is male homosexuality the result of a difference in brain structure?") arise because there may be several possible causes of a given effect or several possible effects of a given cause. An argument that attempts to demonstrate a causal connection between male homosexuality and brain structure would have to show that a particular difference in brain structure between male homosexuals and heterosexuals exists and is capable of causing the effect in question.

Events that merely follow each other in sequence should not be confused with true cause and effect. Writers should also be wary of attempting to oversimplify events that have complex causes. In seeking to answer a complicated question such as "Does violence portrayed on television cause aggression in children?" the burden is on the writer to clearly demonstrate the existence of a plausible means by which a specific cause (violence portrayed on television) could have produced a particular effect (aggression in children).

These theoretical considerations become very important in any "real-world" causal analysis. For example, a specialist in forensic medicine, brought in to help investigate a murder, will use causal analysis to determine the time and method of death. The approximate time of death can be estimated from the temperature of the body, the amount of clothing worn, the temperature of the surroundings, and the rate at which a dead body normally loses heat. Forensic techniques can also determine the cause of death. Analysis of a stab wound can disclose the size and shape of the weapon used, while analysis of a gunshot wound can reveal the distance and angle from which the bullet was fired, the caliber of the bullet, and even the type of gun used. By the same token, forensic chemists can identify from bits of paint the year, make, and model of a car that struck a hit-and-run victim.

Causes and effects can occur in connecting sequences of "chains of causation." For instance, the chain of consequences resulting from the ever-increasing cost of college was the subject of a 1985 report by the Carnegie Foundation for the Advancement of Teaching. As found by the report, (1) the cost of college, as reflected in tuitions, is rising faster than the inflation rate. The high cost of college makes it necessary for students to depend increasingly on outside support. As a consequence, (2) students borrow about ten billion dollars a year from the federal Guaranteed Student Loan program. The Foundation also discovered that (3) colleges increasingly offer students loans rather than scholarships or grants.

The immediate results are that (a) the proportion of undergraduates borrowing money for college rose from 11 to 30 percent from 1975 to 1984 and (b) average student indebtedness rose from $2,100 in 1975 to $7,900 in 1984. Next, the Foundation investigated some probable long-term effects. A student graduating with $8,000 in federal loan debt repayable at 8 percent interest would owe $1,192 a year over ten years, or $11,920. That amount would be 11 percent of a beginning engineer's discretionary annual income, 21 percent of a beginning nurse's disposable income, 26 percent of a beginning social worker's income, and 33 percent of a beginning teacher's income.

These facts produced two disturbing effects. The most obvious was that (1) students who borrow money for education often study in fields that will lead to jobs with high starting salaries so that they can pay back their loans faster, and (2) undergraduates frequently do not pursue careers in their field of prime interest; instead, economics is often the deciding factor. For instance, the Foundation discovered that (a) only one-third of those whose expected major was engineering or computer science declared these as areas of prime interest, (b) while 19 percent said they planned business careers, only 47 percent of these declared business to be their field of prime interest, and (c) while only 2 percent selected music as their career choice, 83 percent of these said music was their prime interest.

The Foundation did not look into the long-term consequences for society when so many students enter professions that do not hold much interest for them, influenced by the economics of having to repay sizeable debts originally incurred to attend college. In this chain of causation, each effect itself becomes the cause of a further effect that can be studied by educators and economists.

Causal analysis is an invaluable analytical technique used across the disciplines. Because of the complexity of causal relationships, researchers try to identify, as precisely as possible, the contributory factors in any causal sequence. The direct or immediate causes of the event are those most likely to have triggered the actual event. Yet, behind direct causes may lie indirect or remote causes that set the stage or create the framework in which the event could occur. By the same token, long-term future effects are much more difficult to identify than are immediate, short-term effects.

Determining with any degree of certainty that x caused y is more complicated in situations where one cause may have produced multiple effects or the same effect could have been produced by multiple causes.

To understand how useful this kind of claim is in various disciplines, consider the following: Historians use causal analysis to put events into perspective. Barbara W. Tuchman's investigation of the fall of Troy, the mismanagement of the American Revolution by the British, and the debacle in Vietnam in *The March of Folly* (1984), led her to believe that "folly" has always been a major cause of disastrous governmental policies. The leaders in bureaucracies are particularly prone to fall back on automatic ways of doing things precisely at those times when creative decision making is required to avoid disastrous consequences. Ironically, says Tuchman, this is often true just at those moments in history when leaders are under the greatest pressure to make wise policy decisions. Throughout history, time and time again, overburdened leaders fall back on traditional solutions that might have worked for past crises but are inappropriate in their circumstances. This phenomenon, which Tuchman calls "folly," is the most common cause of political disasters.

Causal analysis is an indispensable analytical method employed in the physical and biological sciences. In "How Flowers Changed the World," in *The Immense Journey* (1957), a fascinating application of this technique can be seen in Loren Eiseley's analysis of the chain of cause and effect that began with the appearance of flowering plants, or angiosperms, and led to the eventual existence of warm-blooded mammals. Flowers and vegetation played an indispensable role in preparing the way for mammalian life by adding great quantities of oxygen (through photosynthesis) to the atmosphere. The importance of this can be appreciated when, says Eiseley, we realize that:

A high metabolic rate and the maintenance of a constant body temperature are supreme achievements in the evolution of life. They enable an animal to escape, within broad limits, from the overheating or the chilling of its immediate surroundings, and at the same time to maintain a peak mental efficiency. Creatures without a high metabolic rate are slaves to weather. Insects in the first frosts of autumn all run down like little clocks. Yet if you pick one up and breathe warmly upon it, it will begin to move about once more.

Eiseley points out how the appearance of flowers and vegetation produced more oxygen, which in turn made it possible for mammals with higher metabolic rates to exist. If flowers had not appeared, animals would have remained reptilian, slow-moving, and completely dependent on the temperatures of their world. By contrast, higher metabolic rates unchained animals from the climate. And, all this, says Eiseley, is due to the flower.

ARGUMENTS THAT MAKE VALUE JUDGMENTS

As distinct from arguments that debate matters of fact or those that seek to establish plausible connections between causes and effects, *value arguments* in the disciplines apply ethical, moral, aesthetic, or utilitarian criteria to produce judgments that measure a subject against an ideal standard. This type of argument directly challenges underlying assumptions that ordinarily remain unquestioned by making explicit what is usually hidden. A writer who contended that "bilingual education" was or was not worthwhile, or that "euthanasia" was or was not immoral, would be obligated to clearly present the ideal standard against which the subject was being evaluated.

Many arguments in the humanities, which offer interpretive analyses, are of this type. For example, Ursula K. Le Guin, the author of many works of science fiction, claims that, contrary to popular belief, most science fiction is not progressive but regressive and authoritarian in its depiction of women. Le Guin reminds her audience that the women's movement fought for the application of equal standards for men and women, and then presents evidence that science fiction does not meet these standards. Le Guin brings forward examples of the stereotyped depiction of women as "squeaking dolls," "old-maid scientists," and "loyal little wives or mistresses of accomplished heroes" in "American SF and The Other" (1975):

> The women's movement has made most of us conscious of the fact that SF has either totally ignored women, or presented them as squeaking dolls subject to instant rape by monsters—or old-maid scientists desexed by hypertrophy of the intellectual organs or, at best, loyal little wives or mistresses of accomplished heroes. Male elitism has run ram-

pant in SF. But is it only male elitism? Isn't the "subjection of women" in SF merely a symptom of a whole which is authoritarian, power-worshiping, and intensely parochial?

Le Guin urges her audience to share her indignation, not merely to agree with her views. This illustrates how an emotional appeal can be used to strengthen the effect of a logical argument. Value arguments are never made in a vacuum. It is important for the writer to assess what beliefs or attitudes (receptive, hostile, or neutral) the audience holds in relationship to his or her argument. The use of emotional appeals to support a value argument is perfectly legitimate as long as the emotional appeal does not replace the logic of the argument.

For social scientist David Hoekema, in his essay "Capital Punishment: The Question of Justification," (1979), the crucial issue is whether the justice system is arbitrary and capricious in the way it selects those who will be executed for capital crimes. Arguments that evaluate whether something is good or bad must provide (1) sufficient and verifiable evidence of a phenomenon and (2) an appropriate standard by which to measure value. Hoekema cites statistics to show that among all those convicted of capital crimes, the poor and minorities are executed disproportionately in comparison with those who have money for good legal counsel. Hoekema then measures these statistics against the ideal standard of "equal punishment under the law" for the same crime:

> Because of all these opportunities for arbitrary decision, only a small number of those convicted of capital crimes are actually executed. It is hardly surprising that their selection has little to do with the character of their crimes but a great deal to do with the skill of their legal counsel. And the latter depends in large measure on how much money is available for the defense. Inevitably, the death penalty has been imposed most frequently on the poor, and in this country it has been imposed in disproportionate numbers on blacks.

Hoekema asserts that capital punishment should not be permitted because the justice system is, in practice, incapable of administering the punishment fairly. Hoekema bases this conclusion on statistics that show that the amount of money for legal defense is more important than the character of the crime in determining punishment. Note how Hoekema's argument gains force through the cumulative summary of the evidence ("Because of all these opportunities...") he cites to support his thesis.

Appeals by the author to the emotions of an audience (through connotative language and characterization) are encountered frequently in value arguments because this kind of argument requires the selection of a standard to use when deciding whether something is good or bad. Clinical psychologist Thomas S. Szasz, in "A Critique of Skinner's Behaviorism" (1976), assails B. F. Skinner's theories of behaviorism on the grounds that the most essential value by which to measure a psychologist's contribution is the "humanistic" standard—of providing the sense of significance that people need to live their lives more meaningfully. Szasz argues that B. F. Skinner's theories of behaviorism deprive people of the incentives needed to live a meaningful life:

> Hence, I believe that those who rob people of the meaning and significance they have given their lives kill them and should be considered murderers, at least metaphorically. B. F. Skinner is such a person and, like all of the others, he fascinates—especially his intended victims.

Szasz's principle objection is that Skinner's theories of behaviorism arbitrarily characterize all emotions as simply forms of learned behavior, which have no intrinsic meaning, sense, or significance. Szasz feels so strongly on this issue that some readers may react to what they perceive as an excessive use of emotionally charged language, guilt by association, and other techniques of audience manipulation by rejecting any valid points contained in Szasz's argument.

ARGUMENTS ABOUT POLICY

In addition to arguments that characterize situations, make value judgments, or seek to establish causes or consequences, there are arguments that recommend policy changes. Many arguments in law and politics are of this kind, but the range of *policy arguments* extends through the entire spectrum of the liberal arts, political and social sciences, and sciences and technology.

Policy arguments are more complex than other kinds of arguments, since the argument must include a causal analysis pointing out the negative consequences of the *status quo*. The policy claim recommends an action that will remedy the situation without producing new negative consequences.

Earl Warren, former Chief Justice, used this pattern to demonstrate the negative effects of segregated public schools before proposing a course of action—the famous 1954 *Brown* v. *Board of Education of Topeka* decision—intended to remedy the defects of what was then current policy. Warren cites results of studies showing that segregated schools not only instill a sense of inferiority but deprive minority students of educational opportunities they should rightfully enjoy under the Fourteenth Amendment (which guarantees "equal opportunity" under the law):

> Today, education is perhaps the most important function of state and local governments. Compulsory school attendance laws and the great

expenditures for education both demonstrate our recognition of the importance of education to our democratic society.... In these days, it is doubtful that any child may reasonably be expected to succeed in life if he is denied the opportunity of an education. Such an opportunity, where the state has undertaken to provide it, is a right which must be made available to all on equal terms.

After demonstrating the existence of the problem—that is, the detrimental effects on those educated in segregated schools—Warren applies standards based on the Fourteenth Amendment and recommends abolishing segregation in public schools. Warren thus defines the issue as one of "equal protection" under the law and proposes a course of action that will remedy the defects of current policy.

Despite the fact that the liberal arts, political and social sciences, and sciences rely on their own distinctive theoretical models to generate new knowledge, researchers across the disciplines often rely on many of the same strategies to solve problems they encounter within the context of their particular fields of study.

The process by which problems are solved across the disciplines usually involves recognizing and defining the problem, using various search techniques to discover a solution, verifying the solution, and communicating it to a particular audience, who might need to know the history of the problem, the success or failure of previous attempts to solve it, and other relevant information.

Recognizing the Existence and Nature of the Problem

The first step in solving a problem is recognizing that a problem exists. Often the magnitude of the problem is obvious from serious effects that the problem is causing. To Thor Heyerdahl, who originated the famous *Kon-Tiki* and *Ra* expeditions, the dramatic effects of midocean pollution were warning signals, as he describes in "How to Kill an Ocean" (1975):

> We treat the ocean as if we believed that it is not part of our own planet—as if the blue waters curved into space somewhere beyond the horizon where our pollutants would fall off the edge, as ships were believed to do before the days of Christopher Columbus.... What we consider too dangerous to be stored under technical control ashore we dump forever out of sight at sea, whether toxic chemicals or nuclear waste. Our only excuse is the still-surviving image of the ocean as a bottomless pit.

Rachel Carson, too, in her study of pesticides (*Silent Spring* [1962]), looked beyond the immediate short-term solutions to spotlight disastrous long-term effects most people never considered:

> The chemicals to which life is asked to make its adjustment are . . . the synthetic creations of man's inventive mind, brewed in his laboratories, and having no counterparts in nature.
>
> To adjust to these chemicals would require time on the scale that is nature's; it would require not merely the years of a man's life but the life of generations. And even this, were it by some miracle possible, would be futile, for the new chemicals come from our laboratories in an endless stream; almost five hundred annually find their way into actual use in the United States alone. The figure is staggering and its implications are not easily grasped—500 new chemicals to which the bodies of men and animals are required somehow to adapt each year, chemicals totally outside the limits of biologic experience.

Although DDT worked quickly and was inexpensive to use, Carson reveals in "The Obligation to Endure" that unforeseen side effects included illness in those who used the pesticide, destruction of species of helpful insects, and contamination of the entire food chain.

Defining the Problem

In all disciplines, definition of the problem must include a description of the initial state, the goal to be reached, the actions that can be performed, and the restrictions that limit what can and cannot be done. Recognizing constraints is crucial. Some limits can be clearly defined, whereas others are merely implied by the givens of the situation and must be inferred if the problem is to be successfully attempted. Thus, Leon R. Kass, a bioethicist, looks beyond the immediate benefits that advances in biotechnology have brought in "The New Biology" (1971). He discovers a problem that will inevitably confront all those who must decide who should receive the benefits of this new technology:

> The introduction of any biomedical technology presents a new instance of an old problem—how to distribute scarce resources justly. We should assume that demand will usually exceed supply. Which people should receive a kidney transplant or an artificial heart? Who should get the benefits of genetic therapy or of brain stimulation? Is "first-come, first-served" the fairest principle? Or are certain people "more worthy," and if so, on what grounds?

Inevitably, the costly nature of these procedures will make choices necessary. How much is a human life worth and who should be given the power to decide whether, for example, a playwright or a NASA technician will receive a needed kidney transplant? Such constraints or limits on how problems can be solved make it necessary to identify which are the most important criteria—economic or moral, for instance—by which to make decisions.

Representing the Problem in Relevant Form

Often problems are so complex that it is useful to represent them in simplified form. Translating the problem into a sketch or other visual representation is valuable because it lets the problem solver perceive the overall shape of the problem without being overwhelmed by its details. Expert problem solvers find it useful to construct a mental picture of the problem or to put it on paper, whether in the form of a mathematical equation, displayed as a diagram, or represented conceptually in language. For example, in "Learning to Think Like a Lawyer" (*The High Citadel: The Influence of Harvard Law School* [1978]), the case study reported by Joel Seligman is one that first-year law students at Harvard used to learn the principles of contract law:

> Like many cases in first-year law casebooks, the facts in *Hamer* v. *Sidway* seem slightly ridiculous. At a family gathering in 1869, an uncle promised his nephew that if he refrained from drinking, using tobacco, swearing, and playing cards or billiards for money until he turned twenty-one the uncle would pay him $5,000. The nephew agreed and six years later wrote to his uncle that he had lived up to his promise. "Dear Nephew," the uncle replied, "I have no doubt but you have, for which you shall have $5,000, as I promised you." But before the nephew collected the money, the uncle died. The almost comic-opera question of the lawsuit was: Can the virtuous nephew collect the $5,000 from the recalcitrant executor of his uncle's estate? The case is included in virtually every modern American contracts casebook because it illustrates some of the most fundamental principles of contracts law.

Experts differ from inexperienced problem solvers in their ability to draw on a greater range of knowledge and recognize a variety of distinct problem "types" important in their particular disciplines. The better the problem solver, the greater the repertoire of "types," "models," "scripts," or "concepts" (as they have been variously termed) from which he or she can draw. Furthermore, experts use their greater understanding of problem "types" to run through mental simulations of different potential solutions.

An ingenious hypothetical scenario was designed by Alan Turing, as Douglas R. Hofstadter tells us in his essay, "The Turing Test" (in *Godel, Escher, Bach* [1979]). The central problem in the development of artificial intelligence still remains that of devising a way to know whether a machine can think. Turing's classic formulation of the problem placed a machine in a closed room to test whether people would be fooled into thinking it was a human being on the basis of its responses, communicated by teletype into a nearby room. Turing's ingenious experiment makes it possible to evaluate different paths by which the solution can be reached. These paths reflect search techniques that problem solvers use to find their way through the maze of the problem.

Frequently, the results will depend on using an entire range of search techniques, because the more alternatives generated the better the chances of finding a solution to the problem. Also, any search may uncover facts that require the problem to be redefined; this is typical of the process of scientific analysis whereby observation of facts leads to a hypothesis, which additional facts either support or refute.

The range of problem-solving techniques that writers in diverse areas use to identify problems, apply theoretical models, define constraints, use various search techniques, and check solutions against relevant criteria are an important part of all academic and professional research.

✦ Questions for Discussion and Writing

1. How might different disciplines approach any of the following issues in ways that would make them suitable subjects of study for that particular discipline? For example, if the issue were "Can needle exchange programs help slow the spread of AIDS?", an ethicist might examine the morality of giving needles to drug addicts, an epidemiologist might look at the mechanism of disease transmission, a sociologist might look at the effects on various groups in society, and an economist might assess the costs and benefits involved if such a program were federally funded. The class might wish to divide into three groups whose interests correspond with the liberal arts, social and political sciences, and science and technology. Each group may develop a statement related to its line of inquiry and present its position to the whole class for discussion. Select three to five of the following:

   a. How do Saturday morning cartoons differ thematically in terms of characterization and ideological content (which some observers have termed "pro-social") from traditional fairy tales or folk tales?

   b. What are the teachings of major world religions (Buddhism, Judaism, Christianity, Hinduism, Islam) regarding the relationships between human beings and animals?

   c. In what way has a widely used term changed its meanings or shifted its connotations in recent times (for example, "Palestinian homeland," "nationalism," "safe sex")?

   d. Does sex education and/or the distribution of condoms in public high schools decrease teen pregnancies?

   e. Are privately operated prisons a good idea?

   f. Do television commercials reflect a shift in gender, age, and minority roles in American society?

g. What are the consequences of the presence of "gangs" in any major city in the United States?

h. Is it possible to create a machine smart enough to persuade people it is human (known as the Turing Test)?

i. Do advances in medical technology such as in-vitro fertilization and/or surrogate parenting require a new definition of "mother"?

j. Which arguments on the issue of wilderness use do you find are more compelling: those of preservationists or those of conservationists (favoring multiple use)?

k. Should both evolution theory and creationism be taught in public schools?

THREE SHORT ARGUMENTS
FOR ANALYSIS

James Baldwin

If Black English Isn't a Language, Then Tell Me, What Is?

---◆---

James Baldwin's "If Black English Isn't a Language, Then Tell Me, What Is?" originally appeared on the Op-ed page of The New York Times *(July 29, 1979). The distinguished American essayist, novelist, and playwright is author of many books, including* The Fire Next Time *(1963),* Notes of a Native Son *(1956), and* Just Above My Head *(1979). In this article Baldwin formulates an impassioned defense of the role played by black English as a "political instrument," "a proof of power, " and "the most vivid crucial key to identity." He relates the development of black English to the history and experience of blacks in the United States and uses a stipulated definition of "language" to develop his claim that black English is a language, not merely a dialect. Baldwin doesn't suggest that black English be spoken instead of standard English but that it be accepted as a different but equal language.*

ST. PAUL DE VENCE, France—The argument concerning the use, or the status, or the reality of black English is rooted in American history and has absolutely nothing to do with the question the argument supposes itself to be posing. The argument has nothing to do with language itself but with the *role* of language. Language, incontestably, reveals the speaker. Language, also, far more dubiously, is meant to define the other—and, in this case, the other is refusing to be defined by a language that has never been able to recognize him. 1

People evolve a language in order to describe and thus control their circumstances, or in order not to be submerged by a reality that they cannot articulate. (And, if they cannot articulate it, they *are* submerged.) A Frenchman living in Paris speaks a subtly and crucially different language from that of the man living in Marseilles; neither 2 sounds very much like a man living in Quebec, and they would all have great difficulty in apprehending what the man from Guadeloupe, or Martinique, is saying, to say nothing of the man from Senegal—although the "common" language of all these areas is French. But each has paid, and is paying, a different price for this "common" language, in which, as it turns out, they are not saying, and cannot be saying, the same things: They each have very different realities to articulate, or control.

3   What joins all languages, and all men, is the necessity to confront life, in order, not inconceivably, to outwit death: The price for this is the acceptance, and achievement, of one's temporal identity. So that, for example, though it is not taught in the schools (and this has the potential of becoming a political issue) the south of France still clings to its ancient and musical Provençal, which resists being described as a "dialect." And much of the tension in the Basque countries, and in Wales, is due to the Basque and Welsh determination not to allow their languages to be destroyed. This determination also feeds the flames in Ireland for among the many indignities the Irish have been forced to undergo at English hands is the English contempt for their language.

4   It goes without saying, then, that language is also a political instrument, means, and proof of power. It is the most vivid and crucial key to identity: it reveals the private identity, and connects one with, or divorces one from the larger, public, or communal identity. There have been, and are, times, and places, when to speak a certain language could be dangerous, even fatal. Or, one may speak the same language, but in such a way that one's antecedents are revealed, or (one hopes) hidden. This is true in France, and is absolutely true in England: The range (and reign) of accents on that damp little island make England coherent for the English and totally incomprehensible for everyone else. To open your mouth in England is (if I may use black English) to "put your business in the street": You have confessed your parents, your youth, your school, your salary, your self-esteem, and, alas, your future.

5   Now, I do not know what white Americans would sound like if there had never been any black people in the United States, but they would not sound the way they sound. *Jazz*, for example, is a very specific sexual term, as in *jazz me, baby*, but white people purified it into the Jazz Age. *Sock it to me*, which means, roughly, the same thing, has been adopted by Nathaniel Hawthorne's descendants with no qualms or hesitations at all, along with *let it all hang out* and *right on! Beat to his socks*, which was once the black's most total and despairing image of poverty, was transformed into a thing called the Beat Generation, which phenomenon was, largely, composed of *uptight*, middle-class white people, imitating poverty, trying to *get down*, to get *with it*, doing their *thing*, doing their despairing best to be *funky*, which we, the

blacks, never dreamed of doing—we *were* funky, baby, like *funk* was going out of style.

Now, no one can eat his cake, and have it, too, and it is late in the   6
day to attempt to penalize black people for having created a language that permits the nation its only glimpse of reality, a language without which the nation would be even more *whipped* than it is.

I say that this present skirmish is rooted in American history, and it   7
is. Black English is the creation of the black diaspora. Blacks came to the United States chained to each other, but from different tribes: Neither could speak the other's language. If two black people, at that bitter hour of the world's history, had been able to speak to each other, the institution of chattel slavery could never have lasted as long as it did. Subsequently, the slave was given, under the eye, and the gun, of his master, Congo Square, and the Bible—or, in other words, and under these conditions, the slave began the formation of the black church, and it is within this unprecedented tabernacle that black English began to be formed. This was not, merely, as in the European example, the adoption of a foreign tongue, but an alchemy that transformed ancient elements into a new language: *A language comes into existence by means of brutal necessity, and the rules of the language are dictated by what the language must convey.*

There was a moment, in time, and in this place, when my brother,   8
or my mother, or my father, or my sister, had to convey to me, for example, the danger in which I was standing from the white man standing just behind me, and to convey this with a speed, and in a language, that the white man could not possibly understand, and that, indeed, he cannot understand, until today. He cannot afford to understand it. This understanding would reveal to him too much about himself, and smash that mirror before which he has been frozen for so long.

Now, if this passion, this skill, this (to quote Toni Morrison) "sheer   9
intelligence," this incredible music, the mighty achievement of having brought a people utterly unknown to, or despised by "history"—to have brought this people to their present, troubled, troubling, and unassailable and unanswerable place—if this absolutely unprecedented journey does not indicate that black English is a language, I am curious to know what definition of language is to be trusted.

A people at the center of the Western world, and in the midst of so   10
hostile a population, has not endured and transcended by means of what is patronizingly called a "dialect." We, the blacks, are in trouble, certainly, but we are not doomed, and we are not inarticulate because we are not compelled to defend a morality that we know to be a lie.

The brutal truth is that the bulk of the white people in America   11
never had any interest in educating black people, except as this could serve white purposes. It is not the black child's language that is in question, it is not his language that is despised: It is his experience. A child

cannot be taught by anyone who despises him, and a child cannot afford to be fooled. A child cannot be taught by anyone whose demand, essentially, is that the child repudiate his experience, and all that gives him sustenance, and enter a limbo in which he will no longer be black, and in which he knows that he can never become white. Black people have lost too many black children that way.

12   And, after all, finally, in a country with standards so untrustworthy, a country that makes heroes of so many criminal mediocrities, a country unable to face why so many of the nonwhite are in prison, or on the needle, or standing, futureless, in the streets—it may very well be that both the child and his elder have concluded that they have nothing whatever to learn from the people of a country that has managed to learn so little.

✦ Questions for Discussion and Writing

1. How does Baldwin develop his argument by stipulating a definition of language that states that only a language rather than a dialect made it possible for blacks to survive? Specifically, how was black English created as a form of communication between blacks who were brought from different tribes in Africa and did not speak the same language?

2. In essence, what is Baldwin's thesis about the role of language? In what way is language a "political instrument," a "proof of power," and "the most vivid and crucial key to identity"?

3. How does Baldwin use examples of the experiences of those who still speak varieties of French, Basque, Welsh, and Irish (Gaelic) to stress the importance of political and cultural contexts on questions of linguistic acceptability? How does dialect serve to confirm or reject the identity of certain groups?

4. What role did black English play in Baldwin's own life in enabling him to survive?

5. What role did the evolution of black English play in establishing and consolidating a common identity for "blacks [who] came to the United States chained to each other, but from different tribes"?

6. How might the same issue Baldwin discusses in his essay be treated by different disciplines? For example, what approach would a linguistic scholar take? How might a historian's account of how black English evolved differ in method from that used by Baldwin?

7. For a research project, investigate the connection between Baldwin's novels and his assertion that language is a "political instrument" and a

"proof of power." To what extent do his novels deal with the issues of identity and collective history?

8. For a research project, read any of the novels of Toni Morrison, including *Song of Solomon* (1977) and *Beloved* (1988), and discuss the role of black English in these novels. Would these works have been as effective had Morrison substituted standard English for black English?

William A. Henry III

In Defense of Élitism

◆

William A. Henry III was the drama critic for Time *magazine and frequently wrote on social issues. Henry's belief that an antielitist trend in American society has debased higher education is developed in his last book* In Defense of Elitism, *1994. The following excerpt from this book first appeared in the August 29, 1994 issue of* Time.

1   While all the major social changes in postwar America reflect egalitarianism of some sort, no social evolution has been more willfully egalitarian than opening the academy. Half a century ago, a high school diploma was a significant credential, and college was a privilege for the few. Now high school graduation is virtually automatic for adolescents outside the ghettos and barrios, and college has become a normal way station in the average person's growing up. No longer a mark of distinction or proof of achievement, a college education is these days a mere rite of passage, a capstone to adolescent party time.

2   Some 63% of all American high school graduates now go on to some form of further education, according to the Department of Commerce's *Statistical Abstract of the United States,* and the bulk of those continuing students attain at least an associate's degree. Nearly 30% of high school graduates ultimately receive a four-year baccalaureate degree. A quarter or so of the population may seem, to egalitarian eyes, a small and hence élitist slice. But by world standards this is inclusiveness at its most extreme—and its most peculiarly American.

3   For all the socialism of British or French public policy and for all the paternalism of the Japanese, those nations restrict university training to a much smaller percentage of their young, typically 10% to 15%. Moreover, they and other First World nations tend to carry the élitism over into judgments about precisely which institution one attends. They rank their universities, colleges and technical schools along a prestige hierarchy much more rigidly gradated—and judged by standards much more widely accepted—than Americans ever impose on their jumble of public and private institutions.

4   In the sharpest divergence from American values, these other countries tend to separate the college-bound from the quotidian masses in early adolescence, with scant hope for a second chance. For them, higher education is logically confined to those who displayed the most aptitude for lower education.

The opening of the academy's doors has imposed great economic   5
costs on the American people while delivering dubious benefits to
many of the individuals supposedly being helped. The total bill for
higher education is about $150 billion per year, with almost two-thirds
of that spent by public institutions run with taxpayer funds. Private
colleges and universities also spend the public's money. They get
grants for research and the like, and they serve as a conduit for subsi-
dized student loans—many of which are never fully repaid. President
Clinton refers to this sort of spending as an investment in human capital. If that is so, it seems reasonable to ask whether the investment pays
a worthwhile rate of return. At its present size, the American style of
mass higher education probably ought to be judged a mistake—and
one based on a giant lie.

Why do people go to college? Mostly to make money. This reality is   6
acknowledged in the mass media, which are forever running stories
and charts showing how much a college degree contributes to lifetime
income (with the more sophisticated publications very occasionally
noting the counterweight costs of tuition paid and income forgone during the years of full-time study).

But the equation between college and wealth is not so simple. Col-   7
lege graduates unquestionably do better on average economically than
those who don't go at all. At the extremes, those with five or more
years of college earn about triple the income of those with eight or fewer years of total schooling. Taking more typical examples, one finds
that those who stop their educations after earning a four-year degree
earn about 1½ times as much as those who stop at the end of high
school. These outcomes, however, reflect other things besides the impact of the degree itself. College graduates are winners in part because
colleges attract people who are already winners—people with enough
brains and drive that they would do well in almost any generation and
under almost any circumstances, with or without formal credentialing.

The harder and more meaningful question is whether the medioc-   8
rities who have also flooded into colleges in the past couple of generations do better than they otherwise would have. And if they do, is it
because college actually made them better employees or because it simply gave them the requisite credential to get interviewed and hired?
The U.S. Labor Department's Bureau of Labor Statistics reports that
about 20% of all college graduates toil in fields not requiring a degree,
and this total is projected to exceed 30% by the year 2005. For the individual, college may well be a credential without being a qualification,
required without being requisite.

For American society, the big lie underlying higher education is   9
akin to Garrison Keillor's description of the children in Lake Wobegon:
they are all above average. In the unexamined American Dream rheto-

ric promoting mass higher education in the nation of my youth, the implicit vision was that one day everyone, or at least practically everyone, would be a manager or a professional. We would use the most élitist of all means, scholarship, toward the most egalitarian of ends. We would all become chiefs; hardly anyone would be left a mere Indian. On the surface, this New Jerusalem appears to have arrived. Where half a century ago the bulk of jobs were blue collar, now a majority are white or pink collar. They are performed in an office instead of on a factory floor. If they still tend to involve repetition and drudgery, at least they do not require heavy lifting.

10   But the wages for them are going down virtually as often as up. And as a great many disappointed office workers have discovered, being better educated and better dressed at the workplace does not transform one's place in the pecking order. There are still plenty more Indians than chiefs. Lately, indeed, the chiefs are becoming even fewer. The major focus of the "downsizing" of recent years has been eliminating layers of middle management—much of it drawn from the ranks of those lured to college a generation or two ago by the idea that a degree would transform them from the mediocre to magisterial.

11   Yet U.S. colleges blithely go on "educating" many more prospective managers and professionals than the country is likely to need. In my own field, there are typically more students majoring in journalism at any given moment than there are journalists employed at all the daily newspapers in the U.S. A few years ago, there were more students enrolled in law school than there were partners in all law firms. As trends shift, there have been periodic oversupplies of M.B.A.-wielding financial analysts, of grade school and high school teachers, of computer programmers, even of engineers. Inevitably many students of limited talent spend huge amounts of time and money pursuing some brass-ring occupation, only to see their dreams denied. As a society America considers it cruel not to give them every chance at success. It may be more cruel to let them go on fooling themselves.

12   Just when it should be clear that the U.S. is already probably doing too much to entice people into college, Bill Clinton is suggesting it do even more. In February 1994, for example, the President asserted that America needs a greater fusion between academic and vocational training in high school—not because too many mediocre people misplaced on the college track are failing to acquire marketable vocational skills, but because too many people on the vocational track are being denied courses that will secure them admission to college. Surely what Americans need is not a fusion of the two tracks but a sharper division between them, coupled with a forceful program for diverting intellectual also-rans out of the academic track and into the vocational one. That is where most of them are heading in life anyway. Why should

they wait until they are older and must enroll in high-priced proprietary vocational programs of often dubious efficacy—frequently throwing away not only their own funds but federal loans in the process—because they emerged from high school heading nowhere and knowing nothing that is useful in the marketplace?

If the massive numbers of college students reflected a national 13 boom in love of learning and a prevalent yen for self-improvement, America's investment in the classroom might make sense. There are introspective qualities that can enrich any society in ways beyond the material. But one need look no further than the curricular wars to understand that most students are not looking to broaden their spiritual or intellectual horizons. Consider three basic trends, all of them implicit rejections of intellectual adventure. First, students are demanding courses that reflect and affirm their own identities in the most literal way. Rather than read a Greek dramatist of 2,000 years ago and thrill to the discovery that some ideas and emotions are universal, many insist on reading writers of their own gender or ethnicity or sexual preference, ideally writers of the present or the recent past.

The second trend, implicit in the first, is that the curriculum has 14 shifted from being what professors desire to teach to being what students desire to learn. Nowadays colleges have to hustle for students by truckling trendily. If the students want media-studies programs so they can all fantasize about becoming TV news anchors, then media studies will abound. There are in any given year some 300,000 students enrolled in undergraduate communications courses.

Of even greater significance than the solipsism of students and the 15 pusillanimity of teachers is the third trend, the sheer decline in the amount and quality of work expected in class. In an egalitarian environment the influx of mediocrities relentlessly lowers the general standards at colleges to levels the weak ones can meet. When my mother went to Trinity College in Washington in the early 1940s, at a time when it was regarded more as a finishing school for nice Catholic girls than a temple of discipline, an English major there was expected to be versed in Latin, Anglo-Saxon and medieval French. A course in Shakespeare meant reading the plays, all 37 of them. In today's indulgent climate, a professor friend at a fancy college told me as I was writing this chapter, taking a half semester of Shakespeare compels students to read exactly four plays. "Anything more than one a week," he explained, "is considered too heavy a load."

This probably should not be thought surprising in an era when 16 most colleges, even prestigious ones, run some sort of remedial program for freshmen to learn the reading and writing skills they ought to have developed in junior high school—not to mention an era when many students vociferously object to being marked down for spelling or grammar. Indeed, all the media attention paid to curriculum battles at Stanford, Dartmouth and the like obscures the even bleaker reality of American higher education. As Russell Jacoby points out in his book *Dogmatic Wisdom,* most students are enrolled at vastly less demanding institutions, where any substantial reading list would be an improvement.

17   My modest proposal is this: Let us reduce, over perhaps a five-year span, the number of high school graduates who go on to college from nearly 60% to a still generous 33%. This will mean closing a lot of institutions. Most of them, in my view, should be community colleges, current or former state teachers' colleges and the like. These schools serve the academically marginal and would be better replaced by vocational training in high school and on-the-job training at work. Two standards should apply in judging which schools to shut down. First, what is the general academic level attained by the student body? That might be assessed in a rough-and-ready way by requiring any institution wishing to survive to give a standardized test—say, the Graduate Record Examination—to all its seniors. Those schools whose students perform below the state norm would face cutbacks or closing. Second, what community is being served? A school that serves a high percentage of disadvantaged students (this ought to be measured by family finances rather than just race or ethnicity) can make a better case for receiving tax dollars than one that subsidizes the children of the prosperous, who have private alternatives. Even ardent egalitarians should recognize the injustice of taxing people who wash dishes or mop floors for a living to pay for the below-cost public higher education of the children of lawyers so that they can go on to become lawyers too.

18   Some readers may find it paradoxical that a book arguing for greater literacy and intellectual discipline should lead to a call for less rather than more education. Even if college students do not learn all they should, the readers' counterargument would go, surely they learn something, and that is better than learning nothing. Maybe it is. But at what price? One hundred fifty billion dollars is awfully high for deferring the day when the idle or ungifted take individual responsibility and face up to their fate. Ultimately it is the yearning to believe that anyone can be brought up to college level that has brought colleges down to everyone's level.

✦ *Questions for Discussion and Writing*

1. How, according to Henry, has a misguided egalitarianism led to present abuses in the educational system in the United States? Why does he mention the proportion of students going to college in other, even more socialized, countries?

2. What function does statistical evidence play in supporting Henry's claims? Do the inferences Henry draws from these statistics appear to be warranted?

3. How does Henry counter the widely perceived claim that a college degree leads to better-paying jobs? Why is it important for him to undercut this belief in the development of his argument?

4. How does Henry make the case for the virtues of elitism in a society that has increasingly come to champion the values of egalitarianism? How does he base his defense of elitism on the willingness to assert that one idea, contribution, or attainment is better than another?

5. According to Henry, how have the political correctness and multicultural movements promoted egalitarianism?

6. What reasons does Henry present to support his claim that educational reforms are necessary to restore a balance between elitism and egalitarianism? Do Henry's recommendations about separating college from vocational tracks make sense? What currently championed social values would have to be given up?

7. How might the same issue Henry discusses be treated by different disciplines? For example, how might a sociologist investigate the interactions between educational establishments and society as a whole? What kinds of approaches might be used by researchers (such as economists or historians) in other disciplines?

8. As class, look closely at the issues generated by Henry's argument. Form groups to identify the interests of conflicting views generated by Henry's article. Each group should prepare a brief statement of its position and share it with the entire class. One student may be appointed as a mediator to steer the discussion. Are there principles on which all members of the class might agree as a basis for a compromise position?

Donald R. Griffin

Wordy Apes

———————◆———————

Donald R. Griffin is Professor of Animal Behavior at the Rockefeller University in New York. His original discoveries in the field of animal communication revealed the echolocation techniques of bats and the principles by which birds navigate. Listening in the Dark, *1958, won the Elliot Medal from the National Academy of Sciences in 1961. Griffin was awarded the Phi Beta Kappa Science Prize for* Bird Migration, *1964. His later research examines the linguistic abilities of chimpanzees and the possibility of human communication with whales and porpoises. The results of his research first appeared in* Animal Thinking, *1984, from which the following article is reprinted.*

1   Some of the most convincing recent evidence about animal thinking stems from the pioneering work of Alan and Beatrice Gardner of the University of Nevada (1969, 1979). The Gardners had noted that wild apes seem to communicate by observing each other's behavior, and they suspected that the extremely disappointing results of previous efforts to teach captive chimpanzees to use words reflected not so much a lack of mental ability as a difficulty in controlling the vocal tract. Captive chimpanzees had previously demonstrated the ability to solve complex problems and, like dogs and horses, they had learned to respond appropriately to many spoken words. The Gardners wanted to find out whether apes could also express themselves in ways that we could understand. In the late 1960s they made a concerted effort to teach a young chimpanzee named Washoe to communicate with people using manual gestures derived from American Sign Language. This language, one of many that have been developed in different countries for use by the deaf, consists of a series of gestures or signs, each of which serves the basic function of a single word in spoken or written language. To permit fluent conversation, these signs have evolved into clearly distinguishable hand motions and finger configurations that can be performed rapidly.

2   Washoe was reared in an environment similar to that in which an American baby would be raised. All the people who cared for Washoe "spoke" to her only in American Sign Language, and used it exclusively when conversing with each other in her presence. They signed to Washoe, much as parents talk to babies who have not yet learned to speak, but always in sign language rather than spoken English. Washoe was encouraged to use signs to ask for what she wanted, and she was

helped to do this by a procedure called molding, in which the trainer gently held the chimpanzee's hand in the correct position and moved it to form a certain sign.

The Gardners were far more successful than most scientists would have predicted on the basis of what was previously known about the capabilities of chimpanzees or any other nonhuman species, although Robert Yerkes had anticipated such a possibility (Bourne, 1977). During four years of training Washoe learned to use more than 130 wordlike signs and to recognize these and other signs used by her human companions. She could make the appropriate sign when shown pictures of an object, and on a few occasions she seemed to improvise new signs or new two-sign combinations spontaneously. The best example of this was Washoe's signing "water bird" when she first saw a swan. She also signed to herself when no people were present.

3

Following the Gardners' lead, several other scientists have trained other great apes to use a quasilinguistic communication system. This work has been thoroughly and critically reviewed by Ristau and Robbins (1982) and widely discussed by many others, so I will give only a brief outline here. Most of the subjects have been female chimpanzees, but two gorillas (Patterson and Linden, 1981) and one orangutan (Miles, 1983) have also been taught gestures based on American Sign Language. Because gestures are variable and require the presence of a human signer, who may influence the ape in other ways that are difficult to evaluate, two groups of laboratory scientists have developed "languages" based on mechanical devices operated by the chimpanzees. David Premack of the University of Pennsylvania used colored plastic tokens arranged in patterns resembling strings of words. His star chimpanzee pupil, named Sarah, learned to select the appropriate plastic "words" to answer correctly when the experimenter presented her with similar chips arranged to form simple questions. Questions such as "What is the color of—?" were answered correctly about familiar objects when the objects were replaced by their plastic symbols, even if the colors were different from those of the objects they represented. Sarah thus learned to answer questions about *represented* objects (reviewed by Premack, 1976; and Premack and Premack, 1983). This type of communication has the property of displacement, as in the case of the honeybee dances.

4

In another ambitious project at the Yerkes Laboratory of Emory University, Duane Rumbaugh, Sue Savage-Rumbaugh, and their colleagues have used back-lighted keys on a keyboard (Rumbaugh, 1977; Savage-Rumbaugh, Rumbaugh, and Boysen, 1980). Their chimpanzee subjects have learned to press the appropriate keys to communicate simple desires and answer simple questions. In some significant recent studies, two young male chimpanzees, Sherman and Austin, have not only learned to use simple tools to obtain food or toys but have learned

5

to employ the keyboard to ask each other to hand over a certain type of tool. These investigations, as well as extensions of the Gardners' original studies using words derived from American Sign Language, have been extensively reviewed (Ristau and Robbins, 1982) and discussed by Patterson and Linden (1981) and Terrace (1979). Despite disagreement about many aspects of this work, almost everyone concerned agrees that the captive apes have learned, at the very least, to make simple requests and to answer simple questions through these wordlike gestures or mechanical devices.

6   A heated debate has raged about the extent to which such learned communication resembles human language. Sebeok and Umiker-Sebeok (1980) and Sebeok and Rosenthal (1981) have argued vehemently that the whole business is merely wishful and mistaken reading into the ape's behavior of much more than is really there. They stress that apes are very clever at learning to do what gets them food, praise, social companionship, or other things they want and enjoy. They believe that insufficiently critical scientists have overinterpreted the behavior of their charges and that the apes have really learned only something like: "If I do this she will give me candy," or "If I do that she will play with me," and so forth. They also believe that the apes may be reacting to unintentional signals from the experimenters and that the interpretations have involved what behavioral scientists call "Clever Hans errors." This term refers to a trained horse in the early 1900s that learned to count out answers to arithmetical questions by tapping with his foot. For instance if shown 4×4 written on a slate board, the horse would tap sixteen times. More careful studies showed that Hans could solve such problems only in the presence of a person who knew the answer. The person would inadvertently nod or make other small motions in time with Hans' tapping and would stop when the right number had been reached. Hans had learned to perceive this unintentional communication, not the arithmetic. The Sebeoks argue that Washoe and her successors have learned, not how to communicate with gestural words, but rather how to watch for signs of approval or disapproval from their human companions and to do what is expected.

7   Although students of animal behavior must constantly guard against such errors, many of the experiments described above included careful controls that seem to have ruled out this explanation of all the languagelike communication learned by Washoe and her successors. In many cases the ape's vocabulary was tested by having one person present a series of pictures that the animal was required to name, while a different person, who could not see the pictures, judged what sign Washoe used in response. Furthermore the sheer number of signs that the apes employed correctly would require a far more complex sort of Clever Hans error than an animal's simple noticing that a person has stopped making small-scale counting motions.

Another criticism of the ape language studies has been advanced   8
by Terrace and colleagues (1979). Terrace, aided by numerous assistants, taught a young male chimpanzee named Nim Chimpsky to use
about 125 signs over a forty-five-month period. He agrees that Nim,
like Washoe and several other language-trained apes, did indeed learn
to use these gestures to request objects or actions he wanted and that
Nim could use some of them to answer simple questions. But when
Terrace analyzed videotapes of Nim exchanging signs with his trainers,
he was disappointed to find that many of Nim's "utterances" were copies of what his human companion had just signed. This is scarcely surprising, inasmuch as his trainers had encouraged him to repeat signs
throughout his training.

Terrace and his colleagues also concluded that Nim showed no   9
ability to combine more than two signs into meaningful combinations
and that his signing never employed even the simplest form of rule-
guided sentences. It is not at all clear, however, whether Nim's training
provided much encouragement to develop grammatical sentences. In
any event, he did not do so, and Terrace doubts whether any of the other signing apes have displayed such a capability. But Miles (1983) reports that her orangutan Chantek's use of gestural signs resembled the
speech of young children more closely than Nim's, and Patterson believes that her gorilla Koko follows some rudimentary rules in the sequence of her signs. Yet even on the most liberal interpretation there
remains a large gap between the signing of these trained apes and the
speech of children who have vocabularies of approximately the same
size. The children tend to use longer strings of words, and the third or
later words add important meaning to the first two. In contrast, Nim
and other language-trained apes seem much more likely to repeat signs
or add ones that do not seem, to us at least, to change the basic meaning of a two-sign utterance. For instance, the following is one of the
longer utterances reported for the gorilla Koko: "Please milk please me
like drink apple bottle"; and from Nim, "Give orange me give eat orange give me eat orange give me you." But grammatical or not, there is
no doubt what Koko and Nim were asking for. To quote Descartes and
Chomsky (1966), *"The word is the sole sign and certain mark of the presence
of thought."* Grammar adds economy, refinement, and scope to human
language, but words are basic. Words without grammar are adequate
though limited, but there is no grammar without words. And it is clear
that Washoe and her successors use the equivalent of words to convey
simple thoughts.

The enormous versatility of human language depends not only   10
on large vocabularies of words known to both speakers and listeners
but on mutually understood rules for combining them to convey additional meaning. George A. Miller (1967) has used the term "combinatorial productivity" for this extremely powerful attribute of human

language. By combining words in particular ways we produce new messages logically and economically. If we had to invent a new word to convey the meaning of each phrase and sentence, the required vocabulary would soon exceed the capacity of even the most proficient human brains. But once a child learns a few words, he can rapidly increase their effectiveness by combining them in new messages in accordance with the language's rules designating which word stands for actor or object, which are modifiers, and so forth.

11   Signing apes so far have made very little progress in combinatorial productivity, although some of their two-sign combinations seem to conform to simple rules. The natural communication systems of other animals make no use of combinatorial productivity, as far as we know. But the investigation of animal communication has barely begun, especially as a source of evidence about animal thoughts. What has emerged so far has greatly exceeded the prior expectations of scientists; we may be seeing only the tip of yet another iceberg. Extrapolation of scientific discovery is an uncertain business at best, but the momentum of discovery in this area does not seem to be slackening. The apparent lack of any significant combinatorial productivity in the signing of Washoe and her successors might turn out to be a temporary lull in a truly revolutionary development, which began only about fifteen years ago. Perhaps improved methods of investigation and training will lead to more convincing evidence of communicative versatility.

12   One relevant aspect of all the ape-language studies to date is that the native language of all the investigators has been English, and the signs taught to apes have been derived from American Sign Language. In English, word order is used to indicate actor or object, principal noun or modifying adjective, and many other rule-guided relationships. But this is very atypical; most other human languages rely much more on inflections or modifications of principal words to indicate grammatical relationships. No one seems to have inquired whether signing apes or naturally communicating animals might vary their signals in minor ways to communicate that a particular sign is meant to designate, for instance, the actor rather than the object. This would be a difficult inquiry, because the signals vary for many reasons, and only a laborious analysis of an extensive series of motion pictures or videotapes would disclose whether there were any consistent differences comparable to those conveyed by inflections of words in human speech.

13   Regardless of these controversies, there seems no doubt that through gestures or manipulation of tokens or keyboards apes can learn to communicate to their human companions a reasonable range of simple thoughts and desires. They also can convey emotional feelings, although an ape does not need elaborate gestures or other forms of symbolic communication to inform a sensitive human companion that it is afraid or hungry. What the artificial signals add to emotional

signaling is the possibility of communicating about specific objects and events, even when these are not part of the immediate situation. Furthermore, when Washoe or any other trained ape signs that she wants a certain food, she must thinking about that food or about its taste or odor. We cannot be certain just what the signing ape is thinking, but the content of her thought must include at least some feature of the object or event designated by the sign she has learned to use. For instance, the Gardners taught Washoe to use a sign that meant flower, to them. But Washoe used it not only for flowers but for pipe tobacco and kitchen fumes. To her it apparently meant smells. Washoe may have been thinking about smells when she used the sign, rather than about the visual properties of colored flowers, but she was certainly thinking about something that overlapped it with the properties conveyed by the word *flower* as we use it.

The major significance of the research begun by the Gardners is its 14 confirmation that our closest animal relatives are quite capable of varied thoughts as well as emotions. Many highly significant questions flow from this simple fact. Do apes communicate naturally with the versatility they have demonstrated in the various sorts of languagelike behavior that people have taught them? One approach is to ask whether apes that have learned to use signs more or less as we use single words employ them to communicate with each other. This is being investigated by studying signing apes that have abundant opportunity to interact with each other. Few results have been reported so far, although some signing does seem to be directed to other apes as well as to human companions. When scientists have been looking for something, and when we hear little or nothing about the results, we conclude that nothing important has been discovered. But the lack of results may only mean that chimpanzees can communicate perfectly well without signs. The subject obviously requires further investigation, and we may soon hear about new and interesting developments.

REFERENCES

Bourne, G. H., ed. *Progress in ape research*. New York: Academic Press. 1977.

Chomsky, N. *Cartesian linguistics*. New York: Harper and Row. 1966.

Gardner, R. A., and B. T. Gardner. Teaching sign language to a chimpanzee. *Science* 165:664–672. 1969.

Gardner, R. A., and B. T. Gardner. Two comparative psychologists look at language acquisition. In *Children's language*, ed. K. E. Nelson. New York: Halstead. 1979.

Miles, H. L. Apes and language: The search for communicative competence. In *Language in primates: Implications for linguistics, anthropology, psychology, and philosophy*, ed. J. de Luce and H. T. Wilder. New York: Springer. 1983.

Miller, G. A. *The psychology of communication*. New York: Basic Books. 1967.

Patterson, F. G., and E. Linden. *The education of Koko*. New York: Holt, Rinehart and Winston. 1981.

Premack, D. *Intelligence in ape and man*. Hillsdale, N. J.: Erlbaum. 1976.

Premack, D., and A. J. Premack. *The mind of an ape*. New York: Norton. 1983.

Ristau, C. A., and D. Robbins. Language in the great apes: A critical review. *Advances in Study of Behavior* 12:142–225. 1982.

Rumbaugh, D. M. *Language learning by a chimpanzee: The Lana Project.* New York: Academic Press. 1977.

Savage-Rumbaugh, E. S., D. M. Rumbaugh, and S. Boysen. Do apes use language? *Amer. Sci.* 68:49–61. 1980.

Sebeok, T. A., and R. Rosenthal. The Clever Hans phenomenon: Communication with horses, whales, apes, and people. *Ann. N. Y. Acad. Sci.* 364:1–311. 1981.

Sebeok, T. A., and J. Umiker-Sebeok, eds. *Speaking of apes, a critical anthology of two-way communication with man.* New York: Plenum. 1980.

Terrace, H. S. *Nim.* New York: Knopf. 1979.

Terrace, H. S., L. A. Petitto, and T. G. Bever. Can an ape create a sentence? *Science* 208:891–902. 1979.

✦ *Questions for Discussion and Writing*

1. What experiments have led some animal researchers to conclude that chimpanzees can be taught to communicate with humans?

2. What reasons do other scientists give for concluding that "lever-pressing" and "signing" activities by primates are not evidence of true communication, but merely imitative behavior that has been misinterpreted by their overenthusiastic colleagues?

3. What flaws contaminated the results of an early experiment conducted by the Gardners; how was this experiment redesigned by later researchers to eliminate possible sources of error?

4. What significance does Griffin derive from the fact that children can routinely combine "longer strings of words" than can apes with a comparable size signing vocabulary?

5. Because apes may use different inflections to convey different meanings, why might the attempt to teach apes a sign language based only on word order not be successful?

6. How does Griffin organize his summary of research around the question of what criteria should be used and what evidence should be accepted as proof of the ability of primates to communicate with humans?

7. How did the so-called "Clever Hans error" call into question the interpretation of the spectacular results that were obtained with Washoe?

8. How effectively does Griffin take into account both sides of the argument before putting forward his own "middle of the road" position that leaves the basic questions still open to further research?

9. What characteristics or features define this essay as a scientific argument in terms of whether the phenomena are worthy of investigation,

the scientific model advanced to explain the phenomena, predictions based on this model, data obtained from experiments, and the persuasiveness of the match between the model and the data? In what way is consideration of other plausible models and redesign of experiments to take these models into account an integral feature of arguments in science?

4

The Role of Logic in Argument

$$\blacklozenge$$

Why study logic? The answer is simply that most audiences expect an argument to rest on a rational foundation, and logic is the method used to study the nature and features of effective reasoning. Although the study of logic is often opposed to emotional appeals by which writers persuade their audiences, arguments that ring true are usually based on clear reasoning. The following discussion may not help you become the ever-logical Vulcan, Mr. Spock, or his android successor, Mr. Data, but it will spell out the distinctive features of correct reasoning and show some signs by which you can recognize arguments based on faulty logic. Traditionally, the study of logic has centered on two methods of reasoning, induction and deduction, and the analysis of fallacies that short-circuit the rules of logic.

Methods of Reasoning

INDUCTIVE REASONING

Reasoning that moves from the observation of specific cases to the formulation of a hypothesis is called inductive reasoning (from the Latin *in ducere,* to lead toward). Inductive reasoning depends on drawing inferences from particular cases to support a generalization or claim about what is true of all these kinds of cases (including those that have not been observed).

Many inferences we draw every day follow this pattern. For example, if three friends tell you independently of each other that a particular movie is worth seeing, you infer that the movie in question is probably good. Or, if you bought two pairs of the same brand of shoes on two separate occasions and found them to be comfortable, you might reasonably infer that a third pair of the same brand would prove equally satisfactory. Drawing inferences about a movie you have not yet seen or shoes you have not yet bought typically involves what is called an *inductive leap*. Thus, inductive reasoning strives toward a high degree of probability rather than absolute certainty.

The ability to generalize is a fundamental reasoning skill based on discerning common qualities shared by groups of things. For example, consider this traditional form of inductive reasoning:

Fred is human and mortal.

John is human and mortal.

Mary is human and mortal.

Therefore it is reasonable to infer that all human beings are mortal.

Since it would be impossible to observe every human being in the world, the inductively reached conclusion can only suggest what is probably true (even if the conclusion in this particular case seems certain). Inductive reasoning extrapolates that all human beings are mortal based on the three particular cases that have actually been observed.

Because inductive reasoning generalizes from specific cases, the conclusion will be stronger in proportion to the number of relevant examples the writer can cite to support it. Arguments based on atypical or sparse examples are less convincing than those based on conclusions drawn from a greater number of representative examples.

Conclusions reached by inductive reasoning can be stated only in terms of relative certainty because it is unlikely that all instances in a particular class of things can ever be observed. A generalization based on the observation of any phenomenon, from a virus to a spiral nebula, does not rule out the chance that new observations made in the future will require the formulation of totally new hypotheses.

Writers use inductive reasoning to draw inferences from evidence in order to convince an audience to accept a claim. Evidence may take the form of historical documents, laboratory experiments, data from surveys, the results of reports, personal observations, and the testimony of authorities. When our ability to draw conclusions based on firsthand observations is limited, we frequently rely on the opinion of authorities whose field of expertise includes a greater depth of knowledge about the instances, examples, or case histories under investigation.

Writers draw on specific cases and a wide range of empirical evidence to form a generalization that asserts what is true of specific instances is also true of the whole. As an argumentative strategy, the more different kinds of evidence are used as the basis of an inductive generalization, the stronger the argument will be. An argument that generalizes from a variety of sources, including personal experience, observation, the results of experiments, statistics, and historical research, will provide stronger support for a generalization from an audience's point of view than an argument that generalizes from fewer kinds of evidence.

Because inductive reasoning makes predictions or draws inferences about an entire class of things, writers must be careful not to draw conclusions from so limited a sample that these conclusions extend far beyond what the available evidence warrants and thus seem improbable.

The process of forming a generalization always involves making this inductive leap. Inductive arguments therefore aim at establishing a sense of high probability rather than certainty. There are three main kinds of inductive reasoning: analogy, sampling, and causal generalization. They vary according to their ability to persuade audiences to accept the likelihood of the connection made in the claim. We will examine these forms from the weakest to the strongest.

Analogy

The weakest kind of inductive argument requiring the greatest inductive leap is based on analogy or precedent. Here, the argument must persuade the audience that what is true for A is also true for B because of similarities the arguer claims exist between A and B.

Arguments from analogy rely on inductive reasoning to suggest that things or events that are alike in some ways are probably similar in other ways as well. The use of analogy in argument differs from the purely illustrative use of analogy to clarify subjects that otherwise might prove to be hard to visualize or be difficult to understand. For example, in his book *The Revolution Begins* (1979), Christopher Evans uses an ingenious analogy to help his readers realize the incredible processing speeds of which modern integrated circuits are capable:

> Imagine a British billionaire who decides that he is going to hand out a pound note to everyone who comes up to him—just one pound each. A long line forms and the billionaire starts handing out his pounds. He moves quickly and manages to get rid of them at the rate of one every ten seconds, but being human he can only keep it up for eight hours a day, five days a week. How long will it take him to dispose of his billion?...Does it seem conceivable, for example, that the billionaire could have started as far back as the Battle of Waterloo? Well, in fact he would have had to start before that. The Great Fire of London? No, he would have been counting away while Old St. Paul's blazed. The execution of Anne Boleyn? No, he would have been counting then too. Agincourt? No. Battle of Hastings? No, further still. To cut a long story short, you would have to go back to the year 640 or thereabouts before you would see the billionaire handing over his first pound note. But that is

just a taste of the cake. A billion times per second is no longer considered to be anything like the upper limit of computer processing speeds.

Think how very difficult it would be to try to imagine this mind-boggling speed without Evans's clever and entertaining analogy.

A writer uses analogy for argumentative (rather than descriptive or illustrative) purposes to show how evidence serves to support a particular conclusion. An instance of arguing by analogy can be observed in Abraham Lincoln's famous rebuttal silencing the critics who condemned his administration for dragging its heels in settling the Civil War. Notice how Lincoln structures the analogy to bring out similarities between his own situation and the one faced by Blondin (the famous tightrope walker who crossed Niagara Falls three separate times—in 1855, 1859, and again in 1860):

> Gentlemen, I want you to suppose a case for a moment. Suppose that all the property you were worth was in gold, and you had put it in the hands of Blondin, the famous rope-walker, to carry across the Niagara Falls on a tightrope. Would you shake the rope while he was passing over it, or keep shouting to him, "Blondin, stoop a little more! Go a little faster!"? No, I am sure you would not. You would hold your breath as well as your tongue, and keep your hand off until he was safely over. Now, the Government is in the same situation. It is carrying an immense weight across a stormy ocean. Untold treasures are in its hands. It is doing the best it can. Don't badger it! Just keep still, and it will get you safely over.

Lincoln asserts that none of the spectators would have dreamed of distracting Blondin while he was attempting to cross the falls. Nor would anyone in the audience have dared to "shake the rope" while Blondin was crossing the falls, especially since Lincoln has stipulated that Blondin is carrying "all the property you were worth . . . in gold." Next, Lincoln points out the similarities between Blondin's situation and the government's own precarious circumstances. Lincoln says that the government, too, is walking a tightrope bearing the burden of trying to resolve the Civil War. Lincoln concludes that "it [his administration] is doing the best it can." The inductive inference based on the number of ways in which the two situations are analogous is quite clear: critics should refrain from "shaking the rope" and let Lincoln strive to settle the war as he sees fit. Doubtless Lincoln did not depend on this analogy alone to make the case against interference; most likely he supported the same conclusion with other evidence (reports from generals in the field, attempts at behind-the-scenes negotiations, and so on). Although some analogical arguments are better than others, it is important to remember that like other forms of inductive reasoning, the conclusions are probable, not certain.

✦ *Questions for Discussion and Writing*

1. Evaluate the strengths of analogies in the following mini-arguments. Are the analogies literal (drawn from the same class of subjects) or figurative (drawn between different classes of things). Do similarities outweigh dissimilarities? If the analogy is weak, how might it be strengthened?

   a. With jails and prisons overflowing, those convicted rarely serve out their sentences. In California, state prisons release 20,000 of their inmates within three months; 40,000 are released after six months; and 60,000 in less than a year. Then they recirculate. In 1989, for instance, 11,040 parolees were returned to prison. The way the system is designed, the police, the courts, and the jails just keep coming in to perform the same job over and over. If you had a leaky pipe, you wouldn't keep calling a plumber to patch it up—you'd get a new pipe. It would be fixed, and the leak controlled. We need to begin to control our criminal leaks, too, putting an end to the faulty patchwork. (Daryl F. Gates, *Chief: My Life in the LAPD,* 1992.)

   b.

FIGURE 4-1

Source: Copyright 1984, USA Today. Reprinted with permission.

Sampling

Sampling arguments draw inductive inferences or generalizations from specific instances that realistically can never exhaust all the samples from the pool of instances. Sampling must always involve an extrapolation or inductive leap from the unknown to the highly probable. For example, a poll can never ask every single individual in a population about his or her opinion but must project the results from a representative sample.

Inductive generalizations depend on a process known as sampling, based on the selection of a sample drawn from a group. The sample must be drawn so as to accurately represent the composition and makeup of the entire group from which it is taken. All other things being equal, the larger the sample, the more probable it is that important characteristics in the larger population will be represented. For example, if the subject of a study were a small town with a population of 10,000, the sample should not be less than 200 townspeople lest the sample not be broad enough to be significant. Furthermore, because the townspeople that constitute the whole population can be categorized into different subgroups or strata, a reliable sampling must reflect that stratification. No survey of townspeople should fail to take into account small but important segments of different racial, cultural, or ethnic groups. The sample procedure should be random to ensure that a true cross section of townspeople is selected to represent the entire group about which the generalization or prediction is made. Just how this works can be seen on election nights, right after the polls have closed, when commentators report that "on the basis of a very small percentage of the vote" in sample precincts, candidate X or Y is declared the winner. More often than not these predictions turn out to be correct because the sample precincts accurately represent the district, state, or region as a whole.

The sample (1) must be randomly selected, (2) must be broad enough to be significant, and (3) must accurately reflect the general population from which it is taken. Evidence presented to support an inductive generalization must be clearly relevant to the conclusion drawn, objectively presented, and supported strongly enough to withstand challenges from opposing evidence. This last point is crucial since writers of arguments must always assume that evidence can be brought forward to challenge their conclusions.

✦ Questions for Discussion and Writing

1. Evaluate the strength of the following mini-argument. What would you need to know about the way the study was conducted to find the conclusions plausible? How would you assess the random distribution

of lefties among baseball players compared with the general population and the reliability of baseball encyclopedia statistics? How would this affect the conclusions drawn from the sample?

Lefty Longevity: Another Study

Do left-handed people have shorter life spans? Studies have come up with conflicting results. Now a soon-to-be-published study of baseball players—using the largest study population yet examined—takes the middle ground, suggesting that lefties die earlier, but only by a year.

Peter Rogerson, chair of the geography department at SUNY-Buffalo, looked at 4,448 baseball players born before 1920. Rogerson included only players who threw and batted with the same hand. Unlike other studies, instead of focusing only on deaths, he included the living: 19% of the righties were still alive as were 16.4% of the lefties. Survival rates of the two groups were the same for players between 25 and 65, but after 65, southpaws passed on one year sooner, on average.

—*Science,* March 18, 1994

2. What might an archeologist in the year 2025 conclude about the civilization in which you are living now based on a survey of the contents of your most cluttered desk or dresser drawer? Sketch out the likely hypotheses as to the ritual or functional purposes of any three items he or she has found. Explain the pattern of reasoning that would lead to inferences drawn from these three items.

Causal Generalization

Inductive reasoning can take the form of a causal argument that makes a claim about cause and effect, or correlation. The argument is inductive because it still requires an inference to explain the connections between events.

Causal analysis attempts to persuade an audience that one event caused another. Like other kinds of inductive reasoning, causal analysis aims at establishing probability rather than certainty. Writers may work backward from a given effect and seek to discover what might have caused it or work forward and predict what further effects will flow from the known cause. Argument based on causal analysis must identify as precisely as possible the contributory factors in any causal chain of events. The direct or immediate causes of the event are those that are likely to have triggered the actual event. Yet, behind the direct causes may lie indirect or remote causes that set the stage or create the framework in which the event could occur.

It often helps to distinguish between several meanings of the word *cause.* First, the concept of cause may refer to a *necessary condition* that must be present if a specific effect is to occur. For example, buying a lottery ticket is a necessary condition for winning the lottery. Yet, a necessary condition does not by itself guarantee the effect will occur. For the effect to be produced, there must be a *sufficient condition,* that is, a condition in whose presence the effect will always occur. If, for example, you bought a lottery ticket with the winning numbers, that alone would be a sufficient condition to ensure the effect (winning the lottery).

A claim that one event could have caused another is expressed as a generalization. This generalization either explains why an event has happened or predicts why it will happen in the future. For example, a medical writer, Judith Glassman, in "Beating the Odds" (*New Age Journal* [November 1985]) asserts that there is a direct relationship between emotional states of patients and the immune responses of the body. She argues that attitudes directly affect the body's response to disease. She cites research to support her claim that studies show a clear causal relationship between mental states and cancer survival:

> The widely influential Simontons [oncologist Carl Simonton and psychotherapist Stephanie Simonton-Ashley] use an amalgam of group therapy, meditation, and visualization—teaching their patients to picture their cancer cells as weak and disorganized and their treatment and immune systems as powerful. The Simontons' method has amassed impressive statistics. Of 240 incurable patients treated between 1973 and 1979, the median survival time was double the national average, and 10% of those patients had dramatic remissions.

Glassman concludes that the median survival time of double the national average for this group is directly due to the Simonton method for altering the attitudes of cancer patients. This kind of claim would require the author to demonstrate that the technique of changing attitudes was capable of producing these results.

Readers might also expect Glassman to demonstrate exactly how a change in attitudes affects the body's ability to fight cancer. Readers might also wonder whether the attitude change in the patients was the real cause of their high survival rate or whether it just preceded it in time. Might not the connection be just coincidental? Was the Simonton method the only cause of higher survival rates in this group? Might not there be other causes of equal or greater importance, such as a change in diet? A complete causal analysis would be more persuasive if it covered these points.

✦ *Questions for Discussion and Writing*

1. In a short essay, present a plausible account that might persuade an audience to accept your explanation for the causes or consequences of a single or repeated event, puzzling phenomena, or social trend. Try to

take into account alternative hypotheses, and suggest reasons why these other explanations should not be seen as credible.

Puzzling Phenomena

Recently W. Y. Megaw of York University in Toronto compiled a surprising table that lists, by country, the percentage of academic physicists in 1990 who were women. Hungary is first; 47% of its academic physicists were women. The Philippines is second, with 31%; the former Soviet Union is third, with 30%; Turkey, Italy, and France each have 23%; Brazil has 18%; India has 10%; and tied with Korea for dead last is the United States: 3%. What is going on here?

—Ann K. Finkbeiner, "Women Who Run with Physicists," *The Sciences,* September/October 1994

Repeated Events

People who suffer cardiac arrest in New York City have only a 1 in 100 chance of survival, a much lower rate than in several smaller cities and rural areas that have been studied, new research shows. The researchers studied 2,329 consecutive cardiac arrests in New York City during a six-month period in 1991. They found that the median time from patient collapse to the first electrical shock was more than twelve minutes in New York, compared with 8 to 10 minutes in suburban Seattle, where the chances of surviving cardiac arrest are 1 in 5.

—Adapted from the *New York Times,* March 2, 1994

Trends

The percentage of articles in *The New York Times* mentioning the "information superhighway" has increased by 2000 percent since 1992. (*Change,* Vol. 7, No. 3, Summer 1994.)

The percentage of Visa cards issued in China since 1991 has increased by 300 percent. (*Change,* Vol. 7, No. 3, Summer 1994.)

2. How might one of the following claims and questions be developed by showing causal relationships? Evaluate the strength of the resulting mini-argument in terms of the probability that A could have caused B to occur. Is the causal claim a reasonable generalization that can be inferred from the data supplied? Why or why not? What other causal influences might have played a role in producing the effect? Be prepared to defend your position in class or in a one-to-one exchange. Alternatively, the class might wish to brainstorm possible solutions or invent a proposal for resolving a conflict between positions developed by various members of the class.

a. It is or is not likely that within the next ten years a woman could be elected president of the United States. What if the claim said "fifty years"? Could you sketch out a chain of cause and effect over the intervening time period that would account for this happening?

b. I.Q. tests are or are not a reliable predictor of success in school, success in life, and so on.

c. "No other democracy protects the rights of criminals over society's right to peace and security—and no other democracy has anywhere near America's drug problem" (Charles Brandt, *L.A. Daily Journal,* Jan. 5, 1990).

d. From a historical perspective, what accounts for the enormous popularity of country music?

e. What explains the high dropout rate for Native American students?

f. What might be the consequence of Asian Americans being stereotyped as a "model minority"?

g. What factors have resulted in the unprecedented number of children being born to single mothers?

h. How have men's roles in the family changed since women have entered the work force (division of household chores, caring for children, economic decisions)?

i. What are some of the consequences of the rise of Islamic fundamentalism in the Middle East?

A SAMPLE ARGUMENT
FOR ANALYSIS

Garrett Hardin

Lifeboat Ethics: The Case against Helping the Poor

◆

Garrett Hardin is a biologist who was Professor of Human Ecology at the University of California at Santa Barbara. His works include Exploring New Ethics for Survival, 1972. *This essay originally appeared in the September 1974, issue of* Psychology Today. *In this article, Hardin compares a country that is well off to a lifeboat that is already almost full of people. Outside the lifeboat are the poor and needy, who desperately wish to get in. Hardin creates an inductive argument to support his claim that the sharing ethic will swamp the lifeboat unless its inhabitants keep additional people out.*

1   Environmentalists use the metaphor of the earth as a "spaceship" in trying to persuade countries, industries and people to stop wasting and polluting our natural resources. Since we all share life on this planet, they argue, no single person or institution has the right to destroy, waste or use more than a fair share of its resources.

2   But does everyone on earth have an equal right to an equal share of its resources? The spaceship metaphor can be dangerous when used by misguided idealists to justify suicidal policies for sharing our resources through uncontrolled immigration and foreign aid. In their enthusiastic but unrealistic generosity, they confuse the ethics of a spaceship with those of a lifeboat.

3   A true spaceship would have to be under the control of a captain, since no ship could possibly survive if its course were determined by committee. Spaceship Earth certainly has no captain; the United Nations is merely a toothless tiger, with little power to enforce any policy upon its bickering members.

4   If we divide the world crudely into rich nations and poor nations, two thirds of them are desperately poor, and only one third comparatively rich, with the United States the wealthiest of all. Metaphorically

194

each nation can be seen as a lifeboat full of comparatively rich people. In the ocean outside each lifeboat swim the poor of the world, who would like to get in, or at least to share some of the wealth. What should the lifeboat passengers do?

First, we must recognize the limited capacity of any lifeboat. For example, a nation's land has a limited capacity to support a population and as the current energy crisis has shown us, in some ways we have already exceeded the carrying capacity of our land.

5

Adrift in a Moral Sea

So here we sit, say fifty people in our lifeboat. To be generous, let us assume it has room for ten more, making a total capacity of sixty. Suppose the fifty of us in the lifeboat see 100 others swimming in the water outside, begging for admission to our boat or for handouts. We have several options: We may be tempted to try to live by the Christian ideal of being "our brother's keeper," or by the Marxist ideal of "to each according to his needs." Since the needs of all in the water are the same, and since they can all be seen as "our brothers," we could take them all into our boat, making a total of 150 in a boat designed for sixty. The boat swamps, everyone drowns. Complete justice, complete catastrophe.

6

Since the boat has an unused excess capacity of ten more passengers, we could admit just ten more to it. But which ten do we let in? How do we choose? Do we pick the best ten, the neediest ten, "first come, first served"? And what do we say to the ninety we exclude? If we do let an extra ten into our lifeboat, we will have lost our "safety factor," an engineering principle of critical importance. For example, if we don't leave room for excess capacity as a safety factor in our country's agriculture, a new plant disease or a bad change in the weather could have disastrous consequences.

7

Suppose we decide to preserve our small safety factor and admit no more to the lifeboat. Our survival is then possible, although we shall have to be constantly on guard against boarding parties.

8

While this last solution clearly offers the only means of our survival, it is morally abhorrent to many people. Some say they feel guilty about their good luck. My reply is simple: "Get out and yield your place to others." This may solve the problem of the guilt-ridden person's conscience, but it does not change the ethics of the lifeboat. The needy person to whom the guilt-ridden person yields his place will not himself feel guilty about his good luck. If he did, he would not climb aboard. The net result of conscience-stricken people giving up their unjustly held seats is the elimination of that sort of conscience from the lifeboat.

9

10   This is the basic metaphor within which we must work out our solutions. Let us now enrich the image, step by step, with substantive ad-
ditions from the real world, a world that must solve real and pressing
problems of overpopulation and hunger.

11   The harsh ethics of the lifeboat become even harsher when we consider the reproductive differences between the rich nations and the
poor nations. The people inside the lifeboats are doubling in numbers
every eighty-seven years; those swimming around outside are doubling, on the average, every thirty-five years, more than twice as fast as
the rich. And since the world's resources are dwindling, the difference
in prosperity between the rich and the poor can only increase.

12   As of 1973, the U.S. had a population of 210 million people, who
were increasing by 0.8 percent per year. Outside our lifeboat, let us
imagine another 210 million people (say the combined populations of
Colombia, Ecuador, Venezuela, Morocco, Pakistan, Thailand and the
Philippines), who are increasing at a rate of 3.3 percent per year. Put
differently, the doubling time for this aggregate population is twenty-
one years, compared to eighty-seven years for the U.S.

Multiplying the Rich and the Poor

13   Now suppose the U.S. agreed to pool its resources with those seven
countries, with everyone receiving an equal share. Initially the ratio of
Americans to non-Americans in this model would be one-to-one. But
consider what the ratio would be after eighty-seven years, by which
time the Americans would have doubled to a population of 420 million. By then, doubling every twenty-one years, the other group would
have swollen to 354 billion. Each American would have to share the
available resource with more than eight people.

14   But, one could argue, this discussion assumes that current population trends will continue, and they may not. Quite so. Most likely the rate
of population increase will decline much faster in the U.S. than it will in
the other countries, and there does not seem to be much we can do about
it. In sharing with "each according to his needs," we must recognize that
needs are determined by population size, which is determined by the
rate of reproduction, which at present is regarded as a sovereign right of
every nation, poor or not. This being so, the philanthropic load created
by the sharing ethic of the spaceship can only increase.

The Tragedy of the Commons

15   The fundamental error of spaceship ethics, and the sharing it requires, is that it leads to what I call "the tragedy of the commons." Under a system of private property, the men who own property recognize
their responsibility to care for it, for if they don't they will eventually

suffer. A farmer, for instance, will allow no more cattle in a pasture than its carrying capacity justifies. If he overloads it, erosion sets in, weeds take over, and he loses the use of the pasture.

If a pasture becomes a commons open to all, the right of each to use   16
it may not be matched by a corresponding responsibility to protect it. Asking everyone to use it with discretion will hardly do, for the considerate herdsman who refrains from overloading the commons suffers more than a selfish one who says his needs are greater. If everyone would restrain himself, all would be well; but it takes only one less than everyone to ruin a system of voluntary restraint. In a crowded world of less than perfect human beings, mutual ruin is inevitable if there are no controls. This is the tragedy of the commons.

One of the major tasks of education today should be the creation of   17
such an acute awareness of the dangers of the commons that people will recognize its many varieties. For example, the air and water have become polluted because they are treated as commons. Further growth in the population or per-capita conversion of natural resources into pollutants will only make the problem worse. The same holds true for the fish of the oceans. Fishing fleets have nearly disappeared in many parts of the world, technological improvements in the art of fishing are hastening the day of complete ruin. Only the replacement of the system of the commons with a responsible system of control will save the land, air, water and oceanic fisheries.

The World Food Bank

In recent years there has been a push to create a new commons   18
called a World Food Bank, an international depository of food reserves to which nations would contribute according to their abilities and from which they would draw according to their needs. This humanitarian proposal has received support from many liberal international groups, and from such prominent citizens as Margaret Mead, U.N. Secretary General Kurt Waldheim, and Senators Edward Kennedy and George McGovern.

A world food bank appeals powerfully to our humanitarian impuls-   19
es. But before we rush ahead with such a plan, let us recognize where the greatest political push comes from, lest we be disillusioned later. Our experience with the "Food for Peace program," or Public Law 480, gives us the answer. This program moved billions of dollars' worth of U.S. surplus grain to food-short, population-long countries during the past two decades. But when P.L. 480 first became law, a headline in the business magazine *Forbes* revealed the real power behind it: "Feeding the World's Hungry Millions: How It Will Mean Billions for U.S. Business."

And indeed it did. In the years 1960 to 1970, U.S. taxpayers spent a   20
total of $7.9 billion on the Food for Peace program. Between 1948 and

1970, they also paid an additional $50 billion for other economic-aid programs, some of which went for food and food-producing machinery and technology. Though all U.S. taxpayers were forced to contribute to the cost of P.L. 480, certain special interest groups gained handsomely under the program. Farmers did not have to contribute the grain; the Government, or rather the taxpayers, bought if from them at full market prices. The increased demand raised prices of farm products generally. The manufacturers of farm machinery, fertilizers and pesticides benefited by the farmers' extra efforts to grow more food. Grain elevators profited from storing the surplus until it could be shipped. Railroads made money hauling it to ports, and shipping lines profited from carrying it overseas. The implementation of P.L. 480 required the creation of a vast Government bureaucracy, which then acquired its own vested interest in continuing the program regardless of its merits.

Extracting Dollars

21   Those who proposed and defended the Food for Peace program in public rarely mentioned its importance to any of these special interests. The public emphasis was always on its humanitarian effects. The combination of silent selfish interests and highly vocal humanitarian apologists made a powerful and successful lobby for extracting money from taxpayers. We can expect the same lobby to push now for the creation of a World Food Bank.

22   However great the potential benefit to selfish interests, it should not be a decisive argument against a truly humanitarian program. We must ask if such a program would actually do more good than harm, not only momentarily but also in the long run. Those who propose the food bank usually refer to a current "emergency" or "crisis" in terms of world food supply. But what is an emergency? Although they may be infrequent and sudden, everyone knows that emergencies will occur from time to time. A well-run family, company, organization or country prepares for the likelihood of accidents and emergencies. It expects them, it budgets for them, it saves for them.

Learning the Hard Way

23   What happens if some organizations or countries budget for accidents and others do not? If each country is solely responsible for its own well-being, poorly managed ones will suffer. But they can learn from experience. They may mend their ways, and learn to budget for infrequent but certain emergencies. For example, the weather varies from year to year, and periodic crop failures are certain. A wise and competent government saves out of the production of the good years in anticipation of bad years to come. Joseph taught this policy to Pharaoh in Egypt more than 2,000 years ago. Yet the great majority of the gov-

ernments in the world today do not follow such a policy. They lack either the wisdom or the competence, or both. Should those nations that do manage to put something aside be forced to come to the rescue each time an emergency occurs among the poor nations?

"But it isn't their fault!" some kindhearted liberals argue. "How can we blame the poor people who are caught in an emergency? Why must they suffer for the sins of their governments?" The concept of blame is simply not relevant here. The real question is, what are the operational consequences of establishing a world food bank? If it is open to every country every time a need develops, slovenly rulers will not be motivated to take Joseph's advice. Someone will always come to their aid. Some countries will deposit food in the world food bank, and others will withdraw it. There will be almost no overlap. As a result of such solutions to food shortage emergencies, the poor countries will not learn to mend their ways, and will suffer progressively greater emergencies as their populations grow. 24

Population Control the Crude Way

On the average, poor countries undergo a 2.5 percent increase in population each year; rich countries, about 0.8 percent. Only rich countries have anything in the way of food reserves set aside, and even they do not have as much as they should. Poor countries have none. If poor countries received no food from the outside, the rate of their population growth would be periodically checked by crop failures and famines. But if they can always draw on a world food bank in time of need, their populations can continue to grow unchecked, and so will their "need" for aid. In the short run, a world food bank may diminish that need, but in the long run it actually increases the need without limit. 25

Without some system of worldwide food sharing, the proportion of people in the rich and poor nations might eventually stabilize. The overpopulated poor countries would decrease in numbers, while the rich countries that had room for more people would increase. But with a well-meaning system of sharing, such as a world food bank, the growth differential between the rich and the poor countries will not only persist, it will increase. Because of the higher rate of population growth in the poor countries of the world, 88 percent of today's children are born poor, and only 12 percent rich. Year by year the ratio becomes worse, as the fast-reproducing poor outnumber the slow-reproducing rich. 26

A world food bank is thus a commons in disguise. People will have more motivation to draw from it than to add to any common store. The less provident and less able will multiply at the expense of the abler and more provident, bringing eventual ruin upon all who share in the commons. Besides, any system of "sharing" that amounts to foreign 27 aid from the rich nations to the poor nations will carry the taint of charity, which will contribute little to the world peace so devoutly desired by those who support the idea of a world food bank.

28   As past U.S. foreign-aid programs have amply and depressingly demonstrated, international charity frequently inspires mistrust and antagonism rather than gratitude on the part of the recipient nation.

Chinese Fish and Miracle Rice

29   The modern approach to foreign aid stresses the export of technology and advice, rather than money and food. As an ancient Chinese proverb goes: "Give a man a fish and he will eat for a day; teach him how to fish and he will eat for the rest of his days." Acting on this advice, the Rockefeller and Ford Foundations have financed a number of programs for improving agriculture in the hungry nations. Known as the "Green Revolution," these programs have led to the development of "miracle rice" and "miracle wheat," new strains that offer bigger harvests and greater resistance to crop damage. Norman Borlaug, the Nobel Prize winning agronomist who, supported by the Rockefeller Foundation, developed "miracle wheat," is one of the most prominent advocates of a world food bank.

30   Whether or not the Green Revolution can increase food production as much as its champions claim is a debatable but possibly irrelevant point. Those who support this well-intended humanitarian effort should first consider some of the fundamentals of human ecology. Ironically, one man who did was the late Alan Gregg, a vice president of the Rockefeller Foundation. Two decades ago he expressed strong doubts about the wisdom of such attempts to increase food production. He likened the growth and spread of humanity over the surface of the earth to the spread of cancer in the human body, remarking that "cancerous growths demand food; but, as far as I know, they have never been cured by getting it."

Overloading the Environment

31   Every human born constitutes a draft on all aspects of the environment: food, air, water, forests, beaches, wildlife, scenery and solitude. Food can, perhaps, be significantly increased to meet a growing demand. But what about clean beaches, unspoiled forests, and solitude? If we satisfy a growing population's need for food, we necessarily decrease its per-capita supply of the other resources needed by men.

32   India, for example, now has a population of 600 million, which increases by 15 million each year. This population already puts a huge load on a relatively impoverished environment. The country's forests are now only a small fraction of what they were three centuries ago,

and floods and erosion continually destroy the insufficient farmland that remains. Every one of the 15 million new lives added to India's population puts an additional burden on the environment, and increases the economic and social costs of crowding. However humanitarian our intent, every Indian life saved through medical or nutritional assistance from abroad diminishes the quality of life for those who remain, and for subsequent generations. If rich countries make it possible, through foreign aid, for 600 million Indians to swell to 1.2 billion in a mere twenty-eight years, as their current growth rate threatens, will future generations of Indians thank us for hastening the destruction of their environment? Will our good intentions be sufficient excuse for the consequences of our actions?

My final example of a commons in action is one for which the public has the least desire for rational discussion—immigration. Anyone who publicly questions the wisdom of current U.S. immigration policy is promptly charged with bigotry, prejudice, ethnocentrism, chauvinism, isolationism or selfishness. Rather than encounter such accusations, one would rather talk about other matters, leaving immigration policy to wallow in the crosscurrents of special interests that take no account of the good of the whole, or the interest of posterity.   33

Perhaps we still feel guilty about things we said in the past. Two generations ago the popular press frequently referred to Dagos, Wops, Polacks, Chinks and Krauts, in articles about how America was being "overrun" by foreigners of supposedly inferior genetic stock. But because the implied inferiority of foreigners was used then as justification for keeping them out, people now assume that restrictive policies could only be based on such misguided notions. There are no other grounds.   34

A Nation of Immigrants

Just consider the numbers involved. Our Government acknowledges a net inflow of 400,000 immigrants a year. While we have no hard data on the extent of illegal entries, educated guesses put the figure at about 600,000 a year. Since the natural increase (excess of births over deaths) of the resident population now runs about 1.7 million per year, the yearly gain from immigration amounts to at least 19 percent of the total annual increase, and may be as much as 37 percent if we include the estimate for illegal immigrants. Considering the growing use of birth-control devices, the potential effect of educational campaigns by such organizations as Planned Parenthood Federation of America and Zero Population Growth, and the influence of inflation and the housing shortage, the fertility rate of American women may decline so much that immigration could account for all the yearly increase in population. Should we not at least ask if that is what we want?   35

36   For the sake of those who worry about whether the "quality" of the average immigrant compares favorably with the quality of the average resident, let us assume that immigrants and nativeborn citizens are of exactly equal quality, however one defines that term. We will focus here only on quantity; and since our conclusions will depend on nothing else, all charges of bigotry and chauvinism become irrelevant.

Immigration vs. Food Supply

37   World food banks *move food to the people,* hastening the exhaustion of the environment of the poor countries. Unrestricted immigration, on the other hand, *moves people to the food,* thus speeding up the destruction of the environment of the rich countries. We can easily understand why poor people should want to make this latter transfer, but why should rich hosts encourage it?

38   As in the case of foreign-aid programs, immigration receives support from selfish interests and humanitarian impulses. The primary selfish interest in unimpeded immigration is the desire of employers for cheap labor, particularly in industries and trades that offer degrading work. In the past, one wave of foreigners after another was brought into the U.S. to work at wretched jobs for wretched wages. In recent years, the Cubans, Puerto Ricans and Mexicans have had this dubious honor. The interests of the employers of cheap labor mesh well with the guilty silence of the country's liberal intelligentsia. White Anglo-Saxon Protestants are particularly reluctant to call for a closing of the doors to immigration for fear of being called bigots.

39   But not all countries have such reluctant leadership. Most educated Hawaiians, for example, are keenly aware of the limits of their environment, particularly in terms of population growth. There is only so much room on the islands, and the islanders know it. To Hawaiians, immigrants from the other forty-nine states present as great a threat as those from other nations. At a recent meeting of Hawaiian government officials in Honolulu, I had the ironic delight of hearing a speaker, who like most of his audience was of Japanese ancestry, ask how the country might practically and constitutionally close its doors to further immigration. One member of the audience countered: "How can we shut the doors now? We have many friends and relatives in Japan that we'd like to bring here some day so that they can enjoy Hawaii too." The Japanese-American speaker smiled sympathetically and answered: "Yes, but we have children now, and someday we'll have grandchildren too. We can bring more people here from Japan only by giving away some of the land that we hope to pass on to our grandchildren some day. What right do we have to do that?"

40   At this point, I can hear U.S. liberals asking: "How can you justify slamming the door once you're inside? You say that immigrants should

be kept out. But aren't we all immigrants, or the descendants of immigrants? If we insist on staying, must we not admit all others?" Our craving for intellectual order leads us to seek and prefer symmetrical rules and morals: a single rule for me and everybody else; the same rule yesterday, today, and tomorrow. Justice, we feel, should not change with time and place.

We Americans of non-Indian ancestry can look upon ourselves as   41
the descendants of thieves who are guilty morally, if not legally, of stealing this land from its Indian owners. Should we then give back the land to the now living American descendants of those Indians? However morally or logically sound this proposal may be, I, for one, am unwilling to live by it and I know no one else who is. Besides, the logical consequence would be absurd. Suppose that, intoxicated with a sense of pure justice, we should decide to turn our land over to the Indians. Since all our wealth has also been derived from the land, wouldn't we be morally obliged to give that back to the Indians too?

Pure Justice vs. Reality

Clearly, the concept of pure justice produces an infinite regression   42
to absurdity. Centuries ago, wise men invented statutes of limitations to justify the rejection of such pure justice, in the interest of preventing continual disorder. The law zealously defends property rights, but only relatively recent property rights. Drawing a line after an arbitrary time has elapsed may be unjust, but the alternatives are worse.

We are all descendants of thieves, and the world's resources are in-   43
equitably distributed. But we must begin the journey to tomorrow from the point where we are today. We cannot remake the past. We cannot safely divide the wealth equitably among all peoples so long as people reproduce at different rates. To do so would guarantee that our grandchildren, and everyone else's grandchildren, would have only a ruined world to inhabit.

To be generous with one's own possessions is quite different from   44
being generous with those of posterity. We should call this point to the attention of those who, from a commendable love of justice and equality, would institute a system of the commons, either in the form of a world food bank, or of unrestricted immigration. We must convince them if we wish to save at least some parts of the world from environmental ruin.

Without a true world government to control reproduction and the   45
use of available resources, the sharing ethic of the spaceship is impossible. For the foreseeable future, our survival demands that we govern our actions by the ethics of a lifeboat, harsh though they may be. Posterity will be satisfied with nothing less.

✦ *Questions for Discussion and Writing*

1. What measures does Hardin use to deal with his readers' emotional reluctance to think of themselves as the kind of people who would turn a deaf ear to pleas for help by the world's starving poor?

2. What extended analogy does Hardin use as a graphic illustration of his thesis that affluent nations have no obligation to share their food and resources with the world's starving masses? How does this analogy function in the context of his argument?

3. What reasons, evidence, and statistics does Hardin advance to support is thesis that any attempts to help the world's starving masses would ultimately threaten the human species?

4. What features of Hardin's argument require his audience to make an inductive leap to accept his analysis that forces operating in situation A will also operate in situation B?

5. What does Hardin mean by the expression "the tragedy of the commons"? How is the idea underlying this phrase related to the assumption that human beings are not capable of responsible, voluntary restraint?

6. How does Hardin use Public Law 480, intended to set up a world food bank, illustrate how past governmental programs have functioned?

7. What function does Hardin's introduction of the concept of environmental quality of life serve in the development of his overall argument? For example, how is this issue related to his discussion of the effects of humanitarian assistance to India, and the consequences of legal and illegal immigration?

8. Where does Hardin state the arguments that opponents might raise against his position, and what reasons and examples does he give for rejecting these arguments? For instance, how does his account of "a recent meeting of Hawaiian government officials in Honolulu" serve as a specific example of what he believes should be adopted as a policy by the entire United States?

9. How have immigration policies in the United States and elsewhere responded to the kinds of arguments Hardin presents? For example, in your view, was the 1994 California initiative (Prop. 187), conceived to deprive undocumented immigrants of welfare and other benefits that were previously extended, a good idea?

10. Draw on your personal experience to illustrate how the concept of the "tragedy of the commons" can occur on a smaller scale in different con-

texts. For example, what if a teacher allowed students to register for a class already oversubscribed? What would happen to books placed on reserve in the library that could be taken out only for one day?

11. To put Hardin's scenario into terms of a personal moral choice, consider the following dilemma: Would you be willing to add five years to your lifespan even though it meant taking five years away from the lifespan of someone in the United States chosen by chance? How would it change your decision if you knew who the person was?

12. In an essay, discuss your views of one or more of the following assumptions underlying Hardin's argument: (a) Aside from emergency famine or disaster relief, long-term assistance to Third World countries would ultimately do more harm than good; (b) Any attempt by the West to help the world's starving masses would ultimately threaten the entire human species; (c) Affluent nations have a moral obligation to the species and to future generations that takes precedence over helping starving masses in the present.

13. Write an essay directed at your classmates that responds to Hardin's argument. You might wish to formulate your essay as a letter to the editorial page of your campus newspaper or as a letter to the editor section of your local newspaper.

14. The class might wish to form groups that agree or disagree with Hardin's argument. Each group should create a brief summarizing the opposing position or generate questions to be posed to the other side. Are there principles on which all members of the class might agree as a basis for a compromise position?

DEDUCTIVE REASONING

Whereas inductive reasoning at best can only establish a sense of high probability, deductive reasoning can offer audiences a sense of certainty. This difference in effects on audiences is due to the differences between the two forms in their methods of drawing conclusions. Inductive reasoning always requires an inductive leap or inference of some kind, whether based on an analogy, sampling procedures, or causal argument. The generalization that is reached by inductive reasoning can never be proved to be absolutely certain. By contrast, deductive reasoning begins from a generalization that is widely agreed upon and then applies this axiom, or *major premise*, to a specific case to draw a valid conclusion about the particular case. If the premises are taken to be true, the conclusion must invariably also be certain. Looked at in this way, deductive reasoning is a method of reasoning that complements inductive reasoning. Rather than moving from the evidence provided by specific cases to a conclusion, deduction allows us to infer the validity of a particular case from generalizations or *premises*. The generalization "therefore it is reasonable to infer that all human beings are mortal" can be used deductively to predict that all as yet unobserved human beings will also be mortal. The classic form illustrating the relationship between the *premises* and the conclusion is known as a *syllogism:*

MAJOR PREMISE: All human beings are mortal.

MINOR PREMISE: John is a human being.

CONCLUSION: Therefore, John is mortal.

Notice how deductive reasoning applies a general statement to a particular case to draw a logical conclusion (whereas inductive reasoning uses individual cases, facts, and examples to create a hypothesis or generalization). The statements on which deductive reasoning is based appear as categorical propositions, or *laws*. If inferences from the original statements or premises are drawn correctly according to the rules of logic, then the conclusion is valid.

In contrast to inductive reasoning (which draws inferences or generalizes from specific cases), deductive reasoning (from the Latin *de ducere*, to lead from) draws inferences from statements called premises that are assumed to be true or "self-evident." Conclusions drawn via deductive reasoning are both logically necessary and certain (in contrast to the merely probable conclusions reached via inductive reasoning).

Deductive logic assumes that the truth of the premises is sufficient to establish the truth of the conclusion. No external evidence is required beyond the statements from which the conclusion is drawn. The conclusion is logically certain or valid because it follows necessarily from the premises. The term *validity* here refers only to the way in which the conclusion is drawn. If either the major or the minor premise is not true, then the conclusion, although logically valid, will not be true either.

It is frequently overlooked that many of the self-evident truths taken as premises in deductive reasoning are generalizations that have been previously established by inductive reasoning from empirical evidence and observation. **The process of inductive reasoning supplies the generalizations that appear as the starting point or major premise in deductive reasoning.**

To see how this works, examine the following passage from Arthur Conan Doyle's story "The Red Headed League" (1892), one of the innumerable exploits of his legendary character Sherlock Holmes:

"How, in the name of good fortune, did you know all that, Mr. Holmes?" he asked.

"How, did you know, for example, that I did manual labor? It's true as gospel, for I began as a ship's carpenter."

"Your hands, my dear sir. Your right hand is quite a size larger than your left. You have worked with it and the muscles are more developed."

Diagrammed in the form of a syllogism, Holmes's reasoning might appear thus:

MAJOR PREMISE: All men in whom at least one hand has more developed muscles do manual labor.

MINOR PREMISE: This man's right hand is a size larger than his left, and the muscles are much more developed.

CONCLUSION: Therefore, this man has done manual labor.

This deductive syllogism comprises a major premise that generalizes about an entire group or class, a minor premise that identifies the individual as a member of that class, and a conclusion expressing the inference that what is true of all manual laborers must be true of the man Holmes has encountered.

The major premise is a generalization reached by Holmes inductively; after all, Holmes had observed many instances where the hand muscles of manual laborers were more highly developed than the average person's. The minor premise places this particular man in the general category of all those whose hands exhibit signs of unusual muscular development. The conclusion Holmes draws is valid in its reasoning; that is, his process of reasoning from the premises to the conclusion is correct. However, if one or both of the premises were false, the argument would be untrue even though the process of reasoning is correct and the conclusion is validly drawn.

For example, Holmes's major premise might be untrue; perhaps there are men whose right hands are more muscular than their left who do not do manual labor. For instance, squash or tennis might produce unusual muscular development of the one hand used to grip the racquet. His minor premise could also have been untrue. For example, the "manual laborer" might have actually been Moriarty, Holmes's arch-nemesis in disguise, wearing a prosthetic device to lead Holmes to his erroneous conclusion.

Since major premises are often assumed to express self-evident truths, value arguments use deductive reasoning. In these arguments, the major premise states an absolute moral or ethical obligation. The minor premise specifies an instance or individual that falls within the scope of this obligation. The conclusion connects the general obligation to the individual case.

For example, the following syllogism illustrates how an absolute moral obligation can be applied to a specific case to produce a value judgment (adapted from "Medical Paternalism," by Allen E. Buchanan, in *Paternalism,* edited by Rolf Sartorius [1983]):

MAJOR PREMISE: The physician's duty—to which he or she is bound by the oath of Hippocrates—is to prevent or at least minimize harm to his or her patient.

MINOR PREMISE: Giving the patient information X will do greater harm to the patient, on balance, than withholding the information will.

CONCLUSION: Therefore, it is the physician's duty to withhold information X from the patient.

This example illustrates that deductive reasoning is useful in developing an argument leading to a conclusion that might be disputed if it were presented as a starting point. This application of deductive reasoning allows the writer to build an argument step by step that will lead an audience to consider the possibility of a claim they might have rejected initially. In this case, the claim is that in certain circumstances physicians are justified in withholding information from patients even if it means deceiving them.

The syllogisms we have been discussing are known as *categorical* syllogisms because the major premise sets up classes or categories ("all men" in the Sherlock Holmes syllogism, and "all physicians"). The minor premise identifies an individual or instance as part of that class, and the conclusion affirms that the specific case shares characteristics with the general class.

Except for the ever-logical Mr. Data, most people do not think in the form of syllogisms. In deductive arguments expressed in ordinary language (not syllogisms), one premise is usually implicit and understood rather than actually stated. Occasionally, the conclusion is implied rather than being explicitly stated. The result is called an *enthymeme.*

More typically, an enthymeme takes for granted the warrant or unexpressed major *premise.* For example, Charles de Gaulle was quoted in *Newsweek,* October 1, 1962, as saying, "How can you be expected to govern a country that has 246 kinds of cheese?" De Gaulle takes for granted the unexpressed major premise that might be stated thus: any country whose citizens have hundreds of preferences in cheese is unlikely to unite behind one political leader.

It is often helpful to make the unexpressed major premise explicit in order to evaluate the soundness of different parts of the argument. For example, suppose you and a friend were driving past a factory and your friend said, "Look at the picket line over there; there must be a strike at the factory." The unexpressed major premise here would be that picket lines are present only at strikes. The premise expresses a sign warrant: a picket line indicates the presence of a strike.

Consider how deductive reasoning works in the following argument, "Nuclear Power: The Fifth Horseman" (1976) by Denis Hayes:

> Increased deployment of nuclear power must lead to a more authoritarian society. Reliance upon nuclear power as the principal source of energy is probably possible only in a totalitarian state. Nobel Prize–winning physicist Hannes Alfven has described the requirements of a stable nuclear state in striking terms: Fission energy is safe only if a number of critical devices work as they should, if a number of people in key positions follow all of their instructions, if there is no sabotage, no hijacking of transports, if no reactor fuel processing plant or waste repository anywhere in the world is situated in a region of riots or guerrilla activity, and no revolution or war—even a "conventional one"—takes place in these regions. The enormous quantities of extremely dangerous material must not get into the hands of ignorant people or desperados....
>
> Nuclear power is viable only under conditions of absolute stability. The nuclear option requires guaranteed quiescence—internationally and in perpetuity. Widespread surveillance and police infiltration of all dissident organizations will become social imperatives, as will deployment of a paramilitary nuclear police force to safeguard every facet of the massive and labyrinthine fissile fuel cycle.

Diagrammed as a syllogism, Hayes's argument would appear this way:

MAJOR PREMISE: Nuclear power is viable only under conditions of absolute stability.

MINOR PREMISE: Widespread surveillance and police infiltration of dissident organizations and deployment of a paramilitary police force are required to produce absolute stability.

CONCLUSION: Therefore, a more authoritarian society (with widespread surveillance) will result from increased reliance on nuclear power.

Hayes uses deductive reasoning to try to persuade his audience to accept the claim that "increased deployment of nuclear power must lead to a more authoritarian society." His major premise states the assumed truth that "nuclear power is viable only under conditions of absolute stability." Hayes then builds his argument on this premise as follows: (1) nuclear power is viable only under conditions of absolute security, and (2) absolute security can be achieved only by widespread surveillance, police infiltration, and deployment of a paramilitary nuclear police force. From these premises Hayes draws the conclusion that (3) increased deployment of nuclear power must lead to a more authoritarian society.

As we have seen, deductive reasoning is useful as a rhetorical strategy in situations when an audience might reject a conclusion if it were stated at the outset. A writer who can get an audience to agree with the assumptions on which the argument is based stands a better chance of getting them to agree with the conclusion if he or she can show how this conclusion follows logically from the premises.

✦ Questions for Discussion and Writing

1. Locate the major premise, minor premise, and conclusion in the following mini-arguments. In which cases would you disagree with the major premise but have to accept the conclusion as valid?

   a. If suicide is a right, then it is one that has remained undiscovered throughout the ages by the great thinkers in law, ethics, philosophy, and theology. It appears nowhere in the Bible or the Koran or the Talmud. Committing suicide wasn't a "right" 1,000 years ago, and it isn't one now. That's why most societies—including our own—have passed laws against it. The two women who went to Dr. Kervorkian and took a strong dose of his hemlock were fully aware of the consequences of their actions. Now Dr. Kervorkian must take the legal consequences of his. (*Washington Times,* October 30, 1991.)

   b. Many of us care more about making the United States a "shining city on the hill" than about the origins of the people who helped obtain that goal. For those who care about the strengthening of American values, liberty, constitutionalism, and democracy so that they will spread throughout the world, the most effective step is to bring persons from the rest of the world here, so that their light can go back to where they came from, and make those places more like "us." (Julian L. Simon, *National Review,* February 1, 1993.)

   c.

FIGURE 4-2

Source: PEANUTS reprinted by permission of UFS, Inc.

d. The sign of the ascendant is a determining factor in the outward appearance of a person. People who have two signs ruling the first house, commonly called an interception, will take on the characteristics of both signs. One woman who has Capricorn on the ascendant with Aquarius intercepted in the first varies in appearance between the two signs. For a number of years, she looked very nontraditional, dressing like a free spirit and letting her long brown hair flow behind her. As she grew older and became more involved in the business world, the Capricorn ascendent became prominent. She cut her hair and dressed in conservative business suits. (*Horoscope*, Vol. 60, No. 10, October 1994.)

e. Young men have strong passions and tend to gratify them indiscriminately. Of the bodily desires, it is the sexual by which they are most swayed and in which they show absence of self-control. They are changeable and fickle in their desires, which are violent while they last but quickly over: their impulses are keen but not deep rooted, and are like sick people's attacks of hunger and thirst. They're hot-tempered and quick-tempered and apt to give way to their anger; bad temper often gets the better of them, for owing to their love of honor they cannot bear being slighted and are indignant if they imagine themselves unfairly treated. (Aristotle, "Youth and Old Age," from *The Rhetoric*, trans. by W. Rhys Roberts, 1925.)

2. Make explicit and state the implicit or unstated major premise in the following enthymemes. How might this unstated assumption connect the arguer to the audience in terms of the values and beliefs they share?

a. I am a Born Again Christian. I believe marijuana should be legalized, and I have Scripture to back me up. (Kat Marco, St. Petersburg, Florida, reported in *Parade Magazine*, July 31, 1994.)

b. Compare the attitude of Michael Fay's parents and Shiu Chi Ho's parents [both were caned in Singapore for vandalism]. Fay's parents were outraged instead of being ashamed. They went on radio, T.V., talk shows, blaming everyone but themselves. Shiu's parents showed pain, avoided publicity and considered leaving Singapore because of a sense of shame. On the other hand, Michael Fay back in America, got drunk and when his father protested, he tackled the father and wrestled him to the ground. I cannot imagine a Chinese son or any other Asian son, physically tackling his father. But that may happen when sons call their fathers by their first names and treat them as equals. (Prime Minister Goh Chok Tong's National Day speech, August 21, 1994, reported in the *Singapore Straits Times*.)

3. Write a short deductive argument expanding the lines of reasoning laid out in either of the following mini-arguments:

a. The traditional school calendar was not designed to be an educational calendar. It has no particular instructional benefit. It was designed solely to support the 19th-century agricultural economy. Change is long overdue. (Charles Ballinger, *USA Today,* January 12, 1990.)

b. There is nothing immoral about renting or selling your body. The idea that there is something wrong with this is rooted in the same tradition as the fantasy that "if you work hard enough someday the boss will notice you and promote you." In other words, it serves the purposes of those folks who have no problem with breaking your back all your life then, when you are dead, mining your corpse for life-saving organs. On the contrary, one could make a very good case that refusing to allow people to sell the most personal of all property is immoral, resulting in the waste of valuable resources and the loss of life. (Jim Hogshire, from *Sell Yourself to Science,* 1992.)

4. Create a deductive argument drawing on either or both of the following responses to a June, 1991, telephone poll of 1,000 Americans conducted by the Yankelovich organization on the subject of organ transplants.

a. Is it ethical to ask a child under the age of 18 to give up a kidney for transplant to a relative? Yes 45%, no 42%.

b. Is it morally acceptable for parents to conceive a child in order to obtain an organ or tissue to save the life of another one of their children? Yes 47%, no 37%. (Yankelovich, reported in *Time,* June 17, 1991.)

A SAMPLE ARGUMENT
FOR ANALYSIS

Marilyn French

Gender Roles

◆

Marilyn French is a frequent writer on feminist issues in works such as The Women's Room, *1977, and* Her Mother's Daughter, *1987. This selection is from* Beyond Power: On Women, Men, and Models, *1985. French creates a deductive argument to support her claim that sex roles are ultimately determined by culture rather than biology.*

Although many people believe it is women who work harder to maintain gender roles, to teach their daughters to be "ladies," and their sons to be "gentlemen," studies have revealed that in late twentieth-century America, men are more concerned than women that their children adopt "proper" behavior—that is, dictated, traditional sex-role behavior.[1] Other studies show that boys have more difficulty accepting their appropriate sex role. David Lynn, who has conducted a number of these studies, attributes boys' difficulties to three sources: lack of male models, the rigidity and harshness of masculine roles, and the negative nature of the requirements.[2] Boys especially appear to suffer from the fact that fathers are absent, whether emotionally or physically, and from the lack of other significant males in their young lives. And the male role in patriarchal society consists, as we have seen, largely of sacrifices—men must give up the hope of happiness, the ideal of home, emotional expressiveness and spontaneity, in order to become members of an elite that values power, wandering isolation, individuality, and discipline (order in obedience). 1

The fact that the male role does not gratify a boy, does not arise from primary desire but from the secondary desire of wanting to be like other boys or wanting to be a man like others he sees (on television, in films, in comic books, in history books), may account for the rigid, almost ritualistic way in which many adult men "play" their roles. Lynn discovered that boys who lack fathers entirely are more likely to entertain exaggerated and stereotypical images of masculinity than boys who have fathers, no matter how absent or violent.[3] 2

3   What Westerners mean when they say they want to make a man out of a boy is that they want a boy to learn that the sacrifices mentioned above are essential, are *the* characteristics of men. And the schools, or gymnasia, or army training camps to which people send boys to "make men of them" specialize in brutalization: rigid discipline, emphasis on physical hardness and strength, and contempt for sensitivity, delicacy, and emotion. Fortunately, not all boys are subjected to such treatment, but no boy escapes knowledge of the severities of "manliness" in our society, and those who feel they have not achieved it live with lingering self-doubt, self-diminishment. On the other hand, those men who score highest on tests of "masculinity" refuse to restrain their aggressiveness even when by expressing it they lose the approval of their community.[4]

4   "Manliness," as defined by patriarchy, means to be or appear to be in control at all times. But remaining in control prevents a person from ever achieving intimacy with another, from ever letting down his guard; it thus precludes easy friendship, fellowship, community. Men may have "buddies," acquaintances with whom they can engage in the ritual competition of banter, sport, or game, but they rarely possess intimate friends. I mentioned before that on tests administered by Carol Gilligan, in which a set of pictures was submitted to male and female subjects, men offered the most violent and threatening narratives as explanations of the photographs showing people close to each other, and the least threatening stories to explain photographs of men in isolation.[5] Shut out from the most nourishing parts of life, men seek what they need in the channels they have been told are "theirs": work, achievement, success. They imagine that success, or the demonstration of "manliness," will bring them love; instead, it often alienates those they love.[6] They feel cheated: and they blame women.

5   And men have, through patriarchal forms, achieved power-in-the-world. Men own 99 percent of the world's property and earn 90 percent of its wages, while producing only 55 percent of the world's food and performing only one-third of the world's work.[7] Men rather exclusively direct the course not just of states and corporations but of culture: religion, arts, education. Despite the assaults of various waves of feminism, men have been able to retain their control over the people, creatures, plants, and even some of the elements of this planet. Many men wish to retain these powers.

6   Yet psychological, sociological, and philosophical studies describe men as deeply unhappy. Writers like Philip Slater, R. D. Laing, Theodore Roszak, for instance, have described men of our time as alienated, fragmented, suffering from anomie, conflict over role, or identity crises.[8] In projective tests like the Rorschach, men from a number of different cultures showed more insecurity and anxiety than women.[9] Men seem to fall ill more frequently than women—at least they lose

more work days through illness than women do; they are more vulnerable than women to diseases that are associated with stress; and they die younger.[10] These statistics do not necessarily reflect *only* biological differences: when more women died in childbirth, men lived longer than women. Part of the reason why men are physically vulnerable is the stress they live with. And some of that stress is caused by attempting to live up to a definition of manliness that is unattainable for any human.

Sex-role behavior is learned. Whatever qualities we possess "by nature," from our genes, sex role is not among them. If it were, men could not feel and act as differently as they do from culture to culture, and especially from patriarchal society to societies that are not fully patriarchal. The range of behavior within one sex is as great as that between the two sexes; nondeterminist scientists point out that we have no substantive knowledge about the meaning of genetic and hormonal differences between the sexes.[11] The research of John Money and of Hampson and Hampson shows that hermaphrodites who are chromosomally and hormonally of one sex but are raised as if they were the opposite sex lead normal lives, including sex lives, as members of the sex in which they have been reared.[12]

Most men in Western societies work in some form of institution. Institutions breed competitiveness and inculcate an instrumental relation to everything, even personal relationships. One has contacts, not friends. One chooses to cultivate people not (as many women do) because of a sense of rapport with them, but because they might be useful. It also inculcates a focus upward, implicitly teaching men to see life as a power struggle directed at dominance. Men thus tend to see their bosses as masters not only over their working lives but over all of life. Such structures impose dependency, making people feel helpless, powerless; and this in turn arouses rigid, rule-bound behavior, making people act like petty tyrants in the realms which they control. Moreover, the structure is absorbing, and tends to make people regard the other parts of life as secondary. Rosabeth Kanter, who has observed this style in depth, believes it is not a male style but a corporate one; that it is not related to maleness itself, but is a response to the order imposed and the values implicit in large hierarchical organizations.[13]

What is learned can be learned differently. Because men overwhelmingly sit in seats of access to power, there is little possibility of altering the morality of our world unless men are willing to contribute to that alteration, unless men adopt a new set of values. Many men have been reaching toward such a change—witness the many books published in the past two decades offering self-help for men, suggesting broader ways of thinking adapted from Eastern religions, or recounting a personal change toward greater integration of self and of self with world. Whether men desire to change their lives depends upon two

7

8

9

major factors: the degree to which they are conscious of misery in their present condition; and the degree of contempt they feel for women. Many enlightened men will be offended by the suggestion that they feel contempt for women at all: but no one in patriarchal society, woman or man, is free from that feeling. If you imagine you are, imagine how you would feel if someone told you you were "womanly," or asked you to dress and act as a woman for a day. You are a rare creature if you are male and do not react with horror.

10   The grounds of this pervasive contempt for women have been suggested throughout this book. Basically, they lie in women's reproductive functioning, in menstruation, conception and pregnancy, and lactation, none of which men experience, and all of which men have been taught to see as disgusting or worse. But only creatures who have been taught to despise the body would see such things as disgusting; and beings who urinate, excrete, vomit, exude pus and other issue cannot justify disgust at menstruation, the production of nourishing milk, and the wondrous process of pregnancy and birth.

11   If men's disgust with women's reproductive functioning is the basis on which patriarchy taught contempt, it is women's mothering that allowed patriarchy to diminish women. For power is irrelevant to mothering, and vice versa. It is received wisdom that women's capacity for mothering is innate: this alone makes them unfit to participate as full partners in patriarchal society. Fatherhood, on the other hand, is seen as hardly biological at all, but as a "cultural phenomenon."[14] This contrasts conveniently with women's capacity for motherhood, considered as nonvolitional, making women "naturally" subject to coercion into other nonvolitional labors.

12   Yet studies show that there is no evidence of an instinctual or biological basis for mothering: there is no harm to infants, or to their mothers, if the infants are not reared by their biological mothers. There is nothing in the physiology of the parturient woman that makes her particularly suited to later child care, nor any instinctual basis for the ability to perform it. There is no biological or hormonal element differentiating a male "substitute" mother from a female one.[15] Nor is there any evidence that exclusive mothering is necessarily better for children than mothering by a group.[16]

13   Mothering is learned, just as aggression is learned. We often see among women that those who lacked mothers in their childhood cannot mother in turn, and are distant or abusive to their children. Among animals this has been shown frequently. Female animals who were deprived of their own mothers do not mother their babies but abuse and sometimes even kill them.[17] If a female baby rat is removed from her mother just after birth, before the mother has licked the offspring clean, that baby will not, as a new mother, lick her own offspring clean. Education in mothering occurs so early that we confuse it with "instinct,"

genetically programmed knowledge. But as Erving Goffman pointed out in another context, "there is no appreciable quid pro quo" between parents and children; "what is received in one generation is given in the next."[18] This is true of deprivations as well as of gifts.

Although women care for children in all cultures, men actively participate in child care in nonpatriarchal societies. Even in patriarchal ones, men are involved in rearing children in communities that live on the land, that work in or near the home. Our present notion of motherhood is quite recent, having been institutionalized only in the past couple of centuries—that is, separated from other dimensions of life, conceived of as an occupation, named, circumscribed, and prescribed as women's work, and to some degree regulated. 14

Exclusive mothering tends to produce more achievement-oriented men, and people with psychologically monogamic tendencies. Dorothy Dinnerstein and Nancy Chodorow, among others, believe it also creates men's dread and resentment of women, and their search as adults for nonthreatening, undemanding, dependent, even infantile women. Dinnerstein hypothesizes that men's pervasive fear of women—a fear she believes is shared by women—arises from the fact that women do most of the early mothering, that we emerge into consciousness facing a woman who appears huge, all-powerful, and awe-ful, in control of all our pleasures, all our pains. Although as we grow, we bury this sense of her and, indeed, belittle her, the sense is triggered when we encounter a mature woman in a position of authority or control. Such a woman arouses a symbolic dread and fear, preconscious emotions.[19] "Psychologists have demonstrated unequivocally that the very fact of being mothered by a woman generates in men conflicts over masculinity, a psychology of male dominance, and a need to be superior to women." As they reject the control of a woman because it seems overpowering, they also come to reject and devalue "feminine" qualities in general.[20] Sidney Bolkowsky suggests that societies that reject mothers may create their own misery, may be "unnatural," and that "precivilized" societies in which a child is raised by a series of "mothers," all offering extended loving contact, display low incidence of the psychological disorders found in "civilized" societies."[21] 15

A study of Russian and American children demonstrated that the Russian children were better socialized, having been cared for in group centers since infancy; there was more companionship between parents and children, and parents spent more time with their children than the American parents.[22] Collective child-rearing situations—on kibbutzim, in China, in Cuba—seem to produce children who have a greater sense of commitment to and solidarity with a group, less individualism and competitiveness, and who are less likely to form possessive, exclusive adult relationships.[23] 16

17   If we want a society that learns early to live together in harmony, collective child rearing is essential. To participate in child rearing would enlarge and enrich men's experience. It would also enlarge and enrich women's by allowing them to participate in both private and public life. Exclusive gender identity is not an expression of natural differences between the sexes but a suppression of natural similarities.[24] The unhappiness of many women would be eliminated or modified if their men provided them with the same nurturance they offer men, if their children had loving fathers, and if they were able to use their other talents in the world. It is even possible, as Gayle Rubin suggests, that if children were raised by people of both sexes, human social and sexual arrangements would be far richer, sexual power would disappear, and with it the Oedipus complex: she believes feminism must call for a revolution in kinship.[25] We cannot now predict what kind of people would result from such an integration, but it is only reasonable to assume that since they would be more integrated within themselves, people would be more content; and since they would be in greater harmony with each other, people would be more peaceful. To assume that contentment and peaceability would produce less brilliance, less art, less uniqueness than our own society possesses is unwarranted: what we would lose is the brilliance, uniqueness, and art that arises from utter isolation, self-hate, and the atrophy of personal qualities. The world as a whole has to be better off with greater integration and harmony.

18   Power has for too long gone unmodified and in defiant disregard of basic human feelings and needs. The exclusion of women from the public world is at once symbolic of its character and a reason for its character. Women are trained for private virtue, men for public power; and the severance between the sexes and the two realms is responsible for much of our irrational thinking and behavior, as Elshtain has shown.[26] In each realm, one is requested to close the eyes to what the other realm is doing and signifies and to connections between the two. *To disconnect virtue from power is to ensure that virtue will be powerless, and licenses power to be without virtue.* Yet there is no position of virtue for anyone who lives in a world as cruel and ugly as our own; nor any position of power for people who do not even know how to live with themselves. As Dietrich Bonhoeffer wrote, "Here and there people flee from public altercation into the sanctuary of private *virtuousness*. But anyone who does this must shut his mouth and his eyes to the injustice around him. Only at the cost of self-deception can he keep himself pure from the contamination arising from *responsible* action.[27] Bonhoeffer, a Catholic priest who persisted in opposing the Nazis, and died while imprisoned by them, was living his morality, not talking it.* Those who

---

*French is incorrect. Bonhoeffer was a Protestant theologian [editor's note].

closet themselves in a fugitive and cloistered virtue must remain adamantly ignorant or confess themselves participants in evil; those who stand only in the world and never gaze at the inner life, at connections among people, at the sharing and bonding that make all life possible, stride off and become the evil. For millennia, men have possessed fairly total worldly control over women. They have owned women, bought and sold them, forbidden them any form of independence at a cost of death. They have enslaved women, treated them as minors, defectives. In some cultures fathers had the right to kill their daughters, husbands their wives. Women's bodies have been imprisoned, removed from their own control, beaten, tortured, destroyed; women's minds have been constrained and deprived of nourishment by morality and enforced ignorance.

Yet despite all this control, men have remained anxious. As we have seen, some of the worst vituperation against women occurred in periods in which men had the greatest control over them. Wife beating does not cease in societies in which law gives men almost total control over women. It is claimed by some that feminism creates a male backlash against women; but no one can point to a culture in which women are subordinate yet are treated well. It seems that women have a choice between having some power over their lives and being hated and feared by men—and being hated and feared and having no power whatever. Whatever position women occupy in a society, men experience them as threatening; however great men's control, they do not feel in control.   19

Men do not attempt to establish control over women because they hate and fear them; rather, men hate and fear women because they *must* control them, because control over women is essential to their self-definition. Forced to demonstrate superiority, they can do so only by cheating, stacking the deck, by imposing on women deprivations which imprison them in a condition seen as inferior by the male culture.[28]   20

In hubris, bravado, and self-aggrandizement, men have declared themselves superior to other creatures. So they necessarily hate and fear the one creature who could disprove their claim, and attempt to put her in a position of such dependency that she will fear to do so. There are men who acknowledge this, yet cannot change. Their entire *human* identity rests on a manhood that is defined as control. Such men are in the deepest sense deprived, dehumanized: for they cannot find significance within nature, within their bodies and emotions, as part of a human-natural context. For them, significance is located only in that which transcends the natural context and offers something more enduring than life. Deluded by the notion that power offers what endures, they ignore the fact that nothing endures, not even art, except culture itself—the children we make, and the world each generation in   21 turn makes. Searching for meaning in what is superhuman, men have ignored their humanity, the only possible ground for human meaning.

NOTES

1. Evelyn Goodenough, "Interests in Persons as an Aspect of Sex Differences in the Early Years," *Genetic Psychological Monograph* 55 (1957):287–323.

2. David Lynn, *Parental and Sex Role Identification: A Theoretical Formulation* (Berkeley, Calif., 1969), p. 24.

3. David Lynn, "A Note on Sex Difference in the Development of Masculine and Feminine Identification," *Psychological Review* 66, 2 (1959):126–135.

4. D. B. Leventhal and K. M. Shember, "Sex Role Adjustment and Non-sanctioned Aggression," *Journal of Experimental Research in Personality* 3 (1969): 283–286.

5. Carol Gilligan, *In a Different Voice* (Cambridge, Mass.: Harvard Univ. Press, 1982), pp. 39–40.

6. Myron Brenton, *The American Male* (New York, 1966), p. 22.

7. Statistics taken from International Labor Organization study presented at the United Nations Women's Conference in Copenhagen, 1980, but reversed.

8. Glennon, Linda M., *Women and Dualism* (New York, 1979), pp. 170–199, discusses some of these complaints.

9. Roy D'Andrade, "Sex Differences and Cultural Institutions," in Eleanor Maccoby, ed., *The Development of Sex Differences* (Stanford, Calif.: Stanford Univ. Press, 1966), p. 202.

10. D'Andrade, "Sex Differences," Maccoby, *Development*, p. 216; David A. Hamburg and Donald Munde, "Sex Hormones in the Development of Sex Differences in Human Behavior," Maccoby, *Development*, p. 19; and Jane E. Brody, "Some Disorders Appear Linked to Being Left-Handed," *New York Times*, April 19, 1983.

11. Rose Lewontin, and Leon Kamin, *Not in Our Genes* (New York: Pantheon, 1984), Chapter Six.

12. John Money, "Sex, Hormones, and Other Variables in Human Eroticism"; J. L. Hampson and Joan G. Hampson, "The Ontogenesis of Sexual Behavior in Man"; both in *Sex and Internal Secretions*, Vol. 2, ed. W. C. Young (Baltimore, 1961).

13. Rosabeth Moss Kanter, *Men and Women of the Corporation* (New York: Basic Books, 1977), pp. 163, 170, 255ff.

14. See David M. Potter, *American Women and the American Character*, Stetson University Bulletin LXIII (Jan. 1962), p. 21.

15. Nancy Chodorow, *The Reproduction of Mothering* (Berkeley and Los Angeles: Univ. of Calif. Press, 1978), pp. 23–30.

16. Chodorow, *Mothering*, p. 75.

17. Warren Farrell, *The Liberated Man* (New York: Random House, 1974), p. 122.

18. Erving Goffman, "Gender Display," Lionel Tiger and Heather T. Fowler, eds., *Female Hierarchies* (Chicago: Beresford Book Service, 1978), p. 70.

19. Dorothy Dinnerstein, *The Mermaid and the Minotaur* (New York: Harper/Colophon, 1977), especially pp. 188–191.

20. Chodorow, *Mothering*, pp. 75–76, 185, 214; Dinnerstein, *Mermaid*.

21. Sidney Bolkowsky, "The Alpha and Omega of Psychoanalysis," *Psychoanalytic Review* 69, 1 (Spring 1982):131–150. See also Stanley Diamond, "The Search for the Primitive," *In Search of the Primitive: A Critique of Civilization* (New Brunswick, N.J.: Transaction Books, 1974), pp. 116–175; and Meyer Fortes, "Mind," *The Institutions of Primitive Society*, ed. E. E. Evans-Pritchard (Glencoe, Ill., 1956), pp. 90–94.

22. Rosalyn F. Baxandall, "Who Shall Care for Our Children? The History and Development of Day Care in the United States," in Jo Freeman, ed., *Women: A Femi-*

nist Perspective (Palo Alto, Calif., Mayfield, 1979), pp. 134–149. The study was conducted by Urie Brofenbrenner, *Two Worlds of Childhood: U.S. and USSR* (New York: Simon & Schuster, 1970).

23. Chodorow, *Mothering,* p. 217.

24. Gayle Rubin, "The Traffic in Women," in Rayna R. Reiter, ed., *Toward an Anthropology of Women* (New York: Monthly Review Press, 1975), p. 180.

25. Rubin, "Traffic," Reiter, *Anthropology,* p. 199.

26. Jean Bethke Elshtain, *Public Man, Private Woman* (Princeton, N.J.: Princeton Univ. Press, 1981), passim.

27. Dietrich Bonhoeffer, *Letters and Papers from Prison,* ed. Eberhard Bethge (New York, 1967), p. 27. The emphasis is Bonhoeffer's.

28. Philip Slater, *The Glory of Hera* (Boston: Beacon Press, 1971), p. 8.

✦ *Questions for Discussion and Writing*

1. In what ways are the kinds of requirements governing male sexual identity so much more difficult, according to French, than for female sexual identity? How does French use the results of Lynn's research as the major premise of her argument? State this major premise in your own words. How does this premise serve as an underlying assumption or warrant for her interpretation of various aspects of gender roles in American culture?

2. What specific conclusions does French draw through deductive reasoning? How are these conclusions logically necessary rather than merely being probable given the major premise from which she starts and the various minor premises that she introduces along the way. Does she take any truths as self-evident which appear questionable to you? Identify these and state your objections, if any.

3. What inferences can be drawn from the kinds of interpretive narratives men supply to explain two categories of photographs in a study by Carol Gilligan?

4. Where does French's argument rely on premises that are unstated with which her audience could be expected to agree?

5. Where in French's argument does she use inductive reasoning to draw analogies, generalize from specifics, or argue for causal connections in the context of her deductive argument?

6. What evidence does French offer to support the claim that "mothering" is a culturally defined rather than an innate biological instinct?

7. How can French's argument be understood as a policy argument that is built on claims of fact, cause, and value? How does she characterize the nature of masculinity, explore societal causes, evaluate it and find it wanting, lament its deplorable consequences, and recommend chang-

es that would make men more human? In your view, are there any disadvantages that would outweigh the benefits of the solutions she offers?

8. For what kind of audience does French's argument seem to be intended—those who already agree with her, are neutral, or would be skeptical of her claims? How persuasively in your view does French build a case for persuading her readers that gender roles are culturally, rather than biologically, determined?

5

The Role of Language in Argument

———————◆———————

The words a writer uses play a vital role in making any argument more effective for a given audience. By adapting the style of the argument to a particular audience, writers can increase their chances of not only getting a fair hearing for their case but also convincing the audience to share their outlook. For some audiences, tone, style, and syntax that are colloquial may work best. For others, a more formal, literary style may be more appropriate. Of all the stylistic means a writer can use to develop an argument, three areas deserve a close look: (1) definition, (2) tone, and (3) persuasive techniques. Definition covers broad questions of what boundaries a writer chooses to draw around the issue, as well as specific meanings of key terms. Tone reveals a writer's attitude toward the subject, and persuasive techniques include every means a writer uses to encourage an audience to share this viewpoint.

Definition

PURPOSES AND USES OF DEFINITION

Definition is the method of clarifying the meaning of words that are vague or ambiguous. These words may be important terms either in the claim of the argument or elsewhere in the essay. In other cases, you may wish to devote an entire essay to exploring all the connotations and denotations that have accrued to an unusual or controversial term, or challenge preconceptions attached to a familiar term.

In everyday life, arguments on a whole range of issues are really arguments about how terms ought to be defined. There are several reasons why a writer should clarify the basic nature of key terms on which an argument depends. First of all, as a practical matter the audience must understand what the writer means by certain unfamiliar terms crucial to the argument before they can even begin seriously considering the writer's thesis, or the evidence brought forward to support the claim. The writer must define ambiguous terms that might be mistaken to mean something other than what he or she intended. Otherwise, audiences may bring their own assumptions, preconceptions, and associations to the meaning of the terms in question. Definition offers a writer a method by which to clarify the meaning of a term so that it will be free from extraneous associations and undesired connotations.

For example, an argument about whether the government should censor pornographic materials would have to clarify exactly what is meant by such terms as *pornographic* or *obscene*. In *Roth* v. *U.S.* (1957), the United States Supreme Court defined "obscene and pornographic" material as material that is "patently offensive because it affronts contemporary community standards relating to the description or representation of sexual matters in a way that appeals only to 'prurient interests' and is without 'social value.'" Critics have responded that the Supreme Court's definition has itself raised questions about just how key terms such as *community, prurience,* and *social value,* in turn, ought to be defined. How is one really to gauge a community's standards—through a poll, or the testimony of leading citizens? And what type of "community" did the Supreme Court have in mind—a neighborhood, a town, a city, an entire county, a state, or a region of the country? Moreover, might not an evaluation of what constitutes prurience be merely a matter of personal taste? And how is one to identify characteristics that make it possible to say a work has or has not social value?

Likewise, an argument focusing on any of several issues surrounding organ transplantation would have to stipulate what is meant by the concept of death. A clear definition of death is important, since new developments in biomedical technology now make it possible to sustain life by artificial means long after an individual would normally have died. The crux of the issue is that someone who would have been declared dead in the past might now be declared living. Until recently, the courts would have relied on the traditional definition of death as "the cessation of life; the ceasing to exist; defined by physicians as a total stoppage of the circulation of blood and a cessation of the animal and vital functions consequent thereon such as respiration, pulsation, etc." (*Black's Law Dictionary,* revised Fourth Edition [1968]).

In other words, death was defined as occurring only when respiration and circulation of blood ceased. New machines, however, can sustain heartbeat and respiration indefinitely, even in individuals who show no signs of brain activity. For this reason, the Ad Hoc Committee of the Harvard Medical School, in "A Definition of Irreversible Coma" (1968), proposed a new definition of death based on the criterion of irreversible coma. From the committee's point of view, this more accurate definition makes it possible to determine if and when respirators and other devices should be withdrawn, when a patient should be considered dead, and at what point still viable organs might be removed for transplantation.

Besides eliminating ambiguity and vagueness, or defining a term important to the development of the argument, definitions in argument can be used to influence the attitudes of an audience toward a particular issue. Definition becomes important in arguments where the ability to control the way a central term is perceived is equivalent to winning the argument. A writer who convinces an audience that abortion should be "defined" (and perceived) as synonymous with murder has won the debate. Definition of controversial terms not only defines the terms but effectively shapes how people will perceive the issue.

For example, during hearings by the Hawaiian State Legislature on a proposal to abolish the state's law against abortion, the following letter appeared in the February 14, 1970, *Honolulu Advertiser:*

> Dear Sir: You ask me how I stand on abortion. Let me answer forthrightly and without equivocation.
>
> If by abortion you mean the murdering of defenseless human beings; the denial of rights to the youngest of our citizens; the promotion of promiscuity among our shiftless and valueless youth and the rejection of Life, Liberty and the Pursuit of Happiness—then, Sir, be assured that I shall never waver in my opposition, so help me God. But, Sir, if by abortion you mean the granting of equal rights to all our citizens regardless of race, color or sex; the elimination of evil and vile institutions preying upon desperate and hopeless women; a chance for all our youth to be wanted and loved; and, above all, that God-given right for all citizens to act in accordance with the dictates of their own conscience—then, Sir, let me promise you as a patriot and a humanist that I shall never be persuaded to forego my pursuit of these most basic human rights.
>
> Thank you for asking my position on this most crucial issue and let me again assure you of the steadfastness of my stand.
>
> Mahalo and Aloha Nui.

Definitions not only can change perceptions of an event by influencing the attitudes and emotions of an audience but can affect the perception of facts as well. For example, in "The Shrinking Middle Class" (*New England Economic Review* [September/October 1986]) Katharine L. Bradbury, an economist with the Federal Reserve Bank of Boston, addresses the question whether the middle class is shrinking, that is, whether there was a decline in the percentage of families with middle-class incomes between 1973 and 1984. Her argument must first establish what she means by the term *middle class*. She writes:

> the family income range from $20,000 to $49,999 in 1984 dollars is used to define the middle class in this study. This choice implies that one-half of families are in the middle class, about one-third have lower incomes and the remainder (roughly 15%) have higher incomes.

Bradbury explains the limitations of using a simple money income cutoff to define the middle class. She is aware that families of different sizes have different income requirements to achieve the same standard of living, and that living costs vary with regional location. Based on her definition of middle class, she reports:

> using this definition the fraction of families with middle class incomes did indeed decline between 1973 and 1984, from 53% to less than 48%. Most of the decline in the middle class share was picked up by the lower income class which increased from 32% of families to 36%; the upper income class grew slightly, from 15% to 16%.

She employs this particular definition and the accompanying evidence to support her claim that "increasing affluence was not the general case between 1973 and 1984." Of course, a different definition of what constitutes middle class would not only alter an audience's perception but change the "facts" in question and alter any conclusions that might be drawn. For example, in an election year both political parties might be expected to define middle class in a way favorable to their candidate.

It is important for the writer to establish clearly a set of criteria and to list the distinctive characteristics of the term in question, especially if the definition is really an argument for a different interpretation of the term. For example, the following discussion from *Re-making Love: The Feminization of Sex* (1986) by Barbara Ehrenreich, Elizabeth Hess, and Gloria Jacobs calls into question the conventional definition of *sex*. They argue for a reinterpretation of the traditional definition of sex and present a rationale for asking the reader to accept this new definition:

> First, we challenged the old definition of sex as a physical act. Sex, or "normal sex," as defined by the medical experts and accepted by mainstream middle-class culture, was a two-act drama of foreplay and intercourse which culminated in male orgasm and at least a display of female appreciation. We rejected this version of sex as narrow, male-centered, [and] unsatisfying. In its single-mindedness and phallocentrism, this form of sex does imitate rape; it cannot help but remind us

of the dangers and ambiguities of heterosexuality. At best, it reminds us simply of work: "Sex," as narrowly and traditionally defined, is obsessive, repetitive, and symbolically (if not actually) tied to the work of reproduction. We insisted on a broader, more playful notion of sex, more compatible with women's broader erotic possibilities, more respectful of women's needs. Our success in redefining sex can be measured not only in the reported proliferation of "variations" (not all of which are women's innovations, of course) or surveys documenting changes in sexual routine and practice, but in expectations: Twenty years ago the woman dissatisfied with sex was made to believe she was lacking something; the woman who selfishly advanced her own pleasure was made to worry about being less than normal. Today, it is the woman whose marriage still confines her to phallo-centered sex who knows she is missing something; and it is the woman who does not know how to negotiate or find her own way to pleasure who wonders if she is different, abnormal.

Notice how the authors set up a standard, identify criteria, apply them to traditional ideas about sex, and argue that their view is much better suited to characterize the changes wrought by the sexual revolution. In many arguments that seek to persuade an audience to reject or adopt certain values, definition is a way of identifying the criteria that ought to be used in making value judgments. That is, definition is required not because the terms are vague or ambiguous but because the writer rejects familiar and traditional standards and argues for the acceptance of a new set of criteria.

✦ Questions for Discussion and Writing

1. Explain why it is important to be able to define one of the following terms or why the meaning of the term itself has become problematic.

   a. What would you suggest as a more accurate descriptive term to define the age group described here?

   So what does it mean to be a part of "Generation X?" What should we expect as our generation grows older? More importantly, why must we and other generations be labeled and what does it mean to us (if anything)? This phenomenon was given birth by Douglas Coupland with the release of his 1990 novel *Generation X*. From it we have adopted such buzzwords as McJob—"a low-pay, low-prestige, low-dignity, low-benefit, no-future job in the service sector"—and developed an annoyingly new way of defining the twenty something generation. Once this novel of catch phrases and semi-truisms took off, those in the media and, subsequently the advertising and business worlds began selectively programming its campaigns for a generation commonly thought of as pessimistic, cynical, and apathetic. (Dan Roberts, Jr., "The Labelling of a Generation," *Inside BEAT,* September 15, 1994.)

b. What are the defining attributes of the term *African American?*

Whether blacks should now call themselves African-American surfaces as a result of Reverend Jesse Jackson's declaration: "To be called Black is baseless.... To be called African-American has cultural integrity." Little that is meaningful, in the way of agreement or disagreement, can be said about the proposal of a new name. After all, people can call themselves anything they wish and blacks have exercised this option having called themselves: colored, Negro, black, and Afro-American.

But suppose we concede there is a benefit to a name change that has "cultural integrity." It is not clear that African-American is the correct choice. (Walter E. Williams, "Myth Making and Reality Testing," *Society,* vol. 27, no. 4, May/June 1990.)

c. Where do you draw the line in the issue discussed here? How does where you draw the line distinguish between and define *tissue, fetus,* and *baby?* Why is it important to develop criteria?

Common sense, experience, and linguistic usage point clearly to the fact that we habitually consider, for example, a seven-week-old fetus to be different from a seven-month-old one. We can tell this by the way we respond to the involuntary loss of one as against the other. We have different language for the experience of the involuntary expulsion of the fetus from the womb depending upon the point of gestation at which the experience occurs. If it occurs early in the pregnancy, we call it a miscarriage; if late, we call it a stillbirth.

We would have an extreme reaction to the reversal of those terms. If a woman referred to a miscarriage at seven weeks as a stillbirth, we would be alarmed. It would shock our sense of propriety; it would make us uneasy; we would find it disturbing, misplaced— as we do when a bag lady sits down in a restaurant and starts shouting, or on octogenarian arrives at our door in a sailor suit. In short, we would suspect that the speaker was mad. Similarly, if a doctor or a nurse referred to the loss of a seven-month-old fetus as a miscarriage, we would be shocked by that person's insensitivity: could she or he not understand that a fetus that age is not what it was months before?

Our ritual and religious practices underscore the fact that we make distinctions among fetuses. If a woman took the bloody matter—indistinguishable from a heavy period—of an early miscarriage and insisted upon putting it in a tiny coffin and marking its grave, we would have serious concerns about her mental health. By the same token, we would feel squeamish about flushing a seven-month-old fetus down the toilet—something we would quite normally do with an early miscarriage. There are no prayers for the matter of a miscarriage, nor do we feel there should be. Even a Catholic priest would not baptize the issue of an early miscarriage. (Mary Gordon, "A Moral Choice," *Atlantic,* April 1990.)

METHODS OF DEFINING TERMS

Writers can use a variety of strategies either singly or in combination for defining terms. A description of eight of these strategies follows.

Synonyms

One of the simplest methods of defining words is to cite a synonym, that is, another word that has the same meaning. Thus, a writer who wanted to convey the meaning of *feast* might cite a synonym such as *banquet*. By the same token, a writer who wished to communicate the meaning of *labyrinth* could use the synonym *maze*. This method is efficient and workable but cannot always be used because many words have no exact synonyms.

For a more useful way of defining terms, we need to look at the method first discussed by Aristotle in the *Topica* (one of his treatises on logic), still in use today to define terms in dictionaries.

Dictionary or Lexical Definition

This method, sometimes called analytical definition, puts the thing to be defined into a *genus* or general class and then gives the *differentiae,* or distinguishing features that differentiate the subject being defined from all other things in its class with which it might be confused. For example, *teepee* is defined by *Webster's New Collegiate Dictionary* as "an American Indian skin-tent." The modifiers "American Indian" and "skin" are necessary to distinguish this particular type of tent from all other kinds of tent (for example, a canvas army tent) in the same general class. The terms used to define a word should be more specific, clear, and familiar than the actual term in question. Of course, in many cases a dictionary definition is not adequate because the dictionary does not delve into specific criteria, characteristics, and qualities a writer might need to explore in the course of developing an argument. In these cases, the unabridged *Oxford English Dictionary* (*OED*) may prove useful because this voluminous work gives examples, in context, of how each word has been used down through the centuries.

Etymological Definition

Often a fascinating light is thrown on the meaning of words by studying their etymology, that is, by tracing a word to its origin and following its shift of meaning or acquisition of connotative meanings through the years. For example, William Safire, in *William Safire on Language* (1980), traces the derivation of the word *welfare:*

When words die, they deserve a decent burial, or at least a respectful obituary. One noun bit the dust recently, at least in government usage, and it is herein bid adieu. The noun is "welfare," as in "Department of Health, Education and Welfare." This fine old word was born before 1303, the offspring of the Middle English *wel*, meaning "wish" or "will," and *faren*, meaning "to go on a journey." In its youth, the word enjoyed a period on the stage: "Study for the people's welfare," Warwick advised Henry VI in Shakespeare's play. In middle age, the word was used in the same sense but with more of a governmental connotation, beginning in a 1904 *Century* magazine article about the "welfare manager...a recognized intermediary between employers and employees." About that time, *The Westminster Gazette* was pin-pointing its sociological birthplace: "The home of the 'welfare policy' is the city of Dayton, Ohio." According to the etymologist Sir Ernest Weekly, "*Welfare*, as in 'child welfare,' 'welfare center' and so forth, was first used in this sense in Ohio in 1904."

Figurative Language—Metaphors, Similes, and Analogies

Figurative language is used by writers who wish to define a term in order to persuade an audience to agree with their point of view. This form of definition uses metaphor, simile, and analogy to place a thing in its class and identify atypical properties. For example, Len Deighton, in his book *Mexico Set* (1985), writes:

> In Mexico an air conditioner is called a politician because it makes a lot of noise but doesn't work very well.

In each of the following cases, consider how the writers use extended metaphors, similes, or analogies:

> "Politics is the art of looking for trouble, finding it everywhere, diagnosing it incorrectly, and applying the wrong remedies." (Groucho Marx)

> "Money is like manure. If you spread it around, it does a lot of good, but if you pile it up in one place it stinks like hell." (Clint W. Murchison, Texas financier)

> "Suicide is a permanent solution to a temporary problem." (Phil Donahue, NBC [May 23, 1984])

> "Golf is a good walk spoiled." (Mark Twain)

> "A Jewish man with parents alive is a 15-year-old boy." (Philip Roth, *Portnoy's Complaint* [1969])

> "An actor's a guy who, if you ain't talking about him, ain't listening." (Marlon Brando, *British Vogue* [August 1974])

Stipulation

A stipulative definition proposes a meaning for a term that it did not have before being given it by the definition. In some cases, the writer introduces a brand new term and stipulates that at least for the purposes of the argument, it is to carry a specific meaning. For example, Peter Singer, the director of the Monash Center for Human Bio-ethics, coins the word *speciesism* by analogy with *racism* or *sexism*. This term characterizes an attitude that leads scientists involved in animal experimentation to rationalize their cruelty toward the animals used in their tests on the grounds that human beings, as the apex of all species, have every right to sacrifice other species to obtain information useful to humans. Singer feels that a new term is necessary to dramatize the low value industrial societies place on animal life. He stipulates the definition of speciesism to set the parameters of the debate in a way favorable to his viewpoint.

In other cases, the writer uses a term that has been coined to characterize a situation so as to both identify it and express a judgment about it. One such term is *greenmail* (by analogy with *blackmail*). For example, Gerald L. Houseman argues in "The Merger Game Starts with Deception" (1986) that the use of greenmail has allowed corporate raiders like Carl Icahn, Rupert Murdoch, the Bass Brothers, T. Boone Pickens, and Ivan Boesky, among others, to accumulate millions of dollars at the expense of workers, stockholders, and the general public:

> Many offers to take over a company (so-called "tender offers") are made with little or no thought of actually taking it over. The objective in these cases is to threaten the board and management but, after a variety of financial and legal skirmishes, to withdraw—if the company will pay off with "greenmail." Greenmail, technically speaking, is the premium over market value paid by a company to the raider for its own stock in order to obtain withdrawal from a proxy fight (the fight for control of the firm). Let us assume a market value of $40 per share. The stock goes to $52 on the news of the take-over attempt.... When this occurs, a contract is drawn up which guarantees that the raider will not try to do this again for a set number of years. In exchange for this agreement, he sells his stock back to the company for a price of, say, $62. (The terms of the agreement outlined in this example are quite typical.) The take-over artist, or "broker," which is his usual title, has been well rewarded for notifying the SEC about buying into the company "for investment purposes" and for carrying out a war of nerves against the firm.

Notice how Houseman not only defines greenmail but explains how it operates and identifies the ways in which it is damaging to the entire economy of the country. Those who favor takeovers, acquisitions, mergers, and leveraged buyouts on the grounds that such mergers are necessary if the United States is to remain competitive in the world market would not use the term *greenmail* because of its negative associations with *blackmail*. They would probably refer to the same events as "financial restructuring."

In still other cases, the writer stipulates an unconventional meaning for a traditional term (as Barbara Ehrenreich, Elizabeth Hess, and Gloria Jacobs do for the word *sex*) to steer the argument in a direction favorable to his or her viewpoint. For example, William F. Buckley's argument in *Execution Eve* (1972) against those "abolitionists" who favor eliminating capital punishment turns on his unconventional definition of the words *cruel and unusual* punishment. Buckley argues that capital punishment is by no means cruel and unusual (the Eighth Amendment to the U.S. Constitution expressly forbids "cruel and unusual" punishment) and goes on to stipulate his own definition for these terms. Buckley interprets the word *unusual* to mean simply *uncommon* or *infrequent*, in contrast to the framers of the Constitution who used it to refer to bizarre methods of execution like death by public stoning, by the guillotine, and so on. Similarly, of the meaning of the word *cruel*, Buckley says:

> Capital punishment is cruel. That is a historical judgment. But the Constitution suggests that what must be proscribed as cruel is (a) a particularly painful way of inflicting death or (b) a particularly undeserved death: and the death penalty, as such, offends neither of these criteria and cannot therefore be regarded as objectively cruel.

While not everyone will be persuaded to accept Buckley's stipulated definitions of these words, we can see how he uses them to control and limit the argument.

Negation

Another useful strategy for defining a term is to specify what it is not. For example, Paul Theroux in *The Old Patagonian Express* (1979) provides this definition by negation of a *good flight:*

> You define a good flight by negatives: you didn't get hijacked, you didn't crash, you didn't throw up, you weren't late, you weren't nauseated by the food so you are grateful.

A negative definition does not release the writer from the responsibility of providing a positive definition of the term, but definition by negation is often a helpful first step in clearing away false assumptions. For example, Jesse Jackson uses both a negative definition and a figurative definition this way:

America is not like a blanket—one piece of unbroken cloth, the same color, the same texture, the same size. America is more like a quilt—many patches, many pieces, many colors, many sizes, all woven and held together by a common thread.

Example

Good examples are an essential part of effective writing. Nowhere is this more true than when a writer wishes to define an abstract term. Well-chosen examples are especially useful in clarifying the meaning of a term because they provide readers with a context in which to understand it. Examples may take the form of anecdotes, case histories, in-depth interviews, statistics, or even hypothetical cases that illuminate the meaning of the term in question. For instance, when Erwin Wickert in *The Middle Kingdom: Inside China Today* (1981) discusses contemporary Chinese culture, he offers clear-cut examples to illustrate the nature and meaning of *shame* in Chinese society, past and present:

> Thus the courts of ancient times did not so much punish a crime definable in terms of evidence as penalize the state of mind that led to its perpetration. Judicial verdicts and sentences are still coloured by this attitude. In the penal code of the *Qing* dynasty, which remained valid until the beginning of the twentieth century, forty lashes were prescribed as the punishment for "shameless conduct." Shameless conduct itself remained undefined because everyone knew what it was. We, on the other hand, live in a shameless society, where it would be difficult to reach a consensus about what is shameless and what is not.

The more abstract the concept the more important it is for the writer to provide a wide range of representative examples to clarify the meaning of the term. These examples may be drawn from personal observation, history, law, literature, or indeed any field as long as they are effective in clarifying the meaning of the term(s) to the audience. Down through the ages, the persuasive use of examples to define key terms can be seen in the writings and teachings of philosophers, poets, and preachers. For instance, St. Paul (in I Corinthians, chapter 13) in his definition of the spiritual dimensions of love uses a range of examples, both real and hypothetical, along with synonyms and figurative language, to define a heightened state of being:

> And now I will show you the best way of all. I may speak in tongues of men or of angels, but if I am without love, I am a sounding gong or a clanging cymbal. I may have the gift of prophecy, and know every hidden truth; I may have faith strong enough to move mountains; but if I have no love, I am nothing. I may dole out all I possess, or even give my body to be burnt, but if I have no love, I am none the better. Love is pa-

tient; love is kind and envies no one. Love is never boastful, nor conceited, nor rude; never selfish, not quick to take offence. Love keeps no score of wrongs; does not gloat over other men's sins, but delights in the truth. There is nothing love cannot face; there is no limit to its faith, its hope, and its endurance. Love will never come to an end. Are these prophets? their work will be over. Are there tongues of ecstasy? they will cease. Is there knowledge? it will vanish away; for our knowledge and our prophecy alike are partial, and the partial vanishes when wholeness comes. When I was a child my speech, my outlook, and my thoughts were all childish. When I grew up, I had finished with childish things. Now we see only puzzling reflections in a mirror, but then we shall see face to face. My knowledge now is partial; then it will be whole, like God's knowledge of me. In a word, there are three things that last for ever: faith, hope, and love; but the greatest of them all is love.

Modern readers might recognize this as a current translation from the New English Bible. In the past, the translation of this same passage in the King James Version of the Bible renders the same word (*agape* in Greek) as *charity*. Without Paul's powerful examples, it would be difficult to see what he means by *love*. The examples broaden the range of associations and make the meaning of the term resonate through specific cases. Paul's definition of love suggests a spiritual depth and richness that goes far beyond what most people normally associate with the term.

✦ Questions for Discussion and Writing

1. What method is being used in defining each of the following terms?

   a. *Addict:* Susan and her friends aren't shooting up; they snort their heroin or sometimes even smoke it. For Susan, the fact that she doesn't use a needle makes it easier to rationalize her dependency on heroin. In thinking that is typical of an addict, she tells herself that real addicts use needles; therefore, they are the only ones in danger of getting hooked on smack (or China White, as it is now called). (Mark Miller, "Fatal Addiction," *Mademoiselle*, November 1991.)

   b. *Speciesism:* How can a man who is not a sadist spend his working day heating an unanesthetized dog to death, or driving a monkey into a lifelong depression, and then remove his white coat, wash his hands, and go home to dinner with his wife and children? How can taxpayers allow their money to be used to support experiments of this kind? And how can students go through a turbulent era of protest against injustice, discrimination, and oppression of all kinds, no matter how far from home, while ignoring the cruelties that are being carried out on their own campuses?

      The answers to these questions stem from the unquestioned acceptance of speciesism. We tolerate cruelties inflicted on members of other species that would outrage us if performed on members of our own species. Speciesism allows researchers to regard the animals they experiment on as items of equipment, laboratory tools rather than living, suffering creatures. (Peter Singer, from *Animal Liberation: A New Ethics for Our Treatment of Animals*, 1975.)

c. *Obitorium:* Such a unique "suicide center" as described above obviously would offer society more than empty, negative death. Its much more important *positive* mission calls for a name worthy of that noble purpose. Because "suicide" and "euthanasia" have ineradicably negative connotations, I coined the word *obitorium* (from the Latin *obitus,* meaning "to go to meet death") for the center, and *obitiatry* (pronounced oh-bit-eye-a-tree, and using *iatros* meaning "doctor" in Greek) for the specialty. Logically its practitioner would then be an *obitiatrist.* (Jack Kevorkian, *Prescription: Medicine: The Goodness of Planned Death*, 1991.)

d. *Workaholic:* While workaholics do work hard, not all hard workers are workaholics. I will use the word workaholic to describe those whose desire to work long and hard is intrinsic and whose work habits almost always exceed the prescriptions of the job they do and the expectations of the people for whom they work. (Marilyn Machlowitz, from *Workaholics*, 1980.)

Extended Definition

An extended definition differs from other methods for defining terms because it is usually much longer and brings into play a greater variety of methods used. This type of definition expands on or uses any or all of the definition strategies previously discussed to clarify and define the basic nature of any idea, term, condition, or phenomenon. The length can range from several paragraphs to a complete essay or, conceivably, an entire book. In this sense, St. Paul's definition of love is an extended definition.

An extended definition can become synonymous with the definition essay, in which a writer delves more deeply into a concept by looking at its connotations, its defining criteria, and the variations in its meaning. For example, Jo Goodwin Parker in "What Is Poverty?" relies on specific details, graphic language, and memorable examples to challenge her audience's assumptions about what it means to be poor. Her poignant account of the humiliation of being poor was first given as a speech in Deland, Florida, on December 27, 1965, and was published in *America's Other Children: Public Schools Outside Suburbia*, edited by George Henderson, 1971. Notice how she builds her extended definition on the theme of the hard choices she is forced to make in an everlosing battle to preserve the health of her three children.

TWO SHORT DEFINITION
ESSAYS FOR ANALYSIS

Jo Goodwin Parker

What Is Poverty?

◆

This account was first given as a speech by Jo Goodwin Parker in Deland, Florida, on December 27, 1965. It is reprinted from America's Other Children, *edited by George Henderson, 1971.*

1   You ask me what is poverty? Listen to me. Here I am, dirty, smelly, and with no "proper" underwear on and with the stench of my rotting teeth near you. I will tell you. Listen to me. Listen without pity. I cannot use your pity. Listen with understanding. Put yourself in my dirty, worn out, ill-fitting shoes, and hear me.

2   Poverty is getting up every morning from a dirt- and illness-stained mattress. The sheets have long since been used for diapers. Poverty is living in a smell that never leaves. This is a smell of urine, sour milk, and spoiling food sometimes joined with the strong smell of long-cooked onions. Onions are cheap. If you have smelled this smell, you did not know how it came. It is the smell of the outdoor privy. It is the smell of young children who cannot walk the long dark way in the night. It is the smell of the mattresses where years of "accidents" have happened. It is the smell of the milk which has gone sour because the refrigerator long has not worked, and it costs money to get it fixed. It is the smell of rotting garbage. I could bury it, but where is the shovel? Shovels cost money.

3   Poverty is being tired. I have always been tired. They told me at the hospital when the last baby came that I had chronic anemia caused from poor diet, a bad case of worms, and that I needed a corrective operation. I listened politely—the poor are always polite. The poor always listen. They don't say that there is no money for iron pills, or better food, or worm medicine. The idea of an operation is frightening and costs so much that, if I had dared, I would have laughed. Who takes care of my children? Recovery from an operation takes a long time. I have three children. When I left them with "Granny" the last time I had a job, I came home to find the baby covered with fly specks,

236

and a diaper that had not been changed since I left. When the dried diaper came off, bits of my baby's flesh came with it. My other child was playing with a sharp bit of broken glass, and my oldest was playing alone at the edge of a lake. I made twenty-two dollars a week, and a good nursery school costs twenty dollars a week for three children. I quit my job.

Poverty is dirt. You say in your clean clothes coming from your   4
clean house, "Anybody can be clean." Let me explain about housekeeping with no money. For breakfast I give my children grits with no oleo or cornbread without eggs and oleo. This does not use up many dishes. What dishes there are, I wash in cold water and with no soap. Even the cheapest soap has to be saved for the baby's diapers. Look at my hands, so cracked and red. Once I saved for two months to buy a jar of Vaseline for my hands and the baby's diaper rash. When I had saved enough, I went to buy it and the price had gone up two cents. The baby and I suffered on. I have to decide every day if I can bear to put my cracked, sore hands into the cold water and strong soap. But you ask, why not hot water? Fuel costs money. If you have a wood fire it costs money. If you burn electricity, it costs money. Hot water is a luxury. I do not have luxuries. I know you will be surprised when I tell you how young I am. I look so much older. My back has been bent over the wash tubs every day for so long, I cannot remember when I ever did anything else. Every night I wash every stitch my school age child has on and just hope her clothes will be dry by morning.

Poverty is staying up all night on cold nights to watch the fire,   5
knowing one spark on the newspaper covering the walls means your sleeping children die in flames. In summer poverty is watching gnats and flies devour your baby's tears when he cries. The screens are torn and you pay so little rent you know they will never be fixed. Poverty means insects in your food, in your nose, in your eyes, and crawling over you when you sleep. Poverty is hoping it never rains because diapers won't dry when it rains and soon you are using newspapers. Poverty is seeing your children forever with runny noses. Paper handkerchiefs cost money and all your rags you need for other things. Even more costly are antihistamines. Poverty is cooking without food and cleaning without soap.

Poverty is asking for help. Have you ever had to ask for help,   6
knowing your children will suffer unless you get it? Think about asking for a loan from a relative, if this is the only way you can imagine asking for help. I will tell you how it feels. You find out where the office is that you are supposed to visit. You circle that block four or five times. Thinking of your children, you go in. Everyone is very busy. Finally, someone comes out and you tell her that you need help. That never is the person you need to see. You go see another person, and after spilling the whole shame of your poverty all over the desk between you,

you find that this isn't the right office after all—you must repeat the whole process, and it never is any easier at the next place.

7   You have asked for help, and after all it has a cost. You are again told to wait. You are told why, but you don't really hear because of the red cloud of shame and the rising black cloud of despair.

8   Poverty is remembering. It is remembering quitting school in junior high because "nice" children had been so cruel about my clothes and my smell. The attendance officer came. My mother told him I was pregnant. I wasn't, but she thought that I could get a job and help out. I had jobs off and on, but never long enough to learn anything. Mostly I remember being married. I was so young then. I am still young. For a time, we had all the things you have. There was a little house in another town, with hot water and everything. Then my husband lost his job. There was unemployment insurance for a while and what few jobs I could get. Soon, all our nice things were repossessed and we moved back here. I was pregnant then. This house didn't look so bad when we first moved in. Every week it gets worse. Nothing is ever fixed. We now had no money. There were a few odd jobs for my husband, but everything went for food then, as it does now. I don't know how we lived through three years and three babies, but we did. I'll tell you something, after the last baby I destroyed my marriage. It had been a good one, but could you keep on bringing children in this dirt? Did you ever think how much it costs for any kind of birth control? I knew my husband was leaving the day he left, but there were no good-bys between us. I hope he has been able to climb out of this mess somewhere. He never could hope with us to drag him down.

9   That's when I asked for help. When I got it, you know how much it was? It was, and is, seventy-eight dollars a month for the four of us; that is all I ever can get. Now you know why there is no soap, no needles and thread, no hot water, no aspirin, no worm medicine, no hand cream, no shampoo. None of these things forever and ever and ever. So that you can see clearly, I pay twenty dollars a month rent, and most of the rest goes for food. For grits and cornmeal, and rice and milk and beans. I try my best to use only the minimum electricity. If I use more, there is that much less for food.

10   Poverty is looking into a black future. Your children won't play with my boys. They will turn to other boys who steal to get what they want. I can already see them behind the bars of their prison instead of behind the bars of my poverty. Or they will turn to the freedom of alcohol or drugs, and find themselves enslaved. And my daughter? At best, there is for her a life like mine.

11   But you say to me, there are schools. Yes, there are schools. My children have no extra books, no magazines, no extra pencils, or crayons, or paper and the most important of all, they do not have health. They have worms, they have infections, they have pink-eye all summer.

They do not sleep well on the floor, or with me in my one bed. They do not suffer from hunger, my seventy-eight dollars keeps us alive, but they do suffer from malnutrition. Oh yes, I do remember what I was taught about health in school. It doesn't do much good. In some places there is a surplus commodities program. Not here. The county said it cost too much. There is a school lunch program. But I have two children who will already be damaged by the time they get to school.

But, you say to me, there are health clinics. Yes, there are health   12
clinics and they are in the towns. I live out here eight miles from town. I can walk that far (even if it is sixteen miles both ways), but can my little children? My neighbor will take me when he goes; but he expects to get paid, *one way or another.* I bet you know my neighbor. He is that large man who spends his time at the gas station, the barbershop, and the corner store complaining about the government spending money on the immoral mothers of illegitimate children.

Poverty is an acid that drips on pride until all pride is worn away.   13
Poverty is a chisel that chips on honor until honor is worn away. Some of you say that you would do *something* in my situation, and maybe you would, for the first week or the first month, but for year after year after year?

Even the poor can dream. A dream of a time when there is money.   14
Money for the right kinds of food, for worm medicine, for iron pills, for toothbrushes, for hand cream, for a hammer and nails and a bit of screening, for a shovel, for a bit of paint, for some sheeting, for needles and thread. Money to pay *in money* for a trip to town. And, oh, money for hot water and money for soap. A dream of when asking for help does not eat away the last bit of pride. When the office you visit is as nice as the offices of other governmental agencies, when there are enough workers to help you quickly, when workers do not quit in defeat and despair. When you have to tell your story to only one person, and that person can send you for other help and you don't have to prove your poverty over and over and over again.

I have come out of my despair to tell you this. Remember I did not   15
come from another place or another time. Others like me are all around you. Look at us with an angry heart, anger that will help you help me. Anger that will let you tell of me. The poor are always silent. Can you be silent too?

Discussion

Throughout her essay, Parker reveals distinctive characteristics of what she is defining. She brings in an extraordinary range of examples that provide concrete, easy-to-understand illustrations that are invaluable in supporting her evolving definition. Her definition of poverty is stipulative to the extent that she is trying to persuade her audience to accept a definition that challenges several traditional assumptions. When we look at specific features of her essay, we cannot overlook how Parker appeals to the reader's senses in depicting what being poor actually means in the most graphic human terms. Of the many details mentioned by Parker, some of the most effective in communicating her predicament include her account of having to remain awake for fear that the newspapers used to cover the walls to keep out the cold would catch fire. Or the time when she returned from work to find that the baby she left with her mother was "covered with fly specks, and a diaper that had not been changed." Parker makes concrete what is often referred to abstractly. For example, poverty is accompanied by a smell connected with spoiled foods, sour milk, and lack of cleanliness. Many of her examples dramatize the lack of any good choice as a defining characteristic of poverty. She must choose between sending her three children to nursery school, which costs $20 of the $22 she earns every week, or endangering their lives by leaving them with her mother. To keep her children clean and fed she must use the little money she has to buy either soap or food, not both, or food or hot water, heat, clothes, medicines, and diapers, but not all of them. Parker answers critics who would recommend plans for self-improvement by citing specific details about the nature of the support she receives. Her meager allowance is consumed in rent, minimal food, heat, and medicine for her children. Although there are schools, she has no money for books or supplies. Nor does she have a way to get her children to a free health clinic eight miles from where they live.

One important phase of her argument explores the psychological costs of poverty. She describes the sacrifice of pride and self-esteem she undergoes in visiting state agencies. She tells of the constant danger of exploitation to which she is subjected. The dominant impression she conveys is one of powerlessness to alter her own life and, more tragically, an inability to help her children have better lives. Overall, Parker's account expands and deepens a simple definition of poverty in ways that allow her audience to really understand the despair and hopelessness of being poor.

✦ Questions for Discussion and Writing

1. In creating this uniquely real and graphic account, how does Parker appeal to the reader's senses?

2. What are the hard choices that confront Parker when she tries to decide whether she should work and send her three children to nursery school or leave them with her mother?

3. What are the obstacles Parker faces in simply trying to keep her three children clean and fed? What are the trade-offs she is constantly forced to consider because of not having enough money?

4. How do environmental conditions, whether it is cold, or raining, have a direct physical impact on everyday life when you are poor?

5. What sequence of events led to Parker's present situation?

6. What evidence does Parker offer to illustrate that being poor and a woman means that you are in constant danger of being exploited by men?

7. What features of this account by Parker suggest that it was originally given as a speech? How might her account change her audience's assumptions about what it means to be poor?

8. In your opinion, what important criteria does Parker rely on in defining poverty? Restate in your own words what poverty does and does not involve in Parker's view.

9. What range of specific technical strategies does Parker use (for example, synonym, example, negation, stipulation) to define poverty? Which of these strategies are most effective, in your view?

10. Apply the criteria Parker relies on for her definition to any other situation (such as unemployment, disability, welfare) in which you have been involved or have observed that might be defined as an instance of poverty.

Ellen Goodman

The "Reasonable Woman" Is an Effective Standard to Establish Harassment

◆

Ellen Goodman is a nationally syndicated Pulitzer Prize–winning columnist based at The Boston Globe. *This article is reprinted from the October 21, 1991 issue of* Liberal Opinion.

1   Since the volatile mix of sex and harassment exploded under the Capitol dome, it hasn't just been senators scurrying for cover. The case of the professor and judge has left a gender gap that looks more like a crater.

2   We have discovered that men and women see this issue differently. Stop the presses. Sweetheart, get me rewrite.

3   On the "Today" show, Bryant Gumbel asks something about a man's right to have a pinup on the wall and Katie Couric says what she thinks of that. On the normally sober "MacNeil/Lehrer" hour the usual panel of legal experts doesn't break down between left and right but between male and female.

Shared Experiences

4   On a hundred radio talk shows, women are sharing experiences and men are asking for proof. In ten thousand offices, the order of the day is the nervous joke. One boss asks his secretary if he can still say "good morning," or is that sexual harassment. Heh, heh. The women aren't laughing.

5   Okay boys and girls, back to your corners. Can we talk? Can we hear?

6   The good news is that women have stopped rolling their eyes at each other and started speaking out. The bad news is that we may each assume the other gender not only doesn't understand but can't understand. "They don't get it" becomes "they can't get it."

7   Let's start with the fact that sexual harassment is a concept as new as date rape. Date rape, that should-be oxymoron, assumes a different perspective on the part of the man and the woman. His date, her rape.

Sexual harassment comes with some of the same assumptions. What he labels sexual, she labels harassment.

This produces what many men tend to darkly call a "murky" area   8
of the law. Murky however is a step in the right direction. When everything was clear, it was clearly biased. The old single standard was male standard. The only options a working woman had were to grin, bear it or quit.

Women's Feelings

Sexual harassment rules are based on the point of view of the vic-   9
tim, nearly always a woman. The rules ask, not just whether she has been physically assaulted, but whether the environment in which she works is intimidating or coercive. Whether she feels harassed. It says that her feelings matter.

This of course, raises all sorts of hackles about women's *feelings*,   10
women's *sensitivity*. How can you judge the sensitivity level of every single woman you work with? What's a poor man to do?

But the law isn't psychiatry. It doesn't adapt to individual sensitiv-   11
ity levels. There is a standard emerging by which the courts can judge these cases and by which people can judge them as well. It's called "the reasonable woman standard." How would a reasonable woman interpret this? How would a reasonable woman behave?

This is not an entirely new idea, although perhaps the law's belief   12
in the reasonableness of women is. There has long been a "reasonable man" in the law not to mention a "reasonable pilot," a "reasonable innkeeper," a "reasonable train operator."

Now the law is admitting that a reasonable woman may see these   13
situations differently than a man. That truth—available in your senator's mailbag—is also apparent in research. We tend to see sexualized situations from our own gender's perspective. Kim Lane Scheppele, a political science and law professor at the University of Michigan, summarizes the miscues this way: "Men see the sex first and miss the coercion. Women see the coercion and miss the sex."

Another Perspective

Does that mean that we are genetically doomed to our double vi-   14
sion? Scheppele is quick to say no. Our justice system rests on the belief that one person can get in another's head, walk in her shoes, see things from another perspective. And so does our hope for change.

If a jury of car drivers can understand how a "reasonable pilot"   15
would see one situation, a jury of men can see how a reasonable woman would see another event. The crucial ingredient is empathy.

16   Check it out in the office tomorrow. He's coming on, she's backing off, he keeps coming. Read the body language. There's a playboy calendar on the wall and a PMS joke in the boardroom and the boss is just being friendly. How would a reasonable woman feel?

17   At this moment, when the air is crackling with hostility and consciousness-raising has the hair sticking up on the back of many necks, guess what? Men can "get it." Reasonable men.

✦ Questions for Discussion and Writing

1. How has the new perception of sexual harassment changed the law? What are the consequences for employers?

2. In what sense does sexual harassment have less to do with sex and more to do with inequalities in power and authority between men and women in the workplace? How do poor recommendations; denial of overtime; demotions; injurious or undesired transfers; reassignment to less desirable shifts, hours, or locations of work; loss of job training; and unrealistic performance standards connect to sexual harassment as a form of impeding equal employment opportunities for women?

3. How does Goodman use analogous "reasonable man" situations to persuade her audience of the validity of using a "reasonable woman" standard?

4. Explain how the "reasonable woman" standard provides the single most important criterion by which to define an occurrence of sexual harassment. How is the "reasonable woman" standard based on the concept of empathy as the crucial ingredient?

5. In what way did the Clarence Thomas/Anita Hill Senate Judiciary Committee hearings in 1991 (alluded to as the judge and the professor) bring the issue of sexual harassment to the attention of the American public?

6. Apply the "reasonable woman" standard to situations you have been involved in or have observed that might have been defined as instances of sexual harassment involving coercion, discrimination, or a hostile work environment.

7. In your opinion, is it fair or unfair to hold employers legally responsible for subjective perceptions of sexual harassment? For example, how should the law be applied in situations (dirty jokes, offensive sexist language) where sexual harassment might be perceived as less blatant than more explicit *quid pro quo* cases of continued employment for sexual compliance, but nonetheless real?

8. Does your college have an official position on sexual harassment? If so, write an essay that evaluates and defends your assessment of your college's position. If your college has no such statement, the class may wish to compose a letter to the editor of the campus newspaper or to an administrator making a case for the establishment of such a code.

9. If conflicts exist among your classmates' positions on the issue of sexual harassment, write a description of the problem that a resolution acceptable to all sides must address. What questions need to be answered? Try to answer these questions collaboratively or decide what additional information could help you reach a concensus.

10. Draw on any of the following examples to create your own essay that illustrates, extends, or adds a different perspective to any of the following terms (or any of the terms mentioned in this chapter). Your essay should establish clear criteria for your definition, use a variety of methods in developing it, and give examples other than those presented to clarify the term for an audience you specify.

   a. *Culture Shock:* We might consider the apocryphal story of the American couple invited to a Moroccan family's home for dinner. Having pressed their host to fix a time, they arrive half an hour late and are shown into the guest room. After a decent interval, they ask after the host's wife, who has yet to appear, and are told that she's busy in the kitchen. At one point their host's little son wanders in, and the couple remark on his good looks. Just before the meal is served, the guests ask to be shown to the toilet so they may wash their hands. The main course is served in and eaten from a large, common platter, and the couple choose morsels of food from wherever they can reach, trying to keep up polite conversation throughout the meal. Soon after the tea and cookies, they take their leave.

   What did they do wrong? Almost everything. They confused their host by asking him to fix the hour, for in the Moslem world an invitation to a meal is really an invitation to come and spend time with your friends, during the course of which time, God willing, a meal may very well appear. To ask what time you should come is tantamount to asking your host how long he wants you around and implies, as well, that you are more interested in the meal than in his company.

   One should be careful about asking after a Moslem man's wife; she frequently does not eat with foreign guests, even if female spouses are present, nor would she necessarily even be introduced. In any case, she belongs in the kitchen guaranteeing the meal is as good as she can produce, thereby showing respect for her guests and bringing honor on her and her husband's house. Nor should one praise the intelligence or good looks of small children, for this will alert evil spirits to the presence of a prized object in the home, and they may come and cause harm. It was not appropriate to ask to be shown the toilet either, for a decorative basin would have been offered for the washing of hands (and the nicer it is the more honor it conveys upon the family). Nor should one talk during the meal; it interferes with the enjoyment of the food to have to keep up a conversation and may even be interpreted as a slight against the cooking. And one should only take food from the part of the platter directly in front, not from anywhere within reach. Not only is it rude to reach, but doing so deprives the host of one of his chief duties and pleasures: finding the best pieces of chicken or lamb and ostentatiously placing them before the guest. Culture shock, clearly, is not just something we experience, it's something we inflict as well. (Craig Storti, *The Art of Crossing Cultures*, 1989.)

b. *Child abuse:* Behavioral indicators of child abuse, according to the prosecutor's handbook put out by the National Center for the Prosecution of Child Abuse, of Alexandria, Virginia, a subsidiary of the National District Attorneys Association, may include overly submissive behavior, aggressive acting out or incorrigible behavior, school related excesses, sleep disturbances, bed-wetting, and "clingingness." Such broadly defined so-called indicators have a grave potential for contributing to a false accusation, because children who have not been sexually molested may exhibit such behavior. (Robert Sheridan, *Issues in Child Abuse Accusations*, Summer, 1990.)

c. *Guan-xi: Guan-xi* is a loose term. It translates directly as "relationship," but it implies a great deal more: influence, access, friendship, connection. It is the basis for the worldwide economic power of overseas Chinese. Guan-xi allows a San Francisco investor to begin a business partnership with a Toronto firm exporting products from a Singapore company through offices in Australia. This incredible social network, historically fostered and extraordinarily efficient, can basically allow a Chinese American to have access to virtually everyone on earth. It can be intimidating to non-Chinese but for Chinese people, *guan-xi* can spell the difference between success and failure. (Nelson Fu, "The Chinese Connection," *Transpacific*, September 1994.)

d. *Quality of life:* Those who so passionately uphold the "sanctity of life" do not ask "what life?" nor see themselves as retarded and crippled in an institution for the rest of that life. If the concept of "sanctity" does not include "quality," then the word has no meaning and less humanity. The rights of birth and death, of life itself require both. Above all, how can the sanctity-of-life argument prevail in a society that condones death in war of young men who want to

FIGURE 5-1
Source: PEANUTS reprinted by permission of UFS, Inc.

live, but will not permit the old and hopelessly ill, craving release, to die? (Marya Mannes, from *Last Rights*, 1974.)

11. Each language we know allows us access to a worldview, to particular ways of thinking, to a range of feeling, to interpretations of reality unique to that language. You have probably had the experience of searching for a foreign word that will communicate the precise meaning of an English word of expression and realizing suddenly that there is no exact equivalent. There is no exact English equivalent, for example, for the Spanish *simpatico* or the Italian *prego*. *Hogar* and home are, technically, synonyms, but they are not really; they carry a somewhat different emotional content which is critical to the meaning. One language makes it possible for a person to see and understand realities that remain veiled—even invisible—in another language. (Rita Esquivel, speech delivered before the California Association of Bilingual Education, 1991.)

   Are there terms with which you are familiar that have no exact synonym in English? Select one of these terms and define it in a phrase or two, conveying its overtones, nuances, and connotations that would not be known to someone who spoke only English. Why would it be important for someone who is bilingual to be able to define the meaning of this or another term for an English-speaking audience?

Tone

Tone is a vital element in the audience's perception of the author. In *Rhetoric,* Aristotle discussed how an audience's confidence in the character and credibility of the writer or speaker was a key element in persuading its members to accept a claim. He emphasized that the audience would most likely reach their estimate of the writer or speaker's character not so much from what they already knew about the writer, which might be very little, but from the speech itself. This is why the question of tone is crucial. Aristotle believed that credibility was created by the audience's perception of the writer or speaker as a person of good sense, moral integrity, and good intentions. Good sense might be shown by the writer's knowledge of the subject, adherence to the principles of correct reasoning, and judgment in organizing a persuasive case. The more intangible qualities of character might be gauged from the writer's respect for commonly accepted values and unwillingness to use deceptive reasoning simply to win a point.

The most appropriate tone is usually a reasonable one. A reasonable tone shows that the writer cares about the subject under discussion and is sensitive to the needs and concerns of the audience.

Tone is produced by the combined effect of word choice, sentence structure, and the writer's success in adapting her or his particular "voice" to suit the subject, the audience, and the occasion. Choosing between a casual or formal tone might be compared with choosing between wearing jeans or a tuxedo to a party. Most likely, the choice of clothes would fall somewhere in the middle. So, too, the most useful tone is neither undisciplined nor formal and pretentious, but one that creates an impression of a reasonable person calmly discussing issues in a natural voice.

When we try to identify and analyze the tone of a work, we are seeking to hear the "voice" of the author in order to understand how he or she intended the work to be perceived. Tone indicates the author's attitude toward both the subject and the audience. Tone is a projection of the writer's self. The entire essay or argument creates an impression of the writer as a certain kind of person. It is important for writers to know what image of themselves they are projecting in their writing. Writers should consciously decide on what kind of style and tone best suits the audience, the occasion, and the specific subject matter of the argument. Although a casual tone might be suited for a conversation between friends, the same tone would be inappropriate for an argument designed to convince an audience to accept the validity of a claim.

For example, consider the tone of George F. Will's comment in his essay "Government, Economy Linked":

The government in its wisdom considers ice a "food product." This means that Antarctica is one of the world's foremost food producers.

Will's point is that the government has inappropriately included ice in its classification of "food products." His purpose in writing is to persuade his audience to protest this senseless bureaucratic categorization. That much is obvious. What is less obvious but is just as important is the tone of Will's comment. His tone reveals a well-developed sarcastic sense of humor, a dry wit, common sense, and a readiness to spot bureaucratic absurdities. Beyond this, we can sense Will's basic conservative position that big government should not wield too much power.

Of all the characteristics of tone, the first and most important to audiences is clarity. Write so that nothing you put down can be misunderstood. Use a natural rather than an artificial vocabulary. Adopt a tone that reinforces what you want your audience to think and feel about the issue. Keep in mind that insight, wit, and sensitivity are always appreciated.

Certain kinds of tone are more difficult for apprentice writers to manage successfully. A writer who is flippant will run the risk of not having the argument taken seriously by the audience. Arrogance, belligerence, and anger are usually inappropriate in argumentative essays. Even if you are indignant and outraged, make sure you have evidence to back up your emotional stance, or else you will appear self-righteous and pompous. By the same token, steer away from special pleading, sentimentality, and an apologetic "poor me" tone—you want the audience to agree with your views, not to feel sorry for you. Keep out buzz words or question-begging epithets ("bleeding-heart liberal" or "mindless fundamentalist") that some writers use as shortcuts to establish identification with readers instead of arguing logically and backing up their position with facts and evidence.

IRONY

A particular kind of tone encountered in many arguments is called irony. Writers adopt this rhetorical strategy to express a discrepancy between opposites, between the ideal and the real, between the literal and the implied, and, most often, between the way things are and the way the writer thinks things ought to be.

Sometimes it is difficult to pick up the fact that not everything a writer says is intended to be taken literally. Authors will occasionally say the opposite of what they mean to catch the attention of the reader. Often the first response to an ironic statement or idea is "Can the writer really be serious?" If that is your response to an argument, look for clues meant to signal you that the writer means the opposite of what is being said. Irony draws the reader into a kind of secret collaboration with the author in a way that very few other rhetorical strategies can accomplish. One clear signal the author is being ironic is a noticeable disparity between the tone and the subject.

For example, in Jonathan Swift's "A Modest Proposal" (1729) the tone in which the narrator speaks is reasonable, matter-of-fact, and totally at odds with his recommendation that Ireland solve its overpopulation problem by encouraging poor people to sell their babies as food to the wealthy:

> I shall now therefore humbly propose my own thoughts, which I hope will not be liable to the least objection.
>
> I have been assured by a very knowing American of my acquaintance in London, that a young healthy child well nursed is at a year old a most delicious, nourishing, and wholesome food, whether stewed, roasted, baked, or boiled, and I make no doubt that it will equally serve in a fricassee, or a ragout.
>
> I do therefore humbly offer it to public consideration, that of the hundred and twenty thousand children already computed, twenty thousand may be reserved for breed, whereof only one fourth part to be males, which is more than we allow to sheep, black-cattle, or swine, and my reason is that these children are seldom the fruits of marriage, a circumstance not much regarded by our savages, therefore one male will be sufficient to serve four females. That the remaining hundred thousand may at a year old be offered in sale to the persons of quality, and fortune, through the kingdom, always advising the mother to let them suck plentifully in the last month, so as to render them plump, and fat for a good table. A child will make two dishes at an entertainment for friends, and when the family dines alone, the fore or hind quarter will make a reasonable dish, and seasoned with a little pepper or salt will be very good boiled on the fourth day, especially in winter.
>
> I have reckoned upon a medium [average], that a child just born will weigh 12 pounds, and in a solar year if tolerably nursed increaseth to 28 pounds.
>
> I grant this food will be somewhat dear, and therefore very proper for landlords, who, as they have already devoured most of the parents, seem to have the best title to the children.

You may have noticed the practical, down-to-earth, and understated voice with which the narrator enumerates the financial and culinary advantages of his proposed "solution." The discrepancy between his matter-of-fact tone and the outrageous content is a clear signal that the writer means the exact opposite of what is being said. If you missed Swift's signals, you might even think he was being serious!

SATIRE

Satire is an enduring form of argument that uses parody, irony, and caricature to poke fun at a subject, idea, or person. Tone is especially important in satire. The satirist frequently creates a "mask" or *persona* that is very different from the author's real voice in order to shock the audience into a new awareness about an established institution or custom. As we have seen, in "A Modest Proposal" Swift creates the persona of a reasonable, seemingly well-intentioned bureaucrat who proposes, in an offhand way, that Ireland solve its economic problems by slaughtering and exporting one-year-old children as foodstuffs. To mistake the voice as that of Swift's would be to miss the ironic contrast between what is said and what is meant. As with other works that rely on irony, the writer must be in full control of the material no matter how strongly he or she feels personally. Satiric works initially seem quite plausible, coherent, and even persuasive on the surface until the reader notices that the writer intends the work to be read ironically.

Enduring satirical works include Aristophanes' *The Birds,* Samuel Johnson's *Rasselas,* Voltaire's *Candide,* Swift's *Gulliver's Travels,* Mark Twain's *A Connecticut Yankee in King Arthur's Court,* and Joseph Heller's *Catch-22.* These works assail folly, greed, corruption, pride, self-righteous complacency, hypocrisy, and other permanent targets of the satirists' pen.

FOUR SHORT ESSAYS ILLUSTRATING HUMOR, IRONY, PARODY, AND SATIRE

Cathy Guisewite and Mickey Guisewite

Blithering by the Rules

---◆---

This article is the result of an unusual collaboration between Cathy Guisewite, the nationally syndicated author of the CATHY™ comic strip, which she has drawn for the past eighteen years, and her sister, Mickey, a writer and businesswoman. This account is drawn from their book Dancing Through Life in a Broken Pair of Heels: Extremely Short Stories for the Totally Stressed, *1993.*

1   I don't want to hear about it. I don't want to think about it. I don't want to talk about it. And yet, after my friend Carol and I have been together for just four minutes, I can see that look in her eyes. And, being an obliging friend, I say those three little words nearly every woman I know right now longs to hear: "How's the baby?"

2   "The baby? Oh, I just took the cutest pictures of her," she says, whipping out a package of photos. "Doesn't she have the most precious face you've ever seen?"

3   "Oh yes, precious," I say. But I can't help thinking how much more expressive my own little Joey's face is. Always bright. Always smiling. Never a tear.

4   "Here she is clapping her hands. The doctor says she's incredibly coordinated for her age."

5   "Wow," I say. But I can't help thinking how much more impressive it is that my little Joey was able to catch a ball in mid-air at age five months.

6   "And here's Madeline eating her birthday cake. She kind of missed her mouth."

7   Of course I can't help thinking how much more amusing my little Joey's experiences with food have been.... Like the time when, five

FIGURE 5-2

Source: From *Dancing Through Life in a Pair of Broken Heels* by Mickey and Cathy Guisewite. Used by permission of Bantam Books, a division of Dell Publishing Group, Inc.

minutes before guests were to arrive, I had to try and make the tail end of my salmon mousse look like a necktie, because my little Joey had eaten the head. Or the time he ate a container of Kentucky Fried Chicken including the box and receipt, but demonstrated extraordinary will-power by leaving the buttermilk biscuits completely untouched.

But I restrain myself. I say nothing. At age thirty-two I have no 8 children to go on and on about. But I do have a dog.

And soon enough I will have my chance to go on and on about 9 him, because we are operating on a basic principle of female friendship here: the one that guarantees equal time to blither on about the obsessions of our lives.

And so I sit patiently waiting for my turn. I lend a sympathetic ear 10 as my friend tells me about Madeline's little problem of roaming the house like a twenty-two-pound human vacuum cleaner, digesting every bug and hair ball that comes into her path. Why? Because soon I'll be describing Joey's little problem of being unable to greet visitors without torpedoing his six-inch nose directly into their crotches.

11   I politely wade through thirty-six nearly identical photos of her little Madeline throwing a tantrum on Santa's lap. Why? Because soon my friend will be politely wading through thirty-six nearly identical photos of my little Joey mutilating his Christmas reindeer antlers.

12   I thoughtfully nod my head up and down and grunt in the appropriate places as my friend describes the scene her daughter makes when she's dropped off at day care each morning. Why? Because soon she'll be doing the same for me when I describe the cute way my Joey sits completely depressed in the coat closet each morning to protest my leaving him.

13   I chuckle along as she— Wait a minute. According to the equal-time-for-blithering rule, we're heading into some serious overtime on the endearing little Madeline stories. I discreetly check my watch and note that forty-five minutes into our conversation, there has been no mention of my little Joey.

14   Has motherhood completely obliterated her memory of the equal time rule that has been one of the hallmarks of our friendship for fifteen years? Is my one-year-old somehow less important than her one-year-old because mine has four legs and hers has two? And more important, could her purse possibly accommodate any more photographs than the seventy-five I've already seen?

15   Just as I find myself drifting into a coma, I hear the word *Joey*.

16   "Joey?" I ask, snapping to attention.

17   "I was just saying how cute it is when our next door neighbor's son Joey plays with Madeline. Here, I've got some pictures of them in my purse..."

18   Oh for crying out loud, who cares! Is it not enough that I've pleasantly sat through fifty minutes of Madeline anecdotes and photos? Must I now fawn over another one-year-old I don't even know to prove I'm a loyal friend? Will the conversation **ever** turn to my Joey? The cute Joey? The Joey with hair??

19   And even if it does, do I care to tell her? Would my friend think I'm completely crazy for believing that a dog capable of eating rotting pot roast remains out of the garbage somehow prefers his dog food warmed in the microwave? Would she think I'm absolutely nuts for insisting he was merely demonstrating his highly cultivated taste in footwear when he chose to destroy my Italian designer boots instead of the $12.00 sneakers sitting right next to them?

20   Certainly no more of a nut than I think she is for dreaming that when her daughter bangs aimlessly on their piano, the child is well on her way to becoming the next Vladimir Horowitz.

It's becoming quite clear to me that while motherhood may be uni- 21
versal, talking about it does not transcend species. And so if she ever
happens to ask about my Joey, I won't even tell her. I'll just nod and say
fine and that will be the—

"So, how's Joey?" 22

"Joey?...My Joey?" 23

"Yeah. How's your dog?" 24

Well, maybe just one picture...No, two...No, she must see all 25
ninety-seven photos, and hear the fascinating anecdote that accompanies each.

I hear a stifled yawn. Almost like magic, her eyes glaze over, and I 26
know she's my captive audience for the next sixty minutes. But then,
isn't that what friends are for?

✦ Questions for Discussion and Writing

1. How would you characterize the tone of this essay in terms of the writer's attitude toward the events and experiences she describes? What
   verbal cues create your sense of her "voice"?

2. Why does Mickey Guisewite allow her audience to believe, for a short
   time, that "her Joey" is a child too? How does delaying this information allow the audience to understand the double standard she protests, albeit humorously?

3. How do the connotations of terms used to describe Joey differ from
   those used to describe Madeline? What implied value judgments do
   these descriptions contain?

4. What unspoken assumptions governing friendship explain why the
   writer is getting so agitated? To what extent are these the same expectations that guide your friendships?

5. How does the humor of this essay ultimately depend on the writer's
   own self-mockery as she becomes aware that she can't resist talking
   about Joey and that Carol now feels just the way she felt earlier when
   Madeline was the center of the discussion?

6. Have you had an experience similar to this with a friend? Were you
   aware at the time of the unspoken rules of reciprocity governing who
   gets to talk about what for how long? What did your friend talk about,
   and what did you want to talk about?

7. To see how connotations shape tone, try writing about a recent experience, using language that conveys one of the following emotions:
   anxiety, blissfulness, envy, ecstasy, boredom, being turned on, determination, paranoia, surprise.

Dave Barry

Just Say No to Rugs

◆

Dave Barry is a Pulitzer Prize–winning author whose essays appear in the Miami Herald *and other newspapers and magazines. At his acerbic best as court jester to the nation, Barry punctures illusions, many of which turn out to be his own. This essay is reprinted from* Dave Barry Talks Back, *with illustrations by Jeff MacNelly, 1991.*

1 Everybody should have a pet. And I'm not saying this just because the American Pet Council gave me a helicopter. I'm also saying it because my family has always owned pets, and without them, our lives would not be nearly so rich in—call me sentimental, but this is how I feel—dirt.

2 Pets are nature's way of reminding us that, in the incredibly complex ecological chain of life, there is no room for furniture. For example, the only really nice furnishing we own is an Oriental rug that we bought, with the help of a decorator, in a failed attempt to become tasteful. This rug is way too nice for an onion-dip–intensive household like ours, and we seriously thought about keeping it in a large safe-deposit box, but we finally decided, in a moment of abandon, to put it on the floor. We there conducted a comprehensive rug-behavior training seminar for our main dog, Earnest, and our small auxiliary dog, Zippy.

3 "NO!!" we told them approximately 75 times while looking very stern and pointing at the rug. This proven training technique caused them to slink around the way dogs do when they feel tremendously guilty but have no idea why. Satisfied, we went out to dinner.

4 I later figured out, using an electronic calculator, that this rug covers approximately 2 percent of the total square footage of our house, which means that if you (not you *personally*) were to have a random diarrhea attack in our home, the odds are approximately 49 to 1 against your having it on our Oriental rug. The odds against your having *four* random attacks on this rug are more than *five million to one*. So we had to conclude that it was done on purpose. The rug appeared to have been visited by a group of specially bred, highly trained Doberman Poopers, but we determined, by interrogating both dogs, that the entire massive output was the work of Zippy. Probably he was trying to do the right thing. Probably, somewhere in the Coco Puff–sized nodule of

FIGURE 5-3
Source: Jeff MacNelly.

nerve tissue that serves as his brain, he dimly remembered that The Masters had told him *something about the rug.* Yes! That's it! *To the rug!*

At least Zippy had the decency to feel bad about what he did, which is more than you can say for Mousse, a dog that belonged to a couple named Mike and Sandy. Mousse was a Labrador retriever, which is a large enthusiastic bulletproof species of dog made entirely from synthetic materials. This is the kind of dog that, if it takes an interest in your personal regions (which of course it does) you cannot fend it off with a blowtorch.   5

So anyway, Mike and Sandy had two visitors who wore expensive, brand-new down-filled parkas, which somehow got left for several hours in a closed room with Mousse. When the door was finally opened, the visibility in the room had been drastically reduced by a raging down storm, at the center of which was a large quivering down clot, looking like a huge mutant duckling, except that it had Mousse's radiantly happy eyes.   6

7   For several moments Mike and Sandy and their guests stared at this apparition, then Mike, a big, strong, highly authoritative guy, strode angrily into the room and slammed the door. He was in there for several minutes, then emerged, looking very serious. The down clot stood behind him, wagging its tail cheerfully.

8   "I talked to Mousse," Mike said, "and he says he didn't do it."

9   People often become deranged by pets. Derangement is the only possible explanation for owning a cat, an animal whose preferred mode of communication is to sink its claws three-quarters of an inch into your flesh. God help the cat owner who runs out of food. It's not uncommon to see an elderly woman sprinting through the supermarket with one or more cats clinging, leechlike, to her leg as she tries desperately to reach the pet-food section before collapsing from blood loss.

10   Of course for sheer hostility in a pet, you can't beat a parrot. I base this statement on a parrot I knew named Charles who belonged to a couple named Ed and Ginny. Charles had an IQ of 260 and figured out early in life that if he talked to people, they'd get close enough so he could bite them. He especially liked to bite Ed, whom Charles wanted to drive out of the marriage so he could have Ginny, the house, the American Express card, etc. So in an effort to improve their relationship, Ginny hatched (ha ha!) this plan wherein Ed took Charles to—I am not making this up—Parrot Obedience School. Every Saturday morning, Ed and Charles would head off to receive expert training, and every Saturday afternoon Ed would come home with chunks missing from his arm. Eventually Ginny realized that it was never going to work, so she got rid of Ed.

11   I'm just kidding, of course. Nobody would take Ed. Ginny got rid of Charles, who now works as a public-relations adviser to Miss Zsa Zsa Gabor. So we see that there are many "pluses" to having an "animal friend," which is why you should definitely buy a pet. If you act right now, we'll also give you a heck of a deal on a rug.

✦ Questions for Discussion and Writing

1. How does Barry's self-deprecating tone make his own unrealistic expectations about his dog project a sense of irony?

2. How are Barry's aspirations toward having higher social class values negated by his dogs?

3. Why are the metaphors with which Barry describes his dogs funny?

4. How does the contrast between Barry's references to training techniques, calculators, and statistics as well as the metaphors applied to

the dogs create an ideal of control of his environment that is undercut by the uncontrollable behavior of the dogs?

5. How does Barry use anthropomorphizing to enhance the humor of the situation?

6. To what extent have your pet-related experiences helped you see, or prevented you from seeing, the humor in this piece?

James Finn Garner

Little Red Riding Hood

———◆———

James Finn Garner's satires have appeared in the Chicago Tribune Magazine. *He is a performer who is regularly heard on Chicago public radio. This hilarious send-up of a classic children's story is reprinted from his best-selling work* Politically Correct Bedtime Stories, 1994.

1   There once was a young person named Red Riding Hood who lived with her mother on the edge of a large wood. One day her mother asked her to take a basket of fresh fruit and mineral water to her grandmother's house—not because this was womyn's work, mind you, but because the deed was generous and helped engender a feeling of community. Furthermore, her grandmother was *not* sick, but rather was in full physical and mental health and was fully capable of taking care of herself as a mature adult.

2   So Red Riding Hood set off with her basket through the woods. Many people believed that the forest was a foreboding and dangerous place and never set foot in it. Red Riding Hood, however, was confident enough in her own budding sexuality that such obvious Freudian imagery did not intimidate her.

3   On the way to Grandma's house, Red Riding Hood was accosted by a wolf, who asked her what was in her basket. She replied, "Some healthful snacks for my grandmother, who is certainly capable of taking care of herself as a mature adult."

4   The wolf said, "You know, my dear, it isn't safe for a little girl to walk through these woods alone."

5   Red Riding Hood said, "I find your sexist remark offensive in the extreme, but I will ignore it because of your traditional status as an outcast from society, the stress of which has caused you to develop your own, entirely valid, worldview. Now, if you'll excuse me, I must be on my way."

6   Red Riding Hood walked on along the main path. But, because his status outside society had freed him from slavish adherence to linear, Western-style thought, the wolf knew a quicker route to Grandma's house. He burst into the house and ate Grandma, an entirely valid course of action for a carnivore such as himself. Then, unhampered by rigid, traditionalist notions of what was masculine or feminine, he put on Grandma's nightclothes and crawled into bed.

Red Riding Hood entered the cottage and said, "Grandma, I have   7
brought you some fat-free, sodium-free snacks to salute you in your
role of a wise and nurturing matriarch."

From the bed, the wolf said softly, "Come closer, child, so that I   8
might see you."

Red Riding Hood said, "Oh, I forgot you are as optically chal-   9
lenged as a bat. Grandma, what big eyes you have!"

"They have seen much, and forgiven much, my dear."   10

"Grandma, what a big nose you have—only relatively, of course,   11
and certainly attractive in its own way."

"It has smelled much, and forgiven much, my dear."   12

"Grandma, what big teeth you have!"   13

The wolf said, "I am happy with *who* I am and *what* I am," and   14
leaped out of bed. He grabbed Red Riding Hood in his claws, intent on
devouring her. Red Riding Hood screamed, not out of alarm at the
wolf's apparent tendency toward cross-dressing, but because of his
willful invasion of her personal space.

Her screams were heard by a passing woodchopper-person (or log-   15
fuel technician, as he preferred to be called). When he burst into the
cottage, he saw the melee and tried to intervene. But as he raised his ax,
Red Riding Hood and the wolf both stopped.

"And just what do you think you're doing?" asked Red Riding   16
Hood.

The woodchopper-person blinked and tried to answer, but no   17
words came to him.

"Bursting in here like a Neanderthal, trusting your weapon to do   18
your thinking for you!" she exclaimed. "Sexist! Speciesist! How dare
you assume that womyn and wolves can't solve their own problems
without a man's help!"

When she heard Red Riding Hood's impassioned speech, Grand-   19
ma jumped out of the wolf's mouth, seized the woodchopper-person's
ax, and cut his head off. After this ordeal, Red Riding Hood, Grandma,
and the wolf felt a certain commonality of purpose. They decided to set
up an alternative household based on mutual respect and cooperation,
and they lived together in the woods happily ever after.

✦ *Questions for Discussion and Writing*

1. How does the humor of this updated fable depend on the audience's
   being able to recognize Garner's satire of the phenomenon of revising
   history in such a way as to be politically correct? How does this project
   depend on overlaying modern-day sensitivities to the effect of words
   that imply prejudice based on ethnic, sexual, social, or racial differences onto works written before these concepts were invented?

2. Where can you see Garner revising words that may suggest a sexual bias or language that stereotypes men and women in terms of outdated roles?

3. How does the humor of Garner's updated version of the story derive from his scrupulous and elaborate verbal contortions to avoid using phrases that might be offensive or insulting?

4. What might you infer to be Garner's attitude toward the assumptions underlying the political correctness movement or the extremes to which its proponents will go to substitute gender-neutral terms for words and phrases now found to be objectionable?

5. In your opinion, has the attempt to avoid sexual, racist, agist, and species stereotyping reached the ridiculous extremes satirized by Garner (for example, spelling woman so that the word "man" does not appear)? Or do you think that the attempt to revise the use of language to avoid subtle and overt stereotyping is worthwhile?

Joe Bob Briggs

The Lesbo Boom

———————◆———————

Joe Bob Briggs is the pen name of John Bloom, a humorist who lampoons cultural trends in the time-honored tradition of Jonathan Swift, Mark Twain, Oscar Wilde, and Ambrose Bierce. Through his invented persona the author spoofs the extremism of activists championing alternative life styles. This satire first appeared in Iron Joe Bob, 1992.

I first noticed the Lesbo Boom about five years ago. Actually, it started out when women started talking about their "biological clocks" all the time. I know this has nothing to do, per se, ipso facto, dipsy doodle, with lesbianism, but hang with me a minute, and I'll explain it. 1

It started when Wanda Bodine told me that since she's so fat, she might as well get pregnant. It would be a good time to do it, she said, especially since she has her law degree now and so she'd be able to figure out how to dump that baby in day care after two, three weeks and force somebody else to pay for it. 2

"My biological clock has done run around the dial three times," is the way she put it. 3

None of this babbling about being pregnant bothered me, particularly, until she started rubbing up against me in the line at Wyatt's Cafeteria and saying stuff like "I just bought a new Posturepedic and pretty soon I'll have money for sheets." 4

Then it occurred to me—she's gonna need a *male individual* to carry this off. 5

I don't know if you've ever met any of the Bodine sisters, but they get em a husband for five, six weeks, use him long enough to plant some seeds where it counts, and then tell him "You, Dwayne, are not fulfilling my potential as a modern woman, you never pick up your socks, and we have nothing in common." 6

Course, by then they do have something in common. Dwayne just doesn't find out till seven months later when she calls him up about "sharing the expenses of our child." 7

I never did understand this until Wanda and her sister Doreen explained it to me one night. I was thinking all my life all a woman wanted was a man she could manipulate into marrying her. What they really want is a man they can manipulate into giving em *babies*. I thought it was *husbands* they wanted, but it's *babies*. This is the thing for the woman of the nineties. Get rid of that turkey just as soon as he's 8

263

done the *one job* in the poor sucker's life that he can't get fired from, then boot his hiney out of there before he does something stupid like *admit he's the father.* That gets you into all kinds of legal problems like being forced to run the kid out to his house on weekends when you don't have a date.

9   Anyhow, the Bodine sisters have had nine babies now—and they're all named Bodine except for little Raul. They call him "Raul Bodino" because nobody'd believe it if you called him plain Bodine. So I think you can see what's going on here. The only reason I bring it up is that I don't give a flip, personally, I know how to protect my personal integrity in the Wyatt's Cafeteria line and not go ape just cause some 260-pound baby-making machine flashes a little thigh while she's shoving a tray full of lemon meringue through the check-out line, but many of you reading this book might not have ever met the Bodine sisters and so when Wanda shows up, you'll be dead meat. After all, she's *real* good looking for a gal that looks like she oughta have an apple in her mouth.

10   Okay, so that's the story on the Bodine sisters, and about five years ago I first started writing about em and pointing out how Wanda and Doreen no longer marry the men they choose to breed with. But when I was writing about this, I thought this was a *new thing*, invented by the Bodine sisters so they could treat men like old dirty dishrags, score some sperm from us, and then hoist our hineys into the street before we know what we've hatched. All these women are *panicked* about their goldurn biological clock turning their fallopian tubes into a pumpkin.

11   Anyhow, some friends of mine out in California started sending me these articles about the "lesbian baby boom." Maybe you're not familiar with the lesbian baby boom. At first I thought it was true what we've thought all along: people in California came here from another planet, and all the people born there since World War II are space-alien science experiments that divide like amoebas. Either that or else all these lesbians have been having a lot of sex with one another and trying *real* hard.

12   But it turns out that the lezzies are showing up at the sperm bank and saying "Gimme one of them test tubes with some of that icky stuff in it that *men* have." And then they get em a lesbo sex partner to frizz up her hair like Anne Murray, and they figure that when the little frog-faced booger is born, he'll never know the difference. They can name him something like Jeremiah—nope, too sexist—how about Noah?—nope, they'd laugh at him when he goes to Montessori School. I've got it! Jessie! Could be a boy. Could be a girl. The perfect name for the kid who's gonna wake up one day and think, "You know, there seem to be way too many sets of panty hose around this house."

13   This stuff is great, though. Soon as I heard about it, I ran over to tell Wanda that all she needs is Artificial Spermatization. "You know," I

told her, "it's like they do with racehorses. You want Secretariat's genes? The vet takes some of them Secretariat genes, sticks em in a hypo, and then he makes sure they get to their destination. Eleven months later, Secretariat doesn't know *which one* belongs to him. It's the exact same thing with humans, only you need to start you out on a strong lesbian relationship in order to give the resulting Bodine child a strong and supportive environment."

"I don't need a lesbian," she said. "I got Doreen around the house all day."   14

"Doreen doesn't count. Your own sister? That would be perverted!"   15

"Oh," Wanda said.   16

Anyway, you probly know where this is leading. You've probly read about it already. From that point forward I became fascinated with the Lesbo Movement, and I stayed hot on the trail of every new lesbian trend, right up until I attended the National Lesbian Conference in the summer of 1991.   17

By the way. I wanna thank everyone for the cards, letters, flowers, and telegrams you sent me during those long few weeks while I was recuperating at Parkland Hospital in Dallas.   18

In retrospect, I *knew* I shouldn't have attended the National Lesbian Conference. You warned me. You told me to stay away. Even Wanda Bodine tried to protect me. She said, "Joe Bob, you ever seen what a two-hundred-and-fifty-pound woman with a burr haircut can do to the human pelvis?"   19

But I told her, "Wanda, I'm a reporter. I've got to check these things out."   20

And so I volunteered to go to the big convention in Atlanta with the Texas delegation. After all, I told em, with that many women in one bus, who was gonna *drive?*   21

That was when I got the first sprained elbow from being sat on by Wendy "the Mattress" Stubbs. She put her knees between my shoulder blades and twisted my arm and wouldn't let go until I yelled "Aunt!"   22

A couple days later I showed up with my notebook and tape recorder at the Handicapped Jewish Lesbian Caucus. They weren't gonna let me in, so I faked the guards out by putting on a dress and riding in a motorized wheelchair and saying the word *schlemiel* a lot. I had one of those little black beanies on my head, which is what gave me away, because I didn't realize that handicapped Jewish lesbians don't wear those little black beanies.   23

This one-armed woman named Shirley Steinberg challenged me. She said, "You're not *Jewish.* No self-respecting lesbian Jew would wear a yammakuller like that."   24

And I tried to fake it. I said, "Well, I realize that, but I thought that since Jewish *men* get to wear em, it was only right that Jewish *women* who *look like men* should get to wear em, too..."   25

26   And she was about to buy this when she noticed I was wearing a pink chiffon taffeta party dress from J. C. Penney's, and she said, "I don't even think you're a lesbian."

27   And I couldn't *believe* I'd done that. *Of course.* I should have worn a polyester pants suit. I could of got away with the whole deal.

28   Anyway, that's how I got the multiple rib fractures, from being kicked out the door by three ladies named Frank, Steve, and Mumbles the Molester.

29   I don't know if you read much about the convention, but it got really interesting around the third day, when all the lesbos started beating one another up. The Elderly Lesbians got mad at the Lesbian Avocado Farmers, and the Lesbians of Color got ticked off because there weren't enough Puerto Rican–Arab Lesbians admitted to the convention floor, and then some Overeating Lesbians who were dressed up in black leather *Star Trek* costumes ambushed some Lesbian Marines and crushed one gal's skull for being a tool of the imperialist American military forces. And then, of course, there was the Dykes on Bikes circus act that had to be canceled because the unicycles they were using were made at a factory in Poland that discriminates against lesbian porpoise trainers.

30   Finally, on the last day of the convention, I managed to get inside by wearing my normal clothes but passing myself off as an eighteen-year-old girl who had taken a *lot* of steroids. *It worked!* I should have done this right from the beginning.

31   And so, when I finally got a firsthand look at what was going on, they were having a debate between the representative of Native American Lesbians, Babs Stumbling Buffalo, and the representative of the Radical African-American Nuclear-War-Now Lesbians of Inner Detroit, whose name was Mahogany Sims. And they were yelling and screaming at one another. Babs was claiming that the American Indian male was the most disgusting, sexist, no-good, abusive sorry excuse for a human being in the universe. But Mahogany said that, no, if you'd ever met her second ex-husband Kaleem "the Scream" Akim, then you would know that she had no choice but to chop his body into thirty-seven pieces and mail him to Armour Beef in Chicago. And when Mahogany mentioned actual *crimes*, that set off the United Lesbian Convicts Who Shouldn't Have Gone to Prison Except Some Worthless Man Sold Drugs in Their House, and they started chanting "Free all lesbian prisoners! Free all lesbian prisoners!"

32   And so I felt the situation was about to get out of hand—call me an idiot, but I decided to step in—and so I asked for permission to speak, and, after everybody quieted down, I stood up and I said, "Y'all would feel a whole lot better if you'd take two Midol."

33   That's how I got the brain injuries.

They say, with physical therapy, I could have a normal life again   34
within two or three years.

Now, right after I went to the lesbo convention that summer, even *be-*   35
fore I was fully recovered, I started reporting on my lesbian experiences
in various American newspapers. And some of the lesbos did *not* like it.

They are Woman, hear them roar.   36

So I'd like to take this opportunity to apologize to the lesbos of   37
America for any remarks they considered vile and degrading. They
were not intended in that spirit.

Evidently there were some lesbians in San Francisco and Aspen   38
who wrote in to the paper demanding that I be strapped into a leather
corset and flogged with a punji stick. Of course, when they found out
this is one of my secret fantasies, they withdrew the offer.

Let there be no mistake about it. I respect the right of lesbians to do   39
any disgusting thing they want to with their bodies and/or farm imple-
ments. After all, this is America. In fact, I would like to make the following public statements, for the benefit of those lesbians who were
offended:

1. I am opposed to the random killing, mutilation, and torture of
   women, unless it's necessary to the plot.
2. Your body belongs to you, except when you sell it.
3. Martina Navratilova is my favorite Romanian.
4. I didn't mean to imply that all lesbians look like men. After all,
   some men wear dresses.
5. Many of the lesbos who wrote in said I shouldn't be abbreviat-
   ing "lesbians" with the term "lesbos." I was merely using the ancient Greek term, which originated on the Isle of Lesbos, home
   of Sappho and other important bohemian females. Since the
   modern lesbian movement seems to have forgotten this, I will
   no longer use either "lesbo" or the corrupt Latin term "lesbian,"
   but the more neutral Mesopotamian term for any woman of this
   persuasion: Naugahyde Sofa Woman.
6. I think Birkenstock sandals are extremely attractive on a size
   14 foot.
7. Several of the professional...er...Naugahyde Sofa Women—
   sorry, but it'll take a while for me to get used to it—several of
   these people wrote in to say that there were certain jokes that
   just should *not* be made about...uh...*those people,* and that anyone who would make those jokes should be banned from print.
   Up till now, there have only been two groups that continually
   argue for actually *removing* unpopular opinions from newspapers and TV—the fundamentalists and the feminists. So I need
   clarification. Is this a *branch* of the feminists, or should we create

a third category? But if you gals have been meeting with the Reverend Donald Wildmon and the Americans for Decency to discuss strategies for getting rid of me, I would like to see a transcript and a seating chart. I'll pay up to $24.95.

8. I read the book *The White Goddess,* even the footnotes in Welsh, and I agree that we should all worship the One Great Big-Breasted Earth Mother. In my dreams her name is Monique.

9. The public image of lesbians is all wrong. Most people think of them as big fat razor-headed snarling wolf-women in biker jackets with hairy armpits and stinky flabby arms. This is completely unfair. Most of them look like Helen Reddy.

10. I'm thinking of becoming a lesbian myself. It's a nineties thing.

40   I hope this has cleared up the misunderstanding.

✦ Questions for Discussion and Writing

1. How does the depiction of the Bodine sisters depend on a reversal of assumptions?

2. How does Briggs use caricature or parody in his depiction of the "plan" that will allow lesbians to have babies and raise them in nontraditional households?

3. How would you characterize the narrator? In what way does his perspective reflect the collision of a much older traditional set of expectations with new social and biological possibilities? Do you detect any clues that suggest that the author John Bloom is making the persona of "Joe Bob Briggs" so extreme as a way of caricaturing the viewpoint he represents (as Jonathan Swift does with the speaker in "A Modest Proposal")?

4. Why is the issue of freedom of speech and the First Amendment alluded to at the end of this essay? How does it serve to define the real issue of the preceding essay as a question of whether views like this should be allowed to appear in print? Can you make a case for why or why not depictions of alternative lifestyles should be the object of satire?

5. As a class, look closely at the preceding essays by Guisewite, Barry, Garner, and Briggs and try to identify each writer's strategy for connecting with his or her audience's experiences, background, knowledge, and concerns. For each essay, compile a class list of the strengths and weaknesses of each writer's attempt to connect with the audience. Use this list as a basis for your own critique and evaluation of any two of the essays.

Language and Persuasion

"And the Lord said: 'go to, let us go down, and there confound their language, that they may not understand one another's speech.'"

—Genesis 11:7

LANGUAGE SHAPES THOUGHT

Language clearly has an influence on our beliefs and actions. Those who have an interest in persuading us to believe or buy something are quite skillful in using language to persuade. Thus, if we are more aware of how others, including politicians and advertisers, use language to manipulate our behavior, the less likely it becomes that we can be deceived into acting against our own best interests.

Emotionally Charged Language

Emotionally charged language is a principal means by which language affects perceptions. Basically, emotive language is designed to elicit certain feelings in an audience.

For example, imagine you saw your three-year-old child playing next to the stove, in danger of tipping over a pan of boiling water. Consider how different your reactions would sound using nonemotive language and emotive language to express your concern:

> Please get away from the stove. It is dangerous to play near the stove when something is cooking. You might get burned.

> My God, you're going to get burned! Get away from there!

Or consider the difference in impact of a factual and an emotive account of the same event:

> Rutgers wins over Penn State

> Rutgers clobbers Penn State

The sports page abounds with accounts of one team *shooting down, jolting, blasting, mauling, bombing,* or *outslugging* another team. Sportswriters purposely choose verbs that will produce the most dramatic effect, such as "the Devils submerge the Penguins." The feelings evoked in the reader are as important as the scores of the games.

Connotations of Words

The connotations of words are often far more persuasive than their explicit or primary meanings. For example, *home* connotes qualities of security, comfort, affection, and caring that ultimately are far more persuasive in influencing perception than the simple denotative meaning of the word.

In the hands of a skilled writer, connotations can be used to arouse positive or negative emotions toward the subject. For example, think of the different feelings you would have about the following subjects depending on which words the writer used:

Youthful offender instead of *juvenile delinquent*

Perspire instead of *sweat*

Sanitation engineers instead of *garbage collectors*

Pass away instead of *die*

Full-figured instead of *fat*

Celebrities often change their names to avoid negative connotations or to elicit positive associations from audiences. To see how this works, compare the person's real name with his or her stage name:

Frances Gumm	Judy Garland
Marion Morrison	John Wayne
Leonard Slye	Roy Rogers
Henry John Deutschendorf, Jr.	John Denver
Issur Danielovitch Demsky	Kirk Douglas
Doris Kappelhoff	Doris Day
Archibald Leach	Cary Grant
Robert Zimmerman	Bob Dylan
Steveland Judkins Morris	Stevie Wonder
Marvin Lee Aday	Meat Loaf
Reginald Kenneth Dwight	Elton John

So, too, advertisers spend considerable time, money, and effort in formulating brand names for products that are designed to trigger favorable connotations. The fashion and cosmetics industries take great care in naming their products. Plain brown carpeting might be marketed as Coffee Buff, Berber Beige, or Plantation Amber. Likewise, red lipstick might be marketed under the brand names Red Hot and Blue, Fire and Ice, or Roseberry. In automotive advertising, car names play an important role in manipulating the emotions of the car-buying public. To appeal to the need for status, cars are named Regal, Le Baron, and Grand Marquis. To conjure up places where the wealthy congregate, cars are named Riviera, Capri, Monte Carlo, and Fifth Avenue. To evoke feelings of freedom, uninhibited expression, and power, cars take on real and mythological animal names, such as Skyhawk, Mustang, Cougar, AMC Eagle, Firebird, and Thunderbird.

Sometimes brand names can take on unintended negative connotations, especially when product names are translated into other languages to be marketed in other countries. Occasionally the original English name takes on entirely different connotations in a different culture. For example, in "What's In a Name?" (*Big Business Blunders* [1983]), David A. Ricks points out that Ford's Pinto was introduced in Brazil under its English name. After Ford discovered that Pinto in Portuguese slang meant "a small male appendage," the company changed the car's name to Corcel (*horse* in Portuguese). In another case, a foreign company introduced its chocolate concoction with the unappetizing English name of Zit. To avoid such negative connotations, companies often conduct extensive research to produce names like Kodak and Exxon that can be pronounced but have no specific meanings in any language.

Euphemisms

Euphemism comes from Greek ("to speak well of" or "to use words of good omen"). Originally these words were used to placate the gods.

Euphemistic language is used to smooth things over, present activities in a more favorable light, and make things seem better than they are. More commonly, euphemisms are used to avoid taboo subjects. For example, in ancient Greece, baby boys were encouraged to call their genitals their "kokko," their "laloo," or their "lizard." Roman nannies taught little girls to call their genitals their "piggy." In the nineteenth century, Victorians used a wide range of euphemisms to avoid explicit references to sex, birth, and bodily functions. Trousers were called "unmentionables," sexual organs became "private parts," and the birth of a baby became the arrival of "the little stranger" or "the patter of tiny feet."

Today, poverty has replaced sex and bodily functions as a taboo subject. The result of using euphemisms to disguise reality was the point of a 1965 Jules Feiffer cartoon, quoted in *Safire's Political Dictionary* (1978), which read

> I used to think I was poor. Then they told me I wasn't poor, I was needy. They told me it was self-defeating to think of myself as needy, I was deprived. Then they told me underprivileged was overused. I was disadvantaged. I still don't have a dime. But I have a great vocabulary.

A principal subject of euphemisms is death, whose implacable reality has been skirted by such phrases as the following:

> to go to a better place, just reward, with God, cash in one's chips, to pop off, to croak, cross over, go to the hereafter, join one's ancestors,

meet the grim reaper, go to the last roundup, bite the dust, pass out of the picture, slip away

In fact, the systematic use of language to mask the reality of death has been the subject of satiric novels like Evelyn Waugh's *The Loved One* (1948) and exposés like Jessica Mitford's *The American Way of Death* (1963). In this profession, the word *coffin* has long since been displaced by the term *casket*, a shroud is called a "slumber robe," and the room in which the dead body is viewed is called the "slumber room" or the "reposing room."

We can see euphemism at work when the Russian government claims that it has eliminated prostitution while acknowledging that there are "priestesses of love," "night stalkers," "ladies of easy virtue," and "ladies who take tips" walking the streets of Moscow and other cities (*The Philadelphia Inquirer*, cited in *Quarterly Review of Doublespeak* [April 1987]). In all these cases, euphemisms are designed to foster favorable perceptions, or at least to neutralize unfavorable ones—as, for example, referring to abortion as "pregnancy reduction" (*Atlanta Constitution*, cited in *Quarterly Review of Doublespeak* [April 1988]).

✦ Questions for Discussion and Writing

1. Why are disabilities and impairments called challenges?

2. What are the connotations of the following terms, and how are they intended to alter perceptions?

   politically correct, new Right, liberal, pro-life, pro-choice

3. In a paragraph, discuss how the connotations of key terms in the next two examples are crucial in developing the author's ideas.

   a. Jones is now ready for casketing (this is the present participle of the verb "to casket"). In this operation his right shoulder should be depressed slightly "to turn the body a bit to the right and soften the appearance of lying flat on the back." Positioning the hands is a matter of importance and special rubber positioning blocks may be used. The hands should be cupped for a more life like, relaxed appearance. Proper placement of the body requires a delicate sense of balance. It should lie as high as possible in the casket, yet not so high that the lid, when lowered, will hit the nose. On the other hand, we are cautioned, placing the body too low "creates the impression that the body is in a box." Jones is next wheeled into the appointed slumber room where a few last touches may be added—his favorite pipe placed in his hand or, if he was a great reader, a book propped into position. (In the case of little Master Jones a Teddy bear may be clutched.) (Jessica Mitford, "Mortuary Solaces," from *The American Way of Death,* 1963.)

b. In their enthusiasm to forward a noble cause in a suspicious, nasty-minded world, naturists have been vigorous devisors of euphemism. *Naturist* has by now virtually ousted *nudist,* which itself could be supposed a sort of euphemism for *nakedist.* Lest the idea of a *naturist beach* seem too jolting to the conventional, naturists have come up with *free beach,* or *clothing-or-swimsuit-optional beach. Sunbathing* is popular as a disarming synonym for *nudism,* and among the *cognoscenti* no elbow nudge is needed to suggest how it differs from *sunning,* which is what you do with a bathing suit on. (Paul Fussell, "Taking It All Off in the Balkans," *GQ,* April 1987.)

4. Decipher the stated versus the implied meaning of the language of a classified ad for an apartment, job, or car, or a personal ad (e.g., cozy = small).

5. How are the connotations of key terms in the following intended to influence the audience's responses?

Ralph Ellison: "Some people are your relatives but others are your ancestors, and you choose the ones you want to have as ancestors. You create yourself out of those values."

Oscar Wilde: "The old believe everything. The middle aged suspect everything. The young know everything."

Virginia Woolf: "Women have served all these centuries as looking-glasses possessing the magic and delicious power of reflecting the figure of man at twice its natural size."

Adrienne Rich: "Abortion is violence: a deep, desperate violence inflicted by a woman upon, first of all, herself."

Jesse Jackson: "America is not like a blanket—one piece of unbroken cloth, the same color, the same texture, the same size. America is more like a quilt—many patches, many pieces, many colors, many sizes, all woven and held together by a common thread."

Alice Walker: "I think it pisses God off if you walk by the color purple in a field somewhere and don't notice it."

Slanting

Information that is edited to reflect a particular point of view is referred to as being *slanted.* Slanting can take the form of selecting facts to purposely mislead, quoting out of context, or presenting facts in a biased way. We might easily accept these biased characterizations without thinking them through. For example, *question-begging epithets* like *flaming liberal* or *arch conservative* attempt to slip value judgments past the reader disguised as objective descriptions.

Slanting can also result from apparently innocuous word choices, use of quotation marks around a word, or exclamation points that draw special attention!!!

People employ a subtle form of slanting when they use words like *nothing but, only, just, mere, little more than, nothing more than,* or some other disparaging qualifier. For example, "her speech was *mere* rhetoric," "he is *only* an adolescent," "she's *just* a freshman," or "she's *little more than* a secretary."

Labels that Stereotype

How a person or event is labeled influences the readers' or listeners' perception of what is being described. Labels can be damaging because they classify people in ways that stereotype or stigmatize. The label creates a stereotyped picture that portrays the person only in terms of a single trait. Perhaps the most dangerous thing about stereotypes is that they create a mind-set that makes it impossible to accept people as they really are. Stereotypes distort our perceptions and make it impossible to acknowledge experiences that conflict with the stereotype. Research shows that if your expectations about members of an entire group are shaped by a stereotyped view, you are more likely to disregard contradictory evidence in order to avoid giving up the stereotype.

Labels act as filters to screen out everything that does not confirm the stereotype. For example, let's say you were asked to complete any of the following statements:

Southerners are . . .	Easterners are. . . .
Texans are . . .	Hairdressers are . . .
Rock stars are . . .	Football players are . . .

Each completed statement reveals one of your attitudes or beliefs. If you were then asked to write down whatever experiences you have had that justify or explain this attitude, you might discover that your ideas are based much more on portrayals and labels conveyed by the media than on your own personal experiences.

One of the most interesting studies of how proper names (literally, how we are labeled) evoke stereotypes that operate without our being aware of them was conducted by Gordon W. Allport (*The Nature of Prejudice* [1954]):

Thirty photographs of college girls were shown on a screen to 150 students. The subjects rated the girls on a scale from one to five for *beauty, intelligence, character, ambition, general likability.* Two months later the same subjects were asked to rate the same photographs and fifteen additional ones (introduced to complicate the memory factor). This time five of the original photographs were given Jewish surnames (Cohen, Kantor, etc.), five Italian (Valenti, etc.), and five Irish (O'Brien, etc.); and the remaining girls were given names chosen from the signers of the Declaration of Independence and from the Social Register (Davis, Adams, Clark, etc.).

When Jewish names were attached to photographs there occurred the following changes in ratings:

decrease in liking
decrease in character
decrease in beauty
increase in intelligence
increase in ambition

For those photographs given Italian names there occurred:

decrease in liking
decrease in character
decrease in beauty
decrease in intelligence

Thus a mere proper name leads to prejudgments of personal attributes.

The unconscious assumptions triggered by students' names meant that each person was no longer perceived as a complete human being. The label set up expectations that would block any conflicting new information and make it probable that only information that could be interpreted to support the preconception would be believed. It is for these reasons that all labels designed to persuade us must be carefully identified and analyzed.

Sexist, Racist, and Agist Language

One form discriminatory labeling takes is sexist language, that is, any language that expresses a stereotyped attitude that presumes the inherent superiority of one sex over the other. As with other kinds of labeling, people placed in the devalued categories are, by definition, stigmatized and treated as less than fully human. Language can also discriminate by omission. For example, the way the English language has tended to make women seem invisible is addressed by Elaine Morgan in the opening chapter, "The Man-Made Myth," of her book *The Descent of Woman* (1972):

All this may sound like a mere linguist quibble or a piece of feminist petulance. If you stay with me, I hope to convince you it's neither. I believe the deeply rooted semantic confusion between "man" as a male and "man" as a species has been fed back into and vitiated a great deal of the speculation that goes on about the origins, development, and nature of the human race.

A very high proportion of the thinking on these topics is androcentric (male-centered) in the same way as pre-Copernican thinking was geocentric. It's just as hard for man to break the habit of thinking of himself as central to the species as it was to break the habit of thinking of himself as central to the universe. He sees himself quite unconsciously as the main line of evolution, with a female satellite revolving around him as the moon revolves around the earth. This not only causes him to overlook valuable clues to our ancestry, but sometimes leads him into making statements that are arrant and demonstrable nonsense.

The longer I went on reading his own books about himself, the more I longed to find a volume that would begin: "When the first ancestor of the human race descended from the trees, she had not yet developed the mighty brain that was to distinguish her so sharply from all other species...."

Of course, she was no more the first ancestor than he was—but she was no *less* the first ancestor, either. She was there all along, contributing half the genes to each succeeding generation. Most of the books forget about her for most of the time. They drag her onstage rather suddenly for the obligatory chapter on Sex and Reproduction, and then say: "All right, love, you can go now," while they get on with the real meaty stuff about the Mighty Hunter with his lovely new weapons and his lovely new straight legs racing across the Pleistocene plains. Any modifications in her morphology are taken to be imitations of the Hunter's evolution, or else designed solely for his delectation.

Casey Miller and Kate Swift suggest in *Words and Women* (1976) that the abbreviation *Miss* (from the seventh-century noun *mistress*) had evolved as a "means of distinguishing married from unmarried women." They believe it came into popular use as a way of supplying

> at least a modicum of information about a woman's sexual availability, and it applied not so subtle social pressure toward marriage by lumping single women with the young and inexperienced...[in this way] the needs of the patriarchy were served when a woman's availability for her primary role as helper and sexual partner was made an integral part of her identity—in effect, a part of her name.

The marriage-neutral term *Ms.* was introduced to remedy this problem. As Miller and Swift note, "the abbreviation Ms. has been around as a title of courtesy at least since the 1940's, but it was largely unused until two things happened: the growth of direct mail selling made the abbreviation an effective time and money saver, and a significant number of women began to object to being labeled to their (presumed) marital status."

The prospect of changing attitudes by changing language (or reflecting changed attitudes in new terminology) has resulted in the *The Government's Dictionary of Occupational Titles* (1977) replacing potentially discriminatory job titles with sex-neutral terms. For example, *telephone linemen* has been replaced by *telephone line installers, firemen* are now listed as *firefighters, airline stewardesses* are now *flight attendants,* and *policewoman* has become simply *police officer.*

Historically, stigmatization always precedes disenfranchisement. Haig A. Bosmajian in "Defining the American Indian" (*The Speech Teacher* [March 1973]) reminds us that "one of the first important acts of an oppressor is to redefine the oppressed victims he intends to jail or eradicate so that they will be looked upon as creatures warranting suppression and in some cases separation and annihilation."

Agist stereotypes, that is, the negative labels used to refer to old age, are as destructive as racist or sexist language. Referring to elderly women as *biddy* or *hag* or to elderly men as *codger, coot, geezer,* or *fogey,* fosters a conception of the elderly as senile, incapable of learning new things, and antiquated. These labels promote a notion of the elderly that makes it difficult for the young and middle-aged to identify with them as human beings. Agist language encourages discriminatory reactions toward the elderly and reinforces a negative self-image among older people. The mechanisms involved are identical to those of racism (based on differences in skin color) or sexism (based on differences in gender). As in these cases, the use of dehumanizing language paves the way for discounting the elderly and treating them as second-class citizens. This issue has been studied by Frank Nuessel in "Old Age Needs a New Name but Don't Look for It in Websters" (*Aging* [August/ September 1984]) who concludes that "in this regard the extensive, pejorative, and agist vocabulary of the English language constitutes a verbal record of this society's fear of getting old."

✦ *Questions for Discussion and Writing*

1. Formulate three short descriptions using neutral, negative, or positive adjectives for the postal service, the National Rifle Association, Greenpeace, the American Civil Liberties Union, the John Birch Society, the National Organization of Women, or any other defined association or organization.

2. Analyze any portion of a recent speech by a public official—an assemblyperson, mayor, governor, or presidential candidate—to see whether

it reveals the presence of slanting, labeling, stereotyping, or guilt or virtue by association.

3. Stereotyping by gender, race, age.

   a. What common labels for men and women rely on metaphors associated with food, pets, or plants? What attitudes do these labels promote; for example, calling someone "buttercup," "cupcake," "you dog"?

   b. Keep a log for a few days of television programs. To what extent do prime-time programs stereotype women, minorities, or old people?

4. How does the editorial cartoon in Figure 5-4 address the issue of stereotyping and self-image?

FIGURE 5-4

Source: Barbara Brandon, copyright Universal Press Syndicate. Used with permission.

Words that Create Images

The ability to create compelling images in picturesque language is an important element in communicating a writer's thoughts, feelings, and experiences. For example, consider how picturesque terms are often used by wine experts to describe different kinds of wines. A wine might be said to be *robust* or *mellow* or *round*; a beaujolais might be described as "witty" or "an amusing little wine" or "a delightful wine."

The way a writer chooses to describe something expresses an opinion that is capable of persuading an audience. In the following description of London, H. G. Wells selects details that reinforce the dominant impression he has of the city, organizes these details in terms of his main impression, and creates a vivid word picture that allows the reader to see the city as Wells does: "London, like a bowl of viscid human fluid, boils sullenly over the rim of its encircling hills and slops messily and uglily into the home counties."

Notice how Wells's description of London's urban sprawl relies on words whose emotive effect is enhanced by his skillful use of picturesque language. The fact that Wells does not make a formal claim does not lessen the impact of this description. The word picture itself expresses his opinion. Or consider how Fred Allen's opinion of Hollywood is strengthened by the unusual image he creates: "You can take all the sincerity in Hollywood, place it in the navel of a fruit fly, and still have room enough for three caraway seeds and a producer's heart."

Creating a vivid picture or image in an audience's mind requires writers to use metaphors, similes, and other figures of speech. Imagery works by evoking a vivid picture in the audience's imagination. A simile compares one object or experience to another using *like* or *as*. For example, if you wrote that "on a trip home the train was crowded and the passengers were packed in like sardines," your audience would be expected to understand the idea rather than literally assume you were accompanied by sardines in the train. A metaphor applies a word or phrase to an object it does not literally denote in order to suggest the comparison. Thus, if you looked into the crowded train and yelled, "Hey, you sardines," most people on the train would know what you meant.

To be effective, metaphors must look at things in a fresh light to let the reader see a familiar subject in a new way. As George Orwell observed in *Politics and the English Language* (1946), "the sole aim of a metaphor is to call up a visual image." When they are first conceived, metaphors can call up pictures in the mind, but worn-out metaphors lack the power to summon these images. What is meant by an effective metaphor can be illustrated by two short descriptions drawn from Henry Allen's "The Corps" (*The Washington Post* [March 1972]). In describing the Marine Corps drill instructors at the marine boot camp, Parris Island, South Carolina, Allen notes "the wry ferocity drill instructors cultivate, the squinted eyes and the mouth about as generous as a snapping turtle's, and the jut-jawed arrogance of their back-of-the throat voices."

Of one particularly feared drill instructor, Allen writes, "He is seething, he is rabid, he is wound up tight as a golf ball, with more adrenalin surging through his hypothalmus than any corner slum rat." And of the new recruits, Allen comments, "fat and forlorn, they look like 60 sex perverts trapped by a lynch mob."

✦ *Questions for Discussion and Writing*

1. How might you complete any of the following, using positive or negative analogies to persuade an audience of the benefits or disadvantages of the proposed action? Develop the thought as an extended analogy that expresses your feelings. Add the phrase "is like" after each of the topics you choose.

   a. Moving to an unfamiliar city is like_____.

   b. Finding an apartment

   c. Screening roommates

   d. Driving cross country

   e. Backpacking through Europe

   f. Attending a fraternity or sorority party

   g. Mastering the language of the classified ads for rentals, cars, personals, help wanted

   h. Making up your own personal ad to meet someone to date or a classified ad to sell something

   i. Moving back home

   j. Defrosting the freezer

   k. Sleep deprivation

   l. Living together before marriage

   m. Furnishing your apartment

   n. Writing your resume

   o. Being interviewed for a job

   p. Being hired as a temp

   q. Getting letters of rejection

   r. Personalizing your office cube, dorm room, etc.

   s. Faxing

   t. Using e-mail

   u. Fixing the copy machine

   v. Taking a vacation with/without your family

   w. Having your best friend get married

   x. Attending a potluck dinner party

   y. Going on a blind date

   z. Attending a high culture event (ballet, symphony, opera)

   aa. Bungee-jumping

Slang

"I have seen the future and it is slang."
—Eric Overmeyer, *On the Verge* (1986)

A particularly vivid, playful, and ephemeral form of picturesque language is called *slang*. Slang does not take itself seriously and expresses itself in down-to-earth, direct idioms. Many slang expressions use picturesque language metaphorically. For example, consider the range of terms used to describe drinking too much:

> blitzed, bombed, blotto, zonked, plastered, tanked, embalmed, sauced, juiced, corked, shellacked, hung over, tight, tipsy, smashed

How slang is created can be seen in the origin of the term *hype* (hyping a movie, product, book). The term originated as a turn-of-the-century abbreviation for a hypodermic needle. *Hype* gradually lost its connection with an actual hypodermic needle but retained the idea of injecting or infusing. Today it refers to artificially stimulated public relations phenomena designed to generate publicity and sales.

Clichés

Words that through overuse lose their power to evoke concrete images become clichés. A cliché is a trite, time-worn expression or outworn phrase that has become commonplace or lost its freshness. Initially, each of the following descriptions of mental deficiency probably seemed quite inventive the first time it was used:

> not playing with a full deck, front porch light is out, out to lunch, asleep at the switch, off his rocker

The fact that these clichés are used so much has made them predictable. Metaphors that are no longer relevant, stereotyped expressions, and overused idioms no longer have the ability to conjure up an image in the hearer's mind. They have been used so often that they become a ready-made way of substituting a phrase to avoid thinking, as in the following list of clichés about money:

> as sound as a dollar, it's money in the bank, don't sell yourself short, stop on a dime, a penny for your thoughts, pay your dues, take it at face value, put your two cents in, worth one's weight in gold

Some clichés depend on effects of alliteration and rhyming to produce sets of words that are easy to remember: bag and baggage, wishy washy, safe and sound, high and dry, fair and square, wear and tear. Other clichés use two words where one would be sufficient: ways and means, null and void, six of one and half a dozen of the other. Still other clichés are really overused similes:

> clean as a whistle, dead as a doornail, cool as a cucumber, fit as a fiddle, flat as a pancake, free as a bird, fresh as a daisy, good as gold, hard as nails, light as a feather, mad as a March hare, quiet as a mouse, slippery as an eel, ugly as sin, sweet as sugar

An even greater sin than using stale metaphors is using them incorrectly, as John Simon complained of the film critic Rex Reed in "Why Reed Can't Write" (*Paradigms Lost* [1980]):

> Reed's brain is incapable of grasping how metaphors work. In perusing some of Reed's pieces in *Vogue* I came upon some truly remarkable formulations. For example: "the note of reigning terror is struck in the first scene (a dull woman's body is being examined by a Fascist doctor)." A dull corpse? How many witty ones has Reed known? But a corpse so dull as to strike a note of terror? That *is* dull, even for a corpse.

Abstract and Concrete Language

Abstract and concrete language plays a crucial role in argument. Concrete words refer to actual things, instances, or experiences. By contrast, writers need abstractions to generalize about experience and discuss qualities or characteristics apart from specific objects or to sum up the qualities of whole classes of things. For example, we have been using the term *warrant* to refer to the rules or principles that allow conclusions to be connected to evidence. The term is used to convey an abstract idea. Yet, the term *warrant* originally referred to a literal document (as in *arrest warrant* or *search warrant*) that gave the possessor authority to take an action. In this book, the term *warrant* preserves the essential idea—of justifying an action (in argument, drawing a conclusion) by referring to a particular principle that authorizes connecting evidence to a claim.

Without being able to call upon abstractions with which to generalize, we would find ourselves in a situation similar to the one described by Jonathan Swift in Book III of *Gulliver's Travels* (1727). There, Gulliver, on a visit to a "school of languages," learns of a "Scheme for Entirely Abolishing All Words Whatsoever." The rationale behind this unlikely enterprise is that "since words are only names for things, it would be more convenient for all men to carry about them, such things as were necessary to express the particular business they are to discourse on." Thus, instead of speaking, citizens would carry sacks filled with the physical objects about which they wished to converse, and a "'conversation" would appear as follows:

> If a man's business be very great and of various kinds, he must be obliged in proportion to carry a greater bundle of Things upon his back unless he can afford one or two strong servants to attend him. I have often beheld two of those sages almost sinking under the weight of their packs like peddlers among us who when they meet in the streets would lay down their loads, open their sacks and hold conversation for an hour together, then put up their implements, help each other to resume their burdens and take their leave.

This amusing caricature of a conversation without speech dramatizes the disadvantages of being unable to use abstractions to symbolize qualities or express ideas.

Arguments are frequently misunderstood because key terms evoke entirely different specifics (or referents) for the writer than they do for the audience. The chances for communicating improve if the writer attempts to discover what the key terms in the argument actually mean to the audience. For example, if a physician were trying to persuade a physicist, a botanist, and an astronomer to change their views on the probable effects of a nuclear winter and used the term *node*, she would know she was referring to a term in anatomy describing a concentrated swelling, as in *lymph node*. However, the physicist would most likely know the term only as a reference to the point in a string where the least vibration occurs, the botanist might think the physician meant the stem joint out of which a leaf grows, and the astronomer might conjecture that the physician was talking about a point where the earth's orbit appears to cross the sun's apparent path.

Although it would be quite literally impossible to think without being able to generalize, it is clear that any argument requires a balance between the use of abstract terms to make generalizations and concrete or literal terms to provide supporting details and evidence.

Concrete terms provide specific details that allow the writer to focus the audience's attention on all the particulars of the case on which generalizations are based. Without a specific frame of reference and supporting details, examples, and anecdotes, abstract terms can be used to conceal rather than to reveal and clarify. In "Politics and the American Language" (*The American Scholar* [1974]) the eminent historian Arthur Schlesinger, Jr. observed that the use of abstractions in politics has long been a problem:

> So words, divorced from objects, became instruments less of communication than of deception. Unscrupulous orators stood abstractions on their head and transmuted them into their opposites, aiming to please one faction by the sound and the contending faction by the

meaning. They did not always succeed. "The word *liberty* in the mouth of Webster," Emerson wrote with contempt after the Compromise of 1850, "sounds like the word *love* in the mouth of a courtezan." Watching Henry Kissinger babbling about his honor at his famous Salzburg press conference, one was irresistibly reminded of another of Emerson's nonchalant observations: "The louder he talked of his honor, the faster we counted our spoons."

Jargon

An important kind of language often encountered in arguments within specialized fields is jargon. Basically, jargon is the specialized language of a trade, field, or profession. It provides a shorthand way of quickly communicating a lot of information. For example, in publishing, horror stories combined with romantic melodrama are called "creepy weepys," and historical romances filled with sex and violence to stimulate sales are known as "bodice rippers." In police work, officers refer to confiscated drug money as "dead presidents."

The word *jargon* comes from the fifteenth-century French term *jargoun* (twittering or gibberish). In its original context, *jargoun* referred to the secret language criminals used to communicate with each other without being understood by the authorities. The impenetrable nature of jargon makes it all too easy for it to be used to disguise the inner workings of a particular trade or profession or to avoid being held accountable.

Part of the function of jargon is to make the ordinary seem extraordinary and to give an air of importance to everyday situations encountered in different fields. For example, Diane Johnson in "Doctor Talk" (*The New Republic* [1979]) reports that new physicians have been told to use "scientific-sounding euphemisms" in the presence of patients. An alcoholic patient might be told he was suffering from "hyperingestion of ethanol." Not only is the use of specialized terms part of the medical shorthand doctors use in communicating with each other, but such jargon has the added benefit of impressing patients, forestalling counterarguments (how can the patient argue without knowing what the terms mean?), and justifying larger fees.

In military jargon, descriptions of objects are blown out of proportion to warrant higher procurement costs. For example, an ordinary pencil is a "portable, handheld communications inscriber" (*Quarterly Review of Doublespeak* [January 1984] quoting Senator Ted Stevens of Alaska), a toothpick is a "wood interdental stimulator" (*Quarterly Review of Doublespeak* [October 1983]), and a shovel is a "combat emplacement evacuator" (in Hugh Rawson, *A Dictionary of Euphemisms and Other Doubletalk* [1981]). A parachute is an "aerodynamic personnel decelerator," and a 13¢ ordinary steel nut is a "hexiform rotatable surface compression unit," which costs $2,043 for just one (in William Lutz, *Doublespeak* [1989]).

We can see the same desire to make high-sounding utterances at work in many other fields as well. For example, the *New York Times* (February 4, 1987) reports on a New York artist, William Quinn, who teaches a course titled "Meeting People at the Great Museums." According to Quinn, an important part of the course is acquiring a basic but critical vocabulary for discussing art. Thus, at the conclusion of the course, a student would not say, "It just looks like a mess to me" when speaking of Jackson Pollock's *Autumn Rhythm (Number 20)*. Instead, the student would say, "Although the words poured and dripped are commonly used to describe Mr. Pollock's unorthodox creative process, they hardly suggest the diversity of Mr. Pollock's movements, namely flicking, splattering and dribbling" (cited in *Quarterly Review of Doublespeak* [October 1987]).

Lawyers, along with academicians, scientists, and bureaucrats, have their own trade talk that often presents what would normally be easy to grasp in language that mystifies and obscures. For example, in Connecticut the *New Haven Register* (August 9, 1986) reports that the estate of a man who was killed when a barn collapsed on him is bringing a suit against the owners of the barn. The legalese of the suit states that the man's death "destroyed his capacity to carry on life's activities, resulting in loss and damage to his estate." According to the suit, death also "curtailed his earning capacity" and caused him to lose "the joy of life" (cited in *Quarterly Review of Doublespeak* [October 1987]).

THE RHETORIC OF ADVERTISING

Whether ads are presented as sources of information enabling the consumer to make educated choices between products or aim at offering memorable images or witty, thoughtful, or poetic copy, the underlying intent of all advertising is to persuade specific audiences. Seen in this way, ads appear as mini-arguments whose strategies and techniques of persuasion can be analyzed just like a written argument. We can discover which elements are designed to appeal to the audience's emotions (*pathos* according to Aristotle), which elements make their appeal in terms of reasons, evidence, or logic (*logos*), and how the advertiser goes about winning credibility for itself or in terms of the spokesperson employed to speak on behalf of the product (the *ethos* dimension). Like arguments, ads can be effective if they appeal to the needs, values, and beliefs of the audience. Advertisers use a variety of visual and verbal means to encourage their audiences to identify with the people in the ads, the experiences the ads depict, and the values the ads promote. Although the verbal and visual elements within an ad are designed to work together, we can study these elements separately. We can look at how the composition of the elements within an ad is intended to function. We can look at the role of language and how it is used to persuade. We can study how objects and settings are used to promote the audience's identification with the products being sold. We can judge ads according to the skill with which they deploy all of these resources while at the same time being critically aware of their intended effects on us.

The Techniques of Advertising

The claim the ad makes is designed to establish the superiority of the product in the minds of the audience and to create a distinctive image for the product, whether it is a brand of cigarettes, a financial service, or a type of gasoline. The single most important technique for creating this image depends on transferring ideas, attributes, or feelings from outside the product onto the product itself. In this way the product comes to represent an obtainable object or service that embodies, represents, or symbolizes a whole range of meanings. This transfer can be achieved in many ways. For example, when Elizabeth Taylor lends her glamour and beauty to the merchandising of a perfume, the consumer is meant to conclude that the perfume must be superior to other perfumes in the way that Elizabeth Taylor embodies beauty, glamour, and sex appeal. The attempt to transfer significance can operate in two ways. It can encourage the audience to discover meanings and to correlate feelings and attributes that the advertiser wishes the product to represent in ways that allow these needs and desires to become attached to specific products. It can also prevent the correlation of thoughts or feelings that might discourage the audience from purchasing a particular product. For example, the first most instinctive response to the thought of smoking a cigarette might be linked with the idea of inhaling hot and dry smoke from what are essentially burning tobacco leaves. Thus, any associations the audience might have with burning leaves, coughing, and dry hot smoke must be short-circuited by supplying them with a whole set of other associations to receive and occupy the perceptual "slot" that might have been triggered by their first reactions. Cigarette advertisers do this in a variety of ways:

> By showing active people in outdoorsy settings they put the thought of emphysema, shortness of breath, or lung disease very far away indeed.

By showing cigarette packs set against the background of grass glistening with morning dew or bubbling streams or cascading waterfalls, they subtly guide the audience's response away from what is dry, hot, congested, or burning toward what is open, airy, moist, cool, and clean.

In some brands, menthol flavoring and green and blue colors are intended to promote these associations.

Thus, ads act as do all other kinds of persuasion to intensify correlations that work to the advertiser's advantage and to suppress associations that would lessen the product's appeal.

The kinds of associations audiences are encouraged to perceive reflect a broad range of positive emotional appeals that encourage the audience to find self-esteem through the purchase of a product that by itself offers a way to meet personal and social needs. The particular approach taken in the composition of the ad, the way it is laid out, and the connotations of the advertising copy vary according to the emotional appeal of the ad.

The most common manipulative techniques are designed to make consumers want to consume to satisfy deep-seated human drives. Of course, no one consciously believes that purchasing a particular kind of toothpaste, perfume, lipstick, or automobile will meet real psychological and social needs, but that is exactly how products are sold—through the promise of delivering unattainable satisfactions through tangible purchasable objects or services. In purchasing a certain product, we are offered the chance to create ourselves, our personality, and our relationships through consumption.

Emotional Appeals Used in Advertising

The emotional appeals in ads function exactly the way value warrants do in written arguments. They supply the unstated major premise that supplies a rationale to persuade an audience that a particular product will meet one or another of several different kinds of needs. Some ads present the purchase of a product as a means by which consumers can find social acceptance.

These ads address the consumer as "you" ("wouldn't 'you' really rather have a Buick?"). The "you" here is plural but is perceived as being individual and personal by someone who has already formed the connection with the product. Ironically, the price of remaining in good standing with this "group" of fellow consumers requires the consumer to purchase an expensive automobile. In this sense, ads give consumers

a chance to belong to social groups that have only one thing in common—the purchase of a particular product.

One variation on the emotional need to belong to a designated social group is the appeal to status or "snob appeal." Snob appeal is not
new. In 1710, the *Spectator*, a popular newspaper of the time, carried an
ad that read:

> An incomparable Powder for Cleaning Teeth, which has given great
> satisfaction to most of the Nobility Gentry in England. (Quoted in
> W. Duncan Reekie, *Advertising: Its Place in Political and Managerial Eco-
> nomics*, 1974.)

Ads for scotch, expensive cars, boats, jewelry, and watches frequently place their products in upper-class settings or depict them in
connection with the fine arts (sculpture, ballet, etc.). The *value warrant*
in these ads encourages the consumer to imagine that the purchase of
the item will confer qualities associated with the background or activities of this upper-class world onto the consumer.

In other ads the need to belong takes a more subtle form of offering
the product as a way to become part of a time in the past the audience
might look back to with nostalgia. Grandmotherly figures wearing
aprons and holding products that are advertised as being "like Grandma used to make" offer the consumer an imaginary past, a family tradition, or a simpler time looked back to with warmth and sentimentality.
For many years, Smucker's preserves featured ads in which the product was an integral part of a scene emanating security and warmth,
which the ad invited us to remember as if it were our own past. Ads of
this kind are often photographed through filters that present misty
sepia-tone images that carefully recreate old-fashioned kitchens with
the accompanying appliances, dishes, clothes, and hairstyles. The ads
thus supply us with false memories and invite us to insert ourselves
into this imaginary past and to remember it as if it were our own. At
the furthest extreme, ads employing the appeal to see ourselves as part
of a group may try to evoke patriotic feelings so that the prospective
consumer will derive the satisfactions of good citizenship and sense of
participation in being part of the collective psyche of an entire nation.
The point is that people really do have profound needs that advertisers
can exploit, but it would be a rare product indeed that could really fulfill such profound needs.

Advertisers use highly sophisticated market research techniques to
enable them to define and characterize precisely those people who are
most likely to be receptive to ads of particular kinds. The science of demographics is aided and abetted by psychological research that enables
advertisers to "target" a precisely designated segment of the general

public. For example, manufacturers of various kinds of liquor can rely on studies that inform them that vodka drinkers are most likely to read *Psychology Today* and scotch drinkers the *New Yorker,* while readers of *Time* prefer rum and the audience for *Playboy* has a large number of readers who prefer gin. Once a market segment with defined psychological characteristics has been identified, an individual ad can be crafted for that particular segment and placed in the appropriate publication.

Ads, of course, can elicit responses by attempting to manipulate consumers through negative as well as positive emotional appeals. Helen Woodward, the head copywriter for an ad agency, once offered the following advice for ad writers trying to formulate a new ad for baby food: "Give 'em the figures about the baby death rate—but don't say it flatly... if we only had the nerve to put a hearse in the ad, you couldn't keep the women away from the food" (Stuart Ewen, *Captains of Consciousness: Advertising and the Social Roots of Consumer Culture* [1976]). Ads of this kind must first arouse the consumer's anxieties and then offer the product as the solution to the problem that more often than not the ad has created.

For example, an advertisement for Polaroid evokes the fear of not having taken pictures of moments that cannot be re-created and then offers the product as a form of insurance that will prevent this calamity from occurring. Nikon does the same in claiming that "a moment is called a moment because it doesn't last forever. Think of sunsets. A child's surprise. A Labrador's licky kiss. This is precisely why the Nikon N50 has the simple 'Simple' switch on top of the camera."

Ads for products that promise to guarantee their purchasers sex appeal, youth, health, social acceptance, self-esteem, creativity, enlightenment, a happy family life, loving relationships, escape from boredom, vitality, and many other things frequently employ scare tactics to frighten or worry the consumer into purchasing the product to ease his or her fears. These ads must first make the consumer dissatisfied with the self that exists. In this way, they function exactly as do *policy arguments* that recommend solutions to problems with measurably harmful consequences. The difference is that these kinds of ads actually are designed to arouse and then exploit the anxieties related to these problems.

Large industrial conglomerates, whether in oil, chemicals, pharmaceuticals, or agribusiness, frequently use advertising to accomplish different kinds of objectives than simply persuading the consumer to buy a particular product. These companies often seek to persuade the general public that they are not polluting the environment, poisoning the water, or causing environmental havoc in the process of manufacturing their products. The emotional appeal they use is to portray themselves as concerned "corporate citizens," vitally interested in the public good as a whole, and especially in those communities where they conduct their operations. In some cases, the ads present products as if they were directly produced from nature without being subjected to intermediary processing, preservatives, and contaminants, thereby lessening concern that they produce harmful byproducts. For example, Mazola might depict a spigot producing corn oil directly inserted into an ear of corn. A Jeep might appear to have materialized out of thin air on a seemingly inaccessible mountain peak. Companies sensitive to accusations that they are polluting the air and water can mount an advertising campaign designed to prove that they are not simply exploiting the local resources (whether timber, oil, fish, coal) for profits but are genuinely interested in putting something back into the community. The folksy good-neighbor tone of these ads is designed to create a benign image of the company.

THE LANGUAGE OF ADVERTISING

We can see how the creation of a sense of the company's credibility as a concerned citizen corresponds to what Aristotle called the *ethos* dimension. For example, Chevron (see Figure 5-5) expresses concern that the light from their oil drilling operations be shielded so that spawning sea turtles won't be unintentionally misdirected and lose their way!

The appeals to logic, statements of reasons, and presentations of evidence in ads correspond to the *logos* dimension of argument. The wording of the claims is particularly important, since it determines whether companies are legally responsible for any claims they make.

Claims in advertising need to be evaluated to discover whether something is asserted that needs to be proved or is implied without actually being stated.

Claims may refer to authoritative-sounding results obtained by supposedly independent laboratories, teams of research scientists, or physicians without ever saying how these surveys were conducted, what statistical methods were used, and who interpreted the results. Ads of this kind may make an impressive-sounding quasi-scientific claim; Ivory Soap used to present itself as "99 and 44/100% pure" without answering "pure" what. Some ads use technical talk and scientific terms to give the impression of a scientific breakthrough. For example, STP claims that it added "an anti-wear agent and viscosity improvers" to your oil. The copy for L. L. Bean claims of one of its jackets that "even in brutal ice winds gusting to 80 knots this remarkable anorak kept team members who wore it warm and comfortable." It would be important to know that the team members referred to are members of the "L. L. Bean test team."

Other claims cannot be substantiated, for example, "we're the Dexter Shoe Company. And for nearly four decades we put a lot of Dexter Maine into every pair of shoes we make."

In an ad for lipstick, Aveda makes the claim that "it's made of rich, earthy lip colours formulated with pure plant pigment from the Uruku tree. Organically grown by indigenous people in the rain forest."

Claims may be deceptive in other ways. Of all the techniques advertisers use to influence what people believe and how they spend their money, none is more basic than the use of so-called *weasel words*. This term was popularized by Theodore Roosevelt in a speech he gave in St. Louis, May 31, 1916, when he commented that notes from the Department of State were filled with weasel words that retract the meaning of the words they are next to just as a weasel sucks the meat out of the egg.

In modern advertising parlance, a weasel word has come to mean any qualifier or comparative that is used to imply a positive quality that cannot be stated as a fact, because it cannot be substantiated. For example, if an ad claims a toothpaste will "help" stop cavities it does not obligate the manufacturer to substantiate this claim. So, too, if a product is advertised as "fighting" germs, the equivocal claim hides the fact that the product may fight and lose.

A recent ad for STP claimed that "no matter what kind of car you drive, STP gas treatment helps remove the water that leads to gas line freeze. And unlike gas line anti-freeze, our unique gas treatment formula works to reduce intake valve deposits and prevent clogged injectors." The key words are "helps" and "works," neither of which obligates STP to be legally accountable to support the claim.

The words *virtually* (as in "virtually spotless") and *up to* or *for as long as* (as in "stops coughs up to eight hours") also remove any legal obligation on the part of the manufacturer to justify the claim.

Other favorite words in the copywriter's repertoire, such as *free* and *new,* are useful in selling everything from cat food to political candidates.

✦ *Questions for Discussion and Writing*

1. How are each of the following ads designed to create a distinctive image for the company, product, or service being promoted? In each case, what function does the picture serve? What psychological needs or values do the advertisers appeal to? How is the ad copy or language designed to manipulate the emotions of the readers in ways that are positive for the advertisers? In your opinion, is the approach taken by each advertiser in the following ads successful? Why or why not?

FIGURE 5-5
Source: Chevron Corporation.

Our Courses Are Limited To 12 Students, But Our Classrooms Are Quite Large.

People who've taken our courses say they learned more about themselves in that

one week than they had in years. Which isn't too surprising, when you consider that we

have incredibly qualified instructors. Limited groups. A challenging curriculum.

And whether you backpack, sail, canoe or even dogsled, our classroom settings just

can't be beat. So call 1-800-243-8520 and we'll send you a free color catalog today.

A nonprofit, nondiscriminatory organization celebrating over 50 years of excellence in education worldwide.

Outward Bound.
THE ADVENTURE LASTS A LIFETIME.

FIGURE 5-6

Source: Outward Bound, created by Ogilvy & Mather.

THERE WILL ALWAYS BE THOSE WHO REFUSE TO SKI MAMMOTH.

Admittedly, with an elevation of 11,053 feet and 3,100 foot vertical, there are those of you who just flat out won't pay us a visit. Guess you probably don't realize we have 150 trails – spread out over 3,500 skiable acres – so there's lots of prime terrain, no matter what your ability. But hey, if you don't want to call 1-800-832-7320 and get the complete story in our free travel planner, far be it for us to insist. We certainly wouldn't want to ruffle anyone's feathers.

MAMMOTH

No other mountain lives up to its name.

FIGURE 5-7

Source: Mammoth.

The fully functional sedan
with Ultra-Zesty Deluxe.™

The Mazda 626 With the help of an unsurpassed "bumper-to-bumper" warranty.* It's more than cruise control, power windows and leather interior.** It's the combination of all these in such a beautiful package that makes the 626 ES what it is. A zesty-deluxe family chariot that would make any garage proud. If we could only find a better way to say that.

modern science, Mazda engineers have brought something extra to 4-door transportation. No, it doesn't actually come in a bottle. It's something that goes a lot further than the minimum daily sedan requirements like dual air bags and anti-lock brakes. It's more than just a powerful V6 and

AS DEVELOPED IN OUR
SECRET LABORATORIES

mazpa
IT JUST FEELS RIGHT.*

*See dealer for limited-warranty details. **Seating surfaces upholstered in leather except for vinyl on seat side panels, rear sides of seatbacks and other minor areas. For a free brochure, call 1-800-639-1000. © 1994 Mazda Motor of America, Inc.

FIGURE 5-8

Source: Copyright (1994) Mazda Motor of America, Inc. Used by permission.

2. How does the ad copy used by the makers of Trojan Brand Latex Condoms attempt to associate their product with an implicit guarantee of safe sex? How does the use of the word "genius" create a relationship between the potential consumer and the advertiser? What is this relationship, and how does it intensify the message of the ad?

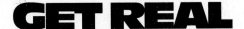

"I didn't use one because I didn't have one with me."
GET REAL
If you don't have a parachute, don't jump, genius.
TROJAN
Helps reduce the risk

FIGURE 5-9

Source: Reprinted with permission of Carter-Wallace Inc. New York, New York. © CWI. All rights reserved.

3. How does the ad for Hamilton watches in Figure 5-10 combine status appeal, nostalgia appeal, and patriotic appeal?

THE ETHICAL DIMENSION OF PERSUASION

As we have seen in our examination of the methods advertisers use to influence consumers, ethical questions are implicit in every act of persuasion. For example, what are we to make of a persuader whose objectives in seeking to influence an audience may be praiseworthy but who consciously makes use of distorted facts or seeks to manipulate an audience by playing on their known attitudes, values, and beliefs. Is success in persuasion the only criterion or should we hold would-be persuaders accountable to some ethical standards of responsibility about the means they use to achieve specific ends? Perhaps the most essential quality in determining whether any act of persuasion is an ethical one depends on the writer maintaining an open dialogue with different perspectives that might be advanced on a particular issue. By contrast, any act of persuasion that intentionally seeks to avoid self-criticism or challenges from competing perspectives will come across as insincere, dogmatic, deceptive, and defensive. The desire to shut down debate or control an audience's capacity to respond to the argument might well be considered unethical. The consequence of this attitude may be observed in the arguer's use of fraudulent evidence,

FIGURE 5-10

Source: Hamilton

illogical reasoning, emotionally laden irrelevant appeals, simplistic representation of the issue, or the pretense of expertise. Standards to apply when judging the ethical dimension in any act of persuasion require us to consider whether any element of coercion, deception, or manipulation is present. This becomes especially true when we look at the relationship between propaganda as a form of mass persuasion and the rhetorical means used to influence large groups of people.

PROPAGANDA:
THE LANGUAGE OF DOUBLESPEAK

Ultimately, it is the intention with which words are used that determines whether any of the techniques already discussed, such as slanting, labeling, and emotionally loaded language, pose a political danger. Of themselves, strategies of persuasion are neither good nor bad; it is the purpose for which they are employed that makes them unethical and offensive. For this reason, the techniques of rhetorical persuasion have been decried throughout the ages. Aldous Huxley in "Propaganda Under a Dictatorship" in *Brave New World Revisited* (1958) discussed how the manipulation of language through propaganda techniques in Nazi Germany conditioned thoughts and behavior. Some of the key techniques identified by Huxley included the use of slogans, unqualified assertions, and sweeping generalizations. Huxley notes that Hitler had said "all effective propaganda must be confined to a few bare necessities and then must be expressed in a few stereotyped formulas.... Only constant repetition will finally succeed in imprinting an idea upon the memory of a crowd." Hitler knew that any lie can seem to be the truth if it is repeated often enough. Repeated exposure encourages a sense of acceptance and familiarity with the slogan. Hitler's use of propaganda required that all statements be made without qualification.

George Orwell commented frequently on the dangers posed by political propaganda. In his novel *1984* he coined the term *doublespeak* to show how political language could be used to deceive, beg the question, and avoid responsibility.

Doublespeak can take forms that can range from the innocuous, such as Lt. Colonel Oliver North's intention to give "a nonvisual slide show" (cited in *Quarterly Review of Doublespeak* [January 1988]), to the deceptive and dangerous, such as the Pentagon's reference to the neutron bomb as "an efficient nuclear weapon that eliminates an enemy with a minimum degree of damage to friendly territory." Or consider a statement by the U. S. Army that "we do not call it 'killing,' we call it 'servicing the target'" (cited in *Quarterly Review of Doublespeak* [January 1988]). In each of these cases language is used against itself to distort and manipulate rather than to communicate.

INTENSIFYING AND DOWNPLAYING:
STRATEGIES FOR PERSUASION

One of the most valuable ways of analyzing forms of public persuasion was suggested by Hugh Rank in "Teaching about Public Persuasion: Rationale and a Schema" (1976). Rank won the 1976 *Orwell Award* (presented by the Committee on Public Doublespeak) for his "Intensifying/ Downplaying Schema." Rank observed that all acts of public persuasion are variations of what he terms *intensifying* and *downplaying*.

Persuaders use intensifying and downplaying in the following ways: (1) to intensify, focus on, or draw attention to anything that would make their case look good; (2) to intensify, focus on, or draw attention to anything that would make counterclaims or their opponent's arguments look bad; (3) to downplay, dismiss, or divert attention from any weak points that would make their case look bad; and (4) to downplay, dismiss, or divert attention from anything that would make their opponent's case look good.

What is meant by intensifying and downplaying can be seen by comparing the words a country uses to refer to actions of the enemy (by intensifying) with those words it uses to describe its own identical activities (by downplaying):

Intensifying	*Downplaying*
Bombing	Air support
Spying	Intelligence gathering
Invasion	Pacification
Infiltration	Reinforcement
Retreat	Strategic withdrawal

The calculated manipulation and conditioning of thought and behavior by propaganda experts is now a fact of everyday life. Professional persuaders have an unequal advantage over those whom they seek to influence and persuade. By contrast, the average citizen has never received any training in critically examining the various techniques professional persuaders use.

The three basic techniques of intensification are (1) repetition, (2) association, and (3) composition.

Repetition.   Slogans, unqualified assertions, and sweeping generalizations seem more true if they are constantly repeated. Much of commercial advertising is built on the repetition of slogans, product logos, and brand names. Political campaigns rely on repetition of candidates' names and messages over the airwaves and on posters and bumper stickers.

Association.   Intensifying by association is a technique that is also known as virtue (or guilt) by association. This strategy depends on linking an idea, person, or product with something already loved or admired (or hated and despised) by the intended audience. That is, an idea, person, or product is put into a context that already has an emotional significance for the intended audience. Once market researchers discover the needs and values of a target audience, political campaigns and advertising for commercial products can exploit the audience's needs by linking their idea, candidate, or product to values already known to be appealing to the audience. Much of advertising exploits this technique of correlating feelings and emotions with purchasable objects.

Composition.   A message gains intensity when it is arranged in a clearly perceivable pattern. Arranging the message can rely on the traditional rhetorical patterns (comparison and contrast, cause and effect, process analysis, classification, analogy, narration, description, and exemplification) as well as inductive or deductive logic or any other distinctive way of grouping the elements of the message.

The three basic techniques of downplaying are (1) omission, (2) diversion, and (3) confusion.

Omission.   If persuaders wish to downplay, or divert attention away from, an issue that is felt to be potentially damaging to their purposes, they can use the opposite of each of the intensifying techniques. If repetition is an effective way to intensify, persuaders can downplay by omitting, biasing, or slanting. Omissions can range from euphemisms that downplay serious issues to acts of overt censorship.

Diversion.   Just as persuaders intensify by associating, they can downplay by diverting attention through an emphasis on unimportant or unrelated side issues. Many of these tactics (discussed in the Appendix A section on logical fallacies) include the *red herring, non sequitur, straw man, argumentum ad hominem, argumentum ad populum, argumentum ad misericordiam* or *appeal to pity, argumentum ad baculum* or *appeal to force, circular reasoning* or *begging the question,* and *appeal to ignorance.* All these techniques are used to divert or distract attention from the main issues to peripheral or entirely unrelated issues.

Confusion.   Just as a message gains intensity when it is well structured and coherent, so persuaders can downplay by using a variety of techniques designed to obscure or cloud the points at issue. These techniques include the calculated use of faulty logic, including the *fallacy of complex question, false dilemma, false cause, post hoc, slippery slope,* and *faulty analogy.* Downplaying via confusion also results from the use of ambiguous terms or phrases, as in the fallacies of *equivocation, amphiboly,* and *accent,* as well as the use of bureaucratese, medicalese, legalese, pentagonese, and all other jargons used to obscure or cloud the real issues.

We should realize that all these strategies of intensifying and downplaying can take place *simultaneously* during any attempt to persuade.

To see how this works in practice, we can apply Rank's "Intensifying/Downplaying Schema" to "The Case of the Non-Unanimous Jury" by Charles Sevilla and "Justice Can Be Served Despite Dissenting Votes" by Robert E. Jones (in this chapter). The point at issue is whether unanimous juries are necessary to the process of reaching fair verdicts. Sevilla *intensifies the virtues of his argument* by using the movie *Twelve Angry Men* to dramatically illustrate how the need for a unanimous verdict compels juries to review facts and evidence carefully. Sevilla uses this classic movie to illustrate his claim that the current system offers a better chance for a correct result by offering dissenters the opportunity to argue points in testimony that other jurors may have missed.

At the same time, Sevilla intensifies *negative aspects of his opponent's* (Jones's) *argument* by arguing that despite the current system innocent people are still convicted; therefore, eliminating the requirement for unanimous verdicts (as Jones recommends) would lead to more mistaken convictions. Sevilla also claims that removing the need for dissenting jurors to justify their decisions would compromise a crucial element of our justice system. Simultaneously, Sevilla *downplays points on which his case might be vulnerable* by claiming that hung juries are statistically such a small fraction of all cases that they do not warrant changing the system and losing the benefits of a unanimous verdict. At the same time, he concedes that requirements for unanimity can lead to inconclusive results but asserts that no verdict is better than an erroneous one. Last, he *downplays what might be seen as a positive point for the other side* by suggesting that if Jones is so interested in saving money, trials might be done away with altogether (*reductio ad absurdum*).

By contrast, Jones, arguing the opposite position, *intensifies the virtues of his own argument* by citing his own twenty years' experience as a trial judge overseeing civil cases where verdicts were reached by ten out of twelve jurors, and not one person convicted by a nonunanimous jury was later found to be innocent. Jones also aids his case by presenting an accurate summary of Sevilla's argument, thereby enhancing his credibility as a thoughtful and objective person taking the opponent's position into account. Jones *intensifies weak points of Sevilla's argument* by asserting that trials may be aborted by one or two kook jurors whose irrationality does not blossom until after the jury is locked up for deliberation.

At the same time Jones *downplays points on which he might be vulnerable* by failing to mention that the mock trials set up to compare unanimous with nonunanimous verdicts were not designed to test for the blossoming of kook jurors. Last, he *downplays what might be seen as good points of his opponent's argument* by arguing that Henry Fonda notwithstanding, it is improbable that one juror could convince eleven others, as is depicted in *Twelve Angry Men.* Jones also *downplays or undercuts his opponent's claim* that hung juries are infrequent by citing research and mock trials to prove that hung juries happen often enough to justify judicial reform.

✦ Questions for Discussion and Writing

1. Locate coverage of a recent event in the school newspaper and analyze how the event was depicted, compared with your own experience. What features were ignored, and what features were focused on and intensified? How did the report differ from your own experience and perception? To what extent are these differences due to a different agenda or purpose on the part of the reporter or the audience for whom the report was written?

2. Analyze the effect of a photograph in a recent newspaper or magazine that played an important role in shaping public response toward a natural disaster, war, or famine.

THREE SHORT ARGUMENTS
FOR ANALYSIS

Charles Sevilla

The Case of the Non-Unanimous Jury

———————◆———————

Charles Sevilla is a former Chief Deputy Public Defender for the state of California who now practices trial law in San Diego. Sevilla believes that the number of cases reaching trial that result in hung juries is so small that it doesn't warrant losing the benefits of a unanimous verdict. This article first appeared in the January 23, 1983 issue of the Los Angeles Times.

One of Henry Fonda's most memorable roles was as one of *Twelve Angry Men* selected to determine the fate of a young Puerto Rican accused of murdering his father. They were angry because the majority's quest for a speedy verdict of guilty was frustrated by Fonda's lone vote for acquittal. Without unanimity, a verdict could not be returned, and the other jurors, anxious to get home to dinner or out to a ballgame, were furious.

In real life, the lone dissenting juror on a first ballot almost always succumbs to the pressure and joins ranks to return a verdict. Fonda's character was different. He convinced the others to pause long enough to discuss the evidence and hear him out. After all, he said, the defendant, a slum youth, had been ignored most of his life. The jury owed him some time for a just verdict.

In the next 90 tension-filled minutes Fonda argued the importance of subtle points of testimony that the others had missed; he proved that the murder weapon, a knife, was not as distinctive as the prosecutor had insisted; he pointed out lapses in the defense attorney's presentation, all the while importuning the others to reach a verdict through reason rather than emotion. One by one, the others came around to join him, the last capitulating only when his underlying motivation was revealed—the defendant reminded him of his wayward son.

Hollywood melodrama though it was, the film's depiction of a jury struggling to do its duty is a rare illustration of unanimity's function in the difficult job of jury decisionmaking.

303

5   Perhaps nothing epitomizes the concept of American liberty as well as the right to a trial by a jury. The jury is one of a handful of institutions that allow individual citizens, not government, to make important societal decisions. A crucial component of the jury trial is the rule that verdicts be unanimous. It has always been the rule in federal criminal trials, in the overwhelming majority of states.

6   Critics of the right to a unanimous verdict in serious criminal cases see it as a costly medieval relic. Los Angeles new district attorney, Robert Philobosian, is the latest to join the chorus. He wants the verdict requirement shrunk from 12 jurors to 10 (in all but capital cases) so that one or two people will not be able to force a retrial.

Hung Juries

7   The costs of hung juries do not warrant losing the benefits of the unanimous verdict. Statistically, jury trials play a minor role in the criminal-justice system. The vast majority of defendants plead guilty and have no trial. In 1981, only about 7 percent of accused felons had jury trials. The incidence of hung juries is thus but a fraction of the already small fraction of cases that go to trial.

8   Some money undoubtedly could be saved by such a reform. Even more could be saved by abolishing jury trials altogether.

9   That juries occasionally are deadlocked does not demonstrate a flaw in our criminal-justice system. Our concept of justice does not require juries to decide every case. Hung juries usually occur when the case is close—that is, when neither side has presented convincing evidence. Further, juries that wind up deadlocked with one or two members in dissent usually start with a more substantial minority of four or five which indicates that the evidence is not clear-cut.

10   Even though the requirement of unanimity may lead to an inconclusive result from time to time, no verdict is better than a wrong one. Despite the protection of unanimous verdicts, we still manage to convict some innocent people each year. Eliminating the unanimity requirement would only increase the opportunity for mistakes. Unanimity guarantees give-and-take among jurors and filters out the biases of individuals. It makes the ultimate decision truly reflective of the community. Most important, it provides a better chance that the result will be correct by affording a counterbalance to the state's inherent advantages, such as the jurors' subconscious presumption that a defendant who is on trial must be guilty.

11   Consider what would have happened if the decision in *Twelve Angry Men* could have been made by 10 jurors instead of 12. After the first ballot, the 11 who voted "guilty" could have put an end to the deliberations, without having to listen to Fonda.

12   What could be more fundamental to justice than verdicts that can be trusted and respected? If even one juror has doubts, that is enough

to undermine society's confidence that a proper verdict has been reached.

✦ *Questions for Discussion and Writing*

1. Evaluate Sevilla's use of the classic film *Twelve Angry Men* to illustrate his thesis that "the jury is one of a handful of institutions that allow individual citizens, not government, to make important societal decisions. A crucial component of the jury trial is the rule that verdicts be unanimous." In what way does the action depicted in the film underscore the central point of Sevilla's argument? How does Sevilla's use of a worst-case scenario, in the next to last paragraph, dramatize what he fears might happen if proposed reforms were enacted?

2. Against what specific proposal is Sevilla arguing, and how would it change the present system?

3. What role does Sevilla's introduction of statistical evidence concerning the percentage of hung juries play in the overall development of his argument? How does this portion of his argument depend on the tactic of extending the opposition's stance to an extreme in order to refute it (reductio ad absurdum)?

4. What reasons does Sevilla present to support his assertion that because "juries occasionally are deadlocked does not demonstrate a flaw in our criminal-justice system"?

5. In an essay, discuss the validity of an important assumption underlying Sevilla's argument: keeping the existing system, which requires all twelve members of the jury to agree on a verdict, is superior to adopting a system that would allow a verdict to be reached if only ten of the twelve jurors agreed because, under the present system, jurors must publicly discuss and justify their decisions and, in the process, reveal latent personal motivations that might otherwise remain hidden. Points to consider in your evaluation include (a) whether the current system provides a better chance for a just result by offering lone dissenters the opportunity to argue subtle points in testimony that other jurors may have missed, (b) whether the doubt of even one juror should be enough to raise the question whether a proper verdict has been reached, and (c) whether the current requirement for a unanimous verdict encourages dissenting members of the jury to support their opinions, reveal their feelings, and disclose any possible biases or prejudices that may have influenced their reasoning in some way. If the obligation for dissenting jurors to justify their decisions were removed, would the system of justice be shortchanged, as Sevilla claims?

Robert E. Jones

Justice Can Be Served Despite Dissenting Votes

——————◆——————

Robert E. Jones has served as a criminal-felony trial judge for over twenty years on the Oregon Supreme Court. Jones draws on his extensive experience on the bench to argue that the present system ought to be reformed to include nonunanimous verdicts where only ten out of the twelve jurors have to agree. This article appeared originally in the January 23, 1983 issue of the Los Angeles Times.

1   After sitting for 20 years as a criminal-felony trial judge in Oregon, where jurors in all but first-degree murder cases are allowed to return a verdict if 10 out of 12 agree, I believe that such a system delivers fair, if not perfect justice to both the state and the defendant. In my experience, no one who was convicted by a nonunanimous jury later was shown to have been innocent.

2   While unanimous verdicts are still required in federal trials, the U. S. Supreme Court ruled in 1972 that the Constitution does not require them in state trials.

3   Those who are opposed to allowing nonunanimous verdicts in criminal trials base their arguments on several assumptions: that the views of the minority will be given less consideration and that there will be less opportunity for persuasion, that jurors will be less inclined to engage in "earnest and robust argument" to quote the late U. S. Supreme Court Justice William O. Douglas; that there will be a less thorough examination of the facts; that jurors will not be as likely to review as much of the testimony or adhere as carefully to the judge's instructions and that the deliberations will be shorter, thereby making it easier to jump to conclusions.

4   Unfortunately for those who make such arguments, there is no scientific evidence to support those claims.

5   Many people cite the example of *Twelve Angry Men,* in which Henry Fonda played a holdout juror who managed to bring around 11 bigoted or misguided jurors to a verdict for the defense. I doubt that this occurs very often in real life, but stranger things have happened.

6   The main argument for nonunanimous verdicts is that no matter how carefully the jury is picked, a trial in which a unanimous verdict is

required may be aborted by one or two kook jurors whose irrationality does not blossom until after the jury is locked up for deliberations. I think this is a pretty convincing claim.

You have to wonder about the mentality or motives of certain jurors when you see cases, usually involving hardened criminals, in which the prosecution's witnesses remain unimpeached, the defense offers nothing and still the jury returns a guilty verdict of 11–1 or 10–2.   7

Experiment

In 1976, Alice Padawer-Singer and Allen Barton of Columbia University's Bureau of Applied Social Research set up an experiment with actual jurors participating in mock trials under different rules in order to compare unanimous and nonunanimous verdicts. The 23 12-member juries that were required to reach unanimous decisions returned 10 not-guilty and eight guilty verdicts with five winding up deadlocked. Of the 23 panels that were not required to reach unanimity, nine returned not-guilty verdicts, nine guilty and five deadlocked. The average deliberation time for reaching a verdict was 178 minutes for the unanimous juries and 160 minutes for the nonunanimous.   8

From a statistical standpoint the differences between the two groups were insignificant. In short, the study did not prove that one system was better than the other. They were indistinguishable.   9

Last year I took a random sample of 164 felony cases tried before 12-person nonunanimous juries in Portland and found that 155 had resulted in verdicts—128 convictions and 27 acquittals. Of the convictions, 52 were unanimous, 35 were reached on a vote of 11–1 and 41 were 10–2. Of the acquittals, 9 were unanimous and 18 were split. Of those 18, seven were 11–1 and 11 were 10–2. Nine juries were deadlocked.   10

Chief Justice James Burns of the U. S. District Court in Oregon has had the rare opportunity to view both verdict systems in operation, first on our state court and then for the last decade on the federal trial court where unanimous verdicts are required. When I asked him to compare the two, his conclusion surprised me.   11

"I don't think it makes a bit of difference," he said. "A good or bad case will be spotted by either type of jury. The only difference seems to be that unanimous juries deliberate several minutes or sometimes several hours longer." He said that hung juries were rare—occurring only in about one out of 200 trials—something I have also observed in the Oregon state courts.   12

In sum, I believe that nonunanimous jury verdicts have no harmful consequences for our criminal-justice system. And, since such verdicts speed the jury-selection process and protect the system from irrational jurors, they provide a model that other states should follow.   13

✦ *Questions for Discussion and Writing*

1. Initially, how does Jones draw upon his personal experience "as a criminal-felony trial judge" to support his thesis that nonunanimous jury verdicts are not incompatible with justice?

2. Evaluate Jones's summary of the opposition's viewpoint by comparing it with reasons Sevilla presents to support his thesis. Is it a fair restatement of Sevilla's argument and its underlying assumptions?

3. Discuss Jones's claim that "the main argument for nonunanimous verdicts is that no matter how carefully the jury is picked, a trial in which a unanimous verdict is required may be aborted by one or two kook jurors whose irrationality does not blossom until after the jury is locked up for deliberations." Where in his article does Jones present evidence of the number of times this situation has occurred (resulting in hung juries), either in his personal experience or in mock trials set up to compare unanimous versus nonunanimous jury verdicts?

4. Jones describes an experiment conducted by Alice Padawer-Singer and Allen Barton. What were the results of this experiment and how does Jones use them to support his thesis? Evaluate the design of this experiment and discuss whether or not it was constructed to test for the occasional irrational kook juror.

5. To what extent does Jones's argument depend on assertions and evidence as to the frequency with which deadlocked juries occur?

6. What function does Jones's use of the testimony of Chief Justice James Burns have in supporting Jones's argument?

7. If you were a defendant on trial for murder, or another capital crime, which jury system would you want to decide upon your guilt or innocence: one requiring the unanimous consent of twelve jurors, or one in which a guilty verdict could be returned by ten or eleven jurors? Discuss your reasons in an essay, citing relevant arguments from either Sevilla's or Jones's articles or both.

8. Analyze Sevilla's and Jones's arguments in terms of Rank's "intensifying/downplaying schema." How do both Sevilla and Jones intensify both the virtues of their own arguments and the negative features of their opponent's views while at the same time downplaying points that might undercut the persuasiveness of their own cases and also downplaying what might be seen as positive points for the other side? For example, how does each deal with the issue of the statistical frequency of hung juries and "kook" jurors?

9. In your judgment, to what extent was the way in which the O. J. Simpson trial was conducted an illustration for either Jones's or Sevilla's thesis? The class may wish to form two groups for purposes of discussing the merits and disadvantages of the present jury system.

Alfred Adask

"Democracy" vs. "Republic"

◆————————

Alfred Adask is the editor and publisher of AntiShyster: A Critical Examination of the American Legal System. *Although Adask is not a lawyer, he has written numerous works on legal and constitutional issues, including* The Missing 13th Amendment, 1992. *When he ran for the Texas Supreme Court in 1992, Adask received over 200,000 votes. This article is reprinted from the Vol. 4, No. 2, 1994 issue of* AntiShyster.

1   Black's Law Dictionary (4th ed.) defines a **"Commonwealth"** as "...generally...a *republican* frame of government—one in which the welfare and rights of the *entire mass of people* are the main consideration, rather than the *privileges* of a class or the will of a monarch...." [emphasis added]

2   This definition offers an interesting insight into the fundamental difference between a Republic and a democracy:

3   In a Republic, all persons enjoy equal, inalienable Rights and the laws must therefore apply *equally to all;*

4   However, under a *democracy,* the laws may be biased to favor the "special interests" of specific groups or classes, usually at the expense of the majority. Therefore, one of the hallmarks of democracy is "special interest legislation" which, in virtually every case, constitutes *theft* of wealth, property, or Rights from one class to benefit another class.

5   In all cases, by definition, "special interest" legislation *does not apply equally to all.* Hence, since democracies can treat their citizens "specially" (i.e., *unequally*), the citizens of any democracy *cannot* have *any* inalienable, God-given, Constitutionally-guaranteed Rights. If they did, those Rights would have to apply *equally to all* and be beyond government's power to modify or rescind. "Equal, inalienable" Rights for *all* renders "special interest" legislation virtually *impossible.*

6   For example, if you and I have *equal, inalienable* Rights, how can Congress pass a law that compels *you* to surrender some of the money *you* earned and possess by *inalienable* Right, in order to enrich *me* with money (yours) which I have not earned and to which I have no Right whatsoever?

7   No matter that I might be black, or hispanic, or poor, or be a major corporation (like Chrysler). If your Right to your property (including the fruits of your labor) is both 1) *inalienable* and 2) *equal* to the Rights of every other Citizen, then there can be no lawful basis for any law that

benefits me, my class, or my corporation, at the expense of even a single Citizen.

Democracy is antithetical to inalienable Rights and Freedom. More   8
precisely, *inalienable* Rights cannot co-exist for long with a democracy, cannot *survive* in a democracy since there can be *no* God-given, inalienable Rights in a democracy, only government-granted *privileges* of temporary, conditional duration. Therefore, it follows that *all* "democracies" must eventually confront and seek to destroy not only the political *concept* of "equal, inalienable Rights", but the *source* of those Rights, as well—i.e., God, Himself. (If this notion sounds bizarre, ask yourself if God was driven from the public schools under a Republic or under a democracy. . . .)

Like democracy? Then kiss your Constitution, your inalienable   9
Rights, and your Freedoms goodbye.

On the other hand, would you be Free? Would you bequeath Free-   10
dom to your children and grandchildren? Would you do God's bidding and fight for the Rights He's given you?

Then stand up, speak out, hiss, boo, and jeer every time some poli-   11
tician, bureaucrat or fool starts praising "democracy". Don't sit there silently. If you would be Free, open some books and *learn* the *meanings* of "democracy" and "Republic". Once you understand, DEMAND the restoration of our Republic. Make it absolutely clear that if government won't respond to your demands, you are prepared to FIGHT—to the death, if necessary—for your Rights and a Republic.

Don't have the nerve for it? Then prepare yourself and your chil-   12
dren to wear chains. And prepare, also, to one day explain your cowardice to God.

Reprinted with permission from the *AntiShyster,* POB 540786, Dallas, Texas, 75354-0786.

✦ *Questions for Discussion and Writing*

1. In your own words, restate the most important characteristic or trait that Adask seeks to uphold as the defining quality in the American form of government.

2. How does Adask seek to persuade his audience of the importance of this characteristic by emphasizing how current definitions of democracy are antagonistic to this specified feature?

3. Is this argument merely a linguistic quibble over nearly identical terms, or are there profound philosophical differences between the two? Explain your answer.

4. How does Adask use the framework of deductions drawn from stipulated definitions to reach the seemingly paradoxical conclusion that a

democracy is antagonistic to the rights and welfare of an overwhelming majority of its citizens? What flaws can you discover in his reasoning process that might invalidate his conclusion?

5. To what extent does the author's use of language intended to arouse the emotions of his audience enhance or diminish the force of his argument?

6

Strategies for Writing Arguments

◆

The process of writing an argumentative essay is similar to that of writing other kinds of essays in that it requires you to find a subject, define your approach to the topic, establish a thesis sentence, decide on your purpose, identify your audience, plan your essay (with or without an informal outline), write a rough draft, revise, edit, and proofread to produce a final paper.

Argumentative essays differ from other kinds of essays in that they are designed to achieve at least one of the following purposes: (1) persuade others to accept your position on a clearly defined issue, (2) accept your argument refuting someone else's position, or (3) endorse a solution you propose to a problem.

The process of writing can best be thought of as a series of operations you perform. These actions or steps encompass prewriting activities that precede the first draft, including a variety of invention strategies useful for discovering a topic, identifying your purpose, analyzing your audience, and organizing the material before writing a first draft.

Although this chapter will spell out the different steps in the writing process, writers know that it is impossible to take a prescriptive approach to writing. Writing is a recursive process without clearly defined beginnings and endings. You should feel free to do any of the following steps in a different order from the way they are presented or to return to any of the earlier steps at any time. You should also feel free to follow the developing idea in whatever direction it may lead, whether or not it means departing from a predetermined sequence of steps. You may discover, as many writers do, that the act of writing requires you to substantially rethink your thesis and perhaps even change your entire essay as you discover a new topic or come to a radically different

313

conclusion about your original topic. What is valuable about the process approach is that it gives you many opportunities to get a clear idea of what you want to write about and a way to test your developing essay in order to correct basic oversights and add new insights.

Prewriting

Finding something to write about (if you have not been assigned a topic in class) can be helped along if you consider some of the following sources for likely argumentative essay subjects.

Differences of opinion on issues with friends are a potential starting point, as are other issues drawn from your personal experiences. For example, you might address a problem that needs solving. How should fraternities deal with the alcohol-related problems that have caused injuries and deaths during fraternity hazings? Is the problem so unsolvable that colleges should even consider banning fraternities from their campuses?

You might begin with experiences that frustrate you or make you dissatisfied with the way things are being done. What do you complain about a lot? You might propose that your school provide more parking facilities for students, since there is always a rush for the few spaces that are available.

For another source, you might consider topics of current controversy reported in the news. For example, in a 1988 book Albert Goldman wrote a biography of John Lennon that portrayed Lennon as a heroin addict and a bisexual. Yoko Ono and the remaining members of the Beatles protested Goldman's unsavory characterization of Lennon, especially since none of them was interviewed by Goldman for the book. You might wish to argue that something should be done to change the current libel laws to protect deceased celebrities and other people who cannot defend themselves.

Consider issues that have come up in your reading for other courses. In a psychology course you might have read different arguments by Desmond Morris, Ashley Montagu, or Sigmund Freud claiming that human aggression is either innate or learned. Your thesis could be that human aggression is not genetically determined but is a form of learned behavior.

The issue you choose to write about must be genuinely debatable. Rule out arguments over facts that could be settled by looking in a reference book. Also eliminate questions of personal taste. What you are looking for is an issue about which knowledgeable people disagree. The assumption is that if people who know a lot about the issue disagree, then the facts of the situation can be interpreted in different ways, and therefore that issue would make a good, debatable subject to

explore in your essay. For example, people still disagree about whether
the Supreme Court 1966 Miranda decision (which requires the police to
inform those being arrested of their right to remain silent unless an attorney is present) should be amended to make it less likely that hard-
core criminals can be released on procedural technicalities. You might
wish to argue that the Miranda decision should be modified to rectify
this problem.

SELECTING AN ISSUE

To get started, you might begin by listing possible topics you already
know about. For example, you might have been in Little League and
experienced a lot of pressure to compete, both from the coaches and
from your parents. Some children later think the experience was worthwhile, whereas others think the pressure parents put on them to win
was too traumatic. If you felt this latter way, you might make a case
that parents who wish to live vicariously through their children's suc-
cesses put an unfair burden on their children.

The next step in selecting an issue is to consider whether it requires
research just to find out what is entailed. You might need to discover
the range of arguments that already exist to determine what your own
position might be. For example, police officers occasionally pose as students to find out who is using and selling drugs on campus. What
exactly does the law say on this issue? Where does posing as an under-
cover student leave off and entrapment begin?

To discover whether you have found a genuinely debatable topic,
consider whether the same facts are open to more than one interpretation. Most college students have heard about the increasing incidence
of date rape (a 1988 study, reported by Robin Warshaw in *I Never Called
It Rape: The Ms Report on Recognizing, Fighting, and Surviving Date and
Acquaintance Rape,* found that "1 in 4 women surveyed were victims of
rape or attempted rape") where women are not attacked by some anonymous stranger but by their dates or romantic acquaintances. Yet many
of these men do not see themselves as rapists. The question of what is
considered permissible sexually in the context of modern male–female
relationships has contributed to the problem. For instance, men who
hold traditional views of sex roles may believe that if the woman asks a
man for a date, goes to his apartment, or allows him to pay for all expenses, a sexual invitation is implied that the woman has no right to
withdraw. The whole question is obviously subject to more than one
interpretation.

Genuinely debatable topics are found when people bring two competing sets of values to the same situation, perhaps without even being
aware of it. Thus, a tradition of the Christmas season may have been a
manger scene in front of the town hall, yet, recently, groups have pro-

tested that having such a scene on a municipally owned piece of property violates the First Amendment's "establishment clause" separating church and state. This is an emotional issue precisely because people bring competing sets of values to bear on the same set of circumstances.

You might consider moral questions you have debated with friends regarding what is right and what is wrong. What if you discover that athletes at your school are receiving special academic tutoring that is not equally available to other students, or that a particular athlete has received an under-the-table cash payment to induce him or her to attend a particular college? Although you can appreciate that college athletics bring big money and prestige to schools, you may wish to argue that school administrations apply one set of standards to athletes and another to all the other students.

Aside from maintaining an inquisitive perspective to discover a potential starting point for your essay, you might be the type of person who wonders what caused certain things to be the way they are. Let's say you lived abroad and recently immigrated to the United States or that your grandparents and other relatives came from another culture. You might wonder why the elderly are often treated as disposable citizens in the United States when they are treated with veneration and respect in many other cultures. Why should this be so? You might wish to argue a thesis that many people would find controversial: our culture does not value old people because many are poor and cannot afford to participate in the consumer culture. You might develop your thesis by looking at how our culture encourages young people starting out in life to assume debt of monumental proportions. You might further claim that since old people are unwilling or unable to take on large debts, they are automatically viewed as second-class citizens.

You might consider what started a fad. For example, what explains the increase in popularity of New Age fads such as channeling, crystal healing, flower essences, and reflexology? Or you might consider what started a certain trend. For example, statistics show an increasing trend in the numbers of children who are abused physically and emotionally each year. Are more accurate identification procedures responsible for the greater numbers of cases reported, or are greater numbers of children actually being abused? If the latter, what is causing this trend to accelerate?

You might be aware of implications or far-reaching effects about which others seem unaware. For example, you read that crops are going to be sprayed with biogenetically produced frost-inhibiting bacteria. You wonder what precautions have been taken to prevent this and other genetically engineered substances from wreaking havoc on the environment.

Even if you are not assigned a specific subject, topics that can become sources of good arguments are all around you. All that is required is that you discover a situation that is subject to more than one interpretation and where it is probable that neither side has a lock on the truth. For example, you read about a case where strict Christian Scientists would not permit doctors to give a blood transfusion to their severely injured child. The hospital appealed to a judge who allowed the transfusion despite the parents' religious convictions. Who made the correct decision in this case? Do you think the court was warranted in overstepping the parents' wishes?

INVENTION STRATEGIES

After selecting the issue that is most interesting to you from your list, excluding those that are too broad, are matters of fact, or are simple disagreements over personal preferences, consider whether this issue can be investigated within the amount of time you have to write about it and within the number of pages you have been assigned.

At this point, you might wish to consider any or all of the following invention strategies that have proved useful to many writers in discovering their particular aspect of a topic and how best to approach it in developing an essay. The basic invention strategies we will discuss include

Free-writing
Five W's
Discovering different perspectives
Mapping
Writing a dialogue
Discovering the pros and cons

Free-Writing

Free-writing is a technique for setting down whatever occurs to you on the topic within a few minutes to a half hour. There are no restrictions whatsoever on what can or cannot be put down. Free-writing serves a sound psychological purpose. It lets you find out what you already know about the issue without imposing any editorial constraints on your thought processes. Simply free-associate everything you think of that has to do with this issue. Write without stopping to edit or correct. The only rule is to keep writing without stopping to think or to criticize what you are writing. You will find that your thought processes will function more fully and creatively when you are not being critical. Also, the very act of expressing your thoughts in writing compels you to clarify what you think. Simply free-associate, allowing your mind to come up with any thoughts without stopping to censor, evaluate, or edit them. Don't worry about spelling or punctuation or rules of grammar.

Free-writing is meant to be casual, informal, and tentative. You write to define the issue. Your goal is to get as clear a perception as you can of the key aspects of the issue in order to discover how you should focus your argument. For example, let's say that in your social psychology class you read an account of the Kitty Genovese case (in which a young woman was stabbed to death while her neighbors watched and did not call the police) and have decided to try to focus on the components of the case to discover a genuinely debatable topic.

Your free-writing might appear thus:

> Why would 38 people ignore a woman's cries for help, maybe afraid to get involved, what were they thinking, hassles with the police, legal proceedings, open court and criminal would get off and come back and kill them, what did they say to themselves, why did they do nothing, isn't plausible that all 38 were apathetic, maybe each thought another called police, rationalize not doing anything, wonder if the number of people has anything to do with the decision, how aware were these people of each other.

✦ Questions for Discussion and Writing

1. To generate your own ideas for free-writing, use the following starters as lead-ins:

   My pet peeve is . . .

   I wish I could talk my (brother, sister, boyfriend, girlfriend, professor, mother, father) into . . .

   The last argument I had with someone was about . . .

   Current rules at my college require . . .; I believe they should be changed in the following way. . . .

2. Make the subject of your free-writing an account of your past efforts to use any prewriting or invention strategies. What worked for you and what did not work?

Five W's

Next, you might wish to ask and answer questions journalists often use to define what can be known about the subject.

WHO is involved in this situation?

WHAT is at stake? WHAT action or outcome is hanging in the balance?

WHERE did the action take place?

WHEN did the action take place?

WHY is what happened an important issue?

In the Genovese case, your answers might be:

WHO—38 people, Kitty Genovese, the murderer

WHAT—Kitty Genovese is attacked as she returns home from work at 3 A.M. 38 of her neighbors in Kew Gardens, New York come to their windows when she cries out in terror. Not one comes to her assistance even though her assailant takes one-half hour to murder her. The murderer is twice frightened away and returns. No one so much as calls the police. She dies.

WHEN—1968

WHERE—apartment building in Kew Gardens, Queens, New York.

WHY—why did none of the 38 people help the woman or call the police at any time during the 35 minutes? Why did the witnesses continue to look out of their windows at the scene only to ignore what was happening?

Use the five W's to analyze different elements connected with the personal experiences you have had with a particular issue. In answering "why" tell how your experience has influenced the opinions you now hold (for example, sexual harassment, drug-testing, etc.).

Discovering Different Perspectives

The next step is to explore your topic from different angles. Discovering different perspectives (DDP) is an invention strategy to help you generate and develop material for your essay by looking at an issue from several angles. It requires you to take the topic and write for a few minutes from each of the following perspectives:

1. What is the issue connected to or related to? What does this issue bring to mind? What common elements does this situation share with other situations that I am familiar with?
   Your answer might be:

   For me, the issue is connected with urban violence, crime in the subways, and the baffling question why people don't help victims of crime.

2. What is the issue similar to or different from? What distinguishes this situation from other situations that at first glance might look very similar?
   Your answer might be:

   Is this situation similar to the Holocaust? Does it involve the same phenomenon of being indifferent to what is happening to people around you? On the other hand, it is different from the Holocaust because then the German state acted criminally and here the government is against the criminal. It seems more similar to other cases of bystander noninvolvement, for example, subway riders not coming to the assistance of fellow passengers, even after the attackers have left the subway car.

3. Analyze the different elements involved. Break the topic into its component parts. How might the same event appear through the eyes of each of the people involved? How do they relate to each other?
Your answer might be:

By running away, the killer revealed he could have been scared off and it would not have taken very much to scare him. If the people watching literally did anything at all, the murder would not have taken place. There was no way for the people in the apartment building to know if the person being murdered was a friend or not. She could have been someone they knew. Or was there enough light to recognize her and no one cared that she was being murdered since they did not know her personally? Has our society made life so difficult for witnesses, in terms of police lineups, testimony in open court, endless trial delays, taking time off from work, that witnesses end up being victims of the system? The key point is that, psychologically, 38 people from very different backgrounds shared something in common that prevented all of them from taking any action. What could this be?

4. Define the issue. The purpose of defining is to try to arrive at a working definition of the topic. What are the distinctive elements in this particular situation that give it its unique quality or meaning? Try to isolate the most important qualities of the issue and discuss what they mean. Write for a few minutes. (You can use any of the techniques under "Definition" in Chapter 5.
Your answer might be:

Why didn't any of the 38 witnesses feel a sense of personal responsibility and intervene or at least call the police? Were they merely indifferent to the violence they were watching? Does living in a city make you not care about what is happening to others? Would I react the same way they did in the same situation? If asked before the event, most of the 38 people would probably have said they would have helped the victim, or at least called the police before this incident. What caused all of them not to do anything? So, the issue is what prevented each of them individually and collectively from acting?

Mapping

Mapping, another effective prewriting strategy, allows you to perceive the relationship between important ideas visually. To do this, simply create a map, circling the key ideas and letting their spatial relationships to each other and the connecting lines give you a way of representing or charting groups of related ideas. When you group ideas in this way you discover connections and patterns that will help you when you decide which ideas are central and which are subordinate. Mapping out your observations on the topic in this way will allow you to see more clearly what you have to say. The map in Figure 6-1 will be especially useful in letting you see how your thesis will emerge from materials that can be used to support it.

Writing a Dialogue

Writing a dialogue is another invention strategy useful in discovering what is at stake in the issue. You invent a drama in which you discuss the issue from both sides, playing yourself as well as a devil's advocate to represent different viewpoints fairly. This technique depends on your ability to create an imaginary dialogue where you take both sides. To get started, you might wish to use a tape recorder and then transcribe your dialogue later. We all have had the experience of rehearsing conversations in order to clarify what we would say in differ-

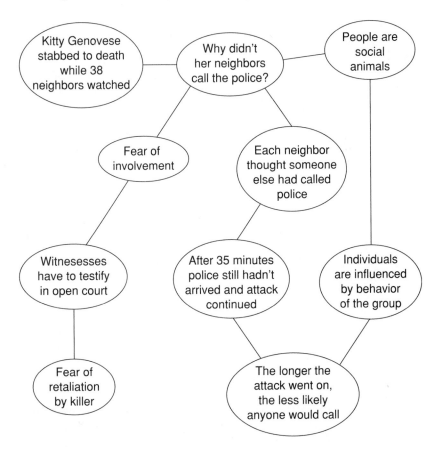

FIGURE 6-1

ent situations and how we would answer someone who held the opposite view.

To construct the dialogue, simply begin by making an assertion that expresses your view on any aspect of the issue. Then swing around and put yourself in the position of someone with an opposing viewpoint. Next, put down what you would reply as yourself. Then challenge that view by putting yourself in the frame of mind of your opponent, who views the issue from a totally different angle or perspective. The technique is an old one, used by Socrates (as reported by Plato in the *Dialogues*) to challenge people to discover whether they had good reasons for supporting their beliefs. Being cross-examined forces you to look critically at assumptions you might take for granted and pressures you to come up with reasons to support your views. Any reason able to survive objections raised by an opponent would qualify as a sound reason with which to support your belief.

You will know you are on the right track when the dialogue assumes a momentum of its own. It is important to avoid getting bogged down. If you get stuck, ask yourself a question, taking the part of the other person. You will find this a valuable technique for anticipating the counterarguments of those who would react negatively to the points you raise.

After you create your informal dialogue, identify and rank the reasons you have discovered on both sides of the issue, from weakest to strongest.

For example, what follows is an imaginary dialogue between you and you-as-your-opponent. Your purpose in making up this dialogue was to systematically focus on each aspect of the topic of the Kitty Genovese case in order to discover a point of view to encapsulate in your thesis statement.

> *Opponent:* The issue is apathy; people simply didn't care.
> *You:* People were not apathetic; they were aware and did care but were inhibited from acting.
> *Opponent:* Maybe they rationalized not acting because each person believed someone else had called the police.
> *You:* It's just not credible that in a group of 38 people not one person would care that someone was screaming for help while being murdered. It is much more likely that people did care but were afraid to get involved for some reason.
> *Opponent:* I understand why they would be afraid to go down there and confront a killer personally, but why would they be afraid to call the police?
> *You:* It isn't so simple as calling the police. They knew they would have to identify themselves, testify in open court, and if the killer got off or got out of jail he could return to kill them.

Opponent: Not true. All they had to do was phone in without giving a name and the police still would have come. How do you explain that?

You: You're right. Good point. Maybe each witness thought someone else had called the police and rationalized not calling for that reason.

Opponent: That might seem plausible at first, but what about when they saw that the police did not arrive and the murderer returned, was frightened away again, and returned again. Remember, this whole attack took over 35 minutes.

You: Let's look at it from another angle. Would any one of these people have called if they thought they were the only witness and saw a crime being committed and knew they were the only one who could possibly stop it or report it to the police? I don't have any hard evidence, but I think chances would have been 38 times greater if any one of them thought they were the only one.

Opponent: So, you're saying that a number of people, all of whom were aware of each other's presence, are less likely to help a victim of street crime than they would be if they knew they were the only one who could call the police.

You: I guess that's what I mean. People are social animals, and the behavior of individuals in a group is strongly influenced by the behavior of the group as a whole. I guess that's my thesis:

I think the 38 people who witnessed the murder of Kitty Genovese were inhibited from helping because as time went on it became obvious that the group had decided not to call the police, so ironically the longer the attack went on, the less likely it was anyone would call.

◆ Question for Discussion and Writing

1. Describe a situation in which two people are exchanging opinions about an issue about which they both have strong views. What do they say to each other?

Discovering the Pros and Cons

The activities of note-gathering and exploration in free-writing, answering the five questions, discovering different perspectives, mapping, and writing your own dialogue should provide you with enough material to let you start looking at the issue in an organized way. You may find that your dialogue has given you some idea of how you would want to go about advancing your views and how you would defend your reasons if someone with an opposing viewpoint challenged them.

You should now be ready to prepare a list of pro and con points on each side, along with accompanying reasons.

List these reasons in two columns under pro and con headings, and then arrange each list of reasons from weakest to strongest or vice versa. From the range of reasons on both sides of the issue, you should be able to discover the idea you believe will be important enough to serve as a focus of your argument. This idea should be expressed in one sentence (called a *thesis statement*) that asserts your view on the issue.

For example: A student who wished to explore the phenomenon of ESP (extrasensory perception) and to look into the cases that could be made for and against its existence might use all the previous invention strategies (free-writing, five W's, discovering different perspectives, mapping, and dialogue) to generate the following list of points for and against the existence of ESP:

PRO
1. Premonitions of disaster, feelings of déjà vu, and strange coincidences suggest ESP exists.

CON
1. Belief in ESP gives people a sense of power, leads them to think the future can be predicted and controlled, and boosts their egos—who wouldn't want to believe in ESP?

PRO
2. One of the conditions of having ESP is that you cannot use it for personal gain.

CON
2. If ESP existed, those who had it would be multimillionaires and would be able to prove it was true.

PRO
3. The evidence found to prove the existence of any new phenomenon in the past has always been scant and the existence of the phenomenon difficult to prove. For example, Galileo was almost killed when he suggested that the sun, not the earth, was at the center of the solar system. When Louis Pasteur introduced his germ theory, medical men scoffed at it as being a "ridiculous fiction."

CON
3. No one has been able to demonstrate the existence of ESP under research conditions. A phenomenon that cannot be replicated in the laboratory does not exist, for scientific purposes.

From this list of reasons, the student chose the concept of being able to replicate ESP under laboratory conditions as the focus of her argument. Her tentative thesis statement would read as follows:

All so-called demonstrations of the existence of ESP simply don't meet any of the criteria required for scientific research.

Notice that the thesis statement is phrased as a complete sentence and is stated in a way that would allow an opponent to be able to make a case for the opposite point of view. For example, in the above instance, an opponent might take the contrary position that laboratory replications of ESP really do meet the traditional criteria required of all scientific research. To test whether your thesis statement will allow you to create an argument, turn it around and see if you can make a case from the opposite side.

✦ *Question for Discussion and Writing*

1. How do you feel about sororities and fraternities? Create a set of pro and con arguments in which you make a claim, add the word "because," and fill in your reasons. For example, the pro view: "Sororities and fraternities are worthwhile because they often raise money for good causes," could be balanced by a counterassertion, or con view: "Sororities and fraternities are not worthwhile because they create an atmosphere that is not conducive to studying."

ARRIVING AT A THESIS: CLAIMS OF FACT, CAUSATION, VALUE, AND POLICY

It may take several tries to arrive at a clear and supportable thesis statement. Arriving at a thesis involves discovering an idea you think is important enough to serve as the focus of your essay. The thesis is stated in the form of a single sentence that asserts your personal response to an issue that others might respond to in different ways. If, for example, the issue were euthanasia, your response might be that "mercy killing, in some circumstances, is not only morally permissible but a humane course of action." Or, you might wish to assert the contrary, that "mercy killing, under any circumstances, is not morally permissible."

If the issue were the crime-stoppers program, your thesis might be "crime-stoppers has proved its value in solving crimes, recovering property, and obtaining convictions in cases that previously baffled investigators." By contrast, you might wish to argue the opposite position, that is, "crime-stoppers should be abolished on the grounds that it invites the erosion of vital civil liberties guaranteed by the Sixth Amendment's provision against anonymous accusations."

The thesis usually is not the first thought that springs to mind on an issue; it should not be an automatic response but rather an idea you have carefully considered. The thesis is an idea that you have arrived at by thinking through an issue or problem until you feel you have come up with an opinion capable of being substantiated with good reasons. Of course, only when you get into the actual process of writing the essay will you discover whether you have enough good reasons and supporting evidence to persuade your audience to agree with your thesis.

The thesis statement should be phrased as an assertion that makes a claim of fact (what is it?), value (is it good or bad?), causation (what caused it?), or policy (what should be done about it?). For example, the thesis statement "mercy killing, under any circumstances, is not morally permissible" expresses a value judgment that requires the writer to persuade the audience to agree with a set of moral criteria and then to judge the phenomenon of mercy killing accordingly.

Obviously, it is helpful to figure out what kind of question your thesis, and consequently your entire essay, will answer, since the methods by which your essay will be developed are keyed to the specific goal you have in mind. The kind of evidence you use and how you develop your argument will, of course, depend on your specific thesis, but here are some examples of different kinds of thesis statements along with possible ways of developing them.

1. A thesis statement that makes a *factual claim:* The material you have gathered in the prewriting and invention stages can be invaluable in helping you focus on what people argue about when they argue about that issue. When people disagree over (1) what happened, (2) what the nature of the event is, or (3) how to define a phenomenon, your argument can best be developed as a claim of fact. Your essay will explain your particular interpretation of the facts and offer evidence to support your interpretation about the nature of X. You may wish to develop your argument through comparisons or analogies that make it easy for your audience to grasp the basic nature of your subject. The first thing to do is phrase your claim as a thesis statement. For example:

> The evidence provided by the accounts of people who have survived near-death experiences is compelling but hardly conclusive proof of some form of life after death.

To develop a factual claim like this you will need to add several "because" clauses that express your own reasons for holding this view. Support for your claim might be in the form of evaluations of available accounts, anecdotal personal experience if appropriate, or theories advanced by scientists and theologians.

2. A thesis statement that makes a *causal claim:* "De-institutionalization programs by the nation's hospitals is the major cause of the hun-

dreds of thousands of homeless people wandering the streets of our major cities." Notice how the thesis statement implies how the paper should be organized. The author would need to show what the hospital policy was before, why it was changed, and exactly what effects the change produced. It is important not to assume that your thesis statement is permanent. In this case, the writer discovered midway into the process of writing the essay that a big part of the homeless population in our big cities were the unemployed and all those who simply could not afford the price of housing. This meant that the thesis would have to be modified, restated, or perhaps even scrapped entirely.

3. A thesis statement that makes a *value claim:* Do the notes and observations from the prewriting and invention exercises suggest that when people disagree it is because they hold completely incompatible or conflicting beliefs that stem from different sets of values? If so, your essay will require that you decide which side, if any, you agree with or offer you the chance to explore the issue without trying to prove that either side is right or wrong. For example, you may assert:

> It is wrong for Hollywood stars to be treated preferentially by being allowed to work off drug sentences in community service whereas ordinary people convicted of the same crimes have to serve jail time.

Notice how this value claim could be organized around a comparison showing how Hollywood stars are treated in contrast to how ordinary people are treated who have committed the same drug-related crimes.

4. A thesis statement that makes a *policy claim:* Let's say that your prewriting observations alerted you to the fact that you were most concerned with the conflict over government subsidies for tobacco companies. At the core of this argument, people disagree about the double standard of requiring health warnings while giving money to the same companies about whose products the public is being warned. You decide that instead of maintaining this complicated roundabout situation, the government should simply cut off the subsidies. You might phrase your claim as follows:

> Since the federal government already requires health warnings on every pack of cigarettes and forbids advertising of cigarettes on radio and television, tax money should not be used to subsidize tobacco growers.

Since you have added "because" clauses to this claim, it will require you to support your recommendation with credible statistics, evaluations of the impact on public health, and projections as to the kinds of effects a change in government policy would produce.

A good thesis statement is like a schematic blueprint of a building that shows what the building will look like before money, effort, and time are spent on its construction. By the same token, it makes more sense to put in extra time in drafting your thesis statement than to spend extra time later extensively rewriting your entire essay, hoping that some central point or thesis will emerge. For instance, a student's essay was originally organized around this thesis:

> The U.S. Department of Agriculture should not help the tobacco producers in their efforts to offset the loss of sales in the United States by encouraging export of cigarettes to Japan, Taiwan, Korea, Thailand, and Third World countries, where they would be sold without the warning labels that are required on cigarette packages sold in the United States.

As it stands, this thesis statement has no central focus. An essay organized around it would go off in all directions, but this would become apparent only after the student had spent considerable time and effort. Think of how much more efficient it would be to revise the thesis statement so that everything in the essay would tie into one central point, the unjustifiable difference between foreign and domestic policies of the Unites States government regarding the sale of cigarettes. In its revised form the thesis statement would read as follows:

> Since the U.S. government requires warning labels on cigarettes to protect U.S. citizens, it is inconsistent and immoral for the Department of Agriculture to promote the sale of cigarettes to countries where they will be sold without warning labels.

The thesis should express the idea that you would want your audience to reach after they had read through your entire essay. Place the thesis statement in the first paragraph or group of paragraphs so that your readers will be able to evaluate each of the reasons you present to support your thesis and be better able to perceive the relationship between these reasons and the main idea of your argument.

✦ Questions for Discussion and Writing

1. When people argue about one of the following issues, what do they disagree about?

   a. Victims' compensation laws

   b. Technological advances in robot production

   c. Behavior modification: stop smoking, overeating, insomnia

    d. History of a famous rock band: Rolling Stones, the E Street Band, the Traveling Wilbury's, Tom Petty and the Heartbreakers

    e. Organ transplants

    f. The right to die issue: a dilemma for religion, law, and medicine

    g. The sharp rise in teenage pregnancies

    h. Psychotherapists on the radio: helpful or harmful?

    i. Fashion industry fads: why do they change?

    j. Television violence and its effect on children

    k. Rights of smokers versus rights of nonsmokers

    l. Preventing, diagnosing, and treating child abuse

    m. The FDA's drug approval procedure: careful or just bureaucratic?

    n. America's fascination with New Age fads: crystals, spirit channeling, and so on

    o. Socialized medicine: will it work in the United States?

    p. History of the Nobel Prize, the Pulitzer Prize, the Academy Awards

    q. Should children be prosecuted as adults for serious crimes?

    r. How do fraternities/sororities help later in life?

    s. Experiments on the intelligence of dolphins

    t. Funeral practices: ancient and modern

    u. The latest chapter in the history of affirmative action

    v. Nostradamus: prophet or fraud?

2. Develop a workable thesis on one of the above topics. Follow this claim with several "because" clauses that express your own reasons. What would an essay written along these lines need to show? If you and some of your classmates have written arguments taking opposing views on the same issue, prepare a summary of your position to share with other classmates. You might also wish to write summaries of the opposing position to see how well you understood what the other side was saying.

3. If you have trouble finding an issue about which people disagree, you might consider one of the following. To develop each claim, follow it with several "because" clauses that express your own reasons. What would an essay written along these lines need to show? How should it be organized? Specify the audience to whom you would be making this argument. Think of an audience (person or group) whose opinion you would want to change.

    a. Factual arguments about the nature of things or how something should be defined:

- Are affirmative action programs reverse discrimination?
- How have views on marriage changed over the past fifty years? What are they now?
- Which professions continue to attract almost all men and which almost all women? Is there any evidence of a change?
- Is the evidence for extrasensory perception (far from) conclusive?

b. Arguments over causation:

- Can humor teach as well as entertain?
- How has the use of photography affected the perceptions of war, famine, and natural disasters?
- What lessons does history have to teach us about what could happen to individual rights and freedoms if genetic information is readily available to employers, insurers, schools, courts, politicians, the military, and others who make far-reaching decisions?
- What are the consequences of programs designed to enforce population control in Third World countries?
- Are the effects of divorce less harmful for children than the effects of living in a conflict-ridden home environment?
- Has the feminist movement benefited society?
- What factors would cause cremation to replace traditional burials?
- Why don't 18-year-olds vote as often as other age groups vote?

c. Value arguments:

- Is patriotism a virtue?
- What is the difference between a just and an unjust war, whether or not it is called an international peacekeeping operation? For example, are there differences between World War II, Vietnam, the 1989 U.S. invasion of Panama, the 1991 war in the Persian gulf, the 1992 intervention in Somalia, Haiti, and wars since then?
- Should the covers of *Playboy* or *Penthouse* magazines be considered art or pornography?
- Is it immoral to keep animals in zoos for our entertainment and edification?
- Is it morally wrong to use human fetal tissue for medical research?
- Is it ethically wrong to implant animal parts in humans (xenografts)?
- Write a review of a recent movie, television program, play, concert, or book, clearly stating your criteria and comparing them with the judgments made by other reviewers.
- Is advertising fundamentally deceptive? Does it create insecurity in order to sell goods? Does it perpetuate stereotypes? Is it a harmful or harmless addition to our lives?
- Does political correctness promote censorship?

- Does an abortion involve killing what may be a human being? Is abortion moral? Does a fetus have the right to life, liberty, and the pursuit of happiness guaranteed by the U.S. Constitution?
- Is drug testing an invasion of privacy? What are the bounds of privacy in the workplace in terms of drug testing, lie detector tests, computer surveillance, or genetic screening?
- Is surrogate mothering a form of exploitation? Should it be permitted?
- Should American sports teams such as the Atlanta Braves, Washington Redskins, Cleveland Indians, Florida State Seminoles, and Kansas City Chiefs take into account the concern for stereotyping expressed by Native Americans?
- Do animals have rights?
- How do the fashion and cosmetic industries create standards for the way Americans should look that contribute to a variety of eating disorders such as anorexia and bulimia?

d. Policy arguments over what should be done:

- Should patients have the right to transfer and sell their body parts?
- Should smoking in public places be prohibited?
- Should campus newspapers publish or suppress false or misleading advertising (for example, for a book or speaker denying the Holocaust)?
- Does freedom of the press outweigh the right to privacy of a rape victim? Should the names of rape victims be published?
- Should bilingual education programs be eliminated? Does the evidence support the benefits of bilingual education?
- How early should the topic of AIDS be addressed in public schools?
- Should children with disabilities be mainstreamed into regular classrooms?
- Should gays and lesbians have the right to marry and to adopt children?
- Should pregnant women who use drugs be prosecuted for "fetal abuse"?
- Under what conditions should physicians be allowed to assist terminally ill patients commit suicide?
- Should the United States adopt a national health care program?
- Should prostitution be decriminalized?
- Should businesses provide on-site day care facilities?
- Is there a case to be made for arranged marriages?
- Should insurance companies be allowed to use genetic screening to set rate structures?

- Should extremely retarded men and women be sterilized to prevent them from having children?
- Should genetic engineering be used to produce insect resistant plants, or food that doesn't spoil, or grass you don't have to mow?
- Should immunization against childhood diseases be mandatory for all children?
- Should public schools distribute condoms to reduce teenage pregnancy and the rate of HIV infection among teenagers?
- Should five-year surgically implanted contraceptives (Norplant) be provided in public schools to reduce teenage pregnancy?
- Should the ban against RU-486, the hormonal birth control pill, be lifted in the United States? It is currently legal in France, Scandinavia, and the United Kingdom.
- Should the U.S. Food and Drug Administration (FDA) suspend rules requiring extensive testing of new drugs to provide seriously ill people with immediate access to the most promising drugs and treatment?
- Make the case for saving any plant or animal (for example, the snail darter or the rhinoceros in Africa).

MAKING UP AN OUTLINE: SUPPORTING YOUR CLAIM

If you have a workable thesis that expresses the conclusion you want your audience to reach, *consider whether it is capable of being adequately supported with evidence in the form of examples, statistics, or expert testimony.* An easy way to do this, and at the same time to see what the structure of the paper you intend to write will look like, is to draw up an outline before writing the rough draft. For example, an outline of a student paper, with the kinds of evidence brought in to support each idea, can appear as follows:

I. Current theories explaining widespread drug use.
   —supported by evidence in the form of expert opinions by a psychologist and a sociologist

II. Increasing drug use in the success-oriented areas of sports, finance, and entertainment.
   —supported by evidence of personal testimony, sports medicine experts, interviews, and surveys

III. Unsuccessful efforts of the government to stop the drug epidemic.
   —supported by statistics, reports by government agencies, testimony of psychologists and lawyers, and court cases

IV. The crucial role of education in preventing drug abuse.
    —supported by government supplied statistics

Even an informal outline, as long as it sets the boundaries for different sections of your paper, will prove invaluable as a blueprint in pointing out structural weaknesses in the organization of your essay. The outline might reveal that two short, partially developed sections in the argument might be better joined together as one complete, fully developed section. Likewise, your outline may disclose an overlong section that might be more effective if it were split into two or more shorter, paragraphs. Check your outline to make sure your essay has covered all the important points necessary to the development of your argument.

CHOICES IN ORGANIZING YOUR ESSAY

Writing the Introduction

The function of the initial paragraph or introduction is to engage the reader in the central issue and to present your claim regarding the question at hand. If you intend to disagree with widely held views, or if the nature of the issue is complex or unfamiliar to your readers, you might use the first few paragraphs to briefly summarize relevant background information before explicitly stating your thesis.

Some writers find it valuable to use the opening paragraphs to briefly acknowledge commonly held views opposed to the position taken in the essay. The introduction alerts readers to the fact that the writer is aware of opposite views and plans to rebut them while providing reasons and evidence supporting his or her own argument as the essay advances. By helping your readers to understand how you will organize your argument you are providing them with a map to follow in reading your essay.

Some writers find that a brief story or anecdote is an ideal way to focus the audience's attention on the subject. For example, Walter Bems introduces his argument for capital punishment "Crime and the Morality of the Death Penalty" (from *For Capital Punishment* [1979]) with an amusing anecdote that focuses the attention of the audience on the issue of capital punishment in a memorable way:

> It must be one of the oldest jokes in circulation. In the dark of a wild night a ship strikes a rock and sinks, but one of its sailors clings desperately to a piece of wreckage and is eventually cast up exhausted on an unknown and deserted beach. In the morning, he struggles to his feet and, rubbing his salt-encrusted eyes, looks around to learn where he is. The only human thing he sees is a gallows. "Thank God," he exclaims, "civilization."

There cannot be many of us who have not heard this story or, when we first heard it, laughed at it. The sailor's reaction was, we think, absurd. Yet, however old the story, the fact is that the gallows has not been abolished in the United States even yet, and we count ourselves among the civilized peoples of the world. Moreover, the attempt to have it abolished by the U.S. Supreme Court may only have succeeded in strengthening its structure.

Other writers use the strategy of opening with an especially apt quotation. Henry David Thoreau opens his famous essay "Civil Disobedience" (1849) with a quotation that sets the stage for his defense of individual conscience on the grounds that when conflicts arise between citizens and the government, "we should be men first and subjects afterward":

> I heartily accept the motto, "That government is best which governs least"; and I should like to see it acted up to more rapidly and systematically. Carried out, it finally amounts to this, which also I believe— "That government is best which governs not at all"; and when men are prepared for it, that will be the kind of government which they will have. Government is at best but an expedient; but most governments are usually, and all governments are sometimes, inexpedient.

Still other writers draw us in by beginning with a personal narrative, as does Richard Rodriguez in "Aria: A Memoir of a Bilingual Childhood" (1980):

> I remember, to start with, that day in Sacramento, in a California now nearly thirty years past, when I first entered a classroom—able to understand about fifty stray English words. The third of four children, I had been preceded by my older brother and sister to a neighborhood Roman Catholic school.

Another effective way to begin is by setting the stage or describing the setting as a backdrop against which to see the conflict the argument will explore. For example, this is the way Byron Dorgan opens his essay "America's Real Farm Problem: It Can Be Solved" (1983):

> Recent scenes from America's farm belt seem like a grainy film clip from the thirties. Young families putting their home and farm machinery on the auction block. Men, choked with emotion, breaking down in tears as they describe their plight. Angry farmers organizing, getting madder and madder. It's not as bad as the thirties yet, no governor has called out the National Guard to stop the foreclosures, the way North Dakota's William "Wild Bill" Langer did in 1933. But the pain is running deep. Losing a farm is not like having a new Chevrolet or a color

TV repossessed. In many cases, what's lost is land that's been in the family for generations—and a way of life that for many is the only one they've ever known or wanted.

Writers may also choose to introduce their arguments in many other ways by defining key terms, offering a prediction, posing a thoughtful question, or using a touch of humor. William Ryan begins an argument (*Blaming the Victim* [1971]), whose thesis is that the poor are blamed for their own poverty, with an amusing, but all too true, story:

> Twenty years ago, Zero Mostel used to do a sketch in which he imper-sonated a Dixiecrat Senator conducting an investigation of the origins of World War II. At the climax of the sketch, the Senator boomed out, in an excruciating mixture of triumph and suspicion, "what was Pearl Harbor *doing* in the Pacific?" This is an extreme example of Blaming the Victim.

Even though your introductory paragraph is the most logical place to state your thesis, you can also put the central assertion of your essay in the title. Suzanne Britt does this in the title of her essay "That Lean and Hungry Look." You might recognize this title as a line from Shakespeare's play *Julius Caesar* (III.iv.5) expressing Caesar's mistrust of Cassius, one of the conspirators. The title immediately alerts readers to Britt's distrust of thin people in her witty defense of "chubbies."

It is best to avoid lengthy and overcomplicated titles that suggest a long, dreary road ahead. Titles do not necessarily have to contain the writer's thesis but should refer to the subject of the essay. For example, one would surmise correctly that William C. Martin's article "The God Hucksters of the Radio" was fashioned as an exposé of religious broad-casters who con the public.

Writing the Middle of the Essay

The choices open to the writer in organizing an argumentative essay depend on the nature of the thesis, the kind of claim on which the the-sis is based, and, most importantly, the anticipated attitude of the audi-ence toward this claim. The traditional argumentative essay has three parts: the introduction, the middle, or body, and the conclusion. If the audience is inclined to agree with the writer's basic assumptions, the essay can be organized deductively, with the thesis declared at the out-set; if the audience is neutral or not inclined to agree with the author's thesis, an inductive pattern of organization that arrives at the thesis af-ter the preliminary exploration would be most effective.

This basic format can be easily modified to accommodate different kinds of arguments. For example, if the argument makes a value judgment, the introduction can describe the subject to be evaluated, provide background discussion, discuss the criteria being applied, and present the writer's opinion on the issue. In some cases the writer may have to stipulate a meaning for key terms (such as *euthanasia*) that appear in the claim.

The middle portion of the essay presents reasons that support the value judgment with persuasive evidence that backs up the reasons. Often an evaluation essay or value argument relies on comparison to establish that something is either good or bad compared with something else. The middle portion may also contain a critical analysis of opposing value judgments along with reasons why the writer's value judgment should be accepted as more compelling.

The conclusion should allude to reasons developed within the essay and end on a note of commonality by emphasizing the concerns, values, and beliefs shared with the audience.

If the argument focuses on a causal claim, the introduction must first describe the phenomenon and demonstrate its importance for the audience by using statistics, authoritative testimony, or illustrative examples.

Keep in mind that audiences are most skeptical about "how" *A* could have caused *B*. Your argument will need to demonstrate in a persuasive way why it is likely that *A* could have caused or will cause *B*.

The main portion of the essay identifies the probable causes of a single event or chain of events, distinguishing immediate causes from those that are remote. Like other forms of argument, a causal claim requires the writer to consider alternative causes and give sound reasons for rejecting them.

The conclusion follows the pattern of other kinds of arguments. The writer concludes the essay by restating important points and by emphasizing how they support the thesis. The conclusion should convey a feeling of closure on the issue.

For policy arguments, a different plan of organization is required. Policy arguments are usually arranged in a problem–solution format that concludes with an appeal for action. Although the basic plan can be as simple as demonstrating the existence of a problem, proposing a solution, and providing reasons supported by evidence for accepting the solution, a fully developed policy argument should delve into a whole range of related issues. The statement of the problem must show that the problem exists, and is serious enough to need solving, by documenting negative effects the problem is causing. In some cases, the writer might discuss the consequences of failing to solve the problem. Next, the writer must identify the cause of the problem, determine who or what has caused it, and provide a history of the problem, including a discussion of past efforts to solve it.

The writer is obliged not only to present reasons showing why the solution is practical but also to present and refute counter objections that may be made to the proposed solution.

The conclusion should stress that the solution is the best, feasible alternative. It may also make an appeal to the audience to act upon the writer's recommendation.

Writing the Conclusion

The conclusion of an argumentative essay may serve a variety of purposes. The writer may restate the thesis after reviewing the most convincing points in the argument. The writer may also choose to support a recommendation by closing with an appeal to the needs and values of the specific audience being addressed. In some cases, the conclusion itself may contain the strongest reasons and supporting evidence of the entire paper. Whatever ending is chosen, it is important for the reader to feel that the essay has completed all the important lines of thought the writer has set out to develop. This sense of closure can be achieved in many different ways. The following examples illustrate a few.

The conclusion can echo the ideas in the opening paragraph. For instance, here are the introduction and the conclusion of an argument "Computer Monitoring and Other Dirty Tricks" (1985) by 9 to 5, National Association of Working Women, which claims that computer monitoring of office workers increases stress and threatens to reestablish an electronic version of "'nineteenth-century garment industry sweat shops'":

Introduction:

From "Chuckle Pops" to electronic surveillance, office computers are being used in absurd and even threatening ways. Today there's a host of computer tools that allow managers to keep tabs on office workers to an extent that was never before possible. The goal is to increase productivity. The results range from the benign to the malevolent but they all add up to the same thing: miserable working conditions for office workers. We call these tools computer dirty tricks, and they are being played on many of the 13 million men and women who work on VDTs [video display terminals or computer screens].

Conclusion (note how this final paragraph recaps the opening):

When, as a data processor tells us, her VDT flashes the message, "You're not working as fast as the person next to you," or when a claims processor logs in in the morning and the screen informs her that she's been fired, it may seem like some bad practical joke. But surveillance, work speed-ups, stress-related heart diseases and possible violation of Constitutional rights are dirty tricks in our book.

And they are not acceptable in the office.

Another strategy writers use is to end on a note of reaffirmation and challenge. Edward Abbey does this in "The Right to Arms" (1979), arguing that countries where citizens are prohibited from owning guns are, for the most part, oppressive police states:

> If guns are outlawed, only the government will have guns. Only the police, the secret police, the military. The hired servants of our rulers. Only the government—and a few outlaws. I intend to be among the outlaws.

Still another way to conclude an argumentative essay is with irony or a striking paradox. For example, C. R. Creekmore cites Brendan Gill in his argument "Cities Won't Drive You Crazy" (*Psychology Today* [1985]) to support his claim that contrary to popular belief, cities are far better places in which to live than rural areas:

> It is a power that gives them the means of meeting the city on its own fierce terms of constant stress. And it is profoundly the case that your true (urbanite) rejoices in stress; the crowds, the dirt, the stench, the noise. Instead of depressing him, they urge him onto an unexpected 'high,' a state of euphoria in which the loftiest of ambitions seems readily attainable.

The most traditional kind of ending is one that sums up the points raised in the argument and brings the essay to a focused conclusion. We can see this in Betty Winston Baye's last paragraph of "You Men Want It Both Ways" (1985), which states that men may say they want educated and independent women but in reality feel threatened by the prospect of a truly equal partner:

> There are dozens of other ways that men send out mixed signals to the women in their lives and show, through their words and deeds, that they really want it both ways. They want us to drive the car—but from the backseat. Mostly what they want is for things to be the way they used to be. That, however, is a pipe dream. Black women, like their counterparts of other races, are liberating their minds and their bodies from the shackles of the past. Increasingly, women are refusing to waste their lives trying to decode men's mixed messages and buying into some man's macho fantasies. Instead, many women who are or want to be high achievers are accepting the fact that the price of success may be temporary loneliness. And even that loneliness is relative, since many of us have learned that having a man isn't all there is to life.

AUDIENCE

The specific audience for whom you are writing your argumentative essay determines, to some extent, what reasons you present to support your claim.

Unless you have inquired into what beliefs and attitudes your audience already hold, you won't be able to determine the best way to present your argument. Try to estimate how much the audience know about the issue in question. If they are unfamiliar with the issue, you might provide a brief summary of background information, to give them a more complete context in which to appreciate why this particular issue is an important one. If your audience already know something about the issue, how do they feel about it?

For most writers, the simplest procedure consists of imagining yourself as part of the audience and then asking what would be necessary to convince you to agree with the assertion stated in the thesis. By being your own most critical reader, you can assess the credibility of the reasons that would change your attitudes. From this viewpoint, you can evaluate whether the reasons given are adequate. If you are not persuaded, consider what better reasons and what additional evidence would convince you.

To understand what writers do to increase the chances that an argument will be accepted by the audience for whom it is intended, we might use a simple analogy: Writing an argumentative essay is rather like cooking and serving a meal. Just as the process of writing an essay moves through the stages of prewriting, writing, and revising, the process of preparing a meal moves through the stages of planning the meal, cooking the food, and serving it in an appetizing way.

Audience considerations play an important part in both processes. Both processes require the writer or chef to look at actions performed in the present with reference to what will be required in the future. The writer uses a variety of invention strategies to generate a thesis while looking at the thesis from the perspective of how well it will serve as a focus for a rough draft. The writer also evaluates the thesis in light of the purpose of the whole essay and the particular audience for whom it is intended. Only by looking to the end point of what can be accomplished by addressing this particular audience can the writer avoid formulating an unrealistic thesis. So, too, the chef looks ahead to the particular audience during the planning stages. Who the audience is and what the occasion is will alter the decision of what to cook. Without these considerations, the chef might begin to prepare a rib roast for vegetarians.

Writing the first draft involves combining the thesis, an outline of the organization of the paper, and any notes generated in the prewriting stage while keeping in mind the particular needs, values, and concerns of the audience for whom the argument is being written. The order in which the writer raises points, the kinds of examples a particular audience would find effective, and questions of tone can be correctly gauged only by keeping in mind potential audience reactions.

The next stage, revising, encompasses everything that must be done in terms of transforming the essay to make it easier to understand: revising ambiguous words or unclear phrases and garbled sentences, checking to see that the essay has an attention-getting introduction and an effective conclusion, and adding transition sentences to help the audience see the relationship between sections of the argument.

The most important shift in perspective relates to seeing what is being prepared from the potential audience's point of view. In our analogy, the chef's attitude toward the food changes so that he or she no longer sees only the ingredients being transformed into this or that kind of a dish but now perceives the task as one of making the food acceptable to others in terms of their needs, anticipated expectations, and satisfactions. So, too, the writer must be able to look at the work as it is being written from the perspective of those who will read and "digest" it.

To put this into practice, try to create an audience "inventory" by answering each of the following questions:

What do I know about the audience's background?

What are they already likely to know about the issue?

Based on what they know, what explanations, definitions of terms, and descriptions of unfamiliar processes would they need to know to better understand the issue?

How might the audience be expected to feel about the issue?

What might be the audience's misconceptions about the issue that I could clarify?

By studying the list of responses to these questions, you will have a clearer sense of which of the following approaches might be the most persuasive for your specific audience.

You might wish to write what is called a traditional argumentative essay that presents your views on the issue, provides a background to set the issue in context, briefly summarizes opposing views, and offers counterarguments for each opposing reason. This is fine for audiences that are neutral or even predisposed to agree with you, but for audiences who might disagree with you, a different kind of an approach is necessary. You risk antagonizing these negative audiences if you use the traditional approach. For this reason, your essay must take a more conciliatory approach by pointing out areas of agreement between you and those opposed to your views by stating the opponent's views fairly, by conceding good points to the opposition, and, most importantly, by basing your argument on those values both you and your audience might share.

✦ Questions for Discussion and Writing

1. To put these principles into practice, select one of the following topics and decide what kind of claim (fact, cause, value, policy) would be the

most appropriate on which to base your argument. Suggest an organizational plan that might be well suited to develop an argument on this topic for neutral, positive, or negative audiences. Should your argument be shaped inductively to work up to the thesis or deductively to explore implications drawn from the thesis? For any topic you choose, try to create a scene or story designed to create an emotional bond with the audience at the outset. Your scene, story, or description should personalize the abstract issue in a way that makes it more meaningful. What would your title be? How would you wish to change your audience's perception of the topic?

a. Should the names of rape victims be published in newspapers?

b. Should public high schools distribute condoms?

c. Do physicians have an ethical duty to treat AIDS patients?

d. Are college athletic programs incompatible with the school's academic mission?

e. Has feminism made a positive contribution to society?

f. Should date rape be defined to include psychological coercion?

g. At what point should the human fetus be considered a person?

h. Should the embryo/fetus be accorded civil rights?

i. Should dial-a-porn numbers be restricted to a subscription-only basis?

j. Is an Afrocentric curriculum necessary?

k. Is pornography harmful to women?

l. Develop an essay based on any topic identified in this chapter, and exchange it with other students in the class. Write a short evaluation of the most effective and least effective features of the essay you are evaluating. How well did the writer connect or fail to connect with the audience? How effective were the writer's strategies in getting the audience to see his or her point of view? What techniques might have worked better?

Writing the First Draft

As you begin your first draft you might find the following suggestions useful:

1. Give yourself enough time to write the rough draft so that you'll have time to look it over and make necessary changes.
2. Try not to get bogged down by questions of spelling and punctuation when you are putting the first draft together.

3. If you are not sure about spelling, punctuation, or a question of grammar, simply make a note and come back to it later.
4. Don't erase or delete what you write. Instead, cross it out lightly on the printout so that you can still use it later if you want to.
5. Keep in mind that this draft is temporary and discardable, and revel in the fact that for once neatness does *not* count.
6. Don't get hung up on how to open or close your argument. Just concentrate on stating your thesis and laying out the points and evidence that support it.
7. If you lose the thread of your argument, or find that you have hit the proverbial brick wall, take some time off and come back to it later. If this doesn't work, go back to notes you accumulated during the prewriting and invention stages and try to find another aspect to the topic that might prove more productive.

The rough draft is the place to go through the progression of reasons and supporting evidence that your readers will need to come to the conclusion you stated at the outset as your thesis. Since the purpose of the argument is to win people over to your side, it is important to look at your rough draft from the audience's point of view.

Whereas the introduction or opening paragraphs state the nature of the problem and may briefly touch on opposing arguments, the body of the essay creates a structure of assertions or claims backed up by evidence in the form of examples, statistics, or the testimony of experts. The exact order in which you acknowledge and respond to counterarguments will, of course, depend on the kind of argument you are presenting.

When you suspect that your audience does not share your viewpoint, your argument should be presented in the spirit of a mutual search for the best reasons to support your claim rather than in a spirit of trouncing the opposition. Your goal should be to present your argument as an open-minded inquiry, expressed in a reasonable tone, for people who may not share your views initially but who you assume will be fair enough to acknowledge any good reasons brought forward to support your argument.

Conclude your essay with the strongest and most persuasive reasons for your point of view.

With audiences who agree with you or who are neutral on the issue, choose the opposite method of organization. Begin the main part of your essay with the strongest reasons you have in order to reinforce the audience's attitudes and win their assent as quickly as you can.

You must make it as easy as possible for your audience to see the relationship among the different parts of your essay so that they can reach the conclusion stated in the thesis sentence at the outset of your argument.

Revising, Rewriting, and Editing

Although revision is often discussed as if it were something you do after writing your essay, it is actually part of the continuous editing process that goes on as you write your paper. Each time you change a word to improve how a sentence sounds, or make your essay more coherent by changing the order in which reasons are presented, or pursue any promising idea that may not have been apparent when you began writing, you are revising your essay.

Read your essay aloud so that you can hear how your writing sounds. Your ear will often tell you what your eye will not. As you listen to what you have written, you may hear inconsistencies in grammar, usage, and syntax that escaped your notice. Reading your work aloud is also a good way to discover repetitious words, sentence fragments, and run-ons.

In looking over your paper for stylistic flaws, be on the lookout for inappropriate, emotionally charged language; melodramatic figures of speech; and flowery metaphors. Writers who hold strong opinions are understandably susceptible to such linguistic excesses; argument is a dramatic form and tends to bring out the theatrical tendencies in some writers.

Ask whether the issues in your argument are raised in the best possible order. Could any paragraph or group of paragraphs be better placed elsewhere? Would some other arrangement contribute more effectively to the overall sense of the paper as expressed in the thesis? The type of development your paper should follow will depend in large part on your thesis, but certain general criteria should be met:

1. Have you offered sufficient evidence to support your assertions?
2. If your approach requires you to attack the credibility of an opposing viewpoint, have you summarized the opposing position before countering its main assertions?
3. Have you effectively questioned the assumptions underlying the opposing argument, disputed the validity of the evidence cited, and pointed out logical fallacies in the process by which the conclusions were reached?
4. Did you support your recommendations or proposed solutions with logical reasoning and compelling evidence?

If this seems like a tall order, keep in mind that all argumentative papers and to a lesser extent all research papers are expected to take into account diverse opinions on the subject. What would someone who holds a view opposite to your own have to say about your argument? What about the assumptions underlying your argument? Does any portion of your essay depend on shaky assumptions, whether implicit or explicitly stated, that would not withstand close scrutiny? Consider whether some of the assumptions you take for granted need to be explicitly stated for your audience.

Often writers are so immersed in formulating the argument that they omit transitional words and connecting phrases that readers will need to understand the relationship between different parts of the essay. These connections may seem self-evident to you, but the reader needs explicitly stated signaling words to perceive the underlying organization of your essay more accurately. Also, you may have inserted words and phrases that give the appearance of logical connections where none exist. Don't be fooled into thinking that a generous sprinkling of *thus*es, *therefore*s, and *moreover*s will lend an aura of coherence to your paper. The contrary is true. Inappropriate use of these words will alert the reader that all is not well and that your conclusions may not really follow from an adequately developed line of reasoning.

REFUTING ARGUMENTS

An important aspect of writing arguments depends on the ability to refute opposing views. In fact, some arguments are entirely refutations of the opposition's argument.

An analysis of someone else's argument, like any argument of your own, must center on a thesis or central assertion. When you evaluate another's argument, the thesis will be your overall assessment of how convincingly the author has succeeded in bringing forward good reasons and persuasive evidence to justify the conclusions reached. Your thesis should not express your opinion of the issue but rather should be an objective evaluation of the skill with which the author uses different strategies of argumentation to present his or her case.

Analyzing Someone Else's Argument and Inventing Your Own

If you have never gone through the process of analyzing someone else's argument before creating your own, you might find it difficult to know what to look for. Fortunately, there are several strategies you can use both for analyzing someone else's argument and for inventing material for your own. For example, you might analyze someone else's argument to determine the author's purpose and how well he or she accomplished it. You might describe the author's tone or voice and try to assess how much it contributed. How effectively does the writer use authorities, statistics, or examples to support the claim? Does the author identify the assumptions or warrants on which the argument is based, and are they ones with which you agree or disagree? To what extent does the author use the emotional connotations of language to try to persuade his or her audience? Do you see anything unworkable or disadvantageous about the solutions offered as an answer to the problem the essay addresses? All these and many other ways of analyzing someone else's argument can be used to create your own case. The entire range of strategies has come to be known collectively as *critical thinking,* which differs from taking things for granted or taking things at face value.

Critical thinking involves becoming aware of the reasoning processes other people use and that you yourself use in thinking about experiences. The central element in critical thinking is the ability to evaluate information critically. This means you must be able to identify the main idea underlying someone else's argument, locate the reasons and evidence that support the idea, be able to express the idea in your own words, and evaluate how well (in terms of formal strategies of argument) the author makes his or her case. You must also be able to see the relationship between the main idea and other things that you already know.

You think critically when you change your views about something from what you first thought. Critical thinking not only involves being willing to change your views when the evidence warrants it, but encompasses being able to see how the same phenomenon can be viewed very differently by people with different perspectives. For example, you might have seen a movie and not liked it initially and then seen it later on television and found it more enjoyable. By the same token, a first reaction of not liking someone you met might have been an automatic response. On reflection, you might have changed your attitude later.

In a different context, thinking critically means being open to new perspectives that add something to your understanding. First, of course, you must be aware of the angle from which you view events and your own preconceptions, expectations, and biases. Critical thinking makes it possible to generate ideas when you take the trouble to review what you think you already know. You may often discover that you have been passively taking in information and making other people's beliefs your own without exploring or testing them. If someone else's argument makes you rethink things and examine your reasons for holding beliefs, you will discover material enough for more essays than you will ever have time to write. In this sense, critical thinking means becoming aware of how you react to an issue. Of course, you must be honest enough to modify your views, if the evidence warrants it, as you go about the process of examining, questioning, and inquiring into the issue at stake in someone else's argument.

The process of evaluating someone else's argument requires you to systematically assess the quality of the argument in terms of its strength and persuasiveness. Draw from your annotations and notes based on your observations of the effectiveness of each part of the argument. You must be able to identify the writer's *claim*, thesis, or proposition and discover where the writer chooses to place the thesis. Does the placement of the thesis suggest that the writer is addressing an audience that is neutral, inclined to agree, or opposed to the thesis? You should also be able to locate any *grounds* the writer presents in the form of data, examples, statistics, testimony, or other kinds of evidence. Try to make explicit the underlying assumptions, or *warrants*, that justify drawing specific conclusions from the evidence presented. Does the writer need to support these assumptions with *backing* that explains why a particular warrant is appropriate? To what extent might the prospective audience find the writer's reasons persuasive because they share the same values? To what extent and how fairly does the writer summarize opposing views? Does the argument provide clear rebuttals to counterarguments or concede good points to the opposition? What kind of impression does the writer create for himself or herself in terms of persona, image, and *ethos*? What use does the writer make of connotations, metaphors, images, and appeals to *pathos* and the audience's emotions?

A signal that the writer is relying more on implicit assumptions than on evidence, statistics, expert testimony, logic, and sound reasoning is the frequent use of words whose emotional connotations are meant to prejudice the reader into automatically agreeing with the author's viewpoint. When you come across one of these loaded terms or phrases, or question-begging epithets, ask yourself whether you agree with the writer's characterizations. Are the assumptions underlying these characterizations supported independently by real reasons and examples elsewhere in the article? When looking for a conclusion, try to identify pivotal terms (*because, likewise, consequently*) that indicate the writer is bringing together various elements of the argument to support an inference or generalization. Is the conclusion warranted by the preceding facts and reasons?

The arguments you are evaluating may not appear legitimate, may contain flawed reasoning, may be impractical, or otherwise may pose unrealistic or unworkable alternatives. To refute these kinds of arguments, look carefully to see whether the claim is based on implausible warrants or assumptions, whether the proposed solutions would produce disadvantageous effects, whether the evidence cited to support the claim is irrelevant or insufficient, or whether the logic underlying the reasoning is faulty. For a discussion of the most common logical fallacies, see Appendix A. Bring the same standards to bear on an argument you are evaluating that you would on an argument you were writing.

Another element of critical thinking requires you to relate your own ideas to those of the person who wrote the argument you are reading. You can use this to generate material for your own essay if you can evaluate your own attitudes at the same time you evaluate someone else's argument. The more you are challenged or even threatened by what the person says, the greater your opportunity to use the conflict, tension, or discomfort being produced to look at your own values and beliefs.

Does the writer you are analyzing make assumptions about human nature, society, religion, or culture that are different from your own? In what way do they differ? Keep in mind that you wouldn't even be aware you had these assumptions if you weren't analyzing why someone else's assumptions are making you uncomfortable. Essentially, this is how the analytical process can be used as an opportunity for critical thinking. The extent to which the argument you are reading forces you to question your own highly personal beliefs and values, or provides you with new perspectives you can use to change your own point of view, depends solely on how you react. The encounter with someone who makes a compelling case for something you do not believe can be unsettling because it forces you to examine the reasons underlying your own beliefs. The point is that you can use any discomfort creatively as an opportunity to engage the issue.

To do this, of course, you must be able to (1) identify the basic issues at stake, (2) summarize in your own words the main points of the arguments, and (3) understand why the writer used particular kinds of evidence to support this specific viewpoint. Most importantly, use the occasion of analyzing someone else's argument as an opportunity to critically examine your own beliefs. Read critically and try to be aware of your own attitudes as they emerge while you are responding to someone else's argument.

AN ARGUMENT
WITH A STUDENT'S
EVALUATION OF IT

The following argument, "The Business World as a Hunting Ground," is a chapter from Esther Vilar's *The Manipulated Man* (1971). It is followed by student Helene Santos's evaluation.

Esther Vilar

The Business World as a Hunting Ground

◆

Born of German parents in 1935 in Buenos Aires, Esther Vilar received a medical degree from the University of Buenos Aires. After moving to Munich, Germany, she practiced as a physician and began a career as a freelance writer. This chapter, "The Business World as a Hunting Ground" (from The Manipulated Man *[1972]), has as its thesis that men from earliest childhood are manipulated by women, first by their mothers and then by their wives. Vilar says, "only women can break this vicious cycle of exploitation. But they will not break it, for they have no rational reason for doing so. Thus, the world will continue to sink into a kitchy, barbaric, and feebleminded morass of femininity."*

1   There are many women who take their place in the working world of today. Secretaries and shop assistants, factory workers and stewardesses—not to mention those countless hearty young women who populate the colleges and universities in ever-increasing numbers. One might even get the impression that woman's nature had undergone a radical change in the last twenty years. Today's young women appear to be less unfair than their mothers. They seem to have decided—perhaps out of pity for their victims—not to exploit men any more, but to become, in truth, their partners.

2   The impression is deceptive. The only truly important act in any woman's life is the selection of the right partner. In any other choice she can afford to make a mistake. Consequently, she will look for a man

348

where he works or studies and where she can best observe and judge the necessary masculine qualities she values. Offices, factories, colleges, and universities are, to her, nothing but gigantic marriage markets.

The particular field chosen by any young woman as a hunting   3
ground will depend to a large extent on the level of income of the man who has previously been her slave, in other words, her father. The daughters of men in the upper income brackets will choose colleges or universities. These offer the best chances of capturing a man who will earn enough to maintain the standards she has already acquired. Besides, a period of study for form's sake is much more convenient than a temporary employment. Girls from less-well-off homes will have to go into factories, shops, offices, or hospitals for a time—but again with the same purpose in mind. None of them intend to stay in these jobs for long. They will continue only until marriage—or, in cases of hardship, till pregnancy. This offers woman one important advantage: any woman who marries nowadays has given up her studies or her job "for the sake of the man of her choice"—and "sacrifices" of this nature create obligations.

Therefore, when women work and study, it merely serves to falsify   4
statistics and furthermore to enslave men more hopelessly than ever, because education and the professions mean something very different when applied to women as opposed to men.

When a man works it is a matter of life and death, and, as a rule,   5
the first years of his life are decisive. Any man of twenty-five who is not well on his way up the ladder can be considered, to all intents and purposes, a hopeless case. At this stage, all his faculties are being developed, and the fight with his competitors is a fight to the death. Behind a mask of business friendship, he is constantly on the watch for any sign of superiority in one of his associates, and he will note its appearance with anxiety. If this same associate shows signs of weakness or indecision, it must be taken advantage of at once. Yet man is only a tiny cog in a gigantic business machine, he himself being in effect exploited at every turn. When he drives others, he drives himself most of all. His orders are really orders from above, passed on by him. If the men at the top occasionally take time to praise him, it is not in order to make him happy: it is only to spur him on, to stimulate him to greater effort. For man, who was brought up to be proud and honorable, every working day is merely an endless series of humiliations. He shows enthusiasm for products he finds useless, he laughs at jokes he finds tasteless, he expresses opinions which are not his own. Not for a moment is he allowed to forget that the merest oversight may mean demotion, that one slip of the tongue may spell the end of his career.

Yet woman, who is the prime cause of all these struggles, and un-   6
der whose very eyes these fights take place, just stands aside and watches. Going to work means to her flirting and dates, teasing and

banter, with the odd bit of "labor" done for the sake of appearances—work for which, as a rule, she has no responsibility. She knows that she is only marking time, and even if she does have to go on working for one reason or another, at least she has had years of pleasant dreams. She watches men's battles from a safe distance, occasionally applauding one of the contestants, encouraging or scolding, and while she makes their coffee, opens their mail, or listens to their telephone conversations, she is coldbloodedly taking her pick. The moment she has found "Mr. Right," she retires gracefully, leaving the field open to her successors.

7   The same applies to university education. American colleges admit more and more women, but the percentage who actually complete their courses is less than before the Second World War. They sit happily in lectures designing their spring wardrobe and between classes flirt with the boys. With their scarlet nails carefully protected by transparent rubber gloves, they play around with corpses in the dissecting rooms, while their male colleagues realize their whole future is at stake. If a woman leaves the university with an engagement ring on her finger, she has earned her degree; man has hardly begun when he obtains his diploma. Degrees are, after all, easy to come by—you have only to memorize. How many examiners can tell the difference between real knowledge and bluff? Man, however, has to *understand* his subject as well. His later success will depend on whether his knowledge is well-founded; his later prestige will be built on this, and often other people's lives are dependent on it.

8   None of these battles exists for woman. If she breaks off her studies and marries a university lecturer, she has achieved the same level as he has without exerting herself. As the wife of a factory owner she is treated with greater respect than he is (and not as somebody who at best would be employable on the assembly line in the same factory). As a wife she always has the same standard of living and social prestige and has to do nothing to maintain them—as he does. For this reason the quickest way to succeed is always to marry a successful man. She does not win him by her industry, ambition, or perseverance—but simply through an attractive appearance.

9   We have already seen what demands the well-trained man makes on a woman's appearance. The best women trainers—without the least effort—catch the most successful fighters among men. The so-called "beautiful" women are usually those who have had an easy life from their childhood days and therefore have less reason than others to develop their intellectual gifts (intelligence is developed only through competition); it follows as a logical consequence that very successful men usually have abysmally stupid wives (unless, of course, one considers woman's skill at transforming herself into bait for man a feat of intelligence).

It has almost become a commonplace that a really successful man, [10] be he a company director, financier, shipping magnate, or orchestra conductor, will, when he reaches the zenith of his career, marry a beautiful model—usually his second or third wife. Men who have inherited money often take such a supergirl as their first wife—although she will be exchanged over the years for another. Yet, as a rule, models are women of little education who have not even finished school and who have nothing to do until they marry but look beautiful and pose becomingly in front of a camera. But they are "beautiful"—and that makes them potentially rich.

As soon as a woman has caught her man, she "gives up her career [11] for love"—or, at least, that is what she will tell him. After all, he could hardly be flattered by the thought that she had been saved in the nick of time from having to sweat her way through examinations. He would much rather get drunk on the idea of the love "that knows no compromise," which this woman pretends to feel for him. Who knows, he thinks, she might have become a famous surgeon (celebrated prima ballerina, brilliant journalist), and she has given it all up for him. He would never believe that she preferred to be the wife of a famous surgeon, to have his income and prestige without having either the work or the responsibility. Therefore, he resolves to make her life at his side as comfortable as possible to compensate for her great sacrifice.

A small percentage (ten to twenty percent) of women students in [12] industrial countries of the West do, in fact, obtain their degrees before they get married. Despite occasional exceptions, they are, as a rule, less attractive and have failed to catch a suitable provider while still in school. But then, this degree will automatically raise their market value, for there are certain types of men who feel bolstered if their wife has a degree—providing they have one themselves. It is clear evidence of his own cleverness if such a highly educated woman is interested in him. If by chance this female mastermind happens to be sexy, he will be beside himself with joy.

But not for long. Even women doctors, women sociologists, and [13] women lawyers "sacrifice" their careers for their men, or at least set them aside. They withdraw into suburban ranch houses, have children, plant flower beds, and fill their homes with the usual trash. Within a few years these new entertainments obliterate the small amount of "expert knowledge," learned by rote, of course, and they become exactly like their female neighbors.

Helene Santos

Are Men Really the Slaves of Women?

◆

What follows is a student's analysis of Vilar's essay:

1   In "The Business World as a Hunting Ground," Vilar substitutes catchy phrases for evidence to develop her argument that women seek an education or employment to find husbands. Vilar claims that women seek education or employment to reach this objective because "offices, factories, colleges and universities are, to her, nothing but gigantic marriage markets."

2   Vilar says that women have to do nothing other than marry someone who will support them for the rest of their lives. Vilar claims that "as soon as a woman has caught her man she 'gives up her career for love'--or, at least, that is what she will tell him." Upon hearing this, the husband, in Vilar's view, is so flattered and guilt-ridden that "he resolves to make her life at his side as comfortable as possible to compensate for her great sacrifice."

3   Vilar fails to provide objective evidence such as surveys, interviews, or case histories, to support her thesis that women have no goals other than finding "Mr. Right." For example, Vilar presents no documentation to support her claim that the percentage of women who graduated from American colleges are "less than before the Second World War." The reader has to depend on Vilar's interpretation because she doesn't give any statistics. She bases her argument on erroneous assumptions and unexamined beliefs. How can Vilar possibly claim to know what motivates all women?

4   First Vilar asserts that the motivation of men and women towards work and education is radically different. She maintains that men view employment and higher education as serious tasks on which their future lives will depend, whereas women see work and study as games to be played while seeking a husband.

5   Furthermore, Vilar says that because of their different attitudes towards education, men and women develop different

352

levels of intelligence. Women, she claims, merely have to memorize enough to get by while men have to understand the material on which their future careers depend. Vilar assumes that no men memorize their way through school, and no women understand what they study unless, as she claims, they are so unattractive that they can't find a man to support them and must become intelligent in order to survive. Innate intelligence exists and does not develop out of the blue at the age of nineteen because one cannot find a husband. Such simplistic reasoning is characteristic of Vilar's argument.

Vilar believes that women attend universities solely to find men. In her view, men achieve social status through their careers whereas women marry to better themselves. For this reason, she thinks women work to observe more closely the money-making potential of prospective husbands. Vilar uses the phrase "hunting ground" to express her thesis that women view the workplace and universities as "arenas" in which to "capture" their "prey." She describes men as having to struggle in a highly competitive work environment while women watch the battle, "cold-bloodedly" taking their pick. Vilar asserts that for a woman, sex-appeal is a commodity that can be translated into marriage and a life of ease. Vilar fails to cite even one case history that might support these claims. 6

Women at work, according to Vilar, will be less capable as employees since husband "hunting" and not work is their primary objective. She uses phrases like "odd bit of 'labor' done for the sake of appearances" and "for a time" to imply that women are not serious about their jobs. Vilar says that for women work means flirting and dates. What of those dedicated and skilled women who take their jobs seriously? How would Vilar account for these women? 7

Moreover, Vilar would have us believe that women choose low-paying jobs with little responsibility because they do not take work seriously. Her tactic of "blaming the victim" fails to acknowledge that very often women are excluded from executive positions and must take menial jobs in order to survive. Vilar often confuses cause and effect in this way. 8

Vilar's stereotyped view of women as sex objects doesn't take into account that beauty is in the "eye of the beholder," and more a matter of subjective choice than Vilar assumes. She also stereotypes men by portraying them as witless dupes who believe their wives have given up possible careers as famous surgeons, celebrated ballerinas, or brilliant journalists to marry them. 9

10   Vilar claims that "very successful men usually have abysmally stupid wives." She reaches this conclusion through a parody of reasoning that runs as follows: (1) "intelligence is developed only through competition," (2) "so-called 'beautiful' women...have had an easy life from their childhood days," (3) "those who have had an easy life...have less reason...to develop their intellectual gifts," (4) "an attractive appearance" acts as "bait" for a "really successful man," therefore (5) "very successful men usually have abysmally stupid wives." Why must beauty and intelligence be mutually exclusive?

11   Vilar bases her argument on unexamined assumptions. For instance, she assumes that no woman wants to be single. She also assumes that no man wants to be married and therefore must be manipulated into a lifetime "obligation." Vilar ignores the many men who want to get married and the large number of women who want to remain single in order to pursue their education and careers.

12   Vilar claims that women obtain degrees in order to "raise their market value" or because they are so unattractive that they cannot find a man to support them. From this, she mistakenly concludes that only unattractive women go on to have successful careers. She also fails to mention the large number of women who complete their degrees after getting married and overlooks the many women who return to work after marriage. In her view, only wives of unsuccessful husbands return to work after marriage.

13   Vilar discounts objections to her argument by using phrases like "might...get the impression," "appear" and "seem." In this way, she suggests that those who believe opposing arguments are being fooled and only she is telling the truth.

14   Instead of citing evidence, examples, statistics, testimony, quotations, and surveys, as support for her claims, Vilar uses imaginative metaphors such as "hunting ground," "prey," "victim," "arena," "capturing," "cold-bloodedly," and "slave." Her strategy is to use words to create images whose connotations imply foregone conclusions. For example, she states, "the particular field chosen by any young woman as a hunting ground will depend to a large extent on the level of income of the man who has previously been her slave, in other words, her father." This statement appears to convey a conclusion, but is actually "begging the question." A closer look reveals Vilar's circular reasoning: Vilar asserts as a proven fact what the argument itself exists to prove—"all men are slaves of women."

15   Despite Vilar's catchy phrases and stylistic flair, the lack of any objective evidence to prove her assertions makes it impossible to perceive her as a reliable observer or take her views seriously. Vilar presents herself as a hard-working, truly emancipated woman surrounded by silly, conniving women who giggle, flirt, play games, and "design their spring wardrobes" while sizing up their "prey."

16   Perhaps women do view the "business world as a hunting ground," but they are "hunting" things other than husbands such as self-esteem and rewarding careers.

This student has done an excellent job in analyzing Esther Vilar's "The Business World as a Hunting Ground":

1. The title of the essay "Are Men Really the Slaves of Women?" is effective in suggesting both the subject and the writer's skeptical attitude.

2. Santos identifies the subject, author, and title of the article early, and she announces the thesis of her essay in the first sentence.

3. She skillfully summarizes Vilar's chief claims in order to give her readers a necessary background against which to understand her analysis and evaluation.

4. She considers and evaluates all of Vilar's main points, identifying contradictions in Vilar's reasoning.

5. She does an exceptionally good job of locating and analyzing the implicit assumptions in Vilar's argument.

6. Santos adroitly incorporates a few brief quotations to let the reader hear Vilar's voice at crucial points in her analysis. This is especially effective when she turns her attention to questions of word choice and emotionally loaded language in Vilar's essay.

7. Her essay has a sensible, easy-to-recognize, consistent organization. She analyzes Vilar's essay without getting sidetracked.

8. Santos's conclusion ties up all the loose ends with some stylistic grace, using the metaphor of a "business world as a hunting ground" to challenge Vilar's main premise.

9. One area for improvement in Santos's essay is sentence structure. Several of the extremely long sentences might be divided into shorter, clearer sentences.

TWO SHORT ARGUMENTS FOR ANALYSIS

Suzanne Britt

That Lean and Hungry Look

———————◆———————

Suzanne Britt teaches at Meredith College and writes a weekly newspaper column for the Dickens Dispatch. *Her essays and articles have appeared in the* Charlotte Observer, Newsweek, *the* New York Times, *the* Boston Globe, Newsday, *and the* Miami Herald. *She is the author of several books, including* A Writer's Rhetoric, *1988 and* Images: A Centennial Journey, *1993. This article first appeared in the October 9, 1978 issue of* Newsweek.

1   Caesar was right. Thin people need watching. I've been watching them for most of my adult life, and I don't like what I see. When these narrow fellows spring at me, I quiver to my toes. Thin people come in all personalities, most of them menacing. You've got your "together" thin person, your mechanical thin person, your condescending thin person, your tsk-tsk thin person, your efficiency-expert thin person. All of them are dangerous.

2   In the first place, thin people aren't fun. They don't know how to goof off, at least in the best, fat sense of the word. They've always got to be adoing. Give them a coffee break, and they'll jog around the block. Supply them with a quiet evening at home, and they'll fix the screen door and lick S&H green stamps. They say things like "there aren't enough hours in the day." Fat people never say that. Fat people think the day is too damn long already.

3   Thin people make me tired. They've got speedy little metabolisms that cause them to bustle briskly. They're forever rubbing their bony hands together and eyeing new problems to "tackle." I like to surround myself with sluggish, inert, easygoing fat people, the kind who believe that if you clean it up today, it'll just get dirty again tomorrow.

4   Some people say the business about the jolly fat person is a myth, that all of us chubbies are neurotic, sick, sad people. I disagree. Fat people may not be chortling all day long, but they're a hell of a lot *nicer* than the wizened and shriveled. Thin people turn surly, mean and hard

at a young age because they never learn the value of a hot-fudge sundae for easing tension. Thin people don't like gooey soft things because they themselves are neither gooey nor soft. They are crunchy and dull, like carrots. They go straight to the heart of the matter while fat people let things stay all blurry and hazy and vague, the way things actually are. Thin people want to face the truth. Fat people know there is no truth. One of my thin friends is always staring at complex, unsolvable problems and saying, "The key thing is..." Fat people never say that. They know there isn't any such thing as the key thing about anything.

Thin people believe in logic. Fat people see all sides. The sides fat 5 people see are rounded blobs, usually gray, always nebulous and truly not worth worrying about. But the thin person persists. "If you consume more calories than you burn," says one of my thin friends, "you will gain weight. It's that simple." Fat people always grin when they hear statements like that. They know better.

Fat people realize that life is illogical and unfair. They know very 6 well that God is not in his heaven and all is not right with the world. If God was up there, fat people could have two doughnuts and a big orange drink anytime they wanted.

Thin people have a long list of logical things they are always spouting off to me. They hold up one finger at a time as they reel off these things, so I won't lose track. They speak slowly as if to a young child. The list is long and full of holes. It contains tidbits like "get a grip on yourself," "cigarettes kill," "cholesterol clogs," "fit as a fiddle," "ducks in a row," "organize" and "sound fiscal management." Phrases like that.

They think these 2,000 point plans lead to happiness. Fat people 8 know happiness is elusive at best and even if they could get the kind thin people talk about, they wouldn't want it. Wisely, fat people see that such programs are too dull, too hard, too off the mark. They are never better than a whole cheesecake.

Fat people know all about the mystery of life. They are the ones acquainted with the night, with luck, with fate, with playing it by ear. One thin person I know once suggested that we arrange all the parts of a jigsaw puzzle into groups according to size, shape and color. He figured this would cut the time needed to complete the puzzle by at least 50 percent. I said I wouldn't do it. One, I like to muddle through. Two, what good would it do to finish early? Three, the jigsaw puzzle isn't the important thing. The important thing is the fun of four people (one thin person included) sitting around a card table, working a jigsaw puzzle. My thin friend had no use for my list. Instead of joining us, he went outside and mulched the boxwoods. The three remaining fat people finished the puzzle and made chocolate, double-fudged brownies to celebrate.

The main problem with thin people is they oppress. Their good intentions, bony torsos, tight ships, neat corners, cerebral machinations and pat solutions loom like dark clouds over the loose, comfortable, spread-out, soft world of the fat. Long after fat people have removed their coats and shoes and put their feet up on the coffee table, thin people are still sitting on the edge of the sofa, looking neat as a pin, discussing rutabagas. Fat people are heavily into fits of laughter, slapping their thighs and whooping it up, while thin people are still politely waiting for the punch line.

11   Thin people are downers. They like math and mortality and reasoned evaluation of the limitations of human beings. They have their skinny little acts together. They expound, prognose, probe and prick.

12   Fat people are convivial. They will like you even if you're irregular and have acne. They will come up with a good reason why you never wrote the great American novel. They will cry in your beer with you. They will put your name in the pot. They will let you off the hook. Fat people will gab, giggle, guffaw, gallumph, gyrate and gossip. They are gluttonous and goodly and great. What you want when you're down is soft and jiggly, not muscled and stable. Fat people know this. Fat people have plenty of room. Fat people will take you in.

Sample Analysis

CLAIM: Britt claims that the stereotyped view of fat people as lazy, poorly adjusted, and unhappy with themselves is off the mark. Britt argues that in reality fat people have their priorities straight, don't oversimplify things, or see the world in a rigidly organized manner as do thin people. Consequently they enjoy a happier and more fulfilling life.

GROUNDS: Evidence in this essay takes a variety of forms, including a quote from Shakespeare's *Julius Caesar* as its title to support Britt's claim that thin people are pessimistic, power-hungry, and not to be trusted. Her strategy consists in playing off the virtues of fat people as convivial, warm, and open against the lack of those qualities in thin people, who by contrast are characterized as dull, worrying about nonexistent problems, and too defensive, paranoid, and rigid to enjoy themselves.

WARRANT: The value warrant that Britt appeals to in moving from the support to the claim is the assumption that many qualities, such as warmth, compassion, kindness, sense of humor, and tolerance, are far more important than superficial appearance.

PERSUADING THE AUDIENCE: There are few segments in the audience to whom Britt's winning good humor would not appeal, irrespective of what shape they are in. Addressing a culture that for the most part believes "thin is in" requires Britt to describe those who are thin as possessing unappealing characteristics. Few people would wish to see themselves as oversimplifying things, being dull, seeing the world in a rigidly organized manner, believing in simplistic answers to complex problems, or being obsessive and morose.

That segment of the audience unhappy about being fat, which diets, exercises, and takes appetite suppressants, might welcome a defender and vicariously enjoy Britt's characterization of thin people. People who are fat and feel good about it (and either cannot lose weight or don't care to try) would find much to praise in this essay. Doubtless, some thin people will take offense; others will perceive obesity as symptomatic of some deeply rooted psychological problem. Other thin people will continue to see themselves as svelte, suave, and sprightly despite Britt's arguments; a few thin readers will be won over to Britt's viewpoint and will hurry to the nearest fast-food emporium.

✦ Questions for Discussion and Writing

1. How does Britt use a phrase from Shakespeare's play *Julius Caesar* (and the supporting reference "Caesar was right") to put forward an opinion about thin people that the rest of her essay will attempt to establish? How is the original context of the quote related to Britt's use of it?

2. Choose any two sections of Britt's essay and state her arguments in the form of syllogisms. Keep in mind that her arguments are often stated in the form of incomplete or abbreviated syllogisms, called *enthymemes,* which will require you to explicitly formulate the two premises on which she bases specific conclusions. For example, in paragraph 2, what major and minor premises lead her to the conclusion that "thin people aren't fun"?

3. How does Britt deal with the counterarguments that the "jolly fat person is a myth" and "all of us chubbies are neurotic, sick, sad people"?

4. Evaluate the quality of Britt's reasoning in defending fat people against societal stereotyping. Keep in mind that there are lazy thin people and energetic fat people.

5. What reasons does Britt give to support her view that fat people have a less simplistic and better grasp of reality than do thin people?

6. Summarize the list of attributes that Britt uses to characterize thin people, on one hand, and fat people, on the other. Whether or not you

agree with her, write an essay in which you defend thin people while keeping in mind that there are just as many stereotypes about them as there are about fat people. Compare your essay with Britt's and decide who makes a better case.

7. If the person to whom you were engaged suddenly, inexplicably, and permanently became very thin or very fat, would you still go through with the wedding? Explain your answer in two short paragraphs exploring both possibilities.

8. To what extent do cultural attitudes shape our perception of fat or thin people? Keep in mind that in some cultures, past and present, food is (or was) very hard to come by, and being fat is a sign of prosperity and wealth. Also, remember that different aesthetic standards have applied at different times; for example, the women painted by Rubens were considered very beautiful because they were large and voluptuous.

9. Discuss how the tone of this essay reinforces the validity of Britt's assertions. That is, in what way does Britt's tone create the impression that she is a jolly, kind, and compassionate (except toward thin people) person with a great sense of humor?

Molly Ivins

The Romance of Football

◆

Molly Ivins has been a journalist for twenty years. She has written for the Texas Observer, Time, *and many other national magazines. She writes a nationally syndicated column for the* Fort Worth Star Telegram. *This essay is reprinted from* Molly Ivins Can't Say That, Can She? *1991.*

Do real feminists like football? Any fool can see it's the ultimate sexist game. Not only do women never get to play, but their only role in the entire proceeding is to stand on the sidelines and root for those who do, not a life-metaphor even Phyl Shlafly would embrace.

I suspect many of us are born liking it; it's a condition consequent to our birthplace. Marlyn Schwartz, who may appear to be a Dallas career woman but who is actually "a Mobile guhl" and always will be, observes, "I can't imagine not liking football because I'm from the South and Texas and I didn't know there was another topic. It was amazing to me when I grew up and finally visited the East and found out people can get through entire dinners without talking about it. But I was also amazed to learn the South had lost the Civil War—we always called it the War of Northern Aggression—which has since led me to suspect there was a lot they left out of my education."

For cultural reasons too complex to go into here, Nebraska women are also congenital football fans, though they are seldom confused about who won the War of Northern Aggression.

Many of us take up football as a lingua franca. If, for example, you live in Dallas, it is possible to strike up a conversation with anyone at all—CEOs, shoeshine boys, your garbageman, or the barkeep—by inquiring, "How about those 'Pokes?" It is useful in the ensuing chat to know whether the Dallas Cowboys have lately won, lost, or are on strike, but not absolutely necessary.

In the reverse-sexism school of feminism, "all those cute asses" is the most commonly cited reason for watching the game. While this may have merit as an aesthetic argument, it is woefully short on principle.

For many women, football is just a social occasion. They enjoy the pageantry if they go in person, and enjoy socializing with their friends even more. They don't give two hoots about the game. Political activist Liz Carpenter, who is sixty-seven, says she liked the game because her late husband Les did. "It is not one of the things I have kept up in wid-

361

owhood," she said. Carolyn Barta, columnist for the *Dallas Morning News*, said, "For women of my generation, those of us who grew up competitive but were discouraged from competing—we were not encouraged to fight for or compete for anything, especially with men—football was a way of letting out those competitive instincts." You can release a lot of pent-up aggression at a football game.

7 In Pat Conroy's very Southern novel *The Prince of Tides*, there is much of the lore and romance of the game, but even his protagonist-coach admits, "the only good thing about football...the only thing good at all, is that it can be a lot of fun to play." And, as previously noted, that rules us out. On the other hand, that we'll never get to play shouldn't rule us out as fans: I'm never going to figureskate either, but I like to watch other people do it.

8 A more typical coach in Conroy's novel tells his high school team:

9 Tonight I'm gonna learn and the town's gonna learn who my hitters are.... Real hitters. Now a real hitter is a headhunter who puts his head in the chest of his opponents and ain't happy if his opponent is still breathing after the play. A real hitter doesn't know what fear is except when he sees it in the eyes of a ball carrier he's about to split in half. A real hitter loves pain, loves the screaming and the sweating and the brawling and the hatred of life down in the trenches. He likes to be at the spot where the blood flows and the teeth get kicked out. That's what this sport's all about, men. It's war, pure and simple. Now tonight, you go out there and kick butt all over that field. If something moves, hit it....

10 "Now do I have me some hitters?" he screamed, veins throbbing....

11 "Yes, sir," we screamed back.

12 "Do I have some fucking hitters?"

13 "Yes, sir."

14 "Do I have me some goddamn headhunters?"

15 "Yes, sir."

16 "Am I going to see blood?"

17 "Yes, sir."

18 "Am I going to see their guts hanging off your helmets?"

19 "Yes, sir."

20 "Am I going to hear their bones breaking all over the field?"

21 "Yes, sir," we happy hitters cried aloud.

22 "Let us pray," he said.

23 As it happens, chess is also a game of war, pure and simple, but it lacks the *je ne sais quoi* so neatly described above.

24 Football has become real Christian in recent years, a source of distress to many fans. Guys like Joe Namath, Don Meredith, Billy Kilmer—when you saw them on their knees you knew it was because they'd been hit. Nowadays it's hard to tell. Other fans are turned off by

the greed and commercialism of the pros and, increasingly, of college ball. High school football remains the last bastion of high-intensity, pure-emotion football. At the recent Texas state championship playoff game between Plano and Houston-Stratford (it's usually between Plano and somebody), a thoughtful fan told me he was rooting for Plano, which is like rooting for Goliath against David. "Because," he explained, "you never forget losing the Big Game, not for your whole life, but even the thrill of being the underdog who wins the Big Game is not as great as the mortification of losing if you are the favorite."

Football is strategically less interesting than baseball but is emo- 25 tionally more gripping because it is violent. All that hitting and pounding and standing up with a crowd and screaming—it's called catharsis. When the game is well played, it looks easy, it has a rhythm, it's like good sex or great dancing, it's really exciting. Besides, it's cheaper than the movies and a lot more interesting than golf.

✦ Questions for Discussion and Writing

1. What criteria does Ivins bring to bear in defining football as a sexist game? What features of the game could be objectively characterized as sexist? What does "sexist" mean in this context?

2. How does Ivins strengthen her case by bringing in testimonies of Marlyn Schwartz, Liz Carpenter, and Carolyn Barta?

3. What use does Ivins make of the excerpts from Pat Conroy's popular novel *The Prince of Tides*?

4. How does one of the main sources of Ivins's humor depend on the contrast between the values surrounding the genteel southern belle and the savagery of a sport of which they are fans?

5. What features of Ivins's argument seem to take into account the interests and values of her audience, readers of *Ms. Magazine* (in which this originally appeared in March, 1988)?

6. Do you feel that some sports are intrinsically more appealing to men or to women as fans? Explain your reasons in a short essay replying to anticipated objections to your position. You might take a conciliatory approach, stating the opposing views fairly, granting good points to the other side, and finding values you both share.

7

Writing an Argument from Sources

◆

Each of the previous chapters has introduced you to ways of analyzing arguments. In the process, you have explored several controversies through essays written by a wide range of professionals including reporters, government officials, syndicated columnists, spokespersons for special interest organizations, book reviewers, and academic researchers. Doubtless, some of these controversies have sparked your curiosity and made you want to delve into the ideas, opinions, facts, and arguments involved in that issue to a much greater degree. This chapter will introduce you to the methods by which you can pursue your inquiry.

The research paper (sometimes called the *library paper, term paper,* or *source paper*) contains the results of your investigation of an important question through an orderly and close examination of a broad range of available sources. Ideally, the results of your research will shed new light on the subject of the inquiry. The process of writing a research paper is an invaluable opportunity for you to develop the ability to discover and limit a research topic, gain skill in using the library, evaluate the usefulness of source materials, read critically, take worthwhile notes, organize information in the arrangement that best illuminates the answer to the research question, and become proficient in putting together and documenting the results of an extended and systematic study.

Finding a Question to Answer

Preparing a research paper requires you to select a subject and come up with a question on it that you would like to answer in a certain number of pages, given the resources of your library and the time available to you. For this reason, the research process begins with careful consideration of a wide range of thought-provoking questions connected with your subject. If, for example, you were assigned the broad subject of "drug use and drug addiction in contemporary society," each question you thought of would limit this wide-ranging subject to a more manageable topic. Some interesting questions that might be asked on this subject are these:

1. What has caused such a massive upswing of drug use in our society?
2. Are legal drugs less addictive or less dangerous than illegal drugs?
3. Should marijuana use be decriminalized?
4. How dependent are the economies of other countries on the billions of dollars generated by producing cocaine that is sold in the United States?
5. Does mandatory drug testing provide reliable results? Does it violate the Fourth Amendment guarantee against "illegal search and seizure" and constitute an invasion of privacy?
6. What level of success has been achieved by the voluntary "just say no" program?
7. Are athletes coerced into using performance-enhancing drugs, such as steroids, in order to remain competitive?
8. What part do drugs play in highly competitive areas such as professional sports, the entertainment industry, and the financial world?
9. How do drugs affect the central nervous system?
10. What part have hallucinogenic substances played in religions down through the ages?

Some topics, such as the one in question 10, are still too wide-ranging to be researched within the time available. Other topics, such as that in question 9, would be too difficult, since they would require you to possess a high level of technical information. Still other topics, such as that in question 6, might be subjects on which sufficient information is not readily available or might be too narrow to be the subject of a research paper. Since the process of writing a research paper often discloses unsuspected relationships, you may discover that different questions focus on different but related aspects of the same topic.

For example, questions 1, 7, and 8 might be combined as a question that asked, "What part does the idea of competition and winning at all costs play in the massive upswing in drug use in professional sports, the entertainment industry, and the world of finance?" Or the research process might create the possibility for an interesting comparative analysis (combining questions 4, 5, and 6) expressed in the question

"Are attempts to curtail the demand side of drug use through 'just say no' programs and mandatory drug testing more effective than governmental efforts to limit the supply side of drug trafficking by encouraging other countries to grow crops other than coca?"

From all the questions you have generated on a subject, choose several that seem especially interesting. The next step is to determine whether adequate material exists in the library to enable you to produce a well-researched paper drawn from a variety of relevant sources. Avoid topics that are either so new or so old that sources may not be readily available. Some questions, such as the more factual ones, will have already been answered. You might discover that a certain percentage of the cocaine coming to the United States is grown in Peru, Bolivia, and Colombia, or that the government spends a certain amount on drug treatment programs. These and any other questions that have already been answered must be eliminated from contention. Only those questions for which satisfactory answers have not been found should be considered as possible topics for your research paper.

Using the Library

The essence of the research process depends on your skill in finding what others have written on your topic. Certain basic general reference works in your library are of great value in providing an informative, balanced overview of your research topic. General works, including encyclopedias, dictionaries, and handbooks, can give you a balanced idea of the accepted views of your subject and make your research easier. Most of these works can be found in the library's reference room and must be used there.

MAJOR ENCYCLOPEDIAS

The encyclopedia is the most useful general-reference work. Articles written by specialists in particular fields cover general, national, religious, and special topics. Although the articles are relatively short, you will find a comprehensive, carefully selected, well-balanced overview of most subjects.

In most cases, one of the following encyclopedias will provide you with the background information you need:

Chambers Encyclopedia
Collier's Encyclopedia
Encyclopedia Americana
Encyclopedia Britannica
New Columbia Encyclopedia

To make full use of the information contained in encyclopedias, you will often find it necessary to consult a separate index, usually contained in the last volume. This main index will provide you with all the cross-references to your topic. For most students the short list of other works, or bibliography, on the same subject at the end of most articles is the ideal starting point for further research. It is a good idea to consult more than one encyclopedia on your topic, since the same subject may be treated differently in each one.

In addition, there are encyclopedias that deal with special subjects whose usefulness is often nearly as great as that of the general encyclopedias.

SPECIALIZED ENCYCLOPEDIAS AND HANDBOOKS IN THE HUMANITIES, SOCIAL SCIENCES, AND SCIENCES

The following list provides many of the standard reference works you will need to get you started with background information in almost any field.

Almanacs, Yearbooks, and Compilations of Facts

The American Annual (1923–date)
The Book of Lists
CBS News Almanac (1976–date)
Collier's Yearbook (1939–date)
Facts on File (1940–date)
Statistical Abstract of the United States (1878–date)
The World Almanac and Book of Facts (1868–date)
Year Book of World Affairs (1947–date)

Resources in the Humanities

Cassell's Encyclopedia of World Literature, revised edition
A Companion to Ethics
Encyclopedia of American History
Encyclopedia of Art
Encyclopedia of Asian History
Encyclopedia of Bioethics
Encyclopedia of Dance and Ballet
Encyclopedia of Philosophy
Encyclopedia of Religion and Ethics
Encyclopedia of World Art
An Encyclopedia of World History: Ancient, Medieval, and Modern
International Encyclopedia of Film

International Standard Bible Encyclopedia
The New College Encyclopedia of Music
Oxford Companion to Art
Oxford Companion to Canadian Literature (also *Oxford Companion* volumes for Classical, English, French, German, and Spanish Literature)
Oxford Companion to Film
Oxford Companion to Music
Penguin Companion to American Literature (also *Penguin Companion* volumes for English, European, Classical, Oriental, and African Literature)
Princeton Encyclopedia of Poetry and Poetics
World Spirituality: An Encyclopedic History of the Religious Quest

Resources in the Social Sciences

American Educators Encyclopedia
The Cambridge Encyclopedia of China
The Cambridge Encyclopedia of Latin America and the Caribbean
CQ Researcher (formerly *Editorial Research Reports*)
Encyclopedia of Adolescence
The Encyclopedia of Aging and the Elderly
The Encyclopedia of Alcoholism
Encyclopedia of the American Constitution
Encyclopedia of Banking and Finance
Encyclopedia of Black America
The Encyclopedia of Censorship
Encyclopedia of Child Abuse
Encyclopedia of Crime and Justice
The Encyclopedia of Drug Abuse
Encyclopedia of Education
Encyclopedia of Gambling
Encyclopedia of Homosexuality
Encyclopedia of Human Behavior
Encyclopedia of Japan
Encyclopedia of Marriage, Divorce and the Family
Encyclopedia of Political Science
Encyclopedia of Psychology
Encyclopedia of Social Work
Encyclopedia of Sociology
Encyclopedia of Suicide
Encyclopedia of the Third World
The Encyclopedia of World Crime
Guide to American Law
International Encyclopedia of Higher Education

International Encyclopedia of the Social Sciences
The New Standard Jewish Encyclopedia
Women's Studies Encyclopedia

Resources in the Sciences

Cambridge Encyclopedia of Astronomy
Encyclopedia of Bioethics
Encyclopedia of Biological Sciences
Encyclopedia of Chemistry
Encyclopedia of Computer Science and Engineering
Encyclopedia of Computer Science and Technology
Encyclopedia of Death
Encyclopedia of Earth Sciences
Encyclopedia of Environmental Studies
Encyclopedia of Health
Encyclopedia of Occultism and Parapsychology
Encyclopedia of Physics
Grzimek's Animal Life Encyclopedia
Grzimek's Encyclopedia of Ecology
Harper's Encyclopedia of Science
International Encyclopedia of Psychiatry, Psychology, Psychoanalysis and Neurology
Larousse Encyclopedia of Astronomy
McGraw-Hill Encyclopedia of Environmental Science
McGraw-Hill Encyclopedia of Science and Technology: An International Reference Work in fifteen volumes including an index
McGraw-Hill Yearbook of Science and Technology
Stein and Day International Medical Encyclopedia
Universal Encyclopedia of Mathematics
Van Nostrand's Scientific Encyclopedia

✦ Questions for Discussion and Writing

1. Drawing on these reference sources, identify which encyclopedias you would most likely consult for information on the following issues:

   a. Analyze the history of a recent public policy or a United States Supreme Court decision.

   b. How has a word in current widespread use evolved from its original meaning from a particular group (computer users, musicians, athletes, drug users, rock music fans, etc.)?

   c. Are prices for pharmaceuticals unconscionably high? Are price controls justified to ensure access to essential medications (by the poor, AIDS victims, etc.)?

d. Does tracking exaggerate initial differences among students from disadvantaged backgrounds?

e. What are the long-term developmental changes that affect children of divorce?

f. What standards have local high school libraries applied in deciding which books ought to be banned or placed in restricted access requiring parental consent?

g. Is alcoholism hereditary?

h. Is too much money being spent on trying to find a cure for AIDS to the detriment of research on noncommunicable diseases such as cancer and heart disease?

i. Which arguments on the issue of wilderness use do you find more compelling: those of preservationists or those of conservationists (favoring multiple use)?

j. What case can be made for the feasibility of shifting energy reliance to solar cell technology?

k. Is it realistic to expect a goddess-centered religion to supplant conventional Judeo-Christian male-centered religious beliefs and practices?

l. How does the literature of war depend on the contrast between fantasy and reality to achieve its effects (for example, Tim O'Brien's *Going After Cacciato*)?

m. How would an understanding of "scaling" theory change our perception of human life?

DEFINING KEY TERMS

Often you will need to know the exact meaning of specialized terms that you come across in your research. Or you may need to know how the meaning of a particular word has developed and changed from the time it was first employed. In both cases, dictionaries of various kinds can be consulted. For example, *Webster's Collegiate Dictionary,* which is condensed from the unabridged *Webster's Third New International Dictionary,* is quite adequate for describing contemporary American word meanings. Under a typical word entry, you will find many kinds of information.

The *American Heritage Dictionary of the English Language,* the *Funk and Wagnall's Standard College Dictionary,* and the *Random House Dictionary of the English Language* are other popular and useful dictionaries providing helpful information on the origins, meanings, usage, and status of hundreds of thousands of words. On the other hand, you may need to use a specialized dictionary for technical terms that are not found in these general dictionaries. For example, if you need definitions of key terms in political science, sociology, social anthropology, economics, and social psychology, you might consult Julius Gould and William L. Kolb's *A Dictionary of the Social Sciences* (1964), which contains long scholarly definitions of approximately 1,000 concepts and terms along with discussions of usage.

The dictionary that dwarfs all the others is the *Oxford English Dictionary*, in thirteen volumes. It deals with the history of the meanings of words over the centuries and cites actual examples. (The OED, as it is abbreviated, is also available in a two-volume reduced-type edition.) In 1986, a four-volume supplement to this work was completed. If you examine the OED, analyzing a word entry or comparing it with the same entry in the *Webster's Third*, you will find that the OED gives illustrations of the usage of words from the time they first appeared to the present.

In addition to the dictionaries listed here, there are bilingual dictionaries as well as those that deal primarily with synonyms and current usage.

Dictionaries: Humanities

Concise Oxford Dictionary of Ballet
Dictionary of American History
Dictionary of American Immigration History
Dictionary of Films
Dictionary of Philosophy
A Handbook to Literature
Harvard Dictionary of Music
Interpreter's Dictionary of the Bible
McGraw-Hill Dictionary of Art
New Grove Dictionary of Music and Musicians

Dictionaries: Social Sciences

The American Political Dictionary
Black's Law Dictionary
Dictionary of the Social Sciences
The Encyclopedic Dictionary of Psychology
McGraw-Hill Dictionary of Modern Economics: A Handbook of Terms and Organizations
The Middle East: A Political Dictionary
The Prentice-Hall Dictionary of Business, Finance, and Law

Dictionaries: Science and Technology

Computer Dictionary and Handbook
Condensed Chemical Dictionary
Dictionary of Biology
Dorland's Medical Dictionary
Encyclopedia and Dictionary of Medicine, Nursing, and Allied Health
McGraw-Hill Dictionary of Scientific and Technical Terms

HOW TO LOCATE
BIOGRAPHICAL INFORMATION

Among the more important books devoted to the lives of people of accomplishment are the *Dictionary of National Biography* (DNB) and the *Dictionary of American Biography* (DAB). Biographical sketches of living people can be found in *Current Biography* and *Who's Who in America*. If your paper concerns a historical figure, you might wish to consult *Who Was Who in America*. Also, there are biographical works that feature people from particular nationalities and professions. There are guides to musicians, artists, and nationally prominent figures in sports and politics. One of the most useful guides is a compiled series called *Contemporary Authors,* which covers more than 85,000 authors who are alive or who have died since 1960.

If what you need is a brief outline of a person's life, you can get the basic facts quickly and conveniently by using a biographical dictionary. The selection of a biographical source depends on the type of information the researcher knows about the person he or she is investigating. For example:

1. If a person's nationality is not known, an international biographical dictionary should be consulted first.
2. If it is known that a person is no longer living, a retrospective source should be consulted first.
3. If it is known that a person is living, a current source should be consulted first.
4. If a person's profession is known, a biographical source for his or her profession should be consulted first.

The following entries give examples of the types of biographical sources available for consultation.

Biographical Sources

American Women Writers: Bibliographical Essays
Asian-American Literature: An Annotated Bibliography

Black American Writers Past and Present

Contemporary Authors

Current Biography (1940–) (Monthly): a well-indexed tool giving biographies of people in the news. Includes portraits.

Dictionary of American Biography (1928–1937): a twenty-volume set that gives nearly 15,000 long evaluations of those "who have made some significant contribution to American life."

Mexican-American Biographies: A Historical Dictionary, 1836–1987

National Cyclopaedia of American Biography (1892–): more comprehensive, albeit less scholarly, than the *Dictionary of American Biography.* Nonalphabetical arrangement. Illustrated. Cumulative index volumes.

Who's Who in America (1879–) (Biennial): gives brief descriptive sketches with addresses of biographees.

Who's Who of American Women (1958–) (Biennial): provides brief descriptive sketches, exclusively of women. To locate biographies of other nationals, check the card catalog under the appropriate subjects. For example:

Canada—Biography

China—Biography

Great Britain—Biography

Biographies of people can be retrieved by professions in the card catalog by looking up the appropriate subjects. For example:

Artists—Biography

Who's Who in American Art (1935–) (Biennial): limited to American artists.

USING THE CARD CATALOG

The card catalog of your college library is a record of all the books and other materials available in that library. While libraries vary in their holdings, the types of materials located in your library that are listed in the card catalog usually include books, newspapers, and periodicals (but not articles in them), theses and dissertations, some government documents (most are not listed), and multimedia items including records, cassettes, filmstrips, and videotapes. Materials usually not listed in the card catalog include college catalogs and annual corporation reports.

Libraries traditionally use one of two systems for classifying information: the Dewey decimal system and the Library of Congress system. The Dewey decimal system classifies books numerically into ten categories that are further broken down into decimals:

000	General Works
100	Philosophy and Related Disciplines
200	Religion
300	Social Sciences
400	Language
500	Pure Science
600	Technology (Applied Science)
700	The Arts
800	Literature and Rhetoric
900	General Geography and History

The system often used in most university and college libraries is the Library of Congress system. This system classifies books according to the alphabet, using numbers for further subdivisions:

A	General Works, Polygraphy
B	Philosophy, Psychology, and Religion
C	Auxiliary Sciences of History
D	General and Old World History (except America)
E–F	American History
G	Geography, Anthropology, Manners and Customs, Folklore, Recreation
H	Social Science, Statistics, Economics, Sociology
J	Political Science
K	Law
L	Education
M	Music
N	Fine Arts
P	Language and Literature
Q	Science
R	Medicine
S	Agriculture, Plant and Animal Industry, Fish Culture, Fisheries, Hunting, Game Protection
T	Technology
U	Military Science
V	Naval Science
Z	Bibliography and Library Science

The card catalog in the library organizes and presents information on each book in a variety of ways. Each book is listed alphabetically on a separate card according to title, subject, and author. An especially useful benefit of using the card catalog is that lists of related subject headings and cross-listed subject areas on the cards make it easy to continue searching for relevant source materials.

The card catalog is usually divided into two alphabetical sections: the author/title catalog and the subject catalog.

Authors are usually individuals (such as Freud, Sigmund), but they may also be corporate bodies such as government agencies, business firms, institutions, or associations (such as U.S. Central Intelligence Agency, General Motors Corporation, American Medical Association). When trying to locate an entry in the card catalog, keep in mind the following filing guidelines:

1. Alphabetization is word-by-word and letter-by-letter within a word. Owing to the rule that nothing comes before something, New York is filed ahead of Newark (the space in New York comes before the *a* in Newark). If, however, you were looking for Newyork, then Newark would come first.
2. Numerals in titles are filed as if written out (for example, *2001: A Space Odyssey* is filed as *Two Thousand One: A Space Odyssey*).
3. Articles (*a, an, the,* and their foreign language equivalents) are disregarded in filing when they come at the beginning of titles (for example, *A Night to Remember* is filed under *N*).
4. Names beginning with "Mc" or "Mac" are filed as "Mac" (for example, McNamara precedes MacRae).
5. Cards beginning with initials are filed before any other cards beginning with the same letter (for example, DNA is filed before Darwin, Charles).
6. Common abbreviations are arranged as though spelled out (for example, Dr. is filed as Doctor, Mrs. is filed as Mistress, Mlle. is filed as Mademoiselle).

The subject catalog is used to locate holdings (1) on a certain topic (such as Psychology, Hot Dog Rolls, Railroad Travel) or (2) about a certain person, place, or group (such as Shakespeare, William; Africa; Pueblo Indians). Usually subjects are listed in a specific rather than a general form (for example, for material on basketball, see Basketball in preference to Sports).

Each book in the library will have a minimum of three cards: an author card, a title card, and a subject card. Books that have more than one author will have an additional card for each author. Moreover, the same book may be listed under several subject cards. Figure 7-1 shows four sample cards for Andrew Weil and Winifred Rosen's book *Chocolate to Morphine: Understanding Mind-Active Drugs.* A sample author card for Winifred Rosen is not shown. Notice that except for a different heading, the information on each card is identical and includes the title of the book, the author (in this case, two coauthors), the city where it was published, the publisher, the date of publication, the number of

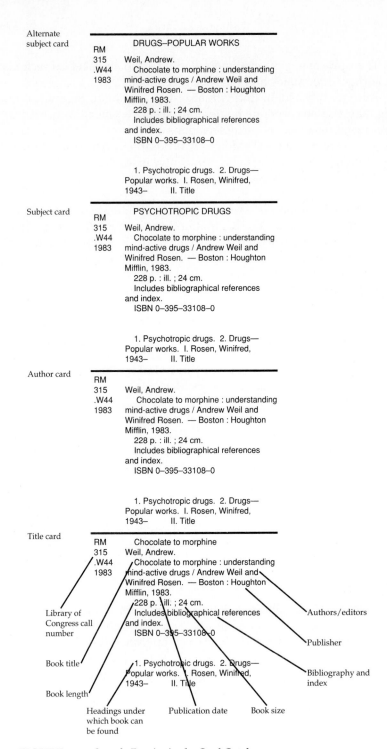

FIGURE 7-1 *Sample Entries in the Card Catalog.*

pages, an abbreviation (ill.) indicating illustrations, the size of the book (24 cm.), and the fact that the book contains both a bibliography and an index. Notice also that the call number appears in the upper left-hand corner on all four cards. The same call number is also found on the spine of the book itself.

The Library of Congress Subject Headings

A particularly indispensable resource you can use to discover relevant headings is the book *Library of Congress Subject Headings,* which provides a comprehensive listing of all phrases used for cataloging materials in all libraries. Since these headings reflect the actual words used in citations and sources, can provide you with valuable leads to finding relevant information.

For example, if you were pursuing an inquiry on the causal relationship between drug use and the effect on adolescents, you would see the following entry:

Drugs and youth (Indirect)
- sa   Alcohol and youth
          Narcotics and youth
          Smoking and youth
- x   Counter culture
          Youth and drugs
- xx   Drug abuse

The bold-faced heading is an entry you would look for in the card catalog. Headings listed as sa (see also) and xx indicate other headings under which material would be listed, if your library has holdings on that subject. The x indicates an unused heading. A skillful researcher can take advantage of these headings to broaden or narrow the search for materials to form the basis of a working bibliography.

USING THE ON-LINE COMPUTER CATALOG

In addition to the traditional card catalog, many libraries have begun to use other means of cataloging information. In newer systems, information on library holdings is available through an on-line computer catalog. The advantage of the on-line catalog is that it allows you to quickly search the library's holdings far more efficiently than would be possible if you were searching through the file cards in a card catalog.

Your search will reveal a list of titles, the location of the materials in the library, and other information including the publisher, date of publication, number of pages, illustrations if any, and the presence of a bibliography for further research. Some on-line systems will also tell you whether or not the book is available or checked out.

The on-line catalogs in some libraries may be connected to other libraries in the same system whose works you may request through interlibrary loans.

A computerized on-line catalog functions much as the traditional card catalog does. The catalog will contain at least three listings for each book: a subject heading, a title heading, and an author heading. When you first press the Enter key, the screen you see may vary from library to library, but the general procedure will require you to type the author symbol (a=) and the author's name to call up a listing of that particular author's works. Take care to type the last name first, followed by a comma and then the first name and initial, if any. You can follow the same procedure by typing the title symbol (t=) and the title of the book you want, or you can search for titles under a specific subject by typing the appropriate symbol (s=) and entering the precise subject that has been narrowed down from a broader heading.

The terms that you use to search (along with titles of works and the names of authors) have been obtained from your previous research using general and specialized encyclopedias, biographical dictionaries, and handbooks in specific subject areas. Here, too, the Library of Congress list of subject headings, available in the reference section of your library, will prove invaluable in providing you with a list of search terms.

When you find a title that offers a promising lead, record its call number on a note card along with all the information you will later need to cite in your bibliography, including the author or editor, title and subtitle, publisher's name and location, year of publication, translator if any, and edition. Search for the book on the shelves. Be sure to look carefully at the books placed on the shelf on either side in case there are other books similar in subject matter that may be useful to you. Always consult the table of contents and index, which will be useful to you in pursuing your inquiry. Books with bibliographies will provide further leads. Keep in mind that if your library still has a card catalog but has installed a computerized on-line card catalog as well, new and future acquisitions will be reflected only through the on-line computerized catalog.

USING PERIODICAL INDEXES

One of the major resources of any college or research library is its periodical and serial holdings. The latest scientific and technological information is usually first available in journals, proceedings of conferences, or society bulletins before the same material appears in book form. The same is true of much of the specialized work in the humanities and social sciences. The student who wishes to keep up to date on various subjects should be aware of the current content of periodicals. Periodicals can refer to any work that appears regularly in print and that has the same title for successive issues. They can be issues of newspapers, of popular magazines such as *Newsweek* or *Sports Illustrated,* or of professional journals such as the *American Journal of Psychology,* published for people in the field.

In putting together your research paper you will most likely use many kinds of sources. Your library's card catalog will give you access to all of the books in the various collections, including the reference room. It will not tell you, however, where to locate articles in the various magazines, journals, and newspapers that your library receives and stores. These are listed separately in what are called *indexes.*

An index is an alphabetical listing of subject and author entries used to locate articles in periodicals. An index is valuable only if it is up to date; virtually all appear at least annually, but most are quarterly, and some appear more frequently. The most commonly used index to periodicals—itself a periodical—is the *Reader's Guide to Periodical Literature,* which indexes more than 150 general magazines and journals by subject and by author. By learning how to use this index you will automatically be learning how to use many other more specialized indexes, such as the *Social Sciences Index* and the *Humanities Index,* which are similarly arranged. Figure 7-2 shows a portion of the listings under "drug abuse" from the February 1987 issue, along with annotations to demonstrate how abbreviations and headings are used.

Although the *Reader's Guide to Periodical Literature* is the best place to start gathering sources on your topic, the nature of the research paper requires you to move beyond these general sources to more specialized ones. In this case, the *Social Sciences Index* would be an ideal next place to look, since it includes specialized investigations into relationships between drugs and society. Figure 7-3 shows some of the listings in the part of the index that provides information on studies produced in one year on drugs and athletes, children, crime, employment, Indians, police, the handicapped, women, and youth.

The *Social Sciences Index* and the *Humanities Index,* which cover scholarly journals, are both more specialized than the *Reader's Guide to Periodical Literature.* As you narrow your topic, however, you will find that you need to search more specialized bibliographies and indexes that provide up-to-date information on highly specific subject areas. The following have proved to be the most valuable; they are listed according to liberal arts, political and social sciences, natural and physical sciences, and technology. The general periodical indexes can be used to locate magazine, journal, and newspaper articles, whereas the

Drug abuse–Conferences–cont.
Preparatory body for international
drug conference calls for draft outline of
future activities. il *UN Chron* 23:84 Ap '86
History
A Yale drug historian sniffs something
familiar in today's cocaine craze [inter-
view with D. Musto] M. Wilheim. il por
People Wkly 26:155–6+ N 24 '86
International aspects
Threat to health from drugs termed
'narco–terrorism'. *World Health* p30 Ag/S
'86
Rehabilitation
See also
Hale House (New York, N.Y.)
Acupuncture used to help crack addicts.
Jet 71:36 D 22 '86
A life of lies, a dance with death—a
recovering addict talks about the cost of
crack. A. Abrahams. il *People Wkly* 26:93–
4 + N 3 '86
Unhooking from drugs. il *Changing Times*
40:113–18 + O '86
Testing
The battle over drug testing [privacy issue]
I. R. Kaufman il *N Y Times Mag* p52 +
O 19 '86
Busting the drug testers [faculty lab results]
S. Budiansky. il *U S News; World Rep*
101:70 O 20 '86
Can test positive for pot by just being near
smoke. *Jet* 71:31 D 15 '86
Courts foil schools' efforts to detect drugs.
T. J. Flygare. *Phi Delta Kappa* 68:329–30
D '86
Danforth urges rules for drug testing of
airline employees. *Aviat Week Space
Technol* 125:47 D 1 '86
Disputed tactics in the war on drugs. M.
Gray. il *Macleans* 99:55 O 13 '86
In school drug tests: right or wrong? K.
Henderson. *Seventeen* 45:84 D '86
NCAA prepares to test athletes for drug
use. *Jet* 71:51 O 13 '86
A new focus on drugs. W. Hoffer. il *Nations
Bus* 74:57–9 D '86
No racial bias found in Cleveland drug case
[surprise urine testing of police] *Jet* 71:22
N 10 '86
"Obsolete" amendments [mandatory drug
testing] D. E. Petzal. *Field Stream* 91:23 +
D '86
Reaganites at risk. R. Vigilante. il *Nat Rev*
38:31–2 + D 5 '86
Test cases. *Time* 128:35 D 15 '86
Testing hair can detect cocaine use,
researchers. *Jet* 71:53 N 10 '86
This is what you thought: 56% say no to
drug testing [results of survey] *Glamour*
84:103 N '86
Anecdotes, facetiae, satire, etc.
Our Puritan dilemma. J. Morley. *New Repub*
195:13–14 D 1 '86

Labels: Article title, Author, Issue date, Periodical title, Page referennce, Volume number, Illustrations, Special feature

FIGURE 7-2 *Sample Page from the* Reader's Guide to Periodical
Literature.

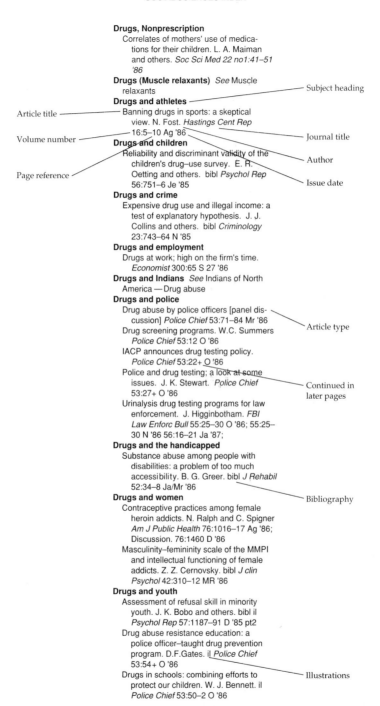

Drugs, Nonprescription
Correlates of mothers' use of medications for their children. L. A. Maiman and others. *Soc Sci Med 22 no1:41–51* '86

Drugs (Muscle relaxants) *See* Muscle relaxants — Subject heading

Drugs and athletes — Subject heading

Article title — Banning drugs in sports: a skeptical view. N. Fost. *Hastings Cent Rep*

Volume number — 16:5–10 Ag '86 — Journal title

Drugs and children
Reliability and discriminant validity of the children's drug–use survey. E. R. — Author
Page reference — Oetting and others. bibl *Psychol Rep* 56:751–6 Je '85 — Issue date

Drugs and crime
Expensive drug use and illegal income: a test of explanatory hypothesis. J. J. Collins and others. bibl *Criminology* 23:743–64 N '85

Drugs and employment
Drugs at work; high on the firm's time. *Economist* 300:65 S 27 '86

Drugs and Indians *See* Indians of North America — Drug abuse

Drugs and police
Drug abuse by police officers [panel discussion] *Police Chief* 53:71–84 Mr '86 — Article type
Drug screening programs. W.C. Summers *Police Chief* 53:12 O '86
IACP announces drug testing policy. *Police Chief* 53:22+ O '86
Police and drug testing; a look at some issues. J. K. Stewart. *Police Chief* 53:27+ O '86 — Continued in later pages
Urinalysis drug testing programs for law enforcement. J. Higginbotham. *FBI Law Enforc Bull* 55:25–30 O '86; 55:25–30 N '86 56:16–21 Ja '87;

Drugs and the handicapped
Substance abuse among people with disabilities: a problem of too much accessibility. B. G. Greer. bibl *J Rehabil* 52:34–8 Ja/Mr '86

Drugs and women — Bibliography
Contraceptive practices among female heroin addicts. N. Ralph and C. Spigner *Am J Public Health* 76:1016–17 Ag '86; Discussion. 76:1460 D '86
Masculinity–femininity scale of the MMPI and intellectual functioning of female addicts. Z. Z. Cernovsky. bibl *J clin Psychol* 42:310–12 MR '86

Drugs and youth
Assessment of refusal skill in minority youth. J. K. Bobo and others. bibl il *Psychol Rep* 57:1187–91 D '85 pt2
Drug abuse resistance education: a police officer–taught drug prevention program. D.F.Gates. il *Police Chief* 53:54+ O '86
Drugs in schools: combining efforts to protect our children. W. J. Bennett. il *Police Chief* 53:50–2 O '86 — Illustrations

FIGURE 7-3 *Sample Page from the* Social Sciences Index.

specialized indexes will direct you to scholarly journals in the relevant discipline.

General Periodical Indexes

Bibliographic Index
Biography Index
Book Review Digest
Book Review Index
Books in Print
Computer Readable Data Bases
Cumulative Book Index
Cumulative Index to Periodical Literature
International Who's Who
Magazine Index
National Newspaper Index
Newspaper Index
New York Times Index
Poole's Index to Periodical Literature
Popular Periodicals Index
Readers' Guide to Periodical Literature
U.S. Government Publications (monthly catalog)
Vertical File Index

Periodical Indexes in the Humanities

America: History and Life
The American Humanities Index
Art Index
Arts and Humanities Citation Index
British Humanities Index
Cambridge Bibliography of English Literature and *New Cambridge Bibliography of English Literature*
Contemporary Literary Criticism
Cumulated Dramatic Index
Drama Criticism Index
Essay and General Literature Index
Explicator Cyclopedia (poetry)
Film Literature Index
A Guide to Critical Reviews
Humanities Index
Index to Book Reviews in the Humanities
Industrial Arts Index
International Index of Film Periodicals

MLA International Bibliography of Books and Articles on Modern
    Languages and Literatures
Music Index
New York Times Film Reviews
Philosopher's Index One: Periodicals
Religion Index
Twentieth-Century Literary Criticism
Year's Work in English Studies

Periodical Indexes in Social Sciences

American Statistical Index
Business Periodicals Index
Current Index to Journals in Education (CIJE)
Education Index
Gallup Poll Monthly
Index to Legal Periodicals
International Political Science Abstracts
Key to Economic Science
Physical Education/Sports Index
Public Affairs Information Service (PAIS)
Social Science Index
Social Sciences Citation Index
Social Sciences and Humanities Index
United Nations Document Index

Periodical Indexes in the Sciences

Agricultural Index
Applied Science and Technology Index
Bibliography and Index of Geology
Biological and Agricultural Index
Cumulative Index to Nursing and Allied Health Literature
Energy Index
Engineering Index
General Science Index
Index Medicus
Index to Scientific and Technical Proceedings
Keyguide to Information Sources in Animal Rights
Science Citation Index
Technical Book Review Index

The best way to find out about a new reference tool such as an index is to read its preface. Unlike the card catalog, which conveniently cross-lists all possible leads, reference indexes may rely only on subject or author listings. Reading the preface will tell you how the index is organized and what materials, subjects, and time periods it includes. All indexing services list articles under subjects, and many list them by author, usually in one alphabetical sequence.

When using indexes, jot down the author, title of the article, complete journal title, volume number, page numbers, and date of the issue. If the journal title is abbreviated, use the list in the front of the index to find the complete tide. To find out whether your library holds the periodical you need, consult a list of currently received periodicals, usually kept as a computer printout or a microfiche list (if available) at the periodical services department or the reference desk.

USING BOOK REVIEWS

Chapters in books can be found in the *Essay and General Literature Index*. To find books on a given subject, try *Books in Print: Subjects*. Remember that out-of-print books are not contained in this volume, but they may be listed in the card catalog. When you have discovered many promising titles of books but don't have the time to pursue each and every one, consult the *Book Review Index, Index to Book Reviews in the Humanities*, or the *Book Review Digest*. The *Book Review Digest* is both a digest and an index of selected reviews of fiction and nonfiction works. More than 6,000 books a year are covered. Excerpts from the book reviews are given, as well as bibliographic information for locating the reviews in full. This work is arranged alphabetically by author with a subject and title index.

The *Book Review Index* is an index to reviews in more than 200 English language journals in the humanities and social sciences. It is arranged alphabetically by author or by title of the book being reviewed and does not contain abstracts. The *Index to Book Reviews in the Humanities* covers books on art and architecture, biography, drama and dance, folklore, history, language, literature, music, philosophy, travel, and adventure. Through 1962, only reviews in English are indexed. Beginning in January 1963, indexes also review in foreign languages. Reviews are arranged alphabetically by author.

The *Library Journal Book Review* also contains full reprints of book reviews as they originally appeared in the *Library Journal*. Current fiction and nonfiction titles are included. An author–title index accompanies each annual volume. Another valuable resource, the *Social Sciences and Humanities Index* (formerly titled *International Index to Periodicals*), indexes about 200 scholarly journals in the humanities and social sciences. Reviews are often cited under author and subject entries.

A compilation of all the *New York Times Book Review* issues published since 1896 appears in the *New York Times Book Review*. Individual reviews may be located by consulting the *New York Times Index*. When you are using the *New York Times Index,* locate book reviews under the heading "Book Reviews." Citations are arranged under this heading by author. Exact references to page, date, and column of the *New York Times* are given.

If the book you are looking for is very recent and is not listed in *Book Review Digest* or other indexes, try the *New York Times Book Review,* the *Times Literary Supplement,* or the *Library Journal.* Reviews will help determine whether the book has been favorably received and will give you a concise overview of the subject and the author's viewpoint. Figure 7-4 illustrates the 1984 *Book Review Digest's* listing of reviews that appeared for *Chocolate to Morphine: Understanding Mind-Active Drugs,* by Andrew Weil and Winifred Rosen.

USING NEWSPAPER INDEXES

A concise, objective and thorough account of all significant international, national, and general news is available in the *New York Times Index.* Entries drawn from the news and editorial matter of the final late city edition of the *Times* are arranged alphabetically under specific subject headings. Summaries of news stories are published in supplements every two weeks and are combined into one volume at the end of every year. Annual volumes of the index have appeared since 1913.

To use the index, simply choose the volume from the year in which you think the subject of your research paper might have appeared in the news. Look through the index for references to your subject. You will notice that entries end with abbreviations that tell you the date, page, and column on or in which the story originally appeared. You may then wish to obtain a copy of the microfilm edition of the *New York Times* and look at it through a microfilm viewer to get the complete story as it appeared on that date. Through the microfilm editions you can gain access to international, national, and general news stories going back to 1851.

The *New York Times Index* provides not only a subject and chronological guide to events but also summaries of *Times* articles and items. Other indexes are available for the *Wall Street Journal* and the *Christian Science Monitor.* Information on articles in the *Chicago Tribune,* the *Los Angeles Times,* the *New Orleans Times-Picayune,* and the *Washington Post* can be located in the *Newspaper Index.*

USING ABSTRACTS

An abstract has the same information as an index and is used in the same way to locate articles in periodicals but also provides a brief summary of the contents for each article it lists. There are comprehensive abstracting services for major subject areas, including

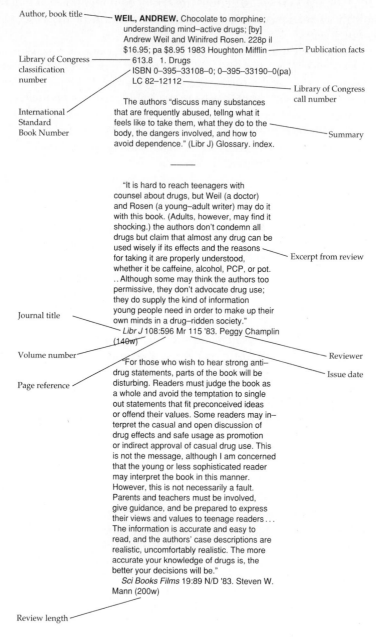

BOOK REVIEW DIGEST 1984

Author, book title —— **WEIL, ANDREW.** Chocolate to morphine; understanding mind–active drugs; [by] Andrew Weil and Winifred Rosen. 228p il $16.95; pa $8.95 1983 Houghton Mifflin —— Publication facts

Library of Congress classification number —— 613.8   1. Drugs

International Standard Book Number / ISBN 0–395–33108–0; 0–395–33190–0(pa) LC 82–12112 —— Library of Congress call number

The authors "discuss many substances that are frequently abused, tellng what it feels like to take them, what they do to the body, the dangers involved, and how to avoid dependence." (Libr J) Glossary. index. —— Summary

"It is hard to reach teenagers with counsel about drugs, but Weil (a doctor) and Rosen (a young–adult writer) may do it with this book. (Adults, however, may find it shocking.) the authors don't condemn all drugs but claim that almost any drug can be used wisely if its effects and the reasons for taking it are properly understood, whether it be caffeine, alcohol, PCP, or pot. ..Although some may think the authors too permissive, they don't advocate drug use; they do supply the kind of information young people need in order to make up their own minds in a drug–ridden society." —— Excerpt from review

Journal title —— *Libr J* 108:596 Mr 115 '83. Peggy Champlin (140w)

Volume number —— "For those who wish to hear strong anti– drug statements, parts of the book will be disturbing. Readers must judge the book as a whole and avoid the temptation to single out statements that fit preconceived ideas or offend their values. Some readers may in– terpret the casual and open discussion of drug effects and safe usage as promotion or indirect approval of casual drug use. This is not the message, although I am concerned that the young or less sophisticated reader may interpret the book in this manner. However, this is not necessarily a fault. Parents and teachers must be involved, give guidance, and be prepared to express their views and values to teenage readers ... The information is accurate and easy to read, and the authors' case descriptions are realistic, uncomfortably realistic. The more accurate your knowledge of drugs is, the better your decisions will be."

Page reference

Reviewer

Issue date

Sci Books Films 19:89 N/D '83. Steven W. Mann (200w)

Review length

FIGURE 7-4   *Sample Page from* Book Review Digest.

Abstracts in Anthropology
Abstracts of English Studies
Abstracts of Popular Culture
Agricultural Engineering Abstracts
Biological Abstracts
Chemical Abstracts
Computer and Control Abstracts
Current Abstracts of Chemistry and Index Chemicus
Dissertation Abstracts International
Economics Abstracts
Food Science & Technology Abstracts
GEO Abstracts
Historical Abstracts
Library Journal Book Review
Physics Abstracts
Pollution Abstracts
Psychological Abstracts
Social Work Research and Abstracts
Sociological Abstracts
Women's Studies Abstracts

An abstract is a bibliographic tool that serves as both an index and a source of concise summaries of original articles. *Psychological Abstracts* (1927–) is one of the most important bibliographies of the world's literature in psychology and related disciplines. It contains listings of books, journal articles, and dissertations with signed abstracts. Abstracts are arranged in seventeen major classification categories. There are author indexes and, beginning in 1983, brief subject indexes to each issue number as well as full author and subject indexes to each volume.

If you were looking for an article by a particular author, you would use the *Cumulated Author Index.* If you were looking for an article on a particular subject, you would use the *Cumulated Subject Index.* You would notice that the *Psychological Abstracts Cumulated Index* covers all the materials that have appeared under an author's name or under a subject during the time period listed on the spine of the volume. Thus, if the author's name appears in the *Cumulated Author Index, 1972–74* or *1969–71,* there will also be the title of the article and the name of the journal in which it appeared as well as the *Psychological Abstracts* volume number and abstract number.

When looking for a subject, find the terms that best describe the material. List these terms. Look through the *Cumulated Subject Index* for each subject. If the desired terminology is found, there will be a brief sentence or phrase describing the articles and giving an abstract number. Copy this information. Do not omit the *Psychological Abstracts* volume number. Next search the annual bound *Indexes of Psychological Abstracts*. Use either an author or a subject approach. Record the abstract numbers and do not forget to include the year and issue number of *Psychological Abstracts*.

After finding an appropriate list of abstract numbers, refer to the proper volume of *Psychological Abstracts,* which are usually located in the periodical collection. Journals are usually shelved here in strict alphabetic order by title from A to Z, with *Psychological Abstracts* toward the end of the collection.

The abstract found under the number written down contains the author's name, the title of the article, the name of the journal, and the issue in which the article appeared. This is followed by the abstract itself, which is a brief description of the article.

Copy the complete citation of the article you wish to read and consult the alphabetic periodicals holdings list, which will be on a printout or on microfiche. If your library received that periodical for the year and issue you need, you would then look for it in alphabetic title order on the bound periodical shelves. In the case of a book or dissertation listing, you would consult the card catalog or ask for help from a reference librarian. Figure 7-5 shows a sample page of summaries from *Psychological Abstracts* along with annotations designed to help you use this essential resource.

USING FIELD RESEARCH—INTERVIEWS

For some research papers you may wish to go beyond the sources available to you in the library (such as *The Gallup Opinion Index,* containing results of national public opinion surveys on topics of current interest, including presidential popularity, elections, and important international and domestic issues); you may wish to conduct interviews or surveys whose results will play a significant role in your research.

For example, faculty members from different specialized fields of study will probably be glad to share their expertise. Or you may want to interview someone whose experiences provide valuable insights into the subject of your study. In any case, you must plan your interview ahead of time by first finding out from your instructor whether information gained from interviews would be considered acceptable and appropriate for the particular assignment. You should have the questions you want to ask already formulated. Carefully check them to see whether you have unintentionally worded them in such a way as to elicit certain answers. What you want are open, honest, and informative responses. If you would like to use a tape recorder, first clear this with the person you plan to interview. Plan to take accurate notes during the interview, including key words and phrases, to make it easier to recall the substance of the interview later. After the interview, review

1032. **Rubio Perez, A. M. et al.** (Facultad de Medicina, Valladolid, Spain) Estudio comparativo del consumo de drogas del medio universitario de Cordoba y Valladolid. [Comparative studies of drug use among students at the Universities of Cordoba and Valladolid.] (Span) *Psicopatologia.* 1984 (Oct–Dec), Vol 4(4), 373–384. –Administered a modified test of psychiatric disorders to a sample of medical and nursing students from the Universities of Cordoba and Valladolid as part of an epidemiological survey on drug usage. The test contained 80 questions on individual, familial, and social traits and on attitudes toward disease and drug use. 1,107 tests from Cordoba and 823 from Valladolid were analyzed. Results were shown as percentages or as a means plus or minus standard deviations. Statistical analyses were performed with an unpaired t–test or chi–square test. Analgesic drug use by nursing students (15%) was lower than that by medical students (21%). 50% of Ss used stimulants, but amphetamines were used by no more than 10% of the medical students and 3% of the nursing students. Only 1% of the Ss used amphetamines to help them perform better on tests. Hypnotics were used in more clinical than preclinical years. 16.6% of the sample used cannibis–related drugs (mainly hashish in Cordoba and marihuana in Valladolid). The decrease in tobacco smokers in the general population was confirmed in the sample. More Ss from Cordoba (70%) than Valladolid (53%) consumed alcoholic beverages. (English abstract) (8 ref)

Language of article

Summary is in English

Entry number corresponding to number from subject index

1033. **Siegel, Ronald K.** (VA Branch, Los Angeles, CA) **Cocaine and the privileged class: A reviev of historical and contemporary images.** *Advances in Alcohol & Substance Abuse.* 1984(Win), Vol 4(2), 37–49. –Discusses the belief that cocaine is a drug associated with privilege and the privileged class, which is frequently cited as a motivating factor for nonmedical use. This association, part myth and part reality, has influenced the perception of cocaine as a glamorous and exotic drug, a drug immune to serious problems, a drug for the successful and wealthy, and, hence, a privileged drug. The origins and development of this myth are examined in terms of both historical and contemporary images in the arts and the media. Alternative competing images of cocaine as a drug associated with severe dependency and toxicity are discussed in terms of their past and future trends. (38 ref)–*Journal abstract.*

Author's institutional affiliation

Article title

Page reference

Journal title

Volume and issue number

Issue date

Bibliography includes 38 sources

FIGURE 7-5 *Sample Page of Summaries from* Psychological Abstracts.

your notes as soon as you can and put down a few sentences that summarize the most important points. Don't forget to record the date, time,
full name, and title, if any, of the person you have interviewed.

USING COMPUTERIZED DATA BASES

Many libraries now provide a variety of services that enable the user to
gain access to computerized data bases. The information supplied by
these data bases may include citations of sources on your subject and
indexes of articles, books, and other materials on specific subjects along
with abstracts drawn from these sources and in some cases the full text
of the source itself.

Computer terminals connected by modems over telephone lines by
means of telecommunication networks, such as Telenet, can provide
the user (at a fee, sometimes hefty) with direct access to many general
and specific data bases. The procedure for using these services requires
you to enter an assigned password or to open an account on a network
provided by your library.

The most widely used services available in university libraries are
BRS (Bibliographical Retrieval Service), DIALOG (which provides access to more than 400 data bases), COMPUSERVE (for business information), LEXIS (for legal information), THE SOURCE (for business
information), NEXIS (for news and public affairs), RLIN (research libraries information network), OCLC (on-line computer library center),
and DOW JONES.

Since computer searching can become very expensive very quickly,
you must work out a strategy in advance so that you can request specific information, using exact terms or key words known as *descriptors.*
Using descriptors that are too broad will produce far too many citations. It is best to make use of the Library of Congress list of subject
headings first to discover the key terms that refer to important concepts. By combining general search terms with more specific ones (for
example, the broad term "genetic" with the more narrow term "screening") you can quickly narrow down your search to produce a small
number of pertinent sources. The information obtained from on-line
services has the advantage of being updated daily. This may be important if your subject requires the latest information.

CD-ROM (Compact Disc, Read Only Memory) data bases are
stored on laser discs in the library, and normally there is no charge to
use them. In most libraries, CD-ROMs are already installed in computers ready to use. In others, you must request the specific data base you
want and install it yourself. Each CD-ROM contains the equivalent of
300,000 printed pages. The process of using these data bases is similar
to that of the on-line services. After selecting a data base, you type in

one or several search terms, call up a list of references and abstracts, and print out a list of materials and accompanying texts that you need. The information services available will vary from library to library, but most students have found it useful to begin their search with general-coverage data bases such as one of the following:

CIS/Masterfile I (an index to Congressional proceedings since 1789) and **CIS/Masterfile II** (index and abstracts for all Congressional Committee Hearings since 1969). These collections provide a wealth of information on current issues and include subject analyses and names of witnesses. **CIS/Statistical Masterfile** is a comprehensive index of federal, state, foreign, and commercial publications providing up-to-date sources for statistical data, beginning with 1973.

ERIC (Educational Resources Information Center) provides a comprehensive system in resources in education including abstracts and indexing for the collection and dissemination of educational resources developed and maintained by the National Institute of Education.

InfoTrac provides several major data bases including the Expanded Academic Index (960+ scholarly journals and general interest publications); the National Newspaper Index, a one-stop source to search references from many national newspapers; the Health Index Plus, which contains summaries, authors, abstracts, and health-related articles (3000+ magazines and newspapers; 130+ publications on health and nutrition with full text for over 80 journals); and the Government Publications Index (an index to a monthly catalog of U.S. government publications).

ProQuest, produced by University Microfilms International, provides data bases including ABI/Inform (indexes 800+ business and trade journals), periodical abstracts (300+ general interest periodicals), and Business Dateline OnDisc.

Silver Platter data bases include PAIS, SocioFile (Sociological Abstracts+), PsycLit (Psychological Abstracts+), Mathsci (Mathematical Reviews+), CIRR (Corporate and Industry Research Reports), and CINAHL (Nursing and Allied Health) and Medline (Biomedics).

UnCover, a data base of information taken from the tables of contents of 15,000+ journals in all disciplines, from fall 1988 to the present.

Wilson Disc data bases include the MLA international bibliography (index to books on literature, from 1981) and indexes published by the H. W. Wilson Company, such as Applied Science and Technology, Art Index, Biography Index, Biological and Agricultural Index, General Science Index, Humanities Index, Social Sciences Index, and Readers' Guide to Periodical Literature. The print equivalents for several of these indexes were described earlier in this chapter.

Some data bases contain a **thesaurus** that is set up in the same way as the Library of Congress list of subject headings. Consulting it will allow you to quickly limit your search by cross-referencing terms. For example, the ERIC data base will prompt a user to check the thesaurus to find a term that can be used to directly search the data base. Thus, a student doing research on "genetic engineering" who used this phrase to search the ERIC data base would discover 135 citations. When the term "screening" was typed in along with "genetic engineering" (a process of cross-referencing called Boolean logic), the resulting search discovered four hits in which both concepts were featured prominently. Abstracts comprising brief summaries of each of the four references could then be printed out to help the student decide whether to locate the full text for all or any of them.

In addition to these general-coverage data base indexes, there are several specialized data bases that are useful for pursuing inquiries within specific academic disciplines. The most widely used are these:

Agricola (agriculture)
America: History and Life
Art Literature International
Arts and Humanities Search
AVE (architecture)
Biography Master Index
Biosis Previews (biology, botany)
CA Search (chemistry)
COMPEN DEX*PLUS (engineering)
Donnelly Demographics (census data)
ENV (environmental sciences and pollution management)
GDCS (Government Documents Catalog Service; includes
     GPO Index)
HAP (Hispanic American Periodicals Index)
IIN (Inside Information/British Library Document Supply Centre)
LIF (life sciences and bioengineering)
Mental Health Abstracts
Metadex (metallurgy)
NPA (newspaper abstracts)
NTIS (National Technical Information Search)
ORBIT (science and technology)
PaperChase (searches four data bases: MEDLINE, HEALTH,
     AIDSLINE, CANCERLIT)
Philosopher's Index
PsychINFO (psychology)
Religion Index
Social Scisearch (social sciences)
Sociological Abstracts
Software Directory (microcomputer software)
SPIN (physics)

Ulrich's International Periodicals Directory
World Translations Index

✦ Questions for Discussion and Writing

1. Drawing on some of the following issues, what key terms would you expect to use to search data bases? What data bases would you search and what terms would you use as *descriptors* in order to produce a small (fewer than ten items) workable list of references?

    a. How is the influence of the Civil War revealed in stories by twentieth-century southern writers?

    b. Do corporations market their products (for example, infant formulas, pesticides, tobacco) to Third World nations in an irresponsible manner?

    c. Do black students need an Afrocentric curriculum?

    d. Does biological and neuropsychological evidence support the claim that gender differences are rooted in the brain?

    e. How important are arms sales to international commerce? Should the global arms trade be restricted? Who is selling what to whom, and what should be done about it, if anything?

    f. How have new discoveries of prehuman ancestors affected theories about the rates of human evolution?

    g. What contemporary or classical works of literature dramatize the consequences to a community if its leader has a tragic flaw (for example, *Things Fall Apart* by Chinua Achebe, *Oedipus Rex* by Sophocles)?

    h. What contemporary works of literature are compelling in the way they give voice to those who cannot speak for themselves (for example, *Song of Solomon* by Toni Morrison, *No Name Woman* by Maxine Hong Kingston, *Schindler's List* by Thomas Kenneally)?

    i. What classic or contemporary works of literature have contributed most to your understanding of the psychological conflicts that racial conflicts produce (for example, *Invisible Man* by Ralph Ellison, *Othello* by Shakespeare)?

    j. What contemporary works of literature have been important in helping audiences understand and deal with the emotional impact of AIDS (for example, *The Band Played On* by Randy Shiltz, *Angels in America* by Tony Kushner)?

    k. What contemporary works of literature do you find especially effective in offering insight into the immigrant experience, the conflict between first- and second-generation immigrants, or the emotional costs of being an immigrant, illegal alien, or migrant worker in the United States (for example, *The Kitchen God's Wife* by Amy Tan, *Jasmine* by Bharati Mukherjee)?

l. Should limits be placed on the awards paid out as a result of malpractice suits?

m. What issues have been raised by recent books on the relationship between race, class, genetics, and intelligence testing?

n. Have scientific tests proved that the Shroud of Turin is genuine?

o. What plausible theories have been advanced to explain the existence or efficacy of channeling, clairvoyance, precognition, telepathy, psychic healing, psychokinesis, astral travel, demonic possession, reincarnation, astrology, the miracle cures at Lourdes, alien abductions, Big Foot, the Bermuda triangle, Nostradamus's prophecies?

EVALUATING SOURCE MATERIALS

Research for an argument-based paper begins with questions about a topic in which you are interested. Becoming familiar with the resources offered in your library makes it easier for you to enter existing debates on the subject. By investigating a topic from many angles, you will see how this topic is viewed from many different perspectives and develop a more complete picture. By discovering how researchers have answered questions in different ways, you will be better able to decide which position merits support. Research should not involve looking for support for a predetermined position but rather should be a process in which you become well enough informed on a topic to express and support an opinion. Your paper will reflect both your search and what you discovered along the way.

DRAWING UP A WORKING BIBLIOGRAPHY

A recommended way of keeping track of the results of your library search to discover which source materials are useful is to draw up a working bibliography. This preliminary or tentative bibliography will contain all the information on books, periodicals, abstracts, newspapers, on-line services, and other source materials held by the library that you consider useful. You can add new source materials or discard those you discover to be irrelevant.

When you have finished your paper you will be ready to make up a final bibliography listing only those works actually cited. A separate 3-by-5-inch or 4-by-6-inch bibliography card needs to be created for each source. This card should record the library call number, the complete title of the work, the author's full name, and the place, date, and publisher of the work. A bibliography card for an article in a journal, periodical, or magazine should record the complete name of the author; the title of the article; the name of the journal or magazine; the volume number, the day, month, and year of publication (if given); and the complete run of page numbers of the article.

On the same card, jot down your impression of how the source might be used in your paper, or where it might fit into the overall investigation. You can begin to evaluate the quality of the source materials by answering the following questions:

1. Does the information presented in the source material bear directly on the question you are interested in exploring?
2. Does the author have appropriate credentials, experience, or expertise in the field?
3. Is the author's research timely, or has it been superseded by more recent research?
4. Are the conclusions presented by the author clearly drawn from well-documented and reliable evidence?
5. Does the book, chapter in a book, article from a magazine or journal, or other source contain a sufficient amount of discussion to warrant its use as a source from which notes will be taken? (Frequently, the best way to determine this for a book is by checking the page numbers on the subject listed in the index. An index entry on "crop substitution programs in Peru" on pages 17–28 would be a more useful source than the same entry followed by pages 17, 28. The first entry covers a discussion of twelve pages, whereas the second indicates that the entire book touches on the subject on only two separate pages.)

THE DANGERS OF UNDOCUMENTED SOURCES

The very nature of the research paper requires you to document all information taken from sources, whether in the form of quotations, paraphrases, summaries, or factual references. This is important even if you are not using the exact language used by the author. It means that you must provide an in-text reference specifying the author, title of the work, and location within the work where the reference can be found. For this reason it is important that you accurately note down the source, including specific page numbers, on each note card you write. Not to do this may later lead you to believe that these were your own ideas, and you may fail to acknowledge that this information derives from an external source. Be especially careful in making sure you have included quotation marks so that you do not, however unintentionally, mistake someone else's words for your own and not give proper credit. It is preferable to overdocument sources that could have been assumed to fall in the category of general knowledge than to underdocument sources and raise the question of plagiarism.

Note-Taking Procedures

To be useful, notes should be legible, written on one side of 4-by-6-inch index cards, and contain information from only one source per card. On each card, write the title of the work from which the note was taken, along with exact page numbers, in the upper right-hand corner. In the upper left-hand corner, write a short phrase identifying the particular aspect of the research question to which the note relates.

Your comments can refer to your evaluation of the source's qualifications; the author's purpose in writing the essay, article, or book in question; the audience being addressed; the methods used; and the conclusions reached. You may wish to comment on how persuasive the evidence is or whether the author agrees or disagrees with others studying the same issue. Most importantly, even at this early stage, try to consider how this piece of information could be used as evidence in your argument. The actual note should be clearly written, preferably in ink, in the center of the card.

Only information on the source and the exact page number need appear on the card, since you have already made up a card with complete bibliographical information. If you are using more than one work by the same author, however, put an abbreviation of the title along with the author's last name and the page number to avoid confusing this note with others drawn from a different work by the same author.

THE VALUE OF DIFFERENT KINDS OF NOTES

Different kinds of notes serve different purposes. Notes can take the form of (1) paraphrases, (2) summaries, (3) quotations, or (4) factual references.

Paraphrases

Paraphrasing requires you to restate the thoughts of the author in your own words. Unlike the shorter summary, a sentence-by-sentence paraphrase will be approximately the same length as the original; the thoughts will be the author's, but the language in which these thoughts are expressed will be your own. A research paper, of course, requires you to footnote any paraphrased material to indicate its source. If you can restate the thoughts, ideas, and opinions of the author in your own words, you demonstrate that you understand what you have read. In both summarizing and paraphrasing, it is a good idea to check what you have written down against the original to see whether you have inadvertently left out anything important.

For example, here is an original passage from Andrew Weil and Winifred Rosen's chapter from *Chocolate to Morphine:*

Many drug users talk about getting high. Highs are states of consciousness marked by feelings of euphoria, lightness, self-transcendence, concentration, and energy. People who never take drugs also seek out highs. In fact, having high experiences from time to time may be necessary to our physical and mental health, just as dreaming at night seems to be vital to our well-being. Perhaps that is why a desire to alter normal consciousness exists in everyone and why people pursue the experiences even though there are sometimes uncomfortable side effects.

The paraphrased entry on a note card might appear this way:

Innate need to alter   **Weil & Rosen, <u>Chocolate,</u>**
consciousness   **page 15**

Drugs allow the user to experience a feeling of vitality,
excitement, loss of ego, and a heightened sense of well-being.
Since people all over the world engage in non–drug-taking
activities to produce this state, we might conclude that
human beings have an innate need to alter consciousness
that is so strong it will make people overlook possible bad
reactions produced by the drugs.

Notice how paraphrasing makes the writer think about the ideas in order to express them in different words. Paraphrasing is a way of thinking through the subject, and in so doing you automatically must take into account what others have had to say about it. Remember that since you are using someone else's ideas, facts, and research as a basis for your own paper, you must always provide a reference that indicates your source. Restating another person's thoughts in your own words not only demonstrates that you have really understood what you read but means that your paper will not be simply a patchwork of connected quotations of many different styles.

Summaries

Summaries are also written in your own words, but unlike paraphrases they tend to be shorter than the original. The length of your summary does not depend on the length of the original passage. A summary simply presents your concise restatement of the author's main ideas. It is important to be careful not to change ideas when you compress and condense them. For example, here is a passage from Philip Slater's article "Want-Creation Fuels Americans' Addictiveness" (1984):

> But in our society we spend billions each year creating want. Covetousness, discontent and greed are taught to our children, drummed into them—they are bombarded with it. Not only through advertising, but in the feverish emphasis on success, on winning at all costs, on being the center of attention through one kind of performance or another, on being the first at something—no matter how silly or stupid ("The Guinness Book of Records"). We are an addictive society. Addiction is a state of wanting. It is a condition in which the individual feels he or she is incomplete, inadequate, lacking, not whole, and can only be made whole by the addition of something external.

Compressed into a note card summary, the above passage might appear this way:

Society encourages   **Slater, "Want-Creation" page 7**
want-creation

Our society encourages drug use by constantly pushing
people to be successful, to win, and to be the best. This
emphasis on competition and success makes people feel
inadequate and leads them to believe that drugs can remedy
the societally induced feelings of dissatisfaction.

Quotations

A third type of note card involves direct quotation, or copying the author's words exactly as they appear in the original. Unlike a paraphrase or summary, you are putting down the exact words of your original source. Quotation marks at the beginning and end remind you that this is a word-for-word copy, including original punctuation and mistakes, if any. Basically, you directly quote a source that you consider especially important, concise, or vivid and want to present in the author's words directly to the reader. Perhaps you discover that the original idea loses its force when you try to paraphrase or summarize it. Or perhaps the distinctive style in which the idea is expressed is unique and memorable. These are all good reasons for using direct quotation.

But the most important reason is that your opinion without the support of the quotation will carry less weight and be less persuasive.

For example, here is what a note card looks like that is quoting from a *Wall Street Journal* article, "High Fliers: Use of Cocaine Grows Among Top Traders in Financial Centers" (September 12, 1983):

Cocaine use in financial   **WSJ, page 1**
centers

"In Chicago, cocaine use is spreading in the city's commodities trading and financial centers. 'A few people take a toot before the trading session and maybe a few times during the day,' says one member of the Chicago Board of Trade, himself a user. 'It's like drinking coffee.' He estimates that 10% of the traders and brokers he knows use cocaine on the job."

Notes where you directly quote an author's actual words exactly as they appear in the original should constitute no more than 25 percent of all your note cards. Although it might seem simpler initially to put down many quotations, you will only be postponing the moment when you have to reread, summarize, comment on, or evaluate each of these quotations. Remember, your research paper should not be little more than a patchwork of stitched-together quoted sources. You would be better off summarizing as many passages as early as possible rather than using your time copying down lengthy quotations that you will not be able to use. The only time quotations should be taken down is when the author's wording is so unique and authoritative that a summary would fail to do it justice.

Notice how each of the preceding examples of note cards not only puts the author's last name and shortened title of the work in the upper right-hand corner but also records the page where the original information appeared. Exact page numbers are necessary, since this information will appear in parentheses, according to the Modern Language Association style of documentation (discussed later in this chapter).

Also, observe that the upper left-hand corner of each note card contains a concise key phrase to remind you how you might want to use this information. You should write down this key phrase before you take the time and effort to put down the entire note. Doing this will compel you to evaluate how useful the information on the card will be. This key phrase will come in handy when you're working with more than thirty cards because it will save you from having to reread the entire contents of each card when you are organizing them into groups before writing a rough draft.

Factual References

Other note cards may be used for recording your own ideas or for keeping track of significant facts you will use to document assertions in your paper. For example, you might record the percentage of Bolivia's gross national product accounted for by cocaine production, or the fact that according to the National Narcotics Intelligence Consumer's Commission "6% of U.S. cocaine users consume 60% of the cocaine" produced in Bolivia, Peru, and Colombia.

Such hard statistical data serve an important function in substantiating your claims. Keep in mind that only one piece of information, whether it is a summary, quotation, combined note (your summary plus a short quotation), fact, or observation should be recorded on each note card.

Using Your Notes to Create an Outline

Once you are satisfied with the results of your initial investigation, you will need to sort your notes to discover the arrangement that will best allow you to develop a coherent structure for the entire paper. To do this, group together index cards with the same or similar headings (indicated in the upper left-hand corner).

These groups represent sections of your paper that should be placed in a logical and coherent order. Since there are so many ways you can arrange the sections, it is imperative that you let the question you wish to explore suggest the direction you should take in developing your topic. Perhaps the most useful for research papers that present and defend an assertion is the problem–solution format. The first section of the paper defines the nature of the problem and offers evidence of its seriousness. This section may also investigate different hypotheses put forward to explain the causes of the problem. In the middle section the writer considers the advantages and disadvantages of alternative solutions. The final section of the paper presents the writer's own recommendation and supports it with appropriate reasons and evidence.

For example, the sample student paper at the end of this chapter, "Why Doesn't the Government 'Just Say Yes' to Funding Prevention Programs Against Drug Abuse?" is organized around the thesis that "short of changing society's attitudes toward using drugs, only federally funded mass education stands a real chance of stopping the drug epidemic." For this student, the note cards he had taken were most effectively organized as follows:

1. Causal explanations put forward to explain widespread drug use in contemporary American society
2. The effects of cocaine use in professional sports, on Wall Street, and in Hollywood
3. Why are attempts to stop the flow of drugs from the supply side by arresting the dealers, intercepting the drugs, and encouraging crop substitution ineffective?
4. Why are attempts to stop drug use by mandatory drug testing ineffective?
5. Why government-funded mass education is a solution that might work

The sequence in which these groups of note cards are arranged follows a straightforward pattern. The student defines the nature of the problem, considers theories put forward to explain what might be causing it, examines the effects of the problem on different areas of society, considers the merits of various solutions put forward to deal with the problem, states his objection to these proposed solutions, and presents arguments that support his recommended solution.

Once the note cards have been organized in groups that define the individual sections of the paper, and cards within groups have been arranged in a sequence that defines the order in which information will be developed within sections, the key phrases on each of the note cards can be used to create a working preliminary outline. You may decide to use a general heading or a key phrase that appears frequently in each group as a main heading in your outline. For example, "causal explanations put forward to explain widespread drug use in contemporary American society" accurately reflects the content of note cards in the first section of the paper. Once the cards with similar content have been grouped together, a working outline created from the headings would begin to give you a more accurate picture of the order, arrangement, and divisions of the sections of your paper. For example, here is how a preliminary outline for the paper at the end of this chapter would appear:

I. Current theories explaining widespread drug use
   A. Weil and Rosen's theory of "innate need"
   B. Philip Slater's theory of societal pressure
II. Evidence of increasing drug use in the success-oriented areas of sports, finance, and entertainment

    A. The effects of cocaine use in professional sports
    B. The effects of cocaine use on Wall Street
    C. The effects of cocaine use in Hollywood
III. Unsuccessful efforts of the government to stop the drug epidemic
    A. Unsuccessful attempts on the "supply" side
        1. Arresting the dealers
        2. Intercepting the drugs
        3. Encouraging crop substitution in countries where produced
    B. Ineffective attempts to stop drug use on the "demand" side
        1. Mandatory drug testing
        2. Voluntary "just say no" programs
        3. Drug treatment programs
IV. The role of education in preventing drug abuse
    A. Studies that suggest drug education programs can reduce drug use
    B. Assessment of conflicting studies
    C. Reductions in funding for drug education programs
    D. Conclusion recommending increased governmental support of drug education programs

The benefit of creating a working outline from your note cards is that it allows you to tinker with different arrangements for the material in your paper. Does any section need to be filled out with more supporting evidence? You can easily spot gaps where information is needed. By the same token, you can see whether you have taken notes that don't bear directly on your research question, are extraneous, and should be eliminated.

Test the ideas expressed in the headings. Material that does not illuminate, support, develop, or explain the main ideas should be omitted. Are there approximately the same number of note cards for each major section? Use your outline to check whether individual sections provide equal levels of support to develop the entire paper. If any sections are insufficiently developed, you may need to return to the library to gather more material.

It is important to have a working outline at this point. Otherwise, you might spend too much time reading and taking extensive notes only to discover that you have no effective means of separating notes that bear directly on the topic from those that are irrelevant. The headings for this preliminary outline may reflect important aspects of the topic that you have discovered by looking through the Library of Congress list of subject headings, the headings and subheadings listed in indexes, and tables of contents of books on the subject for which you have created bibliography cards.

The Preliminary Thesis Statement

The question around which your paper is organized should be stated in the form of a tentative thesis, as a declarative sentence. The thesis statement represents your view on the subject and is stated in such a way that it is apparent to your readers that your research paper will make a case for this point of view. Don't feel that you are locked into a specific formulation of your thesis statement. At this point it is just a means to guide your reading and note taking. What you discover may require you to substantially alter the scope or direction of your paper. If this occurs, you will need to revise your thesis statement accordingly.

Suppose your preliminary thesis was "Moderate alcohol consumption reduces the risk of heart attacks, promotes healthier social relationships, and contributes to longevity." But as you continue your research you discover that the evidence of traumatic lifelong effects suffered by children of parents who become alcoholics contradicts the portion of your original claim that stated that moderate alcohol use "promotes healthier social relationships." In this case, you would have to revise your thesis to reflect the new evidence your research has disclosed.

Revising your thesis in the light of new information will require you to consider the views of others fairly and to offer an opinion that accomodates and takes into account opposing views or differences in perspective on the issue.

Creating the Rough Draft

Different choices are available in the writing of a rough draft. Many students find it helpful to compose the introduction first, informing readers in a straightforward way of the issue, topic, or idea the paper will cover. Asking a provocative question catches the audience's attention and challenges them to reexamine their unquestioned assumptions and beliefs on the subject. Another effective way of introducing readers to the issue is to give a brief review of the controversy—a historical context to help the audience understand the discussion.

A dramatic or attention-getting quotation is another method skilled writers use to capture the audience's attention. For example, a paper exploring the relationship between writing and alcoholism might begin with a quote by Horace: "No poems can please nor live long which are written by water drinkers" (Horace, 65–8 B.C., from *Epistles*, I, 19).

The introduction not only states the question at issue but should also tell the reader how you plan to demonstrate the validity of your hypothesis. If you wish, you may include some general comments on the kinds of sources you intend to use and give an overview of the approach you intend to follow in developing your argument. Before beginning to write the main portion of your paper, be sure to have your outline and note cards in front of you. Detach each group of note cards and spread them out in front of you so you can clearly see the contents of each card. In the rough draft your only concern is with writing or typing the information from your note cards in a coherent order, using the information on each card to illustrate, explain, or substantiate headings from your outline. Don't be concerned about questions of style or grammar. Your primary goal should be to get down the ideas in your outline and support them with the specific quotations, summaries, facts, and observations written on your cards. As you write, be sure to leave extra space between lines and a wide margin on both sides that will give you room to add corrections or make changes in the original text.

Frequently compare what you are writing against the note cards and outline to check that you have not omitted any important points or supporting evidence. Check the wording of any quotations you have copied from your note cards to make sure you have not unintentionally omitted any of the original wording.

Quotations are useful when you wish to support, illustrate, or document important points by citing the opinions of experts or authorities in the field. Quotations are also useful when the language in which ideas are expressed is so vivid, unique, or memorable that a summary or paraphrase would fail to do justice to the original passage. Although most of your paper should be written in your own words, there are occasions when it is important for your readers to hear the voice of your original sources. Quotations of fewer than four lines are normally run into the text but separated from it by sets of double quotation marks. Unless what you quote can be made grammatically part of your own sentence you must reproduce all punctuation and capitalization exactly as it appears in the original. If you change the capitalization to make the quote part of your own sentence, make sure that your introductory phrase and what you are quoting combine to make a complete sentence with the same verb tenses. For example:

> Weil and Rosen's research has led them to conclude that many religions have used marijuana, alcohol, and other psychoactive drugs to enable followers to "transcend their sense of separateness and feel more at one with nature, God and the supernatural."

Quotations of more than four fines should be separated from the text, double-spaced, and indented ten spaces from the left margin. No quotation marks are necessary, as the form here indicates that you are quoting.

The wording of the quotation should be exactly as it appears in the original except that occasionally you may have to insert a word or phrase to correct or clarify the original passage. Words or phrases so added should be placed in brackets to indicate that these are editorial emendations. You may want to add a word or phrase when a word in the original passage is misspelled, when you wish to supply specific names that clarify an unclear pronoun reference, and when you wish to indicate that you have underlined part of a quotation for emphasis. For example, if the original quote was "Coca is being grown all over Brazil, Venezuela, and Argentina too, according to the State Department's Bureau of International Matters," you might feel it necessary to clarify how the production of a coca crop is related to cocaine. An interpolation to clarify the meaning of the original appears in enclosed square brackets:

> Coca [from which cocaine is made] is being grown all over Brazil, Venezuela, and Argentina too, according to the State Department's Bureau of International Matters.

The Latin word *sic* (thus or so) also can be placed in brackets after misspelled words, or words or phrases that are incorrectly used, to let the reader know that the error is in the original material, not in your restatement.

Whenever you omit a part of a sentence from the original you must indicate the omission with an ellipsis (three spaced periods) placed where the omitted passage occurred. If the ellipsis appears at the end of a sentence, these three periods appear in addition to any punctuation in the original. For example:

> Cocaine is one way a growing segment of our society is finding escape from the tedium of daily life. And fame and stardom can be just as tedious as anything else. . . .

If the sentence ends in a question mark, your quote should end with a question mark followed by three spaced periods. If the sentence ends in a period, as in the example just given above, place the ellipsis at the end after one additional period indicating the end of the original sentence. Omission of material in a sentence beginning a quotation should be indicated by three spaced periods, as follows:

> . . . Contac, Sudafed, certain diet pills, decongestants, and heart and asthma medications can register as amphetamines on the test.

Omission of material from a sentence within a quotation is indicated as follows:

> Anti-inflammatory drugs and common pain killers, including Datril . . . and Nuprin, mimic marijuana.

If what you are quoting is a phrase from a sentence, it should be enclosed in quotation marks and unobtrusively blended into your own sentence, making sure that the syntax of the quote and the syntax of your original sentence are in agreement. When you are quoting a passage that you must put within double quotation marks and that also itself contains a quotation, the double quotation marks appearing in the original should be changed to single quotation marks. For example:

> Knowledgeable insiders note the change, "'Cocaine is a negotiable instrument in this town,' said one veteran producer, familiar with drug dealing."

This rule applies only to sentences that are run into the text. In quotations of more than four lines that are separated, double-spaced, and set off from the text as a block without being enclosed in quotation marks, quoted material within the block should be enclosed in double quotation marks even if the source quoted uses single quotation marks. For example:

> Perhaps the most sinister aspect of the growing use of cocaine in the TV industry is the way it is used as a medium of exchange. "Cocaine is a negotiable instrument in this town," said one veteran producer, familiar with drug dealing.

As important as quotations are, they should never exceed 25 percent of your original paper and should be used only in circumstances in which nothing else would substantiate, illustrate, clarify, or dramatize a point as effectively.

While writing the rough draft, look at what you have put down from the reader's perspective. Would a change in the order of the presentation make your ideas clearer?

One of the most important things you can do to help the reader understand the main idea of your paper is to use clear transitional words, phrases, and sentences to signal how parts of the paper are connected to each other. Even though the ideas are presented in an order that is clear to you, you must make every effort to help your reader understand the organization of your paper and perceive the relationships between the sections. Short transitional phrases or even short paragraphs are invaluable in informing the reader how paragraphs are related to each other. These guide words serve as explicit directions signaling the relationship between paragraphs and sections.

Transitions may be of several kinds. Some signal your reader that you are following a chronological order with words such as *now, when, before, after, during, while, next, finally, later, meanwhile,* and *soon.* Other linking words express causal relationships, such as *as a result, since, con-*

sequently, because, therefore, and *thus.* Still other guide words express intensification, such as *furthermore, really, in addition, ultimately,* and *moreover.* Some express limitation, restriction, or concession, such as *although, yet, however, even though, still, despite, but,* and *granted.*

One especially effective kind of transition is an introductory phrase or short transitional paragraph that refers back to prior material while also serving as a connecting bridge into the next section. These short connecting paragraphs allow the writer to sum up the ideas in one section before going on to the next.

As with the introduction, there are many choices available when you are deciding how to end your paper. If your paper has investigated a problem and considered alternative solutions offered by others, your conclusion might present your own solution along with evidence and the reasons required to ensure its acceptance. Some writers prefer to end their papers, especially those that deal with complex issues, with a thought-provoking question intended to keep readers thinking about the implications of the issue. Other writers prefer to use the conclusion to suggest how the issue relates to a wider context. Most frequently, however, writers briefly enumerate the most important points turned up by their research and emphasize how these points prove the validity of the idea expressed by the thesis statement in the introduction.

Revising the Rough Draft into a Final Draft

Careful revision of your rough draft can make your paper many times better. James Michener said, "I never thought of myself as a good writer. Anyone who wants reassurance of that should read one of my first drafts. But I'm one of the world's great revisers."

Transforming a rough draft into a final draft entails testing everything that you have put down—every sentence, every paragraph, every section—to see whether it relates to the central idea expressed in your thesis statement. In fact, some writers find it helpful to write the thesis statement on a separate piece of paper and place it where they can see it while they rewrite their rough draft. Revising consists of eliminating everything from your paper that does not substantiate, exemplify, or explain this thesis sentence.

To evaluate whether any passage really contributes to substantiating or developing the idea contained in the thesis statement, try to see your paper from the viewpoint of a prospective reader. What passages, words, or sentences would the reader see as unnecessary or confusing? At what points would your reader require additional examples or evidence to emphasize an idea, or more effective transitions to signal the relationship between different parts of your paper? You can revise best by going through your paper several times, looking for different kinds of things to improve each time. The first reading should be used to improve the paper's overall organization. Is there any section that would be better placed elsewhere? You may want to rearrange paragraphs if you discover that a change in the order of presentation will make your ideas clearer. Do transitions effectively signal your reader where a paragraph fits in the total organization of the paper? You might need to write short transitional paragraphs, often no longer than a single sentence, to guide your reader smoothly from one section to the next. Transitions should be unobtrusive and make it possible for your reader to follow your line of thought.

If you are satisfied with the overall presentation of your ideas, next consider all the things that might be improved *within* paragraphs. Does each paragraph center on one idea that is clearly related to one aspect of your paper's thesis? Do other sentences in your paragraph clarify this idea by explaining or presenting evidence to support it? Keep in mind that each paragraph must contain a major idea stated in the topic sentence, and supporting sentences that clarify or explain the topic sentence. You may find that some sentences in your paragraphs do not support or illustrate the idea in the topic sentence. Go ahead and delete them.

In addition to relevancy, your paragraphs should be checked to see whether they are equally well developed and supported with effective samples, evidence, and quotations from source documents. Some paragraphs might be so long that they will have to be divided into several shorter paragraphs, each of which must still have its own topic sentence. Conversely, a series of short paragraphs without topic sentences might be consolidated into one coherent paragraph with a topic sentence.

Test your paragraphs for unity and coherence by asking yourself whether these sentences provide facts and details that would lead a reasonable person to believe the truth of your topic sentence. Evidence that illustrates the central idea in your paragraphs can take the form of examples, statistics, citation of authorities, illustrative analogies, or anything else that presents specific, interesting, and relevant information. Also, consider whether you might arrange supporting sentences in a more sensible and logical order.

STYLE

Consider how your choice of words can be improved. Choose words that express clearly, simply, and concretely what you mean to say. Just as every paragraph must clearly support the development of the paper's thesis, and just as every sentence within a paragraph must support, illustrate, or clarify that paragraph's topic sentence, so every word in a sentence must be necessary to express that sentence's thought.

When you revise to improve style, go through your paper and look for sentences that might be recast in the active voice. Find the verb, ask who is doing what to whom, and rewrite the sentence to conform to the basic subject–verb–object (or complement) pattern. When you find prepositional phrases that wander off from the trunk of your sentence, prune them back.

Change your method of editing by reading your paper aloud. Do you hear any sentences that you would not understand if you had not written them? Does the introduction of your paper immediately capture your interest? If you find the opening superfluous, imagine how your readers will feel. The beginnings of most rough drafts are notoriously expendable. Is it easy to tell how the paper is organized at first glance, or do you need to insert clearer signposts letting your reader know that you are defending a thesis, making a value judgment, or recommending a certain course of action to solve a problem? Does each section of your paper contain enough different kinds of evidence from a variety of sources to substantiate your points?

Do any of the sections of your paper bore you to tears? If it fails to keep your interest, pity your audience. See if you can improve these sections through clever analogies, attention-getting quotations, and unusual and interesting examples. No law states that research papers must be dull.

Don't be afraid to experiment with language. Substitute down-to-earth words for abstract jargon. Cut through the fog. Say it simply by using single words for the following circumlocutions:

although	for	in spite of the fact that
because	for	due to the fact that
where	for	in the place that
if	for	in the event that
after	for	at the conclusion of
now	for	at this point in time
when	for	at the time that

Do you hear any clichés, hackneyed expressions, or trite phrases that could be rewritten in your own voice to express your ideas, insights, and opinions? Most importantly, are all the words you have written really necessary? Any words that do not make your thoughts clearer to the reader should be eliminated.

Next, reread your paper, this time double-checking to see whether you have accurately transcribed the information from your note cards. If you have combined direct quotations from one source with supporting interpretations from other sources, make sure that you have not omitted any necessary documentation. Is every source you have cited also included in the list of works cited or bibliography that will be turned in along with your paper?

Are there places where additional direct quotations are necessary to give your ideas greater weight, conviction, and validity? Have you remembered to indicate clearly the source of every quotation at the point where it is introduced in your paper? Check to see whether in re-copying information from your note cards you have mistaken a quotation for your own words.

Using the MLA and APA Styles to Document the Manuscript

THE MLA STYLE OF IN-TEXT CITATION

In 1984 the Modern Language Association (MLA) first introduced a radically simplified method of documenting sources. Complete information for correct models of documentation is now provided by the *MLA Handbook for Writers of Research Papers,* fourth edition (1995).

The MLA style of in-text parenthetical citations has the advantage of providing the reader with documentation when a source is quoted, paraphrased, or summarized directly within the text. This system supersedes older methods of documentation in which footnotes appear at the bottom of the page or at the end of the paper. The parenthetical citations identify sources briefly; provide page references, including the author's name, and a shortened version of the title if necessary; and must follow each occurrence of a source that needs to be documented. A complete description of each source appears in a final alphabetical listing of works cited at the end of the paper. You must identify your source when you quote directly, paraphrase, summarize, or use information that is not common knowledge or has been produced through scholarly effort or research. The brief parenthetical in-text citations must direct the reader to the source in your list of works cited and must include enough information to allow the reader to know where to look in the particular work.

The paper that appears at the end of this chapter uses this system. If the author's name is mentioned in the sentence, you need only provide the page number in parentheses. For example, notice the following sentence taken from the sample student research paper:

> Murray takes the opposite view, claiming that coaches have been known to coerce players into using drugs in order to perform better (28).

The parenthetical reference indicates that this citation refers to material taken from page 28 of a work by Thomas H. Murray. A complete reference on the page listing works cited at the end of the paper gives all necessary information:

Murray, Thomas. "The Coercive Power of Drugs in Sports." *The Hastings Center Report* 13 (1983): 24–30.

A citation should follow the mention of the source and precede your own punctuation. The form the reference will take depends on the nature of the source and the amount of information already provided in your paper.

Author not named in the text: author and page number in parentheses
One archeologist concludes that "Noah's Flood was not a universal deluge; it was a vast flood in the Valley of the Rivers Tigres and Euphrates" (Wooley 242).

Author named in the text: page reference in parentheses
One archeologist, Sir Leonard Wooley, concludes that "Noah's Flood was not a universal deluge; it was a vast flood in the Valley of the Rivers Tigres and Euphrates" (242).

Block quotations
Quotations over four lines in length begin on a new line indented ten spaces from the left margin. They are double-spaced and appear without quotation marks. A parenthetical reference appears after the final punctuation mark.

> without being troubled by the plunges of a
>
> victim who absolutely refuses to be devoured.
>
> A meal liable to interruptions lacks savour (4).

Work with two or three authors or editors
One study investigated the question "How do salmon remember their birth place and how do they find their way back, sometimes from 800 or 900 miles away" (Hasler and Larsen 317).

Work with more than three authors
The concept of *fail-safe* refers to components which, if they fail, do not jeopardize the entire system (Williams, Adamson, Lower, and Nicoll 53).

A multivolume work
Speaking on the rise and decline of civilizations, a historian observes that "In primitive societies, as we know them, Mimesis is directed towards the older generation and towards dead ancestors who stand, unseen, but not unfelt, at the back of living elders, reinforcing their prestige" (Toynbee 7:114).

Newspaper
According to a *Newark Star-Ledger* editorial, peace in the Middle East is still elusive because "Hamas, an Islamic fundamentalist group, continues to fight for the destruction of Israel and refuses to accept the PLO's authority" ("Building Mideast Peace" A26).

Reference work
According to *The Concise Columbia Encyclopedia*, not withstanding the fact that Einstein was a pacifist, "he urged Pres. Franklin Roosevelt to investigate the possible use of atomic energy in bombs" ("Einstein, Albert").

Review
Of demonstrative audiences, the acerbic New York theater critic says "They erupt into promiscuous roars of *bravo* and even *bravi* and *brava* to display either their knowledge of Italian or their deafness in distinguishing the number and sex of the performers" (Simon 17).

Selection in an anthology
"You walk among clattering four-foot marine iguanas heaped on the shore lava, and on each other, like slag" (Dillard 181).

A work by an author with two or more works
In his later years, his cautionary fables concentrate on hypocrisy and greed (Twain, *Hadleyburg* 377–85).

Two or more sources in a citation
There is intense debate over such basic definitional questions as whether the most serious manifestations of alcohol disorders should be treated as "diseases" (Keller 1976, Robinson 1972, Room 1972).

A government document
According to the Congressional Committee on Labor and Human Resources, broader legal definitions of sexual harassment are necessary to combat instances of employment discrimination (*Fair Employment Practices* 13–15).

A work with a corporate author
The use of euphemistic labels to describe nursing homes and retirement villages eases the public's guilt and remorse over accepting the isolation of elders (Understanding Aging, Inc. 35–36).

An indirect source—quoting someone else

Lykken asserts that "more of these unique characteristics than we previously thought may be determined by a particular combination of genes" (qtd. in Holden 35).

Literary works—

Novels

At the beginning of Anne Tyler's novel *Saint Maybe,* the main character, Ian, is introduced: "now Ian was seventeen, and, like the rest of his family, large-boned and handsome and easy-going, quick to make friends, fond of a good time" (2; ch. 1).

Plays

Later in *The Lion and the Jewel* Soyinka has the chief Baroka proclaim, "I change my wrestlers when I have learnt to throw them" (34; act 2).

Poems

Diane Wakowski explores the speaker's sensation of freedom: "Driving through the desert at night in summer/can be/like peeling an orange" ("The Orange" 1–3).

The Bible

St. Paul makes the meaning of the term resonate with spiritual depth: "in a word, there are three things that last forever: faith, hope, and love; but the greatest of them all is love" (I Corinthians 13.13).

Nonprint sources (including interviews, radio and television programs, movies)

A recent documentary explores ancient knowledge of star positions (*Egypt: Quest for Eternity*).

DOCUMENTING SOURCES IN THE
MLA "WORKS CITED" FORMAT

In the following list of examples, the most commonly encountered forms of citation are listed for a wide variety of references.

An article in a journal with continuous pagination of the volume for that particular year

Rockas, Leo. "A Dialogue on Dialogue." *College English* 41 (1980): 570–80.

The issue number is not mentioned because the volume is continuously paginated throughout the year; hence, only the volume number (41) is necessary.

An article from a magazine issued weekly
> Sanders, Sol W. "The Vietnam Shadow Over Policy for El Salvador." *Business Week* 16 Mar. 1981: 52.

Note that all months except May, June, and July are abbreviated in MLA style.

A book by a single author
> Shishka, Bob. *An Introduction to Broadcasting.* Chicago: Wade, 1980.

A book by two or three authors
> Murphy, Mark, and Rhea White. *Psychic Side of Sports.* Reading: Addison-Wesley, 1979.

Only the first author's name, as it is given on the title page, appears— last name first.

A book by more than three authors
> Allen, David Yale, et al. *Classic Cars.* London: Macmillan, 1978.

More than one book by the same author
> Hellman, Leo. *Children Today.* Miami, FL: U of Miami P, 1995.
> ———. *Children Yesterday.* Chicago: U of Chicago P, 1994.

Author unknown
> *How to Raise a Wheaton Terrier for Show and Profit.* Cherry Hill: Solo International, 1995.

Do not use "anonymous" or "anon."

A book by a corporate author
> Modern Language Association. *MLA Handbook for Writers of Research Papers,* 4th ed. New York: Modern Language Association, 1995.

Edited book in a new edition
> Adler, Freda, ed. *Women and Crime.* 4th ed. Cambridge, MA: Harvard UP, 1976.

A collection of essays by different authors compiled by an editor
> Sebeok, Ted, ed. *How Animals Communicate.* Bloomington: Indiana UP, 1977.

A work in an anthology
> Arnold, Charles. "How Monkeys Use Sign Language." *How Animals Communicate.* Ed. Ted Sebeok. Bloomington: Indiana UP, 1977. 40–50.

A book that is translated with both the author and translator named
> Fernandez, Ruth. *The Architectural Heritage of the Moors.* Trans. Wanda Garcia. London: Routledge, 1980.

A book by two or three authors; a revised or later edition
> Reichman, Stuart, and Marsha Deez. *The Washington Lobbyist.* 5th ed. New York: Harcourt, 1978.

A book published in more than one volume
> Thorndike, Lynn. *A History of Magic and Experimental Science.* 3 vols. New York: Columbia UP, 1941.

A republished or reprinted book
> Nilsson, Martin P. *Greek Folk Religion.* 1940. Philadelphia: U of Pennsylvania P, 1972.

A newspaper article
> Petzinger, Thomas J., Gary Putka, and Stephen J. Sansweet. "High Fliers." *Wall Street Journal* 12 Sept. 1983, sec. 1: 1+.

A book review
> Bill Katz. Rev. of *Norman Rockwell: My Adventures as an Illustrator,* by Norman Rockwell. *Library Journal* 85 (1960): 648.

An encyclopedia
> *Academic American Encyclopedia.* 21 vols. Danbury: Grolier, 1987.

A dictionary
> *The Agriculture Dictionary.* Albany: Delmar, 1991.

An unsigned article in a newspaper
> "Executive Changes." *New York Times* 8 Aug. 1991, natl. ed.: C3.

An editorial in a newspaper
> "Breakthrough for Peace." Editorial. *Miami Herald* 2 Dec. 1994, final ed.: 20A.

A letter to an editor
> Mirski, Roberto. Letter. *The Newark Star Ledger* 3 Nov. 1991, A16.

Some Less Common Bibliographic Forms in the MLA "Works Cited" Format

A book published as a volume in a series
> Hochberg, Julian E. *Perception.* Vol. 7 of *Foundations of Modern Psychology Series.* 22 vols. Englewood Cliffs: Prentice Hall, 1964.

A lecture or publicly delivered paper
> Flaye, Sue. "Zen Buddhism and Psychotherapy." Conference on Zen Buddhism. Fargo, 17 March 1988.

A personal interview
> Gold, Mark. Personal interview. December 2, 1987.

The name of the person interviewed should appear first, followed by the kind of interview (personal, telephone) as well as the date.

A reference to an article from dissertation abstracts
> Knutt, Meg. "The Many Masks of Ted Hughes." *DAI* 44 (1984): 474B. Albion U.

An introduction, foreword, preface, or afterword of a book
> Wise, Robert. Foreword. *The Film Director.* By Richard L. Bare. New York: Macmillan, 1971. ii–v.

A radio or television program
> *Egypt: Quest for Eternity.* National Geographic Society. PBS. WNET, Newark. 28 February 1982.

A biblical citation
> *The New English Bible with the Apocrypha.* Oxford Study ed. New York: Oxford, 1970.

An unpublished dissertation
> Stewart, Terry. "Hinduism's Influence on Modern Sex Therapy." Diss. U of Kansas City, 1965.

A personal letter
> Lund, Shanna. Letter to the author. 3 June 1992.

An abstract
> Soucy, Jean-Yves. "Erotic Obsession in French Canadian Literature." Abstract. *PMLA* 106.1 (1991): 175.

A cartoon
> Assy, Chuck. *Colorado Springs Gazette Telegraph* 12 Dec. 1993: 11.

A map/chart
> *Illinois.* Map. Boston: Rand, 1991.
> *Income Distribution.* Chart. New York: Doubleday, 1989.

A pamphlet
> Jacobs, Andrea. *The Abolitionist.* Chicago, 1993.

A telephone interview
> Gold, Mark. Telephone interview. 31 Oct. 1994.

Material from a computer service
> Berger, Charles. "Unresolved Issues from the Gulf War." *The International Courier:* 35 (1994): 125–137. Dialog file 23, item 241372.

Computer software program
> Richman, Richard. *Butterflies.* Computer software. Lancelot Distributing, 1990. 256 KB, disk.

Audiotape and videotape
> Turnbull, Colin M. Music of the Rain Forest Pygmies. New York, LLCT 7157, 1993.
> Brook, Peter. *The Mahabharata.* Videocassette. Prod. Channel 4 Television Co. Ltd. The Parabola Video Library, 1989. 60 min.

Film
> *Sleepless in Seattle.* Dir. Nora Ephron. Prod. Gary Foster. With Tom Hanks, Meg Ryan, Bill Pullman, and Ross Malinger. TriStar Pictures, 1993.

Live play
> *Angels in America.* By Tony Kushner. Dir. George C. Wolf. With F. Murray Abraham. New York, N.Y. 19 Oct. 1994.

Work of art
> Suta, Waylan. *The Balinese Festival.* Ubud Art Gallery, Ubud.

Collaborator
> Brave Bird, Mary, with Richard Erdoes. *Ohitika Woman.* New York: Grove, 1993.

Legal reference
> US v. Rodney. 956 *Federal Reporter* 295–302. St. Paul: West, 1992. 90–3189. US Ct. of Appeals, Dist. of Columbia, 1992.

A recording
> Richardson, Sir Ralph. *The Poetry of Blake.* Caedmon, TC 1101, 1958.

A government publication of the executive branch
> United States. Bureau of the Budget. *Special Analysis: Budget of the United States, Fiscal Year 1967.* Washington: GPO, 1966.

Guidelines for Citing Electronic Media

CD-ROMs and other portable data bases: Periodically published data bases
> Hellman, Leo. "Nutritionists find new growth enzyme in roses." *New York Times* 12 June 1992, late ed.: B1. *New York Times Ondisc.* CD-ROM. UMI-Proquest. Nov. 1992.
> Reeves, Tony. "The Illegal Parrot Trade." *The Consumer's Advocate* Mar./Apr. 1993: 22–24. *Sociofile.* CD-ROM. Silver Platter. Sept. 1993.
> Stewart, Terri. "Islamic Influences in the Mevlana Monastary." *DAI* June 1993. Missouri State University 1993. *Dissertation Abstracts Ondisc.* CD-ROM. UMI-Proquest. June 1993.

Citations in this form should consist of the following items: Author. "Title" of article and publication data. *Title* of the database. Publication medium (CD-ROM). Vendor (distributor). Date of publication (release data, as shown on the title screen or above the menu of the database).

CD-ROMs and other portable data bases: Nonperiodically published data bases
> *The Oxford English Dictionary.* 2nd ed. CD-ROM, Oxford: Oxford UP, 1992.

CD-ROM publications in this form are not continually revised but are issued a single time. The work is cited as you would a book, but add a description of the medium of publication.

A publication on magnetic tape or diskette
> "Missouri State University." *Peterson's College Database.* Magnetic tape. Princeton: Peterson's, 1994.

"Sorrentino, Fernando." Vers. 1.1 *Disclit: World Authors.* Diskette. Dublin: Hall and OCLC, 1994.

A magnetic tape publication or a diskette is also cited as you would a book and includes the following items: Author. "Title" of a portion of the work (if appropriate). *Title* of product. Edition, release, or version (if relevant). Publication medium (magnetic tape or diskette). City: Publisher, Year.

Citing online data bases
McLean, David. "The King of Pop Strikes Again." *Longevity.* Jan. 1995: 62–4. *Magazine Index.* Online. Dialog. 5 May 1995.

Reed, Janice. "Can Alzheimers Be Cured?" *New York Times* 21 Apr. 1993, late ed.: C1. *New York Times Online.* Online. Nexis. 7 Feb. 1994.

An entry for an online information service would include these items: Author. "Title" of article and publication data for printed source. *Title* of the data base. Publication medium (Online). Name of computer service date of access (when you access the file).

Material accessed through a computer network: Internet
Lund, Diana. "New Therapies for Autism." *Journal of Clinical Psychology.* 4 (1994): 8 pp. Online. Internet. 17 May 1994.

Patrick, Deborah. "Third World Population Trends." *World Scope.* 1.1 (1995): 12 pp. Online. U. of Vermont. Internet. 7 Feb. 1995. Available gopher://gopher.vt.edu.

Citations should contain these items: Author. "Title" of article. *Title* of journal or other source. Volume number. (Year or issue data of publication): Number of pages (if given). Publication medium (Online). Name of computer network. Date of access (when you accessed the source). As in the second example, you may also include the electronic address you used to access the document; precede the address with the word *Available.*

Citing an electronic text
James, Henry. *The Aspern Papers.* New York: Scribner's, 1908. Online. Project Gutenberg, Illinois Benedictine Coll. Internet. 15 Jan. 1995. Available hhtp://www.w3.org.

An entry citing an electronic text contains these items: Author. *Title* of text. Year of original publication (if appropriate). Publication data. Publication medium (Online). Repository of text. Computer network. Date of access. Electronic address (if required).

THE APA STYLE OF IN-TEXT CITATION

Although most humanities courses require you to follow the style described by the *MLA Handbook,* most scientific and technical courses require quite different procedures of documentation. Publications in the social sciences (anthropology, education, law, psychology, sociology, etc.) often use the APA style of documentation outlined in the *Publication Manual of the American Psychological Association,* 4th ed. (Washington: APA, 1994). Sources used are listed alphabetically on a separate page titled "References" following the final page of the text.

In-text citations of sources present the *author* and *date* in parenthetical references throughout the paper. Most often the citation consists of the author's name and the year of publication:

> A study of interactions between doctors and nurses (Stewart, 1992) explains...

If the author has already been named in the text, only the year is cited:

> Stewart (1992) analyzes the interactions between doctors and nurses.

Specific page references to a source can follow a quotation or be part of the parenthetical citation:

> The interactions between doctors and nurses, according to Stewart (1992) fit "the non zero sum game model" (p. 77).

> The interactions between doctors and nurses fit "the non zero sum game model" (Stewart, 1992, p. 77).

Other possibilities for the APA in-text citations might include the following:

Work by two authors
> The summary of prior research on genetic factors in crime (Rubinstein & Horowitz, 1992, pp. 35–42) challenges the economic models.

Publications by the same author in different years or within the same year
> Carlson has studied the community policing model in several contexts (1983, 1991a, 1991b).

Work by three to five authors

Names of all authors appear in the first reference. Subsequent references give only the first author's name followed by et al. Use et al. for six or more authors.

> Peterson, Thomas, and Zimbardo (1976) sought correlations between television violence and real-life violence. Like other approaches to the study of violence in the 1970s, the researchers (Peterson et al.) found that portrayals of violence have little impact on inner city residents.

Two or more sources in a single reference

List authors alphabetically and separate multiple sources by a semicolon.

> The question which crimes are victimless and which victims merit concern has been viewed from many perspectives (Adler, 1975; Lambert, 1987; Wilson, 1990).

Personal communication (letter, memo, telephone conversation, fax, e-mail, interview)

> Donald Singletary (telephone conversation, Oct. 11, 1994) stated that...

PREPARING A LIST OF REFERENCES IN THE APA FORMAT

The APA style of documentation provides much of the same bibliographical information as the MLA style but differs from it in some important ways. Note that the author and date sequence begins each entry. Capitals, quotation marks, and parentheses appear differently in the APA style than they do in the MLA style.

The following examples are keyed to the previously shown examples of the MLA style.

An article in a journal with continuous pagination of the volume for that particular year

> Rockas, L. (1980). A dialogue on dialogue. *College English, 41,* 570–80.

An article from a magazine issued weekly

> Sanders, Sol W. (1981, March 16) The Vietnam shadow over policy for El Salvador. *Business Week,* 52.

A book by a single author

> Shishka, B. (1980). *An introduction to broadcasting.* Chicago: Wade Press.

A book by two or three authors
> Murphy, M., & White, R. (1979). *Psychic side of sports*. Reading, Ma.: Addison-Wesley.

A book by more than three authors
> Allen, D. Y., Collins, B., Mirsky, S., & Powell, R. T. (1978). *Classic cars*. London: Macmillan.

A book by a corporate author
> Modern Language Association. (1995). *MLA handbook for writers of research papers* (4th ed.). New York: Author.

APA substitutes *Author* for the publisher's name when a book is published by its author.

More than one book by the same author
Unlike the MLA style, APA style repeats the author's name and puts works in chronological order.

> Hellman, L. (1994). *Children yesterday*. Chicago: University of Chicago Press.
> Hellman, L. (1995). *Children today*. Miami, FL: University of Miami Press.

A collection of essays by different authors compiled by an editor
> Sebeok, T. (Ed.). (1977). *How animals communicate*. Bloomington: Indiana University Press.

A work in an anthology
> Arnold, C. (1977). How monkeys use sign language. In T. Sebeok (Ed.), *How animals communicate*. (pp. 40–50). Bloomington: Indiana University Press.

A book that is translated with both the author and translator named
> Fernandez, R. (1986). *The architectural heritage of the moors* (W. Garcia, Trans.). London: Routledge. (Original work published 1976)

A book by two or three authors; a revised or later edition
> Reichman, S., & Deez, M. (1978). *The Washington lobbyist* (5th ed.). New York: Harcourt.

A new edition of an edited book
> Adler, F. (Ed.). (1976). *Women and Crime* (4th ed.). Cambridge, MA: Harvard University Press.

A book published in more than one volume
> Thorndike, L. (1941). *A history of magic and experimental science.* (Vols. 1–3). New York: Columbia University Press.

A republished or reprinted book
> Nilsson, M. P. (1972). *Greek folk religion.* Philadelphia: University of Pennsylvania Press. (Original work published 1940)

A newspaper article
> Petzinger, T. J., G. Putka, & S. J. Sansweet. (1983, September 12). High fliers. *Wall Street Journal,* sec. 1, pp. 1, 7.

An unsigned article in a newspaper
> Executive changes. (1991, August 8). *New York Times.* p. C3.

A book review
> Katz, B. (1960). [Review of *Norman Rockwell: My adventures as an illustrator*]. *Library Journal, 85,* 648.

An encyclopedia entry
> Albert Einstein. (1992). Concise Columbia Encyclopedia.

Some Less Common Bibliographic Forms in the APA Format

A book published as a volume in a series
> Hochberg, J. E. (1964). *Perception: Vol. 7. Foundations of modern psychology series.* Englewood Cliffs, NJ: Prentice Hall.

A lecture or publicly delivered paper
> Flaye, S. (1988, March). *Zen buddhism and psychotherapy.* Paper presented at The Conference on Zen Buddhism, Fargo.

A personal interview
> Gold, M. (1987, December 2). [Unpublished personal interview].

A reference to an article from dissertation abstracts
> Knutt, M. (1984). The many masks of Ted Hughes. *DAI, 44,* 474B.

An introduction, foreword, preface, or afterword of a book
> Wise, R. (1971). Foreword. In R. L. Bare, *The film director.* New York: Macmillan, ii–v.

A radio or television program
> National Geographic Society. (1982, February 28). *Egypt: Quest for Eternity.* Newark: PBS.

A reference to a recording
> Richardson, R. (1958). *The poetry of Blake.* New York: Caedmon.

A government publication of the executive branch
> United States. Bureau of the Budget. (1966). *Special analysis: Budget of the United States, fiscal year 1967.* Washington, DC; U.S. Government Printing Office.

Material from a computer service
> Berger, C. (1994, July 17) Unresolved issues from the Gulf War. *The International Courier,* pp. 125–37. (DIALOG file 23: MAGAZINE ASAP, item 241372).

Computer software program
> Richman, R. (1990). *Butterflies* [computer program]. Boston: Lancelot Distributing.

Preparing the Manuscript

1. Type or print out your paper on good quality 8½-by-11-inch white paper.
2. Make sure you have a copy for yourself.
3. Type on only one side of each page.
4. Leave at least a 1- to 1½-inch margin at the top, bottom, left-hand, and right-hand sides of each page.
5. Your paper, including the bibliography, should be double-spaced.
6. Indent each paragraph consistently, whether you indent five, six, or seven spaces. Quotations of more than four lines should be separated, double-spaced, indented ten spaces from the left margin, and set off from the text as a block without being enclosed in quotation marks.
7. Starting with the second page, number each page consecutively in the upper right-hand corner. Type your last name in the upper right-hand corner of each page, including the pages of your bibliography and footnotes.
8. The title page should display your name, your teacher's name, the course name and number, and the date submitted as well as the full title of your research paper.

9. To facilitate the reading of your paper, fasten it in a plastic folder or with a paper clip.
10. If it is required by your teacher, make sure you have turned in all your note cards, bibliography cards, and final outline with your final copy.
11. Proofread your paper and make any last-minute corrections neatly in ink.

What follows are two sample research papers, annotated to illustrate typical features of the MLA and the APA formats.

Sample Research Paper (MLA Style)

Manion 1

Jack Manion
Professor Kent
English 102
March 17, 1993

Why Doesn't the Government "Just Say Yes" to Preventive
Education Against Drug Abuse?

    The phenomenon of drug abuse now poses a grave threat
to our country. The extent of damage caused by drugs in terms
of lives and lost productivity is staggering. From elementary
school students to the executive suites of Wall Street, the
insidious effects of the drug epidemic has left no area of
American society untouched. In light of the obvious magnitude
of this problem, why isn't more being done to educate young
people as to the nature and dangers of taking drugs? All
the solutions that have been put forward are plagued with
many obvious disadvantages. In my view, the government
should institute a massive preventative education program
to help children and teenagers understand the dangers of using
drugs.

    Why drug use should have escalated so radically in the
1980's and become such a big part of our society is a question
that many have tried to answer. Perhaps if we understood the
reasons why so many are taking drugs, the solutions proposed
would be more effective.

    Andrew Weil, a professor of addiction studies at the
University of Arizona, and Winifred Rosen, suggest that the
need to alter consciousness is necessary to physical and
psychological well-being; they assert that the need to transcend
the monotony of everyday life and feel at one with the universe
is basic to human nature:

Begin numbering with first page.

Double space. Name, instructor's name, course name, and date.

Title centered.

Introduction of the topic as a problem to be solved.

Student states thesis as claim of policy.

Theory of drug use presented.

Manion 2

> Human beings are pleasure-seeking animals who are very
> inventive when it comes to finding new ways to excite
> their senses and gratify their appetites. . . . Because drugs
> can, temporarily at least, make the ordinary
> extraordinary, many people seek them out and consume
> them in an effort to get more out of life (18).

Weil and Rosen assert that since people all over the world
engage in these activities, human beings are not culturally
influenced to use drugs but rather have an innate need to alter
consciousness.

A more credible explanation for this widespread problem
is offered by the sociologist, Philip Slater, who claims that our
culture conditions us through advertising to expect that our
problems will be resolved within minutes. This leads to an
inability to tolerate frustration and to the belief that all
problems are susceptible to an immediate "quick fix" (7).

Slater reveals that as society's values and norms have
changed, fashions in drug use have also changed. After World
War II, alcohol use was promoted through images of the
"typical suburban alcoholic of the forties and fifties and the
wealthy drunks glamorized by Hollywood" (7). Economic class
and social values determine the kind of substances or drugs to
which people become addicted. Slater observes that "marijuana
and psychedelics" were used by the sixties generation, whereas
"cocaine [is] for modern Yuppies" and "heroin [is used by] the
hopeless of all periods" (7).

Slater's conclusion is a very persuasive one. Advertising
constantly bombards us with messages that we can cope only
by using some substance or product. Although we may flatter

*Writer's name; page
number.*

*Block quotation double-
spaced, indented from
left margin.*

*Competing theory of
drug use presented.
Student establishes
Slater as authority by
identifying him as a
sociologist.*

*In-text citation of page
number of source; cita-
tion is placed at the end
of the sentence before
the period.*

*Student works quota-
tion into his sentence.*

*Material inserted to
clarify put in brackets.*

Manion 3

ourselves that "we may be smart enough not to believe the silly claims of the individual ad, but can we escape the underlying message on which all of them agree?... Can we reasonably complain about the amount of addiction in our society when we teach it every day" (8)?

No one would dispute the fact that drugs have had a profound impact on our society. Crime, much of it drug-related, has gone up dramatically in the last twenty years. Newspapers are filled with stories of those who have had their lives ruined because of their addiction to drugs. Cocaine, in particular, has spread to almost every sector of American life. The extent to which drug use has escalated can be judged by examining its effects in three different areas in our society: in the field of sports, in the financial sector, and in the entertainment industry.

Athletes use drugs for many of the reasons identified by Slater—to remain competitive and to win at all costs. Thomas H. Murray, a professor of ethics and public policy at the University of Texas, points out that many athletes are coerced into using drugs in order to remain competitive with other athletes who are willing to risk addiction by taking performance-enhancing drugs (27). Still other athletes take drugs to numb the pain of injuries and risk permanent physical damage in order to remain competitive.

Student's summary of opposing viewpoints with analysis of underlying assumptions.

This practice is defended by Norman Fost who claims that performance-enhancing drugs pose no higher health risks than taking vitamins. He says that athletes, in any case, always have free choice as to whether or not to use drugs (7). Murray takes the opposite view, claiming that coaches have been known to coerce players into using drugs in order to perform better (28). It is significant that both Murray and Fost take it for granted that the pressure to win is the main cause of drug use by athletes.

Student summarizes sources and questions an unstated warrant in the arguments.

Manion 4

Peter Gent, a former offensive-end for the Dallas Cowboys, and author of <u>North Dallas Forty,</u> notes that drugs are not only used to enhance performance on the field, but are used after the game as well to celebrate a win or numb the pain of a loss. Gent theorizes that:

> Cocaine is one way a growing segment of our society is finding escape from the tedium of daily life. And fame and stardom can be just as tedious as anything else. . . . Today's players seem to be using cocaine to avoid the awful pain of coming down after the tremendous high of game day (15).

Ellipsis shows omitted material.

A producer of television shows, Frank Swertlow, reveals that drugs, especially cocaine, have permeated the entertainment industry. Swertlow observes that:

> Perhaps the most sinister aspect of the growing use of cocaine in the TV industry is the way it is used as a medium of exchange. "Cocaine is a negotiable instrument in this town," said one veteran producer, familiar with drug dealing. "You might not be able to pay a writer or an actor or a director a bonus; so you pay him in cocaine" (10).

Actors under pressure need cocaine to perform. Writers take cocaine because they believe it makes them more creative. Production budgets are frequently altered to accommodate drug costs. Swertlow reports that some producers are successful in getting contracts for their TV pilots solely because of their ability to procure and supply "coke" (12).

Manion 5

Paradoxically, the public continues to admire many of these actors, writers, and producers while disparaging the dismal quality of shows that, ironically, are the result of such widespread cocaine use.

As an article in the <u>Wall Street Journal</u> makes clear, cocaine use has spread beyond the football field and the silver screen to the world of finance. The dimensions of the problem are startling:

> In Chicago, cocaine use is spreading in the city's commodities trading and financial centers. "A few people take a toot before the trading session and maybe a few times during the day," says one member of the Chicago Board of Trade, himself a user. "It's like drinking coffee." He estimates that 10% of the traders and brokers he knows use cocaine on the job (Petzinger, Putka, and Sansweet 1).

Quoted matter within block quotation enclosed in double quotation marks.

The use of drugs by athletes or entertainers may be disturbing but it is not as alarming as the spectre of drug use by brokers, and managers of large portfolios containing the pension funds for millions of Americans. Apparently, those in charge of the securities and financial services industry react in much the same way as do the owners of the NFL teams when cocaine use is exposed. It is first denied and when overwhelming evidence is presented, cocaine abuse is treated simply as "an image problem" (Petzinger, Putka, and Sansweet 22).

Author(s) not cited in text are in parenthesis.

Like athletes and actors, traders use cocaine to eliminate any feelings of inadequacy and to feel more successful. While it is true that people in professional sports, in the

entertainment industry, and on Wall Street are under
tremendous pressure to succeed, these areas simply reflect
more intensely the pressures put on everyone in our society.

Hundreds of times each day we are urged to buy, eat,
drink, or use products that will instantly make us better-
looking, sexier, younger, healthier, more successful and more
desirable. Slater appears absolutely correct when he asserts
that our society glorifies drug use.

Of course, it is ironic that people in the United States hold
other countries responsible for the widespread use of drugs
when the real reasons for increasing drug use are inherent in
our society's values. In essence, we are falling back on the
same "quick fix" mentality that created the problem in our
attempts to stop drug abuse.

The solutions that have been tried thus far—like arresting
the dealers, intercepting the flow of drugs or encouraging crop
substitution in countries where drugs are grown—have proven
ineffective, according to the Editors of Dollars & Sense. They
point out that many countries in South and Central America
are heavily dependent on the revenues produced by the coca
crops (from which cocaine is made) for a significant percentage
of their national income (Editors 6). The profits to be had from
growing coca plants are as much as 29 times greater (up to
$4,000 an acre) than money which could be earned from such
legal crops as corn, rice, and barley ($140 an acre). One-fourth
of Bolivia's gross national product is based on cocaine and
100,000 Bolivians are employed in the cocaine industry.

*Student analyzes
solutions tried thus far.*

Moreover, America remains the primary market for
cocaine since according to the National Narcotics Intelligence
Consumers Commission "6 percent of U.S. cocain users

Manion 7

consume 60% of the cocaine" produced in these countries. The
conclusion is inescapable: cocaine addiction is almost
exclusively the "property" of American society (Editors 7).
Even more disturbing, the amount of cocaine available is now
greater than the demand for it. The cocaine industry has
responded by producing "crack," a cheaper, much more
concentrated, highly addicting and deadly form of cocaine
(Editors 7).

Tragically, efforts to educate people to stay away from
drugs have been undercut; the budget for drug education
programs has been reduced during the Reagan administration
"from 14 million in 1981 to less than 3 million in 1985," and
proposed funding for drug-treatment programs is no higher
than what it was in 1980 (Editors 8).

If economic pressures have doomed attempts to solve the
problem from the "supply" side, attempts to solve the problem
from the "demand" side have centered around the idea of
mandatory drug-testing. Advocates make the case that
although drug-testing is intrusive, it is necessary as a means
of protecting society against a problem that has reached
epidemic proportions.

Anne Marie O'Keefe, a psychologist and lawyer who
specializes in health issues, argues that urinalysis violates the
basic Fourth Amendment guarantees against "unreasonable
search and seizure" (38). She objects to mandatory drug-
testing by employers on the grounds that the use of the results
of drug-testing to evaluate employees, when no shortcomings
in job performance are evident, is a breach of constitutionally
guaranteed civil rights. O'Keefe states that statistics show
drug-testing to be, on the whole, highly inaccurate, producing
both "false negative" results and "false positive" results often
leading to job loss (35). She cites studies to prove that many

*Student cites evidence
to support thesis.*

*Student incorporates
quotation into syntax
of the sentence.*

*Student works part
paraphrase, part direct
quotation into the text.*

over-the-counter drugs give erroneous "false positive" indications of drug use. For example:

> ... Contact, Sudafed, certain diet pills, decongestants, and heart and asthma medications can register as amphetamines on the test. Cough syrups containing dextromethorphan can cross-react as opiates, and some antibiotics show up as cocaine.... Even poppy seeds, which actually contain traces of morphine, and some herbal teas containing traces of cocaine can cause positive test results for these drugs (35).

The right to privacy is a key issue in the whole controversy surrounding drug-testing. Even if the results could be confirmed, what worries most people is the possibility that the test results would not be kept confidential, regardless of the promises of the government or private employers. These issues were at the center of a case in the Carlstadt-East Rutherford School System in New Jersey where students were going to be required to take mandatory urinalysis tests.

Student adds a lead sentence that provides a context for the following discussion.

School officials claimed their policy of mandatory physical examinations would be enacted to determine whether students had "'any physical defects, illnesses or communicable diseases'" (qtd. in Flygare 329). The proposed test included provisions for testing students for drug use. The students brought suit against the school board, arguing that "under the subterfuge of a forced medical examination" drug-testing violated Fourth Amendment rights prohibiting unreasonable "search and seizure" (329).

Lawyers for the students argued that the small percentage of students (28 out of 520) referred for counseling

Manion 9

for drug related problems did not constitute evidence of a
genuine need to institute mandatory testing for the entire
student body. The New Jersey State Court decided mandatory
drug-testing was unconstitutional on the grounds that the
"'comprehensive medical examinations violated the reasonable
privacy expectations of school children'" (qtd. in Flygare 329).

Student cites an indirect source for a quotation.

This case illustrates some of the legal and ethical
problems produced by society's attempt to deal with the drug
crisis solely through the "quick fix" of mandatory drug-testing.
But surprisingly, little has been done to deal with the
underlying causes. The Editors of Dollars & Sense report that
"the Reagan administration has substantially cut funding" for
"drug treatment programs (to help heavy users) and [for]
preventative education." They also note that "instead of these
programs, the administration had made "voluntary" drug-
testing and Nancy Reagan's 'just say no' clubs the real center
pieces of its demand-side strategy" (Editors 8).

By not understanding that the place where you stand the
best chance of stopping drug abuse is in the schools when
people are most vulnerable to peer pressure and form lifelong
habits, the government's reduction of funds is clearly ill-
advised and short-sighted. A variety of studies suggest that
drug education programs are effective in reducing drug abuse
(Galanter, 1992; Jellinek and Hearn, 1991; Shalom, 1992).
Even studies with conflicting results acknowledge that greater
funding might reverse the outcome (Massing, 1991). Clearly,
the single most important action the government should take
would be to support mass-education programs to prevent
children and teenagers from getting involved with drugs in the
first place. The efforts might be modeled on the same kinds of
programs that successfully educated the public about the
dangers of cigarette smoking. A recent report by the Surgeon

Student cites research that education is effective in changing drug abuse behavior.

General states that cigarettes are as addicting as other drugs. Yet, millions of people have stopped smoking because of these programs. Doubtless, there are significant differences between taking drugs and smoking cigarettes, but the fact remains that preventative education programs are one of the few potentially workable solutions that has not been seriously supported.

Manion 11

Works Cited

Editors of <u>Dollars & Sense</u> Magazine. "White Lines, Bottom Lines: Profile of a Mature Industry." <u>Dollars & Sense</u> Dec. 1986: 6–8.

Flygare, Thomas J. "Courts Foil Schools' Efforts to Detect Drugs." <u>Phi Delta Kappan</u> 68 (1986): 329–330.

Fost, Norman. "Banning Drugs in Sports: A Skeptical View." <u>The Hastings Center Report</u> 16 (1986): 5–10.

Galenter, Marc. "The End of Addiction." <u>Psychology Today</u> Nov./Dec. 1992: 7–13.

Gent, Peter. "Between the White Lines: The NFL Cocaine War." <u>The Dallas Times Herald</u> 4 Sept. 1983, Magazine: 13–15.

Jellinek, Paul S. and Ruby P. Hearn. "Fighting Drug Abuse at the Local Level." <u>Issues in Science and Technology</u> Summer 1991: 8–17.

Massing, Michael. "Can We Cope with Drugs?" <u>Dissent</u> Spring 1991: 4–7.

Murray, Thomas H. "The Coercive Power of Drugs in Sports." <u>The Hastings Center Report</u> 13 (1983): 24–30.

O'Keefe, Anne Marie. "The Case vs. Drug Testing." <u>Psychology Today</u> June 1987: 34–38.

Petzinger, Thomas J., Gary Putka, and Stephen J. Sansweet. "High Fliers." <u>Wall Street Journal</u> 12 Sept. 1983, sec. 1:1+.

First line flush left; indent rest of citation five spaces.

Sources arranged alphabetically by author's last name.

Article in a journal with continuous pagination for that year.

Article in a journal with separate pagination for each issue.

Manion 12

Shalom, Stephen R. "Drug Policy and Progress." <u>Z Papers</u> 1
    (1992): 14–20.

Slater, Philip. "Want-Creation Fuels Americans'
    Addictiveness." <u>St. Paul Pioneer Dispatch</u> 6 Sept. 1984,
    sec. 1:7.

Swertlow, Frank. "Hollywood's Cocaine Connection." <u>TV Guide</u>
    28 Feb. 1981: 7–12.

Weil, Andrew and Winfred Rosen. <u>Chocolate to Morphine:
    Understanding Mind-Active Drugs.</u> Boston: Houghton
    Mifflin, 1983.

A signed article in a daily newspaper.

A book by two authors.

Sample Research Paper (APA Style)

Brave New World   1 —— *Abbreviated title begins on cover page. Begin numbering with first page.*

The "Brave New World" of Genetic Engineering —— *Include all information requested by instructor.*

Samantha Clarke

English 103

Professor J. Mathias

April 13, 1994

Brave New World   2

Abstract

The flood of information that will be released by scientists working on the Human Genome Project requires researchers to examine the ethical and moral issues that will ensue from the release of this information.

Short paragraph of less than 150 words presents a concise summary of the argument.

Brave New World   3 —— *Short title and page number.*

The "Brave New World" of Genetic Engineering —— *Title centered.*

> Staring at the walls of doctors' offices while awaiting their turn . . . Americans . . . see a colorful chart hanging next to the traditional diplomas and the renderings of skeletal parts and organs. It will depict the 23 pairs of human chromosomes and pinpoint on each one the location of genes that can predispose people to serious disease. (Jaroff, 1992, p. 58)

Long quotations are set off as block quotations. Indent left margin five spaces, double-spaced, and put author, date of publication, and page number in parentheses after final punctuation. Ellipses (. . .) indicate omitted passage.

More and more, this fictional scenario is coming closer to being a reality. With the dawn of the age of genetic engineering, it is becoming increasingly obvious that, in a little more than a decade, the international group of scientists working on the Human Genome Project, the project which aspires to decipher the entire sequence of genes that make up the human organism, will be able to identify the location of the defective genes that cause certain human diseases and alter the defective genes. This technological "service" seems to be the driving force behind the Project. The goal is, as James D. Watson, head of the project and co-discoverer of the DNA double helix, says, a "public good" because this project is designed "to assist biomedical researchers in their assault on disease" (qtd. in Glass, 1992, p. 2158). The problem is that —— *Indirect source.* along with the benefits that can be derived from genomic information there are serious ethical and moral dilemmas that must be addressed in a timely fashion.

First paragraph ends with thesis stated as a value claim.

How Should We Use Information From Genetic Research?

Headings divide the paper into recognizable sections.

According to the editors of The Economist (1992):

> Beyond today's gene therapy . . . lie far more controversial possibilities: changing genes for non-medical reasons and changing genes wholesale in

Brave New World 4

such a way that the new genes are passed on from generation to generation. (p. 272)

Who decides what genes will be altered? Who decides whether or not genetic information is released to certain agencies? Who decides if a person's genetic information is shared with the rest of his or her family (who also possess that same genetic information) or not? How will we keep genetically flawed persons from being discriminated against in the work place, by insurance companies, or by society itself? How will we keep from repeating the kind of discrimination based on genetics that occurred in the past? All of these questions are central to this new project. They need to be addressed and clearly point to the need for regulation of this project, in terms of its ethical and moral implications.

So far, genetic engineering has been used in two ways: (a) to provide therapy for people with genetic defects and, (b) to produce useful genetically engineered animals and plants. In this sense, genetic engineering has been very beneficial. In treating people with genetic diseases, scientists simply replace the existing defective gene of a person with an altered healthy gene. This process is already being done and can be seen in the treatment of people with diabetes. This involves inserting insulin producing genes into the DNA of defective somatic cells. In producing commercially valuable genetically engineered animals and plants, we have seen how this new technology can make animals into factories which can create vital human proteins, so that "pigs carrying human growth hormone genes produced by USDA scientists were among the first and most widely publicized transgenic animals." (Murphy, 1990, p. 241)

Student summarizes past uses before raising basic questions that she will address.

Brave New World   5

But, what if instead of simply "fixing" defective genes, people begin to "enhance" existing and normal genes? What genes should scientists be allowed to alter? How do we draw the line between gene therapy and gene enhancement? These exact questions are dealt with by W. French Anderson (1990), in his article for <u>The Hastings Center Report:</u>

> Successful... gene therapy also opens the door for enhancement genetic engineering, that is, for supplying a specific characteristic that individuals might want for themselves (somatic cell engineering) or their children (germline engineering) which would not involve the treatment of a disease.... A line... should be drawn between somatic cell gene therapy and enhancement genetic engineering (p. 276). ———

When author and title are mentioned in the text, only the page number is cited.

Releases of Genetic Information Affects Entire Families

With the advent of this technology which will be able to decipher an individual's genetic code comes the problem of the "implications extending beyond the individual to family members and even potential family members" (Glass, p. 2158). This presents a particularly difficult conflict because it hinges on two basic considerations: (1) the individual's ——— freedom, (2) the family's freedom. A person's genetic code is not simply information about that person. Since an individual's genome is made up of the same genetic material as that of his family members how can we say that one person has the right to release genetic information that will violate his family's privacy?

Student presents criteria that should be applied.

This problem is one that is addressed in the book <u>Gene Mapping: Using Law and Ethics as Guides,</u> whose intent was to:

Brave New World   6

> ...assemble a group of the nation's leading experts in
> genetics, medicine, history of science, medical law,
> philosophy of science, and medical ethics for an
> intensive workshop designed to outline where we now
> stand and what is needed to help get the legal and
> ethical studies portion of the human genome project
> focused and off to a reasonable start (Annas & Elias,
> 1992, p. iv).

A prominent concern voiced by the scientific, as well as
the lay community, is the fear that genetic engineering will
result in an increase in discrimination and a possible return to
eugenics. According to Jody W. Zylke (1992), in an article for
JABA (The Journal of the American Medical Association),
"The possibility of discrimination based on genotype was a
theme expressed by many..." (p. 1715). How real is the
possibility that the information genomes could provide would
lead to discriminatory practices by insurance companies and
employers toward people predisposed to genetic diseases?

> The possibility of discrimination can also be addressed
> on a more immediate and practical level. Consider
> health insurance. The private insurance industry relies
> on a system of risk classification, with those people at
> higher risk paying more.... Will the advent of genetic
> testing make it even more discriminatory?... Norman
> Daniels, Ph.D., Chair of the Department of Philosophy
> at Tufts University... says he thinks that information
> from the project will make the insurance system more
> unfair. (Zylke, p. 1715)

Will Genetic Engineering Lead to a Resurgence of Eugenics?

Genetic engineering could very well lead to the idea of
"improving" the human race. Understandably, this raises fear

Student provides a lead sentence that shows what quotations will prove.

Brave New World   7

of a rebirth of eugenics. Such fears are not ill-founded since the
World Press Review (1994) reported the occurrence of the
following event in China in December of 1993:

> China's ministry of public health December 20
> proposed to "avoid new births of inferior quality and
> heighten the standards of the whole population" by
> mandating abortions, contraceptive use and
> sterilizations, if necessary. The measures reportedly
> would be geared towards people identified [as having
> the potential of passing] hereditary diseases or mental
> and physical defects to their children. (pp. 11, 13)

Such events as these are evidence that the impact of the
genome project is affecting us even now. Preventive measures
must thus be taken today in order to forstall any more serious
injustices, "while the science proceeds, most agree that the
ethical and social issues need to be worked on
simultaneously..." (Zylke, p. 1715)

Student reiterates the support for her value claim in her conclusion.

Although genetic engineering has, above all else, the
promise of bettering the lives of many people who truly suffer,
it has the dark possibility of endangering the dignity of human
life as we know it. Genetic engineering, as a new science, has
arrived and is just now beginning to blossom. As intelligent and
moral beings, we are required by the very essence of our
humanity to reflect on the dangers as well as the benefits of
this new technology.

Brave New World   8

References

Anderson, W. F. (1990, January/February). Genetics and human malleability. Hastings Center Report, pp. 59–64.

Annas, G. J., & Elias, S. (Eds.). (1992). Gene mapping: Using law and ethics as guides. New York: Putnam.

Changing your genes. (1992, April). The Economist. pp. 3–6.

Forrest, S. (1994, March 17). Social implications of genetic research. World Press Review, pp. 11–13.

Glass, R. M. (1992). AAAS conference explores ethical aspects of large pedigree genetic research. The Journal of the American Medical Association, 267, 2158.

Jaroff, L. (1992, October). Seeking a Godlike power: genetic science promises to deliver the blueprint for human life. Time, p. 58.

Murphy, C. (1990). Genetically engineered animals. In P. Wheale & R. McNally (Eds.), The Bio-Revolution. (pp. 38–41). London: Pluto Press.

Zylke, J. W. (1992). Examining life's code means re-examining society's long-held codes. The Journal of the American Medical Association, 267, 1715–1717.

References start a new page.

An article from a periodical.

An anthology with two editors.

An article in an anthology.

Glossary

Abstract   designating qualities or characteristics apart from specific objects or events; opposite of **concrete**.

Analogy   a process of reasoning that assumes if two subjects share a number of specific observable qualities then they may be expected to share qualities that have not been observed; the process of drawing a comparison between two things based on a partial similarity of like features.

Argument   a process of reasoning and putting forth evidence on controversial issues; a statement or fact presented in support of a point.

Assumption   an idea or belief taken for granted; see **warrant**.

Audience   the people who read or hear an argument.

Authority   a person who is accepted as a source of reliable information because of his or her expertise in the field.

Backing   authority providing the assurance that the body of experience relied on to establish the warrant is appropriate and justified.

Claim   the assertion that the arguer wishes the audience to discover as the logical outcome of the case being presented.

Cliché   a timeworn expression that through overuse has lost its power to evoke concrete images.

Concrete   pertaining to actual things, instances, or experiences; opposite of **abstract.**

Connotation   the secondary or associative meanings of a word as distinct from its explicit or primary meaning; the emotional overtones of a word or phrase; opposite of **denotation**.

Deduction   a method of reasoning that infers the validity of a particular case from general statements or **premises** taken to be true.

Definition   the method of identifying the distinguishing characteristics of an idea, term, or process to establish its meaning.

Denotation   the literal explicit meaning of a word or expression; opposite of **connotation**.

Enthymeme   an abbreviated syllogism expressed in ordinary language in which the major or minor **premise** is not explicitly stated.

Euphemism from the Greek word meaning *to speak well of*; the substitution of an inoffensive, indirect, or agreeable expression for a word or phrase perceived as socially unacceptable or unnecessarily harsh.

Evidence all material, including testimony of experts; statistics, cases whether real, hypothetical, or analogical; and reasons brought forward to support a claim.

Exception an extraordinary instance or circumstance in which an otherwise valid claim would not hold true.

Fallacy errors of pseudoreasoning caused by incorrect interpretations of evidence and incorrectly drawn inferences.

Ad hominem an attack against the character of the person instead of the issue.

Ad misericordiam an attempt to manipulate the audience through an appeal to pity.

Ad populum an emotional appeal to the audience's feelings for country, class, national identity, or religious affiliation. Variations include *bandwagon, patriotic appeal, just plain folks, common practice* or *appeal to tradition*, and *appeal to status*.

Appeal to force an attempt to intimidate the audience into compliance by holding up a threat of force to compel acceptance of a claim; also known as *scare tactics*.

Argument from ignorance an erroneous belief that the failure to draw a conclusion can be used as evidence to support a claim.

Begging the question a pseudoargument that offers as proof the claim that the argument itself exists to prove; also known as *circular reasoning*.

Fallacy of accent an erroneous impression created by misplaced emphasis or by taking words out of context.

Fallacy of accident a failure to take into account cases that are clearly exceptions to the rule. Also called *sweeping generalization*.

Fallacy of amphiboly an unintended meaning arising from faulty syntax, confusing grammatical structure, or faulty punctuation.

Fallacy of complex question sometimes called the *loaded question*. Occurs when the arguer poses a question ("Have you stopped beating your wife?") in a way that assumes that an implicit first question has already been answered.

Fallacy of composition a failure to recognize that qualities of the individual parts do not automatically characterize the whole.

Fallacy of division an erroneous inference drawn about qualities of the parts based on what is valid for the whole.

Fallacy of equivocation a misleading impression created by using a word that has a double meaning.

False dilemma a simplistic characterization suggesting that there are only two choices in a particular situation; also known as the *either/or dilemma*.

Faulty analogy an unwarranted assumption that two things similar in some respects are also similar in all other ways.

Faulty use of authority a citing of an authority outside the field of his or her relevant expertise.

Hasty generalization an erroneous judgment based on too few instances or on atypical or inadequate examples.

Non sequitur   meaning *it does not follow*; the introduction of irrelevant evidence to support a claim.

Post hoc ergo propter hoc   meaning *after this, therefore because of this*; the incorrect inference that simply because B *follows* A, A *caused* B.

Red herring   the bringing in of a tangential or irrelevant point to divert attention from the real issue.

Slippery slope   a failure to provide evidence to support predictions that one event will lead to a whole chain of events, usually catastrophic.

Straw man   the using of an easily refuted objection to divert attention from the real issue.

Grounds   specific facts relied on to support a given claim.

Hypothesis   a provisional thesis, subject to revision, accepted as a working **premise** in an argument.

Induction   a process of reasoning that reaches a generalization by drawing inferences from particular cases.

Inference   the process of reaching conclusions drawn from the interpretation of facts, circumstances, or statements.

Irony   a way of drawing the reader into a secret collaboration where the writer means something quite opposite to what is being literally said.

Jargon   from the fifteenth-century French term *jargoun*, meaning *twittering* or *jibberish*; usually refers to a specialized language providing a shorthand method of quick communication between people in the same field. Often used to disguise the inner workings of a particular trade or profession from public scrutiny.

Metaphor   a word or phrase applied to an object it does not literally connote to suggest a comparison that evokes a vivid picture in the imagination of the audience.

Persuasion   according to Aristotle, the act of winning acceptance of a claim achieved through the combined effects of the audience's confidence in the speaker's character (*ethos*), appeals to reason (*logos*), and the audience's emotional needs and values (*pathos*).

Picturesque language   Words or phrases that evoke vivid images or pictures in the minds of the audience.

Plagiarism   using someone's words or ideas without giving proper credit.

Premise   statements or generalizations in deductive reasoning taken as self-evidence that have been previously established through the process of inductive reasoning.

Qualifier   a restriction that may have to be attached to a particular claim to indicate its relative strength or certainty.

Rebuttal   a special circumstance or extraordinary instance that challenges the claim being made.

Refutation   showing a position to be false or erroneous in order to lessen its credibility.

Rhetoric   according to Aristotle, the process of discovering all the available means of persuasion in any situation where the truth cannot be known for certain; includes seeking out the best arguments, arranging them in the most effective way, and presenting them in a manner calculated to win agreement from a particular audience.

Satire   an enduring form of argument that uses parody, irony, and caricature to poke fun at a subject, idea, or person.

Simile   a comparison of one object or experience to another using the words *like* or *as* to create a vivid picture.

Slanting   the presentation of information in such a way as to reflect a particular point of view.

Stereotype   labeling a person or a group in terms of a single character trait, usually pejorative.

Support   all the evidence the writer brings forward to enhance the probability of a claim being accepted; can include evidence in the form of testimony of experts, statistics, examples from personal experience, hypothetical cases, appeals to the audience's emotions and values, and the speaker's own character or personality.

Syllogism   a classic form of deductive reasoning illustrating the relationship between a major and a minor **premise** and a conclusion in which the validity of a particular case is drawn from statements assumed to be true or self-evident.

Thesis   an expression of the claim, assertion, or position the writer wishes the audience to accept.

Tone   the voice the writer has chosen to project in order to adapt the argument for a specific occasion and a particular audience; produced by the combined effect of word choice, sentence structure, and the writer's attitude toward the subject.

Values   moral or ethical principles or beliefs that express standards or criteria by which actions may be considered right or wrong, good or bad, acceptable or unacceptable, appropriate or unseemly; value arguments supply ethical, moral, aesthetic, or utilitarian criteria against which proposed actions may be evaluated.

Warrant   according to Stephen Toulmin, a general statement that expresses implicit or explicit assumptions about how the agreed-upon facts of a particular case are connected to the claim or conclusion being offered.

APPENDIX A

Logical Fallacies

———————◆———————

Inappropriate use of strategies of argument can result in arguments that give the appearance of being persuasive but use incorrect ways of reasoning. These methods of pseudo-reasoning often seem quite persuasive: although they appear to be logical, they usually appeal to emotions, prejudices, and existing beliefs.

Writers should be able to identify certain common fallacies both in their own works and in the arguments of others. A familiarity with the main types of fallacies can keep writers from being misled by them. Although we often think of fallacies as being intentionally contrived to lend plausibility to an unsound argument, they may occur accidentally without the writer's awareness. In either case, understanding how arguments go wrong is just as important as understanding the correct relationship among claims, evidence, underlying assumptions, and other elements of sound arguments.

The following discussion covers the more common fallacies that persistently undermine sound reasoning.

FALLACIES THAT RESULT WHEN NO REAL EVIDENCE IS PRESENTED TO SUPPORT THE CLAIM

Begging the Question (**Petitio Principii,** *Circular Reasoning*)

This fallacy occurs when a writer doesn't bring forward evidence to support the claim but simply repeats the main assertion in a disguised form. The argument assumes as already proven the claim that the argument exists to prove. What is offered as proof is only a restatement of the proposition or claim in other words. For example, note the circular pattern of reasoning in the following dialogue:

> How do you know God exists?
> It says so in the Bible.

How do you know the Bible is a reliable source?
Because the Bible is the divinely inspired word of God.

Another form of *begging the question* is *circular definition*, which defines a term by offering a synonym or restatement in other words of the term to be defined. For example, a hero is one who is heroic, hiccup is the sound made by hiccuping, or fermentation is the process of fermenting.

Question-Begging Epithets

This common fallacy occurs in arguments when the writer inserts loaded terms or phrases whose connotations (positive or negative) substitute for the logic of the argument. These phrases often substitute clichéd or stereotyped judgments for sound reasoning, for example, "creeping socialism," "bleeding heart liberal," "city slicker," "country bumpkin," "corrupt politicians," and "irresponsible teenagers."

FALLACIES THAT RESULT WHEN THE EVIDENCE IS NOT RELEVANT TO THE CLAIM

Red Herring (Ignoratio Elenchi, *Arguing Off the Point*)

Writers introduce a *red herring* into an argument when they bring in a point that is tangential or irrelevant to the issue under dispute. The picturesque name stems from the days when it was believed that a pack of hounds would be diverted from following the scent if a herring with its accompanying strong odor were dragged across the trail in front of them. So, too, the *red herring* is a tactic arguers may use to divert the attention of the audience from their pursuit of the real issue at hand. A debate over possible effects on children of witnessing violence on television would *argue off the point* if the arguer started discussing possible dangers of low-level radiation emanating from television screens.

Non Sequitur

Another fallacy involving irrelevant evidence is the *non sequitur*, meaning literally "it does not follow." For example, the statement "My parents raised golden retrievers; therefore I'm against wearing real fur" may make sense to the person making the statement; however, there is no logical connection between being opposed to killing animals to use their skin for coats and the fact that one's parents raised dogs of any kind.

Straw Man

The *straw man* fallacy diverts attention from the real issue onto an easily demolished target. A writer using the *straw man* fallacy would like the audience to believe that the original argument has been disproved when the *straw man* is knocked down. A blatant example of the *straw man* fallacy took place in Richard Nixon's "Checkers" speech, one of the most famous instances of public persuasion in this century. Nixon appeared on television on September 23, 1952, to defend himself against accusations that he had used a political fund for his own personal use. Nixon's situation was especially precarious because Dwight Eisenhower was considering taking him off the Republican ticket as his vice-presidential running mate in the upcoming election. The speech was enormously effective and elicited over two million favorable telegrams from people all over the country. Nixon volunteered the information that "I probably should tell you [about this] because if I don't they'll probably be saying this about me too" as if to suggest that accepting the gift of a puppy, Checkers, was equal in seriousness to dipping into the public coffers. Nixon's strategy of bringing up and then replying to a charge no one had made had the effect of suggesting that all the other charges made against him were equally baseless and absurd.

Inappropriate Use of Authorities (**Argumentum ad Verecundiam***)*

This fallacy is the basis of much advertising featuring testimonials or endorsements by sports figures, movie stars, and other celebrities. The value of expert opinion is that it allows the writer to support conclusions with testimony of someone whose professional expertise is based on greater experience with the issue in question. The opposite of this would be the citation of an authority outside the field that adds nothing in support of the claim. A baseball player might be very credible on the subject of bats, baseballs, and gloves. Yet the same baseball player's endorsement of snow tires, extolling their tread pattern and triple-ply construction, would project him as an authority in an area unrelated to his expertise.

Argument against the Person (**Argumentum Ad Hominem**)

This fallacy can take several forms. In the first, called the *abusive argumentum ad hominem,* the writer attacks the character of the person or his or her personal life rather than providing compelling evidence to disprove the person's argument.

For example, Ashley Montagu, in "Frank Lloyd Wright" (*The American Way of Life* [1967]), veers in the direction of *ad hominem* when he asserts that Wright's architectural theory and practice were determined by his physical stature: "Wright built houses for cave-dwellers, troglodytes, it would almost seem as a practical joke...being a short man Wright designed his rooms with very low ceilings." So, too, William J. Darby in his review of Rachel Carson's *Silent Spring*, titled "Silence, Miss Carson" (*Chemical and Engineering News* [October, 1962]), verges on *ad hominem* when he says "it is doubtful that many readers can bear to wade through its high-pitched sequence of anxieties."

Ad hominem arguments are not off the issue when the character of the person is directly connected to the issue in question. Thus, an argument made by a chief executive officer or a senior partner against certain business practices, such as insider trading, would gain or lose credibility according to the business ethics of the speaker. In this case, it would not be inappropriate for a counterargument to refer to the character of the speaker, especially if it could be shown that the official in question had undisclosed personal interests linked to the acceptance of his argument. Most frequently, however, *ad hominem* argument reflects the inability of the writer to refute points raised by the opposition.

A variation of *ad hominem* is called the *genetic fallacy*, which attempts to disprove an argument by condemning its source or genesis rather than disproving the position itself. Another variation is sometimes referred to as *guilt by association*, which attempts to discredit a claim by linking the person with an already discredited group or a group about whom the audience can be expected to hold a low opinion. For example, Andrew H. Merton writes in the prologue to his book *Enemies of Choice* (1981):

> In its emotional appeals and its disregard of logic, the right-to-life movement resembles many other oppressive crusades in human history, from the earliest witch hunts to the Spanish inquisition to the Nazis persecution of Jews and other *untermenschen* (subhumans). All were based on false logic, and all resulted in widespread misery and loss of freedom. The right-to-life movement differs from these others only in subtlety; it does not directly name the object of its ire—primarily women—but instead would set severe limits on their liberty in the name of saving fetuses.

Here, Merton is using *guilt by association* to put forward evidence that is not directly relevant to the claim. He is trying to manipulate his audience into feeling the way he does by linking anti-abortion groups with discredited groups about which the audience already has negative feelings.

Argument from Ignorance (**Argumentum ad Ignorantiam***)*

This particular fallacy occurs in arguments where the writer's claim is supported by the reason that since "no one knows" what happened or will happen in a given situation, the thesis should be accepted as true. The fact that a hypothesis has not been conclusively proven or disproven cannot itself be used as evidence to support a claim. This fallacy proceeds from the claim that a proposition is true until it is proved false, or false until it is proved true. For example, to argue that UFOs exist on the grounds that no one has ever succeeded in proving they do not, or that there must be ghosts since no one has ever succeeded in disproving their existence, is to commit this fallacy. In short, the failure to draw a conclusion cannot be used as grounds for a conclusion.

Appeal to the People (**Argumentum ad Populum**, *Folksy Appeal, Patriotic, Provincialism, Majority Opinion, Popularity in Numbers, Bandwagon, Status, Snob Appeal, Common Practice)*

This fallacy takes the form of an emotional appeal to the feelings people have for country, class, national identity, or religious affiliation. For example, a political propagandist might appeal to biases, irrational fears, and prejudices by substituting emotional responses for a reasoned set of arguments on the issue. The *ad populum* appeal can take a folksy turn. In fact, this variation is called "just plain folks." Here, the arguer seeks to gain the confidence of his or her audience by seeming to appear as just an ordinary, down-to-earth person whose values are the same as those of most other people.

This appeal is frequently encountered in political campaigns as well as in the world of advertising. For example, Lee Iacocca appeared in Chrysler ads saying in essence that the purchase of an American-made Chrysler was an act of good citizenship. Conversely, not buying a Chrysler might be unpatriotic. To take another case, in the past, Betty Crocker was once presented as "the first lady of desserts."

Sometimes this fallacy takes the form of an appeal to majority opinion, or the idea that the supposed popularity of an idea or product should be sufficient to support its claim. Sometimes this is called the *bandwagon effect*, as in the claim "this product is used in 70 million homes, shouldn't it be used in yours?" Of course, the corollary is that since this idea is believed by X number of millions of people, shouldn't you believe it too?

Advertisers use a variation of this tactic when they appeal to consumers to buy a product by using *snob appeal* or an *appeal to status*. The subgroup here are those who are "in the know." Perhaps the earliest example of the use of *snob appeal* is in an advertisement carried in 1710 in *The Spectator*. The tooth powder so advertised was described as "an Incomparable Powder for cleaning Teeth, which has given great satisfaction to most of the nobility and gentry in England." So, too, today's ads for perfume, Scotch, and luxury cars suggest to readers that by purchasing the product they, too, will be rubbing shoulders with the rich and famous trendsetters.

The fallacy of reasoning underlying these kinds of ads is sometimes called the *fallacy of the undistributed middle term*. This common fallacy can be seen when conclusions draw a wider inference than is warranted by the facts that have been stated. Using our 1710 advertisement, we might diagram the deductive logic as a syllogism designed to expose the flaw in the argument:

MAJOR PREMISE: All members of the nobility in England use X brand of toothpowder.

MINOR PREMISE: All members of the gentry in England use X brand of toothpowder.

CONCLUSION: Therefore, all members of the gentry are also members of the nobility in England.

Obviously, the conclusion is not necessarily true. The argument has failed to establish that the minor term "all members of the gentry" falls within the major term "all members of the nobility in England." In advertising, this translates into the mistaken perception that because wealthy people buy a particular kind of very expensive watch, you will be one of them if you too purchase this watch. When put in this blatant form the fallacy becomes obvious, but advertisers concentrate on the ambiguous area of wishes and fantasies where simply believing something makes it seem true.

Appeal to Pity (**Argumentum ad Misericordiam,** *Appeal to Compassion*)

This fallacy occurs when the arguer seeks to evoke and play on feelings of pity to get his audience to let emotions rather than reason persuade them to accept a conclusion. Again, it should be said that *appeals to compassion* in and of themselves are not necessarily wrong. This fallacy occurs when the arguer seeks to settle a factual matter by using irrelevant appeals to sentiment. Perhaps the most outrageous example is the proverbial case of a defendant on trial for murdering his parents who proceeds to throw himself on the mercy of the court on the grounds that he is now an orphan.

Appeal to Force (**Argumentum ad Baculum,** *Scare Tactics*)

An *appeal to force* is encountered in those arguments that seek to intimidate the audience into compliance or hold up the threat of force to compel acceptance of a claim. The threats posed can include moral or psychological threats as well as ones of physical violence or economic retaliation. For example, Yoshi Tsurumi, writing in *The World Policy Journal* (Spring 1987), argues that the United States should not restrict Japanese imports:

> There's nothing wrong with pressing Japan to open markets that remain closed, but the U.S. cannot expect simply to bully its way to competitiveness. The U.S. needs to recognize that it can no longer dictate the rules of international competition, especially now that it is so dependent on Japanese capital to revive its industries.

It's hard to miss the iron hand in the velvet glove here. In politics the threat of war, and in religion the threat of everlasting damnation (as in Jonathan Edward's sermon "Sinners in the Hands of an Angry God" [1741]), have their counterparts in *scare tactics* used in advertising. For example, an advertising agency head, in the early days of advertising, once proposed an ad based on *scare tactics* for baby food that copywriter Helen Woodward, as quoted by Stuart Ewen in *Captains of Consciousness* (1976), describes as follows:

> "Give 'em the figures about the baby death rate—but don't say it flatly. You know if you just put a lot of figures in front of a woman she passes you by. If we only had the nerve to put a hearse in the ad, you couldn't keep the women away from the food." One such ad did appear. Although there was no hearse, the illustration showed an ominously empty pair of baby shoes.

The unsubtle implication is that her baby will die unless the mother buys a particular brand of baby food.

FALLACIES THAT RESULT WHEN INSUFFICIENT EVIDENCE IS OFFERED TO SUPPORT A CLAIM

Hasty Generalization (**Jumping to Conclusions**)

One of the most common forms of *hasty generalization* involves jumping to a conclusion based on too few instances or inadequate samples. The strength of generalization is that it allows conclusions to be drawn about an entire group or whole category of things based on inferences drawn from observation and analysis of a representative sample. When great care is not taken in selecting the sample, or when the sample does not truly represent the entire group, a fallacy of *hasty generalization* can result.

1. *Generalizing from too few instances.* You would be jumping to a conclusion if you concluded that Maine's summers are always hot and humid based on a week's vacation during an uncharacteristically hot, humid spell.

2. *Generalizing from atypical or unrepresentative examples.* If you read Jerzy Kosinski's novella *Being There* and concluded on the basis of this one story that all his other novels were equally lighthearted, witty, and whimsical, you would be forming a hasty generalization about all his novels based on an atypical example. His other novels, including *The Painted Bird, Steps, Pinball, The Devil Tree, Cockpit, Blind Date,* and *The Hermit of 69th Street,* are rather somber and are centered on the theme of individual survival in a hostile environment.

3. *Stereotyping.* A particularly irrational form of generalizing is called stereotyping. A stereotype is a kind of hasty generalization that expresses a rigid belief about all people in a group based on insufficient evidence, generalized from some members of the group. The logical fallacy involved is moving from some to all in a way that does not take into account individual differences.

Fallacy of Accident (Sweeping Generalization)

A *fallacy of accident* is the direct opposite of *hasty generalization*. It arises from the assumption that if rules exist there can be no exceptions, and it often takes the form of a *sweeping generalization* that fails to take into account cases that are clearly exceptions to the rule. The failure to take into account special circumstances or a particular case—that is, the refusal to admit that circumstances can alter the rule—might result in a *sweeping generalization*. A *sweeping generalization* can take one of two forms: (1) an assertion that something is always good even in circumstances where it clearly is not, or (2) an assertion that something is invariably bad even in situations where it might do some good. For example, most people would agree with the statement that "sunshine contributes to good health," but if this generalization were extended to say that "therefore even people who are fairskinned or allergic should sit in the sun for hours," the writer would be applying a generalization to a specific case whose circumstances prevent the general rule from applying. Conversely, many people would agree with the statement that "marijuana is a harmful drug with negative consequences," but if the writer were then to argue that "therefore marijuana should never be used even for patients suffering from glaucoma," this would be an unjustified application of the general rule to a circumstance clearly regarded as an exception.

FALLACIES THAT RESULT FROM UNWARRANTED ASSUMPTIONS

Fallacies resulting from unwarranted assumptions take a variety of forms.

Oversimplification of Causes

This fallacy results when writers assume that complex events can be explained by pointing to one single cause. For example, a writer might oversimplify the causes of hyperactivity in children by singling out sugar-laden junk foods as the only important factor. Yet, researchers have discovered that metabolism and heredity are just as important.

Complex Questions

The fallacy of the *complex question* occurs when the arguer poses the question in such a manner as to assume or make the unwarranted assumption that an implicit unasked question has already been answered. The most famous example of this fallacy is "Have you stopped beating your wife?" Sometimes this fallacy is called a *loaded question*, for obvious reasons, since it presumes that the person has already been asked the question "Do you beat your wife?" has answered "Yes," and is now answering whether or not he still continues this practice. Trick questions of this kind make a simple *yes* or *no* answer impossible. *Complex questions* enter into legal proceedings when a prosecuting attorney asks a witness, "Where did you hide the axe you used as the murder weapon?" Questions like these can best be handled by separating the issues involved and treating them as two separate questions.

False Dilemma (Either/Or; Black/White Fallacy)

This fallacy results from an unwarranted assumption that there are only two choices in a particular situation. The writer puts the audience in the position of having to pick between one or another of these extreme alternatives. This bumper sticker mentality purveys a simplistic view of the world in terms of black-and-white, right-or-wrong extremes. For example, Noel Keane, the attorney who pioneered the practice of surrogate motherhood, in his book coauthored with Dennis L. Breo, *The Surrogate Mother* (1981), characterizes the phenomenon as follows:

> With surrogate mothers, we are talking about giving life. Those who want to deny life can practice contraception or obtain an abortion.

Keane's characterization suggests that only these two alternatives exist to the problem and does not mention other alternatives, including adoption. Keane's persuasive intent seems to be to characterize the situation in such extreme terms that surrogate parenting appears by contrast to be a more viable option than it otherwise might be. This fallacy depends on acceptance by the audience of the unwarranted assumption that no other options exist, including the alternative of not having to make a choice at all.

False Cause

Overlooking a Common Cause.   This fallacy results from the failure to recognize that two seemingly related events may both be effects of a third common cause.

Suppose, as Darrell Huff (mentioned earlier) has pointed out, some one observes that "there is a close relationship between the salaries of Presbyterian ministers in Massachusetts and the price of rum in Havana." Huff asks, "Which is the cause and which the effect? In other words, are the ministers benefiting from the rum trade or supporting it?" The inference that these two events are connected is improbable, and it is much more likely, as Huff observes, that "in the case of the ministers and the rum it is easy to see that both figures are growing because of the influence of a third factor: the historic and worldwide rise in the price level of practically everything."

Confusing Temporal Succession with Causal Sequence (Post Hoc Ergo Propter Hoc).   This fallacy (from the Latin, "after this, therefore because of this") confuses sequence with causation and infers that simply because B follows A, A has caused B. The cause–effect nature of the relationship is spurious. For example, Roger Blough, former president of U.S. Steel Corporation, once observed that "steel prices cause inflation like wet sidewalks cause rain" (*Forbes* [August 1, 1967]).

Darrell Huff and Irving Geis, in *How to Lie with Statistics* (1954), provide an amusing example of this kind of false correlation:

> The conviction of the people among the New Hebrides [is] that body lice produce good health. Observation over the centuries had taught

them that people in good health usually had lice and sick people very often did not. The observation itself was accurate and sound, as observations made informally over the years surprisingly often are. Not so much can be said for the conclusion to which these primitive people came from their evidence: lice make a man healthy. Everybody should have them . . . more sophisticated observers finally got things straightened out in the New Hebrides. As it turned out, almost everybody in those circles had lice most of the time. It was, you might say, the normal condition of man. When, however, anyone took a fever (quite possibly carried to him by those same lice) and his body became too hot for comfortable habitation, the lice left. There you have cause and effect altogether confusingly distorted, reversed and intermingled.

The nearness or proximity of events may suggest that a causal relationship exists between the two events in question, but true causation always involves the presence of a means (sometimes called *agency*) by which the first event can be demonstrated to have caused the second event.

Mistaking Statistical Correlations for Causal Connections

Simply because two events are linked statistically does not mean that one event has caused the other. The fallacy results from mistaking coincidence for causation. For example, *Science Digest* (August, 1988) featured this tongue-in-cheek account of the discovery of a correlation between storks and babies:

> In 1980, there were 1,000 pairs of breeding storks in West Germany, about half the 1965 census. Helmut Sies of the University of Dusseldorf in West Germany has uncovered a possible clue to that country's falling birth rate: there are not enough storks to go around. Between 1965 and 1980, the decline in the West German birth rate almost exactly matched the decline in brooding [breeding] storks, an explanation that, as Sies says, "every child knows makes sense."

Obviously, it would take more than a statistical correlation between a decline in number of breeding storks and numbers of children to establish that one produced the other. As with the post hoc fallacy, what is required is a demonstration of a means or *agency* by which one event could have caused the other. Even though this is a lighthearted example, many serious arguments rely on statistical correlations to prove a causal relationship. For example, arguments about whether high blood cholesterol causes heart disease, or whether cigarette smoking causes lung cancer, depend on statistical correlations.

Slippery Slope

This fallacy results when writers assume that X will set in motion a series of events that lead to a catastrophe without demonstrating how one step would lead to the next. An example of a *slippery slope* is this turn-of-the-century forecast of the dire consequences of the women's suffrage movement by Henry T. Finck in *The Independent* (January 31, 1901):

> Woman's participation in political life...would involve the domestic calamity of a deserted home and the loss of the womanly qualities for which refined men adore women and marry them.... Doctors tell us, too, that thousands of children would be harmed or killed before birth by the injurious effect of untimely political excitement on their mothers.

Faulty Analogy

Faulty analogy results from the unwarranted assumption that because two things are comparable in some respects, it can be assumed that they are comparable in other ways as well. For example, John McMurtry, a former linebacker who became a professor of philosophy, in his article "Kill 'Em! Crush 'Em! Eat 'Em Raw!" (*Maclean's* [October, 1971]) formulates an analogy between football and war to support his thesis that violence in football might not be a side effect of the game but rather its main point. McMurtry's tactics are based on getting his audience to agree, point by point, that since football and war are so similar in many obvious respects, they may be similar in less obvious ways as well—as expressions of innate human aggression:

> The family resemblance between football and war is, indeed, striking. Their languages are similar: "field general," "long bomb," "blitz," "take a shot," "front line," "pursuit," "good hit," "the draft" and so on. Their principles and practices are alike: mass hysteria, the art of intimidation, absolute command and total obedience, territorial aggression, censorship, inflated insignia and propaganda, blackboard manoeuvres and strategies, drill, uniforms, formations, marching bands and training camps. And the virtues they celebrate are almost identical: hyper-aggressiveness, coolness under fire and suicidal bravery.

Some readers may feel that in his zeal to condemn violence in football, McMurtry has gotten carried away with his analogy. Admittedly, violence in sports is a major problem, but it is not on the same level as war. And it may be true that McMurtry makes a valid point, that violence for its own sake is beginning to eclipse other aspects of football, but the differences between war and football are greater than the similarities. After all, war takes place between countries or nations rather than between individuals or small groups. Furthermore, football games don't include taking prisoners of war from the other team, nor do the football players get killed during the course of the game. At first McMurtry's analogy might seem convincing, but when significant differences begin to outweigh the similarities, the result is a false analogy.

FALLACIES THAT RESULT FROM THE USE OF AMBIGUOUS TERMS OR PHRASES

This class of fallacies occurs when the same word takes on different meanings within the course of the argument. These fallacies may also arise quite unintentionally when the writer has not clearly defined terms crucial to the argument.

Fallacy of Equivocation

This fallacy occurs whenever the writer allows a key term to take on different meanings at different points in the argument. For example, if, in the course of an argument, the writer asserts "the law is on my side," it would be difficult to tell whether the writer meant *law* in the sense of legal statutes, administrative regulations, common law, or constitutional law. Perhaps the writer might even have meant *higher law* in the sense of a moral principle or a divine imperative of the kind contained in the Bible or the Koran. Obviously, important terms need careful definition; otherwise, the argument will quickly unravel because of lack of clarity.

Equivocation has a lighter side when the writer exploits a shift in meaning for humorous effects. For example, Zsa Zsa Gabor was quoted in *Newsweek* (March 28, 1960) as saying that "a man in love is incomplete until he has married. Then he's finished." Gabor's amusing aphorism relies on two different connotations of the word "complete."

A classic example of *equivocation* used for comic effect occurs in Shakespeare's play *Hamlet,* Act V, Scene I. Hamlet has returned secretly to Denmark, and he and his friend Horatio observe a grave being dug in the churchyard by a jocular gravedigger:

> *Hamlet:* ... Whose grave's this sirrah?
> *Clown:* Mine, Sir.
> [Sings] O, a pit of clay for to be made for such a guest is meet.
> *Hamlet:* I think it be thine indeed, for thou liest in't.
> *Clown:* You lie out on't, sir, and therefore 'tis not yours. For my part, I do not lie in't, yet it is mine.
> *Hamlet:* Thou dost lie in't, to be in't and say it is thine. 'Tis for the dead, not for the quick; therefore thou liest.

Clown: 'Tis a quick lie, sir; 'twill away again from me to you.
Hamlet: What man dost thou dig it for?
Clown: For no man, sir.
Hamlet: What woman then?
Clown: For none neither.
Hamlet: Who is to be buried in't?
Clown: One that was a woman, sir; but, rest her soul, she's dead.
Hamlet: How absolute the knave is! We must speak by the card, or
    equivocation will undo us.

The comic effects of this passage are due to the double meaning of
the word *lie*, and the pun on the word *quick* (which means not only
swiftly but *living* as well). So, too, the shift of meaning of the word *man*
(referring to both males and human beings) is the basis for witty repar-
tee. Hamlet aptly observes that on all matters of ambiguity "we must
speak by the card [that is, exactly] or equivocation will undo us."

Fallacy of Amphiboly

The *fallacy of amphiboly* can occur through faulty punctuation, faulty
grammar, or the awkward or careless way in which words are put together. In this case, ambiguity doesn't stem from a term's having two
meanings but from faulty syntax or a confusing grammatical structure.
A classic example is a bequest worded "I hereby leave $20,000 to my
cousins Philip Horton and George Matthews." Imagine being the exec-
utor of the estate trying to decide whether this bequest meant that
(1) each cousin should receive $20,000 or (2) $20,000 should be divided
so that each cousin would receive $10,000. The *New Yorker* magazine
frequently features amusing examples of unintended meaning created
by careless placement of words—for instance, "Do taxidermists make
the most effective decoys?" to which the *New Yorker* (July 18, 1988) replied, "Only when you can get them to hold still."

In the following speech, taken from Willard R. Espy, *The Garden of
Eloquence* (1983), notice how the meaning of the first paragraph is reversed when the same passage is punctuated differently:

Ladies and gentlemen, I bring you a man among men. He is out of
place when among cheaters and scoundrels. He feels quite at home
when surrounded by persons of integrity. He is uncomfortable when
not helping others. He is perfectly satisfied when his fellow human beings are happy. He tries to make changes in order for the country to be
a better place. He should leave us this evening with feelings of disgust
at ineptitude and a desire to do better. I present to you Mr. John Smith.

But somehow the master of ceremonies, or perhaps his secretary, mispunctuated the passage, and it came out this way:

Ladies and gentlemen, I bring you a man. Among men, he is out of place. When among cheaters and scoundrels, he feels quite at home. When surrounded by persons of integrity, he is uncomfortable. When not helping others, he is perfectly satisfied. When his fellow human beings are happy, he tries to make changes. In order for the country to be a better place, he should leave us this evening. With feelings of disgust at ineptitude and a desire to do better, I present to you Mr. John Smith.

Fallacy of Accent

The *fallacy of accent* occurs whenever a secondary meaning is communicated (1) as a result of misplaced emphasis or (2) when an entirely different meaning is created by taking words out of their original context.

Misplaced Emphasis or Accent. For example, the *Philadelphia Inquirer* magazine (cited in *Quarterly Review of Doublespeak* [April 1987]) carried an account of this sign in a restaurant: "Managers Shrimp Special: All you can eat—$5.95." After a couple had eaten the first serving of shrimp they ordered more—only to be told that they couldn't have any more. When the customer pointed out the sign in the window, he was told, "The manager says that's all you *can* eat."

Words Taken Out of Context. The original review of a science fiction film called *The Big Yolk* might appear as follows: "This movie is based on the premise that a big uncracked egg is approaching Earth from outer space and threatens to submerge all the inhabitants in yolk. This so-called film is an astounding bore, is not capable of holding the attention of a gnat, and is for all audiences whose I.Q.s are below the level of house plants. Do anything rather than see this colossal bomb of a movie." Taken out of context, for publicity purposes, this review might become: "Astounding,...capable of holding the attention of...all audiences...do see this colossal...movie."

Fallacies of Composition and Division

The *fallacy of composition* occurs when an inference is drawn about the qualities of a group as a whole based on the evaluations of individual members. For example, the owner of a basketball franchise might pay an enormous amount of money to fill each position on the team with the best players money can buy. Yet, the team composed of these high-priced superstars would not necessarily be the best basketball team in the country. This fallacy overlooks the fact that qualities of the individual parts do not automatically extend to the whole.

To take a hypothetical example, if your favorite foods were chocolate ice cream, tuna fish, tomatoes, and corn, the *fallacy of composition* would imply that a casserole dish combining all your favorite ingredients would be your favorite dish. Inferring that the dish comprised of these ingredients would be even better than the individual parts would be erroneous, and the dish would be inedible.

The *fallacy of division* is the opposite of the *fallacy of composition* and occurs when an inference is drawn about the qualities of the parts based on something that is valid for the whole. Simply that a cake is round does not mean that each piece of the cake can be inferred to be round.

Acknowledgments

———————◆———————

Acknowledgments are continued from page iv.

Alfred Adask, "Democracy" vs. "Republic" *AntiShyster: A Critical Examination of the American Legal System*, Vol. 4, No. 2. 1994. Reprinted with permission from *The AntiShyster*, POB 540786, Dallas, Texas 75354-0786, or call (214) 559–7957.

James Baldwin, "If Black English Isn't a Language, Then Tell Me, What Is?" *The New York Times*, July 29, 1979, Op-Ed. Copyright © 1979 by The New York Times Co. Reprinted by permission.

Dave Barry, "Just Say No to Rugs," from *Dave Barry Talks Back* by Dave Barry. Copyright © 1991 by Dave Barry. Reprinted by permission of Crown Publishers, Inc., a subsidiary of Random House, Inc.

"Beat your parents with a chair." Drawing by Mike Ramirez; COPLEY News Service.

Joe Bob Briggs, "The Lesbo Boom," From *Iron Joe Bob* by Joe Bob Briggs. Copyright © 1992 by John Bloom. Used by permission of Grove/Atlantic, Inc.

Suzanne Britt, "That Lean and Hungry Look." First published in *Newsweek* magazine, October 9, 1978. Reprinted by permission of the author.

Daniel Callahan, "'Aid-in-Dying': The Social Dimensions," *Commonweal* August 9, 1991. Copyright © Commonweal Foundation. Reprinted by permission.

Consumer Reports, "The Dangerous Suzuki Samarai" Copyright 1988 by Consumers Union of U.S., Inc., Yonkers, N.Y. 10703-1057. Excerpted by permission from *Consumer Reports*, July 1988.

The Economist, "The Lays of Ancient ROM." August 27, 1994. Copyright © 1994. The Economist Newspaper Group, Inc. Reprinted with permission. Further reproduction prohibited.

Marilyn French, "Gender Roles," from *Beyond Power: On Women, Men, and Morals*. Copyright © 1985 by Belles-Lettres, Inc. Reprinted by permission of Simon & Schuster, Inc.

Naomi Freundlich, "No, Spending More on AIDS Isn't Unfair." Sept. 17, 1990 *Business Week Magazine*. Reprinted from September 17, 1990 issue of *Business* by special permission, copyright © 1990 by the McGraw-Hill Company.

James Finn Garner, "Little Red Riding Hood," from *Politically Correct Bedtime Stories: Modern Tales for Our Life & Times* by James Finn Garner. Reprinted with the permission of Simon & Schuster from *Politically Correct Bedtime Stories* by James Finn Garner. Copyright © 1994 by James Finn Garner.

Jeremy Rifkin, "Big, Bad Beef." *The New York Times* March 23, 1992, Op-Ed. Copyright © 1992 by The New York Times Co. Reprinted by permission.

Charles M. Sevilla, "The Case of the Non-Unanimous Jury." *The Los Angeles Times,* January 23, 1983. Reprinted with permission.

"STOMP! I thought your motto was 'live and let live'? He wasn't really living!" Drawing by Charles Schultz. PEANUTS. United Feature Syndicate.

Craig Storti, excerpt from "Mad Dogs and Englishmen," from *The Art of Crossing Cultures,* 1990. Reprinted with permission of Intercultural Press, Inc., Yarmouth, ME. Copyright 1990.

"Tell me something Lekesia, is that the name your mother and father gave you?" Drawing by Barbara Brandon. *Where I'm Still Coming From.* 1994 © Barbara Brandon. Distributed by UNIVERSAL PRESS SYNDICATE. Reprinted with permission. All rights reserved.

"Trying to die, eh, Mr. Smith! You could get the chair for this!" Drawing by Don Wright. Reprinted *The Palm Beach Post.*

George E. Vaillant, "We Should Retain the Disease Concept of Alcoholism." *The Harvard Mental Health Letter,* August, 1990. Reprinted with permission from *The Harvard Mental Health Letter,* 164 Longwood Ave., Boston, MA. 02115.

Esther Vilar, "The Business World as a Hunting Ground," from *The Manipulated Man* by Esther Vilar. Copyright © 1972 by Farrar, Straus & Giroux, Inc. Reprinted by permission of Farrar, Straus & Giroux, Inc.

"Whose rights should legislators protect?" Drawing by Chuck Asay. Reprinted *Colorado Springs Gazette Telegraph.*

"Women priests? Nonsense . . . God made man in his own image and likeness. WOMP" Drawing by Mike Peters. Tribune Media Services.

Index